Did British Capitalism Breed Inequality?

Did British Capitalism Breed Inequality?

JEFFREY G. WILLIAMSON, 1935-
Professor of Economics, Harvard University

Boston
ALLEN & UNWIN
London   Sydney

Allen & Unwin Inc.,
Fifty Cross Street, Winchester, Mass. 01890, USA

George Allen & Unwin (Publishers) Ltd,
40 Museum Street, London WC1A 1LU, UK

George Allen & Unwin (Publishers) Ltd,
Park Lane, Hemel Hempstead, Herts HP2 4TE, UK

George Allen & Unwin Australia Pty Ltd,
8 Napier Street, North Sydney, NSW 2060, Australia

First published in 1985

Library of Congress Cataloging in Publication Data

Williamson, Jeffrey G., 1935–
    Did British capitalism breed inequality?
Bibliography: p.
Includes index.
1. Income distribution—Great Britain—History.
2. Capitalism—Social aspects—Great Britain—History.
3. Equality.   I. Title.
HC260.I5W45   1985   339.2′2′0941   84-20413
ISBN 0–04–942186–7

British Library Cataloguing in Publication Data

Williamson, Jeffrey G.
    Did British capitalism breed inequality?
1. Income distribution—Great Britain—History
I. Title
339.2′2′0941   HC260.I5
ISBN 0–04–942186–7

Set in 10 on 11 point Imprint by Paston Press, Norwich
and printed in Great Britain by Butler & Tanner Ltd, Frome and London

Contents

v

Acknowledgements

When this project began in 1978, I knew very little about British economic history since past training and research interests had led me instead to focus on America, the Third World and, briefly, Meiji and Taisho Japan. Peter Lindert (University of California–Davis) and I were both at the University of Wisconsin then. We had finished most of the drafts for our collaborative book *American Inequality: A Macroeconomic History* and were casting our eyes about for another application. Although we thought *American Inequality* offered a convincing explanation for the Kuznets curve, a sample of one did not necessarily make a successful theory. Clearly, to understand what drove inequality through the rising then falling Kuznets curve during so many countries' industrial revolutions required more economic histories. Britain certainly seemed like the most promising candidate, especially given that assertions were abundant, having experienced almost two centuries of public debate on the issue. Professor Lindert and I began a new, exciting and productive collaboration. I learned a great deal from Professor Lindert along the way, not the least of which was the content of his daily instruction on British economic history. Professor Lindert is a marvelous collaborator and, if possible, an even better teacher. I hope readers of this book will find that I have learned my lessons well. While the two of us have decided to write separate books, this one has his intellectual imprint on it too.

Others have shared in my education and have even pointed the way to archival information that turned out to be quite useful in documenting British inequality history. I hope the dozens of helpful colleagues who space makes it impossible to list will not be offended if I single out six: Nick Crafts, Stan Engerman, Charles Feinstein, Joel Mokyr, Nick von Tunzelmann and Patrick O'Brien. In addition, comments and criticisms from participants at the 1982 Conference on British Demographic History (Asilomar, California) and the 1983 Cliometrics Conference (Iowa City, Iowa) were especially helpful, as were those of workshop participants at the following universities: California–Berkeley, California–Davis, Columbia, Harvard, Michigan State, Northwestern, Pennsylvania, Stanford and Wisconsin.

Furthermore, I have never had such an outstanding and devoted group of graduate assistants as those who have participated in this project since 1978. I am pleased to have the opportunity to thank them all publicly: George Boyer (Assistant Professor of Economics at Cornell), Bruce Flory, Howard Metzenberg, Patrice Robitaille, Kenneth Snowden (Assistant Professor of Economics at North Carolina–Greensboro) and Arthur Woolf (Assistant Professor of Economics at Vermont). I am grateful to them all, as well as to Marie Goodman for her typing skills and good humor.

The project has benefited by funding from the National Science Foundation and the National Endowment for the Humanities. Indeed, empirical efforts like that embedded in this book would be almost impossible without the generous support from national agencies like NSF and NEH, which have done so much to foster large-scale quantitative work by cliometricians. I am grateful to them, as well as to the Institute for Research on Poverty at Wisconsin, which supplied so many services along the way.

I would like to thank the Economic History Association, the Economic History Society and the editors of both *Explorations in Economic History* and *Population Studies* for permission to reproduce here some of my work that has appeared in the following publications: Jeffrey G. Williamson, 'Earnings Inequality in Nineteenth-Century Britain', *Journal of Economic History*, 40, 3 (September 1980), 457–76; 'Urban Disamenities, Dark Satanic Mills, and the British Standard of Living Debate', *Journal of Economic History*, 41, 1 (March 1981), 75–83; 'Why Was British Growth So Slow During the Industrial Revolution?', *Journal of Economic History* (forthcoming); 'Was the Industrial Revolution Worth It? Disamenities and Death in 19th Century British Towns', *Explorations in Economic History*, 19, 3 (July 1982), 221–45; 'British Mortality and the Value of Life: 1781–1931', *Population Studies*, 38, 1 (March 1984), 157–72; Peter H. Lindert and Jeffrey G. Williamson, 'Reinterpreting Britain's Social Tables, 1688–1913', *Explorations in Economic History*, 20, 1 (January 1983), 94–109; 'English Workers' Living Standards During the Industrial Revolution: A New Look', *Economic History Review*, Second Series, 36, 1 (February 1983), 1–25.

Most important, I want to thank my wife, Nancy Williamson, for being everything an academic's spouse is supposed to be, and far more. She is a fine computer programmer with a well-developed intuition for social science research. She has always shared these skills unselfishly, even in the face of my frequent impatience. I am very grateful.

Cambridge, Massachusetts
March 1984

1

The Issues

Did British capitalism breed inequality? Opinion has always been in ready supply. The debate still rages in the academic literature; it creeps into most contemporary public debates over taxes, government spending and regulation; and it colors our view of inequality trends that we believe Third World countries should anticipate. This is perhaps because, for the classic British case, the participants in the debate have rarely gathered hard evidence to document inequality trends before World War I. One can sympathize, since few hard data were available then and the distant past offers only indirect clues now. We have the occasional parliamentary income tax and estate tax returns for the nineteenth century used by Marx, Porter and others in the Victorian debate. Around the turn of the century, Arthur Bowley and his colleagues added their impressive compilation of nineteenth-century wages. Beyond these, we have only the rare guesses at the national income distribution by King, Massie, Colquhoun, Baxter and Bowley, limited estimates of the distribution of earnings among 'manual workers', and street-level impressions of the sort that Friedrich Engels used to heat up the debate in the 1840s.

After a two-year visit to England, Engels fired the first public salvo. His first major work deplored the condition of the working class in no uncertain terms, and apologists for capitalism have been on the defensive ever since. Before the industrial revolution, Engels (1974, p. 10) tells us,

> The workers enjoyed a comfortable and peaceful existence. They were righteous, God-fearing and honest. Their standard of life was much better than that of the factory worker today. They were not forced to work excessive hours; they themselves fixed the length of their working day and still earned enough for their needs . . . Most of them were strong, well-built people, whose physique was virtually equal to that of neighbouring agricultural workers. Children grew up in the open air of the countryside, and if they were old enough to help their parents work, this was only an occasional employment and there was no question of an eight- or twelve-hour day.

Three years later, *The Communist Manifesto* (Marx and Engels, 1930, pp. 34–6) added the final touches to the classic description of middle- and lower-class impoverishment in the midst of accelerating economy-wide productivity growth:

Owing to the ever more extended use of machinery and the division of labour, the work of these proletarians has completely lost its individual character and therefore forfeited all its charm for the workers. The worker has become a mere appendage to a machine . . . [Wages] decrease in proportion as the repulsiveness of the labour increases . . . Those who have hitherto belonged to the lower middle class – small manufacturers, small traders, minor recipients of unearned income, handicraftsmen, and peasants – slip down, one and all, into the proletariat . . . Private property has been abolished for nine-tenths of the population; it exists only because these nine-tenths have none of it.

Two decades later, these opinions became a 'General Law of Capitalist Accumulation' in Marx's *Capital* (1947, vol. I, pp. 659–60):

The greater the social wealth, the functioning capital, the extent and energy of its growth . . . the greater is the industrial reserve army . . . and the greater is official pauperism. *This is the absolute general law of capitalist accumulation.*

Like Engels, Marx asserted that the lot of the workers had grown worse, although it can be argued that both had relative 'immiseration' in mind rather than absolute impoverishment.

Engels and Marx were hardly alone in stating publicly that inequality was on the rise in England. Speaking to the House of Commons in 1911, Philip Snowden paraphrased Marx with a statement that has now become part of our common lexicon (cited in Whitaker, 1914, p. 44): 'The working people are getting poorer. The rich are getting richer . . . They are getting enormously rich. They are getting shamefully rich. They are getting dangerously rich.'

Anyone can play the polemic game, and apologists for capitalism rose to the challenge. Porter (1851) and Giffen (1889) countered the radical critique by using limited nineteenth-century tax return data to suggest an egalitarian trend, and the editor of the Economist, F. W. Hirst (cited in Whitaker, 1914, p. 44), said it was still true in 1912. With equally slim evidence, Alfred Marshall (1910, p. 687) added his weighty influence to the optimistic camp:

It is doubtful whether the aggregate of the riches of the very rich are as large a part of national wealth . . . in England, now as they have been in some earlier phases of civilization . . . The returns of the income tax and the house tax, the statistics of consumption of commodities, the records of salaries paid to the higher and the lower ranks of servants of Government and public companies . . . indicate that middle-class incomes are increasing faster than those of the rich; that earnings of artisans are increasing faster than those of professional classes, and that the wages of healthy and vigorous unskilled labourers are increasing faster even than those of the average artisan.

Common to each camp in the debate, of course, is the tendency to denigrate the other's 'evidence'. Thus Eric Hobsbawm (1964, p. 293) counsels us to dismiss Marshall since his 'observations on the subject . . . are exceptionally unreliable (or perhaps wishful)'. The apologists have been equally unkind towards the radicals' use of 'evidence', Hobsbawm included (Hughes, n.d.; Lindert and Williamson, 1983a).

Documenting past inequality trends in Britain seems to be long overdue. Although better and more evidence is unlikely to end the debate, it certainly can help make it better informed. Part I of this book is devoted to that end. Chapter 2 offers new evidence on the standard of living from the late eighteenth to the mid-nineteenth century. Chapter 3 reconstructs earnings distributions between 1827 and 1901, and documents trends in the structure of pay by skill for even longer periods, starting with the 1780s. Chapter 4 collects what is known about income inequality, including the views of the 'social arithmeticians' from Gregory King to Arthur Bowley. As it turns out, the evidence in Part I seems to trace out what has come to be known as the Kuznets curve (Kuznets, 1955) – inequality rising sharply up to somewhere in the middle of the nineteenth century and falling modestly thereafter.

Part II of the book theorizes about potential explanations of the British Kuznets curve. Factor markets are the key, with labor markets playing the central role. Once we understand the impact of changing demographic, technological and world trade conditions on factor rewards in those markets, we understand much about the forces driving the Kuznets curve from 1760 to World War I. Part II suggests how helpful it is to distinguish disequilibrating factor demand forces, which tend to augment inequality during early industrialization, from equilibrating factor supply responses, which tend to produce egalitarian trends during late industrialization. The distinction is especially helpful in organizing the debate between the critics of and apologists for capitalism.

The dialogue between the critics and defenders of capitalism has been going on now for at least 150 years since the British reform debates started to heat up in the 1830s. Furthermore, there is no evidence that the exchange has cooled down, since the same intensity characterizes debate over rising inequality in Latin America and elsewhere in the industrializing Third World today. What appears in Part III is largely motivated by those debates. Thus, the remainder of the book is devoted to developing a model of the British economy that is capable of saying something about growth, industrialization, the standard of living and inequality. The model is developed in Chapter 8 and tested in Chapter 9. It is then used in Chapter 10 to uncover the sources of the British Kuznets curve during *Pax Britannica*, that is from 1821 to 1911. The final step is to explain why British growth was so slow before the 1820s (Chapter 11). Once we understand the impact that the wars had on the British economy, then the sources of the dismal standard-of-living performance up to the 1820s become clearer (Chapter 12). Some peculiar attributes of British inequality trends between the 1780s and the 1820s also become clearer.

We are now equipped to confront three questions motivating this book. Did British capitalism breed inequality? Why? Could Britain have avoided it?

PART I

2

Real Wages and the Standard of Living

(1) The debate

Did real wages rise during the industrial revolution? Who gained from capitalist growth?

The dominant view in the nineteenth century was that common labor gained little during the early years of the industrial revolution. Apologists for British capitalism could concede that real wages failed to improve up to mid-century, while they basked in the abundant evidence of workers' prosperity in the late Victorian era. Capitalism may have had an awkward youth, but it looked good in middle age.

The debate over the standard of living during the industrial revolution[1] heated up again in the 1920s with the appearance of J. H. Clapham's *An Economic History of Modern Britain* (1926). Clapham's contribution was to introduce quantification where anecdotal evidence had served before. On the basis of the work of Bowley, Wood and Silberling, Clapham estimated that real wages of the 'average' industrial worker rose by 60 per cent between 1790 and 1850 (Clapham, 1926, pp. 128 and 561). For every optimist there is a pessimist, and in this case it was J. L. Hammond (1930) who led the counterattack. Hammond conceded the optimists' evidence of real wage improvement up to 1850, but argued that more food and better clothing were poor substitutes for the quality of life that capitalism's 'dark satanic mills' destroyed. While T. S. Ashton (1949) carried the apologists' torch in the interim, the intensity of the modern debate diminished until the appearance of the more recent exchange between Max Hartwell (1959, 1961) and Eric Hobsbawm (1957). Hobsbawm, the pessimist, argued that Hammond gave up far too much ground to Clapham and that the quality of life *and* material standards *both* deteriorated. Hartwell, the optimist, introduced more economic theory into the debate while shifting the attack towards inequality issues – towards relative performance as opposed to absolutes.

The timing of the Hartwell–Hobsbawm exchange should occasion no surprise, for it was in the late 1950s that social scientists began to confront the problem of Third World industrialization, turning for guidance to historical evidence from the early industrializers. Furthermore, it was the pessimists' view that dominated expectations, and the models that development economists brought to Third World experience reflected that view. This was the heyday of W. Arthur Lewis' (1954) model of 'labour surplus', brought to a formal head by John Fei and Gustav Ranis (1964), a position now embedded in models of growth and development. The 'stylized fact' of stable real wages during early industrialization was the pessimists' ultimate intellectual contribution.

Is this 'stylized fact' warranted? As we shall see in this chapter, it certainly is *not*: after the pronounced effects of the French Wars had subsided, real wages of common labor rose rapidly from 1820 to 1850. Nevertheless, there remains the important question of *whose* wages grew fastest. Indeed, that we care in this book at all about real wages implies that the distribution of income is linked closely with the fortunes of the common laborer. So it is that this chapter will also serve to introduce the wage inequality issues that will take so much time in Chapter 3.

(2) Who were the workers?

Which occupations and social classes are of the greatest relevance to the debate? The participants are unlikely ever fully to agree, but a few groups have been of prime concern to both camps in the British nineteenth century debates and in contemporary Third World debates.

Following established conventions in the literature, each group listed in Tables 2.1–2.3 refers to adult male employees; self-employed females, children and chronic paupers are all excluded. The lowest class is dominated by hired farm laborers, a large group of workers who represented the bottom 40 per cent of the earnings distribution in the early nineteenth century,[2] at least among active participants in the labor force. (Paupers are another matter, discussed at length below.) Next come common laborers and miners, their near-substitutes, a 'middle group' dominated by urban occupations requiring little skill. Hobsbawm's (1964) 'labor aristocracy' comes next, a group falling roughly between the 60th and 80th percentiles in the overall distribution of earnings. The 'aristocracy' includes the following artisans: fitters, turners, iron-molders, shipwrights, compositors, bricklayers, masons, carpenters and plasterers. Blue-collar workers comprise all of these listed thus far, a definition that fits 'the working class' most closely.[3] The list is completed by the addition of a diverse white-collar class: messengers, porters, police, teachers, doctors, barristers, clergymen, engineers and many others.

While these class rankings changed very little in the early nineteenth century, they certainly enjoyed very different real earnings growth between 1827 and 1851. Earnings of the bottom 40 per cent declined from 49 to 38 per cent of the average, and blue-collar workers' pay fell from 82 to 70 per cent. The white-collar aristocracy, on the other hand, improved their position from 227 to 343 per cent of the average. These trends reflect a 'stretching' in the wage structure and a rise in earnings inequality that, as it turns out (Chapter 3), was most pronounced during these three decades.

Table 2.1   *1827 estimated earnings distribution for England and Wales: occupations classified by earnings class*

Earnings range £	Mean earnings £	Cumulative frequencies Number %	Income %	Occupations in class (with group mean earnings)	
0–30	25.74	15.52	7.9	*Bottom 40% (£31.04)*	
30–32	31.04	31.09	17.45	Farm labor	
32–38	35.66	40.23	23.89		
38–42	40.30	57.21	37.42		
42–46	44.30	60.94	40.69	*Middle group (£52.36)*	
46–50	48.80	71.62	50.99	Non-farm common	
50–56	53.54	78.49	58.27	labor; miners; cotton spinners	Blue-collar (£51.35)
56–60	58.12	85.37	66.17		
60–66	62.99	88.09	69.55	*Labor aristocracy*	
66–68	66.63	91.70	74.30	*(£70.30)* Skilled in shipbuilding; in engineering; in printing trades; in building trades	
68–90	80.19	95.38	80.14		
90–124	104.70	97.43	84.39	*White collar (£142.62)*	
124–240	154.62	98.64	88.09	Police and guards;	
240–400	302.41	99.52	93.36	messengers; govern-	
400–820	556.19	99.91	97.57	ment; teachers;	
820–2500	1288.95	100.00	99.85	clerks; clergy; other	
2500+	2637.37	100.00	100.00	professionals	

Sources and Notes: This distribution is truncated since it excludes military, tailors, shopkeepers' assistants and some other occupations for which I have been unable to secure information. However, it does include the most important occupations and accounts for 80.5% of those adult males reported as 'occupied' (3,944,000; Mitchell and Deane, 1962, p. 60). The table is constructed from computer output underlying an earlier working paper (Williamson, 1979b). The earnings estimates and the definition of occupations can both be found in Chapter 3 where they are discussed at greater length, or in Table 2.4 below.

These movements in relative earnings between 1827 and 1851 serve to illustrate the importance of examining the wage experience of various laboring classes. Growth was certainly not shared equally by all laborers during the industrial revolution: skilled workers gained the most and unskilled the least.

(3) Real wages and the industrial revolution, 1797–1851

Nominal earnings for eighteen occupations
Quantitative assessments of workers' living standards have always begun with time series on the rates of normal or full-time, 'pre-fisc' pay.[4] This was certainly the starting point for the pioneering contributions by Bowley and Wood, Gilboy, Phelps-Brown and Hopkins, and others. I begin here too,

Table 2.2 *1851 estimated earnings distribution for England and Wales: occupations classified by earnings class*

Earnings range £	Mean earnings £	Cumulative frequencies Number %	Cumulative frequencies Income %	Occupations in class (with group mean earnings)	
0–30	25.56	17.13	7.78	*Bottom 40%* (£29.04)	
30–32	31.60	30.45	15.25	Farm labor	
32–40	36.17	39.85	21.29		
40–42	41.03	58.28	34.72	*Middle group* (£52.95)	
42–48	44.48	61.23	37.05	Non-farm common	
48–50	49.90	70.62	45.37	labor; police and	
50–56.	54.22	77.80	52.29	miners; cotton spinners	Blue-collar (£52.62)
56–60	58.95	84.64	59.44		
60–68	64.55	89.06	64.52	*Labor aristocracy*	
68–78	70.43	92.84	69.25	(£75.15) Skilled in shipbuilding; in engineering; in printing trades; in building trades	
78–98	87.53	95.67	73.65		
98–150	120.75	97.38	77.31	*White collar* (£258.88)	
150–280	203.58	98.63	81.83	Messengers; clergy;	
280–480	347.16	99.34	86.21	government; teachers;	
480–880	619.70	99.76	90.82	clerks; other	
880–1400	1046.79	99.87	92.89	professionals	
1400+	3129.73	100.00	100.00		

Sources and Notes: See Table 2.1.

adding several new pay series along the way, and offering employment weights for aggregation.

The first step is to select appropriate annual pay rates. Most pay series are daily or weekly rates, and there is still only the sketchiest nineteenth-century evidence documenting average days or weeks worked per year. To construct movements in annual earnings, full-time pay rates should be exploited first before turning to independent evidence regarding trends in unemployment or underemployment (see section 2 below). Daily and weekly normal pay rates are aggregated up to a fifty-two-week year,[5] using various estimates of normal days per week by occupations. These annual earnings figures generally exclude payments in kind, but this rule is violated for farm labor, whose large in-kind payments have been included.

The eighteen nominal pay series documented in Table 2.4 reflect a number of additions to and revision in the literature on nineteenth-century British wages.[6] The most conspicuous additions are the service occupations (series 3L, 4L, 1H and 7H–12H). With the important exceptions of clergy and teachers, these service occupation estimates lean heavily on the public salaries published in the 'Annual Estimates' (printed in the *House of*

Table 2.3   *The approximate mean positions of nineteenth-century occupations in the earnings ranks, England and Wales*

Earnings class		Representative occupations used here	Approximate mean-wage percentile positions in the earnings ranks	
			1827	1851
(1) Bottom 40%	(1L)	Farm labor	13th	14th
(2) Middle group	(2L)	Non-farm common labor	38th	35th
	(5L)	Police and guards		50th
	(6L)	Colliers (miners)	55th	51st
	(5H)	Cotton spinners	62nd	58th
(3) Labor	(2H)	Shipbuilding trades	67th	62nd
aristocracy	(3H)	Engineering trades	77th	77th
	(4H)	Building trades	74th	63rd
	(6H)	Printing trades	75th	71st
(4) Blue-collar workers = (1) + (2) + (3)				
(5) White-collar	(3L)	Messengers and porters	78th	71st
employees	(4L)	Other government low-wage	65th	62nd
	(1H)	Government high-wage	87th	80th
	(7H)	Clergy	90th	81st
	(8H)	Solicitors and barristers	95th	100th
	(9H)	Clerks	88th	80th
	(10H)	Surgeons and doctors	86th	79th
	(11H)	Schoolmasters	75th	70th
	(12H)	Engineers, surveyors and other professionals	89th	94th
(6) All workers = (4) + (5)				

Sources and Notes: Derived from Tables 2.1, 2.2 and 2.4.

Commons, Accounts and Papers from 1797 onwards). Annual earnings are reported there for very large numbers of employees in each occupational category, spanning the whole earnings distribution over age, tenure and skill. This information offers time series on a long list of civilian labor inputs hired by the British government: clerks, accountants, porters, messengers, engineers, Post Office letter sorters, doctors, constables and many more. Such information makes it possible to establish the structure of civilian pay *within* the government sector for the century prior to World War I. It offers far more if one is prepared to accept trends in public pay as proxies for trends in private pay for the same occupations. In most cases, there is simply no alternative because the private service sector is so poorly documented. Guy Routh (1954) has presented evidence suggesting competitive public and private labor markets in British service occupations at the time of the Playfair Commission in 1874/5, and similar conclusions were reached by the MacDonnell Commission in 1913. Routh's conclusion was based on clerks' wages in the late nineteenth century, but the same appears to hold for other occupations across the nineteenth century as a whole. It certainly seems to hold for common laborers, agricultural laborers and female domestics. It

Table 2.4 *Estimates of nominal annual earnings for eighteen occupations, 1797–1851: adult males, England and Wales (in current £)*

Occupation	1797	1805	1810	1815	1819	1827	1835	1851
Low-skill:								
(1L) Farm laborers	30.03	40.40	42.04	40.04	39.05	31.04	30.03	29.04
(2L) Non-farm common labor	25.09	36.87	43.94	43.94	41.74	43.65	39.29	44.83
(3L) Messengers and porters	57.66	69.43	76.01	80.69	81.35	84.39	87.20	88.88
(4L) Other government low-wage	46.77	52.48	57.17	60.22	60.60	59.01	58.70	66.45
(5L) Police and guards	47.04	51.26	67.89	69.34	69.18	62.95	63.33	53.62
(6L) Colliers (miners)	47.79	64.99	63.22	57.82	50.37	54.61	56.41	55.44
High-skill:								
(1H) Government high-wage	133.73	151.09	176.86	195.16	219.25	222.95	270.42	234.87
(2H) Shipbuilding trades	51.71	51.32	55.25	59.20	57.23	62.22	62.74	64.12
(3H) Engineering trades	58.08	75.88	88.23	94.91	92.71	80.69	77.26	84.05
(4H) Building trades	40.64	55.30	66.35	66.35	63.02	66.35	59.72	66.35
(5H) Cotton spinners	47.90	65.18	78.21	67.60	67.60	58.50	64.56	58.64
(6H) Printing trades	66.61	71.11	79.22	79.22	71.14	70.23	70.23	74.72
(7H) Clergy	238.50	266.42	283.89	272.53	266.55	254.60	258.76	267.09
(8H) Solicitors and barristers	165.00	340.00	447.50	447.50	447.50	522.50	1,166.67	1,837.50
(9H) Clerks	135.26	150.44	178.11	200.79	229.64	240.29	269.11	235.81
(10H) Surgeons and doctors	174.95	217.60	217.60	217.60	217.60	175.20	200.92	200.92
(11H) Schoolmasters	43.21	43.21	51.10	51.10	69.35	69.35	81.89	81.11
(12H) Engineers and surveyors	190.00	291.43	305.00	337.50	326.43	265.71	398.89	479.00

Sources and Notes: Williamson (1982d, Appendix Table 4). Some of these occupations need no elaboration. Those that do are explained as follows: (4L) – watchmen, guards, porters, messengers, Post Office letter carriers, janitors; (1H) – clerks, Post Office sorters, warehousemen, tax collectors, tax surveyors, solicitors, clergymen, surgeons, medical officers, architects, engineers; (2H) – shipwrights; (3H) – fitters, turners, iron-molders; (4H) – bricklayers, masons, carpenters, plasterers; (6H) – compositors.

also appears to hold for schoolmasters, schoolmistresses and clergymen. I have not, however, been able to test the competitive labor markets hypothesis for the Napoleonic period, or for the majority of white-collar occupations. While the late eighteenth-century public pay data should be treated with special caution,[7] what evidence we do have suggests that wage *trends* (but perhaps not always levels) in public and private employ were pretty much the same after 1797.

Clergymen's mean annual earnings (including the rental value of the vicarage) were estimated for the greater part of the nineteenth century using *The Clerical Guide and Ecclesiastical Directory* and *The Clergy List*. A random sample of 550 clergymen yielded private sector estimates for 1827, 1835 and 1851. For earlier years, the public pay rates for the clergy had to serve, splicing these onto the private series at 1827. This procedure seems to have yielded plausible pay series back to 1797, judging by the similarity in trend between public and private clergy salaries from 1827 on.

Schoolmasters had low monthly cash earnings, both because much of their income was in kind (rents and coals), and because they often received supplementary fees and holiday bonuses. I have assumed that income in kind was a stable share of total income, so that the cash earnings series in Table 2.4 accurately reflects total income trends. For 1797–1835, the estimates rely on schoolmasters' earnings in several charity schools in Staffordshire and Warwickshire. The 1851 figure refers to civilian school-masters in public pay, as reported in the Annual Estimates.

While the well-known estimates of Bowley and Wood will suffice for the nineteenth-century manufacturing and building trades (Bowley, 1898; 1900a,b; 1901; Bowley and Wood, 1899; 1905; 1906; Wood, 1909), there are three very large unskilled occupation groups that are yet to be discussed: miners, non-farm common laborers and farm laborers.

The miners' earnings figures refer to underground coal mining by adult males. The 1851 figure is derived from Wood (Mitchell and Deane, 1962, p. 348). The 1835 figure is from Bowley (1900a), as are the 1810–19 estimates, the latter referring to southern Scotland. For 1797–1805 and for 1835, Ashton and Sykes (1964) supply colliers' daily wages in the northern counties of Lancashire and Derbyshire. These diverse wage estimates are linked together at various dates and converted into annual earnings trends. Common laborers' earnings are based on the Phelps-Brown and Hopkins' (1955, 1956, 1959) estimate for unskilled laborers in the building trades. The farm laborers' figures are based on Bowley's (1898) wages for a 'normal work week', taking into account income in kind and seasonal wage-rate variation. Fifty-two 'normal weeks' are arbitrarily assumed in constructing an annual full-time series.

Table 2.4 represents my best interim view of trends in occupational earnings between 1797 and 1851. It is confined to eight benchmark years simply because the data are more abundant for those years.

Nominal earnings for six classes
Table 2.5 reports average full-time earnings for the six 'target' classes — bottom 40 per cent, middle group, labor aristocracy, blue-collar, white-collar

Table 2.5 Trends in nominal full-time earnings for six labor classes, compared with three previous series, 1797–1851 (1851 = 100)

	(1) Bottom 40%	vs. Bowley's farm laborers	(2) Middle group	vs. Phelps-Brown-Hopkins' building laborers	(3) Labor aristocracy	vs. Tucker's London artisans	(4) Blue-collar	(5) White-collar	(6) All workers
Year									
1797	103.41	93.9	72.92	66.7	64.86	81.0	74.42	32.55	58.97
1805	139.12		98.89	83.3	79.44	87.0	96.58	38.88	75.87
1810	144.76		110.95	97.0	92.03	105.6	107.81	43.01	84.89
1815	137.88		105.55	97.0	95.28	112.1	106.18	46.55	85.30
1819	134.47		99.41	97.0	91.92	103.3	101.84	50.77	84.37
1827	106.89	100.8	98.89	97.0	93.55	105.1	97.59	55.09	83.11
1835	103.41	112.3	96.98	97.0	88.68	98.9	94.11	75.03	88.77
1851	100.00	100.0	100.00	100.0	100.00	100.0	100.00	100.00	100.00
52 weeks' earnings in 1851:	£29.04	£29.04	£52.95	£42.90	£75.15	n.a.	£52.62	£258.88	£75.51

Sources and Notes: Lindert and Williamson (1983a, Table 3). The indices are aggregated up from the occupational wage series in Table 2.4. The employment weights used for the aggregation draw on Lindert (1980b, Table 3) for 1797–1815, while those for 1815–1851 are derived from censuses. For the three previous series, see Bowley (1900a, table in back); Phelps-Brown and Hopkins (1955); and Tucker (1936). The conversion of the Phelps-Brown–Hopkins series from daily to annual wages assumed 312 working days a year.

and all workers. The employment weights applied to aggregate over the eighteen occupations in Table 2.4 are very rough. Those for 1811 and earlier are based on work previously published by Peter Lindert (1980b; see 1980a for a summary), while those for later years are based on manipulations of the imperfect early census enumerations by occupation (see Lindert and Williamson, 1980, Appendix A).

Table 2.5 reveals a striking variety in the earnings history experienced by different classes of workers. From Waterloo to mid-century, the gap between higher-paid and lower-paid workers widened dramatically, a result I have already anticipated when looking at the 1827–51 period (Tables 2.1 and 2.2): farm wages lagged behind, labor aristocracy's earnings improved, while white-collar pay soared. Things were quite different during the French Wars: all six groups pretty much shared the same earnings experience, with the exception of the white-collar group, which fell behind. Obviously, wage inequality and wage stretching were not an inevitable attribute of British industrialization, and we shall need explanations for the variety of experience revealed across these epochs (see chapters 10 and 11).

Table 2.5 also compares my results with the older series that have shaped past impressions of wage trends and that played a key role in Flinn's (1974) survey. The new and the old series exhibit both conformity and contrast. Tucker's artisans approximate my 'labor aristocracy', Bowley's farm laborers pretty much equal my bottom 40 per cent, and the Phelps-Brown–Hopkins' building laborers correspond to my 'middle group'. Where differences do arise (for example, Tucker's London artisans and my economy-wide labor aristocracy), I stand by the present series as improvements. However, the major conclusions of this chapter are not conditional on my preference for the new estimates in establishing trends for nominal full-time pay.

The cost of living
Cost-of-living indices have long been central to the standard-of-living debate. For the 1790–1850 period, the four price indices most often cited are those offered by Gayer, Rostow and Schwartz (1953), Silberling (1923), Rousseaux (1938) and Tucker (1936). Each of these pioneering series has been criticized, and Appendix A offers alternative estimates that respond to three kinds of criticisms.

First, these series have been criticized for their reliance on wholesale and institutional London prices, rather than on the retail prices actually paid by workers' families across England and Wales. In most cases, there appears to be no alternative. An exception is clothing, for which I have used the Gayer–Rostow–Schwartz (GRS) export prices rather than Tucker's institutional prices, leading to a slightly more optimistic view of the cost-of-living trend between 1797 and 1850.

Second, the commodities included in the cost-of-living index also need revision. Some relevant working-class commodities have been added – especially potatoes – and some irrelevant industrial raw materials included in the GRS series – have been removed. The most important change is the addition of house rent. While all four older indices omitted this important component of the cost of living, mine includes rents based on working-class cottages in Staffordshire, a housing stock of virtual unchanging quality (Lindert and Williamson, 1980, 1983a; see Appendix Table A.3 below). The rent series implies that housing costs rose relative to other consumer items throughout the industrial revolution, which throws some new support behind the pessimists' position.

As a final flaw, the traditional cost-of-living indices rarely used actual workers' budgets to weight prices. All exclude any weight for housing, some include industrial inputs, and others are simply vague about their weights. Appendix Table A.1 reports a rural index that draws on workers' household budgets reported in the pioneering work of Davies (1795) and Eden (1797) on the rural poor in the late eighteenth century.[8] An urban index relies on working-class budgets from late eighteenth- and early nineteenth-century towns.[9] Compared with the rural poor, the urban workers' budgets reveal a far lower share spent on food, and a far higher share spent on housing. Fuel, light and clothing shares are more nearly alike.

Choosing the most appropriate set of budget weights could matter a great deal. Cost-of-living trends could differ across classes simply because of differences in budget weights, as often happened in American experience (Williamson, 1976a, 1977; Williamson and Lindert, 1980, Chapter 5). This possibility was pursued with four cost-of-living indices using weights from the rural North, rural South, urban North and urban South (Appendix Table A.2). As it happens, prices moved in such a way that the choice of weights mattered very little. The reason is that, while the price of food rose relative to manufactures (which would have impoverished the rural poor more than the better-paid 'middle group' or labor aristocracy), there was an

Table 2.6   A 'best guess' cost-of-living index, 1797–1850 (1850 = 100)

Year	Index	Year	Index	Year	Index
1797	138.8	1815	182.6	1833	124.7
1798	136.9	1816	192.1	1834	117.6
1799	155.7	1817	197.5	1835	112.8
1800	207.1	1818	192.4	1836	126.4
1801	218.2	1819	182.9	1837	129.2
1802	160.9	1820	170.1	1838	138.2
1803	156.8	1821	155.5	1839	142.3
1804	160.2	1822	139.8	1840	138.4
1805	186.7	1823	146.0	1841	133.3
1806	178.5	1824	154.6	1842	123.4
1807	169.1	1825	162.3	1843	109.6
1808	180.5	1826	144.4	1844	114.5
1809	204.9	1827	140.9	1845	112.0
1810	215.4	1828	143.2	1846	116.4
1811	204.5	1829	143.9	1847	138.0
1812	235.7	1830	141.3	1848	110.9
1813	230.0	1831	141.3	1849	101.2
1814	203.3	1832	133.9	1850	100.0

Source: Lindert and Williamson (1980, Appendix B) and Appendix A below, using southern urban weights.

Table 2.7   *Percentage change in prices, 1788–1850*

Series	1788–92 to 1809–15	1809–15 to 1820–6	1820–6 to 1846–50
Silberling	74.1	−31.2	−16.7
Tucker	85.2	−24.5	−10.0
Rousseaux		−34.8	−16.4
Gayer–Rostow–Schwartz	65.7	−30.7	−19.4
Phelps-Brown–Hopkins	84.6	−23.5	−10.5
Table 2.6 'best guess'	72.5	−27.3	−26.0

Sources: See text.

equally impressive relative rise in house rents (which took a greater toll on urban households). The analysis below sticks with the southern urban weights, confident in the knowledge that the choice makes little difference.

The resulting 'best guess' cost-of-living index is displayed in Table 2.6. Much to my surprise, this series shows mostly similarities when compared with the older ones. Table 2.7, based on Flinn's (1974, p. 404) convenient summary, shows that, between 1788–92 and 1820–6, my index closely corresponds to GRS and Silberling, falling about midway between optimists and pessimists. Between 1820–6 and 1846–50, mine is a bit more optimistic, showing a somewhat bigger drop in living costs than past indices.

Real wage trends for the working classes
Deflating the nominal full-time wages in Table 2.5 by the cost-of-living index in Table 2.6 yields the real wages in Table 2.8 and Figure 2.1. The results support Michael Flinn's conclusion that 'there are relatively few indications of significant change in levels of real wages either way before

Table 2.8   *Trends in real full-time earnings: adult male workers, 1797–1851 (1851 = 100)*

Benchmark year	Farm laborers	Middle group	Artisans	All blue-collar	White-collar	All workers
1797	74.50	52.54	46.73	53.61	23.45	42.48
1805	74.51	52.96	42.55	51.73	20.82	40.64
1810	67.21	51.54	42.73	50.04	19.97	39.41
1815	75.51	57.81	52.18	58.15	25.49	46.71
1819	73.52	54.35	50.26	55.68	27.76	46.13
1827	75.86	70.18	66.39	69.25	39.10	58.99
1835	91.67	85.97	78.62	83.43	66.52	78.69
1851	100.00	100.00	100.00	100.00	100.00	100.00
Period	*Percentage change over entire period*					
1797–1810	−10.2	−11.9	−8.6	−6.7	−14.8	−7.2
1810–51	+48.8	+94.0	+134.0	+99.8	+400.8	+153.7
1797–1851	+34.2	+90.3	+114.0	+86.5	+326.4	+135.4

Sources and Notes: Calculated from Tables 2.5 and 2.6. For more detail, and for discussion of the importance of the deflator used, see Lindert and Williamson (1980, Appendix B and Tables 9 and 11). See also Lindert and Williamson (1983a, Table 5).

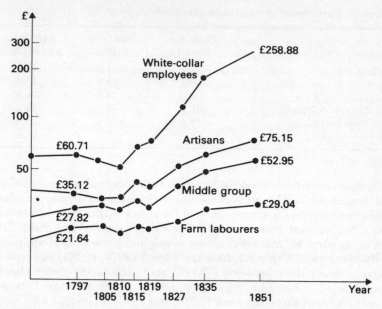

Figure 2.1 *Average full-time earnings for adult male workers, 1797–1851, at constant prices (Source: Table 2.8 and Lindert and Williamson, 1983a, Figure 1)*

1810/14' (1974, p. 408).[10] For later years, however, the results offer revisions. Flinn was struck by the concentration of all real wage improvements into a period of only a dozen years beginning around 1813. Table 2.8 does not confirm Flinn's view.[11] There was general real wage improvement between 1810 and 1815, a fallback between 1815 and 1819, and continuous growth thereafter. After a prolonged stagnation, blue-collar workers' real wages doubled between 1810 and 1850.[12] This is a far larger increase than even past optimists had announced.[13] It is also large enough to resolve most of the debate over whether or not real wages improved during the industrial revolution. Unless new errors are discovered, the debate over real wages in the early nineteenth century is over: the *average* worker was much better off in any decade from the 1830s on than in any decade before 1820. The same is true of *any class* of worker in Table 2.8.

Some dark shadows are cast on this impressive real wage performance by the suggestion of rising inequality. I have already noted some evidence of *wage inequality*, a topic pursued at length in Chapter 3. How about *income* inequality? There is only the slightest clue, but I report it here and explore it further in Chapter 4: between 1797 and 1851, real earnings of blue-collar workers rose at 1.16 per cent per annum, while real product per worker rose at a slightly faster rate (1.23 per cent) between 1801 and 1860 (Feinstein, 1978a, Table 26, p. 86); between 1797 and 1835 the difference was more pronounced – 1.17 versus 1.36 per cent per annum. However, whether the British worker generally – and the common laborer in particular – was falling behind relative to other economic agents in the industrial revolution is an issue I reserve for later. For the present, note that workers made impressive real earnings gains between 1797 and 1851.

Why haven't we heard such announcements before? One might have expected it from any of several devout optimists. The answer lies partly in the steady accumulation of data, including the employment weights so essential for aggregation up to the average worker. Yet past findings have also been muted by the pessimists' allegation that real full-time earnings cannot measure workers' true living standards. Each time a recent writer has come close to announcing a major post-1820 improvement, the report has been disarmed by a confession of ignorance regarding trends in unemployment and in qualitative dimensions of life; perhaps health became poorer, work discipline harsher, employment more uncertain, housing more crowded, environments more polluted, and social injustice more outrageous. Could these qualitative disamenities have cancelled the improvement in workers' real wages?

(4) Mobility, unemployment and pauperism

Occupational mobility and economic progress
Since wage rates differ between occupations, migration from low-paid to high-paid employment can rise average wages for the working class as a whole even if wage rates fail to rise in any one occupation. How much of the wage gains up to 1850 were due to such mobility-induced wage drift? The 'blue-collar' and the 'all worker' wage series in Table 2.8 already capture this mobility effect. It can be factored back out by applying fixed wage rates to shifting employment. Detailed calculations (Lindert and Williamson, 1980, Secton 6) show that occupational mobility contributed less than 5.3 per cent to the rise in average full-time earnings of all blue-collar workers between 1781 and 1851. Virtually all of the average worker's wage gains were gains *within* occupations, not a wage drift attributable to changing employment weights and mobility from low-skill to high-skill occupations. We can reject the pessimists' hypothesis that those migrating to skilled and/or industrial jobs 'were the only workers who were better off, with all other workers remaining at a constantly low standard of living' (Hartwell and Engerman, 1975, p. 205). Real wage gains were universally enjoyed, although some groups enjoyed far bigger gains than others.

Regional migration and economic progress
Migration from low-wage to high-wage regions can also raise wages for the average worker even if wages fail to rise in any region. That nominal wages varied widely across English counties well into the nineteenth century has long been appreciated, at least since Arthur Young's late eighteenth-century tours. The causes of the regional differences in wage rates for agricultural labor have been analyzed at length elsewhere (Lindert and Williamson, 1980, Section 7). It appears that *real* wage gaps persist even after adjustments are made for regional variation in cost of living and disamenities. Furthermore, it has long been appreciated that labor drifted from the low-wage South to the high-wage North during the industrial revolution.[14]

Since the 'blue-collar' and 'all worker' series in Table 2.8 already include most of these regional migration effects, it is now a simple matter to explore their quantitative impact on real wage gains up to 1850.

It appears that regional migration contributed very little to the real wage gains for the average English worker after the 1780s. True, some periods registered far larger migration gains than others: 1841–51 was a decade of impressive gains through migration to high-wage regions; and the late eighteenth century records some small positive gains.[15] But, over the period as a whole, regional migration contributed less than 3.6 per cent to the observed real wage gains.[16] It was real wage gains *within* regions that mattered most.

Unemployment and capitalist instability
Time and again the unemployment issue has pushed the living-standard debate to an impasse. Lacking national unemployment data before 1851, can real wages be trusted as proxies for annual earnings? Are not business cycles an attribute of industrial capitalism? Did not their increased frequency and greater intensity cause unemployment rates to rise as the century progressed? Into this empirical vacuum Hobsbawm has injected fragmentary hints about unemployment in the industrial North, suggesting that the depression of 1841–3 was 'almost certainly the worst of the century' (Hobsbawm, 1964, p. 74), implying that real wage trends up to mid-century overstate real earnings improvements.

Yet no conceivable level of unemployment could have cancelled the near doubling of full-time wages up to 1850. Such a cancellation of gains would have required the national unemployment rate to have risen from 0 to 50 per cent, or from 10 per cent to 55 per cent, jumps that even the most ardent pessimist would dismiss as inconceivable. Even in the 1930s, unemployment was less than a quarter of the labor force. The 1840s lacked the unemployment compensation, the sharp drop in output, as well as the fall in investment that accompanied record jobless rates ninety years later.

One can be more precise about the extent to which the unemployment issue has been overstated in the standard-of-living debate, for there are a number of clues about early nineteenth-century unemployment that have yet to be exploited.

In 1851, 3.9 per cent of engineering, metal and shipbuilding (EMS) union membership were out of work at any one time, and the average was 5.2 per cent for 1851–9. This sector had all the attributes promising untypically high unemployment rates: early unionization, an unemployment insurance scheme, and business cycle sensitivity typical of all capital-goods industries. Indeed from 1851 to World War I the unemployment rate in the EMS sector fell below overall unemployment only twice, both boom years. Between 1923 and 1939, the EMS unemployment rate exceeded that of all insured workers by far (Mitchell and Deane, 1962, pp. 64–7). Thus, the 5.2 per cent EMS unemployment rate clearly overstates unemployment in non-agriculture as a whole. It therefore supplies an upper bound on the extent to which non-agricultural unemployment could have worsened in the half-century prior to the 1850s.

Could unemployment have been worse in the 'hungry forties'? The situation can be inferred by appealing to the behavior of other variables over the business cycle. National unemployment varies inversely with output, but EMS unemployment must have been especially sensitive to the share of capital formation in national product. According to A. W. Phillips' (1958) classic study of the Phillips curve, a tight non-linear relationship between unemployment and wage rate was also present in Britain between 1862 and 1957. Aside from the influence of these three variables (output, investment shares and wages), in addition one might suspect that the structure of the economy drifted over time in a way that influenced the unemployment rate.

These propositions can all be tested for the second half of the nineteenth century. If they are successful, then they can be used to predict non-agricultural unemployment back to the late 1830s. Regression analysis for the period 1851–92 confirms that the unemployment rate in engineering–metals–shipbuilding was lower when GNP was on the rise, when investment was a higher share of national product, and when engineering and shipbuilding wage rates were drifting up.[17] The regression can now predict EMS unemployment rates for the 1840s and late 1830s. It would be unwise to make any predictions earlier than this, given the Poor Law reform of 1834 and other structural changes in the earlier years. For the period 1837–50, the equation generates the following estimates:

Period	Estimate of U_{EMS}	Estimate of U_{EMS} + two standard errors
1837–9	2.70%	0–7.70%
1840–50	4.41%	0–9.41%
1842–3 (two worst years)	(9.44%)	(4.44–14.44%)

Overall, non-agricultural unemployment was probably lower than these estimates, since only brick output showed as bad a slump in the early 1840s as did shipbuilding (Mitchell and Deane, 1962, pp. 348–51). Nor is it clear that the slump of the early 1840s was the 'worst of the century.' Indeed, industrial depression might have been as bad in the immediate postwar years (1814–19) given that the earlier wage–price deflation was far more severe. I conclude that non-agricultural unemployment was not exceptionally high in the 1840s or the 1850s, and, even if it did rise after 1820, that unlikely event could have had only a trivial impact on workers' real earnings gains.

How might employment conditions in *agriculture* have affected the unemployment trends for the economy as a whole? Darkness is nearly total on this front. Seasonal unemployment was surely a more serious problem in agriculture *early* in the century, but structural unemployment may have been worse early in the century as well. To guess when unemployment and underemployment reached crisis proportions, qualitative evidence, grain yields and the terms of trade can all serve to guide us. The signs of distress were strongest during the harvest failures of the 1790s and in the twenty years after Waterloo (Jones, 1974, Ch. 10; Richardson, 1976, pp. 103–16; Hobsbawm and Rudé, 1969). Post-Napoleonic wheat yields were trendless from 1815 to 1840, and then rose (Jones, 1974, Ch. 8). The terms of trade shifted against agricultural products by about 10 per cent from 1812–14 to 1822–4 (Deane and Cole, 1962, p. 91; Mitchell and Deane, 1962, Ch. XIV). The common denominator emerging from this review is that the early postwar period, 1815–24 in particular, witnessed exceptional unemployment in agriculture, followed by overall improvement to 1850.

All of this evidence suggests the plausibility of two inferences: (i) non-agricultural unemployment was considerably less than 9.4 per cent in the 1840s and 1850s; and (ii) agricultural unemployment was no worse in the 1840s or 1850s than around 1820. It is also known that the share of the British labor force engaged in agriculture dropped from 28.4 per cent to 21.7 per cent between 1821 and 1851 (Deane and Cole, 1962, p. 142). This information is sufficient to demonstrate that the net rise in unemployment economy-wide could not have exceeded 7 or 8 per cent, and it was likely to have been far less (Lindert and Williamson, 1980, Section 3; 1983a).

The most 'pessimistic' trend in unemployment could not have detracted significantly from the improvement in workers' real wages. Indeed, depending on conditions in agriculture, an 'optimistic' fall in unemployment may have even *raised* workers' annual earnings.

Pauperism
So much for unemployment trends among the *working* poor. What about paupers? At the very bottom of the household income distribution were female-headed households (widowed by the death of the male head), households headed by the aged and infirm, households headed by those dispossessed by agrarian institutional change (the enclosures), and households headed by traditional artisans sufficiently old to have made difficult their re-employment elsewhere following displacement by factory production (the handloom weavers). These were the 'extreme poor' for whom poor relief was most essential to meet basic needs. Colquhoun, Baxter and other social arithmeticians of the time simply lumped them all together under the label 'pauper'. Only tentative estimates exist of their number and persistence in poverty (Lindert and Williamson, 1982, 1983b; Williamson, 1982b), but Irma Adelman and Cynthia Taft Morris (1978, p. 265) recently guessed them to have been 10 per cent of the population in 1850.

How did the pauper host vary in size across the first industrial revolution? Adelman and Morris relied on Rose (1972), Caird (1852), Mayhew (1861/2), Hobsbawm (1957) and others to arrive at their 10 per cent estimate for 1850. These qualitative sources also encouraged their inference that the proportion in extreme poverty rose in the first half of the nineteenth century: '. . . more than a half century elapsed before expansionary influences were sufficient to produce . . . a marked reduction in the incidence of extreme poverty' (Adelman and Morris, 1978, p. 254). Table 2.9, which is based on the estimates of the social arithmeticians, suggests, on the contrary, a significant decline in the incidence of pauperism across the nineteenth century. True, the Napoleonic conflict tended to raise the share in the late eighteenth century between Massie's 1759 and Colquhoun's 1801–3 estimates, but the incidence declined thereafter. The figure at the turn of the century was 19.9 per cent, declining to 14.8 per cent towards the end of the French Wars, to 10 per cent in 1850, and 6.2 per cent in 1867.

Trends in pauperism must be treated with great caution. After all, social observers changed their view of what constituted the poverty threshold, which surely affected trends in the pauper counts. Furthermore, mobilization of young adult males during the French Wars almost certainly pushed many 'near poor' households into pauperism, while demobilization presented all kinds of postwar absorption problems with additional effects on pauperism. And what about the official counts of those on relief? As Adelman and Morris point out, 'poor relief statistics in Great Britain tended to overstate those *relieved* prior to 1848 and to understate them thereafter' (1978, p. 265). For all of these reasons, the pauper counts offered by King and Colquhoun may well be a bit high, while those of Massie and Baxter may be a bit low, even after efforts to revise them (Lindert and Williamson, 1982, 1983b). Colquhoun's figures for 1801–3 may define poverty too broadly to be comparable with later nineteenth-century benchmarks. The original poor relief returns for 1802–3 showed 11 per cent of the total population on relief at a particular time of year. Colquhoun assumed there were almost as many other paupers not on relief. Although Table 2.9 has pruned his estimates, it still implies that a very large minority of paupers and vagrants went unrelieved at any one time of the year. Certainly Colquhoun's 1801–3 figure of 19.9 per cent exceeds by far the Webbs' (1909) estimates (8.6 per cent of total population), or those offered by J. D. Marshall (11 per cent of total population and 2 per cent of able-bodied males, in Marshall, 1968, Table 2). By contrast, the figure for 1867 (6.2 per cent) may reflect too narrow a definition of poverty, even after my attempts to revise Baxter's original estimates.

In short, while the incidence of pauperism in Table 2.9 may overstate the downward trend across the nineteenth century, the evidence is certainly inconsistent with the Adelman and Morris thesis: extreme poverty was *not* on the rise following the Napoleonic Wars.

Table 2.9   *Estimating the incidence of 'pauperism' in England and Wales, 1688–1867*

Year	Number of 'able-bodied' income recipients and paupers	Number of paupers	'Pauperism' %	Original source
1688	1,390,586	336,672	24.2	Gregory King (1696)
1759	1,539,140	192,310	12.5	Joseph Massie (1760)
1801/3	2,193,114	435,397	19.9	Patrick Colquhoun (1806)
1812	4,248,018	630,780	14.8	Patrick Colquhoun (1815)
1850	n.a.	n.a.	10.0	Adelman and Morris (1978, p. 265)
1867	9,838,010	610,400	6.2	R. Dudley Baxter (1868)

Source: Except for 1850, the figures are taken from Lindert and Williamson (1983b, Section II), where the original 'social arithmeticians'' estimates are revised. Joseph Massie's estimate is taken from Mathias (1957).

(5) 'Dark satanic mills', mortality and the quality of life

Where in Table 2.8 does one take account of the degradation and demorali-
zation associated with the long hours spent at mind-numbing work for an
insensitive capitalist? The disruption of traditional family roles? The noise,
filth, crime and crowding of urban slums? Disease, sickness and mortality?
Until these qualitative aspects of life can be assessed, one cannot answer
questions about living standards, but rather only questions about real
earnings.

Urbanization, 'dark satanic mills' and the quality of life
The quality of urban life has always played a key role in the debate, and,
since nineteenth-century Britain is the best-known case of 'environmental
decay' associated with industrialization, the pessimists have made much of
the issue. The pessimist stresses, first, that the process of urbanization
involved migration into ghastly towns, a move implying costs that must be
subtracted from the pecuniary gains in nominal wages, and, second, that
deterioration in the quality of life in all cities and towns throughout much of
the first half of the nineteenth century implies additional costs to be
subtracted. But how can one quantify these allegations? How is the voice of
the nineteenth-century British worker to be heard? Many were illiterate,
and most were silent. Most lacked the right to vote. All of them could vote
with their feet, however. To the extent that they did, their response has left
its mark on rates of pay – high nominal wages compensating workers in
locations with ghastly environments (the best proxy for which appears to be
recorded infant mortality rates).

Elsewhere (Williamson, 1980b, 1981, 1982a) hedonic wage functions
have been applied to nineteenth-century town data in much the same way
that William Nordhaus and James Tobin (1972) did in confronting the
modern pessimists – Ehrlich, Meadows, Forrester and the Club of Rome.
These estimates suggest that the urban disamenities premium in the early
nineteenth century ranged from 7 to 13 per cent in the North of England,
where they were highest. These are only tentative estimates, to be sure, but
would a large error matter in forming inferences for the standard-of-living
debate? Would such disamenities seriously deflate the measured real wage
gains of the British worker after the Napoleonic Wars? I think not.

Suppose, for example, that the true disamenities premium separating
'good' rural villages from 'bad' industrial towns was 15 per cent in the North
of England during the decades prior to 1850. Suppose further that the
relative shift of male employment from 'good' to 'bad' locations was at the
same rate as the measured decline in the agricultural employment share,
that is, from 36 to 22 per cent of the labor force between 1801 and 1851
(Deane and Cole, 1962, p. 142). These figures would imply that the average
wage of common labor would have increased by about 2 per cent over the
full half-century solely because of the premium paid for urban disamenities
(i.e. $(0.36 - 0.22) \times 0.15 = 0.021$), a trivial share of the total measured
gains in Table 2.8. Alternatively, consider the rise in the population
'urbanized'. According to Mitchell and Deane's estimates (1962, pp. 8–9

and 24–7), the proportion living in urban places rose from 25.7 to 35.8 per cent between 1805 and 1851, implying that the average wage of common labor would have increased by about 1.5 per cent solely as a result of the premium paid for urban disamenities (i.e. $(0.358 - 0.257) \times 0.15 = 0.015$). Either calculation implies a trivial downward adjustment to the measured improvement in the standard of life in Table 2.8: blue-collar real wage improvements over the 1810–51 period might be reduced from the measured increase of 99.8 per cent to an adjusted increase of 97.8 per cent. It would take an enormous error to reverse that finding.

Perhaps I *have* made some serious (but unknown) error? As a gracious concession to the most ardent pessimist, suppose *all* of the nominal wage gain from migration into the cities was spurious, attributable to disamenities premia and the high cost of city life. Furthermore, suppose one measures the wage differential by selecting an extreme pair of potential migrants' choices between 'good' rural villages and 'bad' industrial towns: rural East Anglia and urban Manchester. In 1839, unskilled adult male laborers in the Manchester metal mills and cotton warehouses got £41.4 for a 'normal' forty-six-week year, and they were the better paid of the unskilled. In 1837, a single male farm laborer averaged £25.1 in East Anglia, implying a wage differential of about 65 per cent. If such differentials are assumed to have applied everywhere in England (an exaggeration), and if they are assumed to reflect cost-of-living and disamenity differences solely (an exaggeration), then the measured rise in the average wage of common labor up to 1851 would have been spuriously inflated by only 7–9 per cent over the full half-century, which is not much when compared with the average blue-collar wage gains of 99.8 per cent.

So, the disamenities incurred by migrating into the ugly cities during the industrial revolution have been far overdrawn by the pessimists. What about their point that there was a steady deterioration in the quality of life in all towns up to 1848 and the Public Reform era? Mortality rates are, of course, the most effective proxies for the quality of life, but all one can do with the existing evidence is to infer from scraps. When such scraps are examined (Williamson, 1982a, Section IV), it is hard to avoid the inference that urban mortality rates either stabilized or continued to decline between the 1820s and the 1850s, an inference reached long ago by Buer (1926), Farr (1885) and other analysts of nineteenth-century urban life.

Inference is one thing, evidence another, and the urban mortality data are much too crude to confirm a rise in the quality of city life up to 1850. Barbara Hammond was quite right when some fifty years ago she stated: 'A close examination of the figures for Manchester does not lead to confidence in statistical proof of *improved* urban conditions in the early nineteenth century' (Hammond, 1928, p. 428; emphasis added). But *improvement* is not the issue. The issue is whether the evidence supports the view of *deterioration*, and Hammond – a pessimist – agrees that it does not.

Unless one believes that mortality (and sickness) poorly reflect quality of life – a position I certainly do not adopt here – it is hard to take the pessimists' thesis of a deterioration in the quality of urban life very seriously. As a final concession to their argument, however, suppose that the infant mortality rate *rose* by as much as a third (a gross exaggeration) in *all* British cities and towns between 1790 and 1850. While the evidence certainly does not support such a premise, what would it imply for trends in the real standard of living of the working class? Using an 1834 elasticity of real wages to infant mortality rates estimated elsewhere (Williamson, 1982a, Table 2, 0.2962), a 33 per cent rise in infant mortality implies a 9 per cent fall in the standard of living for urban workers. But only 36 per cent of the population was living in 'urban places' even as late as 1851. Thus, the impact of the hypothetical deterioration in the quality of urban life would have been to lower the standard of living of the British working class by 3 or 4 per cent (i.e. $(0.33 \times 0.2962) \times 0.358 = 0.035$), a trivial amount.

How, then, does one explain the origin of the urban-quality-of-life-deterioration myth? Upper-class Victorian observers no doubt were distressed that the construction of impressive public monuments and quality housing were forgone to create urban social overhead and jerrybuilt tenements; after all, we hear the same complaints from Third World city planners today (Kelley and Williamson, 1984). No doubt Victorian observers were even more distressed by the pall of coal smoke hanging over Britain's towns, which prompted them to write about urban decay and 'dark satanic mills'. Yet the coal smoke had other, obvious implications: fuel was cheap. Besides keeping industrial costs low, British exports competitive and urban job creation rapid, cheap fuel made for warmer houses, better cooked food and greater cleanliness (Buer, 1926, p. 60), all of which had their salubrious impact. The examples could be multiplied, but the issue appears to be one of environmental ugliness in the eyes of the Victorian middle-class beholder versus jobs and improved living standards for the urban poor. Since clean air, water and uncongested space are luxury goods, the working class quite naturally attached lower importance to them.

In summary, there is no evidence to support the position that the quality of urban life was deteriorating following 1790, and there is some evidence to support the contrary position. It also appears that the urban disamenities incurred by migrations to the environmentally nasty towns cannot account for much of the measured rise in wages documented in Table 2.8. The pessimists' 'dark satanic mills' view of the industrial revolution simply will not wash.

British mortality and the value of life

The previous section focused on the quality of life in the cities, for which an important proxy was the infant mortality rate. But what about overall longevity, not just in the cities, but for Britain as a whole? And if one had information on trends in longevity, how would one value them?

With the appearance of Wrigley and Schofield's *The Population History of England* (1981), longevity trends during the British industrial revolution are no longer in doubt. *The Population History of England* offers informed guesses on age-specific mortality from the mid-sixteenth century to the Registrar General's nineteenth-century *Annual Reports*. With their help, it is now possible to say something quantitatively useful about British mortality experience from the onset of the industrial revolution. Table 2.10 offers

Table 2.10   *Life expectancy at birth (e_0), 1751–1871: based on third English life table extended over age 50 by Princeton model north tables (both sexes)*

Year	Benchmark year $e_0(t)$	Range $e_0(t-5)$ to $e_0(t+5)$
1751	36.57	35.34 to 37.29
1781	34.72	38.17 to 35.93
1811	37.59	38.70 to 37.86
1851	39.54	39.56 to 40.39
1871	41.31	40.32 to (n.a.)

Source: Wrigley and Schofield (1981, Table A3.1).

a partial summary: it seems clear that longevity was on the rise after 1781, although only modestly.

Clearly, one need go no further since the rise in longevity would appear to support the optimists' position in the standard-of-living debate. Or does it? It is possible that the British worker placed a very high weight on longevity, and, to the extent that longevity improvements were far less impressive than the real wage improvements documented in Table 2.8, the 'true' standard of living – some combination of the two – would have grown somewhat less than did the measured real wage.

How, then, should one value human life? How should one weight longevity experience in assessing workers' standard-of-living gains during the industrial revolution? What price did the British worker himself place on extended longevity and lower mortality risk? These questions have been at the heart of the standard-of-living debate at least since Adam Smith raised them in the *Wealth of Nations*. Indeed, William Farr's pioneering work as Registrar General included explicit attention to the 'Economic Value of Population' (1885, pp. 59–64) and the 'Cost, and the Present and Future Economic Value of Man' (1885, pp. 531–7). While Farr would have preferred to calculate the gains in 'human happiness' (e.g. utility), he computed instead the discounted present value of income, net of consumption maintenance. Farr's human capital calculation has been repeated, with increased sophistication, many times in the century since.

While the human capital model may be appropriate for evaluating income losses from premature death, in what sense does it assess an individual's desire to live? In response to this criticism, a veritable flood of papers have appeared over the past decade, applying the willingness-to-pay model to a whole range of problems involving risks to life and limb. But, as far as I know, only Dan Usher (1973) has had the temerity to assess the value of improvements to longevity as an ingredient of economic progress. Elsewhere I applied Usher's model to the Wrigley and Schofield longevity data (Williamson, 1982c), and the results can be summarized here very briefly. Between 1781 and 1851, the 'true' standard of living (including the impact of life expectancy) grew *more* rapidly than did measured real wages (excluding the impact of life expectancy). Although the differences appear to have been minor, the measured real wage growth in Table 2.8 must be viewed as an *understatement* of 'true' living standard growth, at least as regards longevity experience.

(6) Beyond the industrial revolution: real wage gains, 1851–1911

Here I am on much firmer ground, since no one denies that real wage gains (and standard-of-living improvements) were quite persistent and impressive over the late nineteenth century as a whole. Furthermore, there are the *Wage Censuses* of 1886 and 1906 to guide us, rich earnings information that Bowley, Wood and other quantitative wage historians have used since the 1890s. Once again, I have augmented farm labor and the 'manual trades', supplying the nominal earnings estimates for the eighteen occupations listed in Table 2.11. And, once again, these are used to produce the 'blue-collar' and 'all worker' averages reported in Table 2.12. It would appear that my efforts to expand the occupational sample to capture service sector activities make very little difference since the conventional series by Bowley and Wood are pretty much replicated by my blue-collar series.

What, then, happened to real wages over the six decades following 1851? A summary appears in Table 2.13: the series implies that blue-collar workers enjoyed a 1.06 per cent per annum gain in real earnings, gains that compare favorably with the growth in real national income per worker. The gains are even more impressive over the half-century 1861–1911. Here the figure is 1.55 per cent per annum, a rate that exceeds the growth in real national income per worker by quite a bit (the latter from Feinstein, 1972, Table 8, 0.92 per cent per annum). The comparison implies, of course, that the 'blue-collar' worker gained relative to other income recipients in the late nineteenth century. The evidence in the next two chapters will confirm this implication of a leveling in the distribution of income.

(7) Who gains from economic growth?

Real wages rose rapidly during the industrial revolution, and they continued to rise well into the twentieth century. Furthermore, they rose for all workers, everywhere; the rise in the average workers' wage was not the quirk of migration to high-wage regions or mobility to high-wage occupations. Nor does (alleged) capitalist-induced unemployment detract from these gains. Although the quality of life of the average worker did suffer a bit along the way, especially for the increasing numbers touched by ugly urban environments, longevity improved and mortality risk fell.

Yet some gained more than others. Those with skills gained the most, and common farm labor gained the least. It may even be true that the worker of average skills gained somewhat less than those who held property in land or capital. But the evidence in Chapters 3 and 4 will be needed before firmer conclusions can be reached about who gains most from economic growth.

Table 2.11 *Estimates of nominal annual earnings for eighteen occupations, 1851–1911: adult males, England and Wales (in current £)*

Occupation	1851	1861	1871	1881	1891	1901	1911
(1L) Farm laborers	29.04	36.04	41.05	41.52	41.94	46.12	46.96
(2L) Non-farm common labor	44.83	44.18	51.44	55.88	62.68	68.90	74.04
(3L) Messengers and porters	88.88	82.21	87.34	97.05	89.51	110.97	85.91
(4L) Other government low-wage	66.45	67.15	63.72	74.65	70.40	72.20	67.95
(5L) Police and guards	53.62	53.94	55.86	76.73	72.33	68.69	70.62
(6L) Colliers (miners)	55.44	62.89	66.20	59.58	82.75	89.37	83.63
(1H) Government high-wage	234.87	251.33	281.02	275.29	215.01	159.63	161.61
(2H) Shipbuilding trades	64.12	69.11	76.83	81.38	87.80	92.51	102.34
(3H) Engineering trades	84.05	88.77	94.38	96.68	107.06	116.20	125.21
(4H) Building trades	66.35	72.90	83.33	87.18	91.52	103.35	105.14
(5H) Cotton spinners	58.64	63.26	82.55	85.77	93.60	101.40	108.50
(6H) Printing trades	74.72	74.72	79.92	86.42	90.04	92.66	97.29
(7H) Clergy	267.09	272.30	293.84	315.37	336.90	238.00	206.00
(8H) Solicitors and barristers	1,837.50	1,600.00	1,326.67	1,280.00	1,342.60	1,500.00	1,343.50
(9H) Clerks	235.81	248.47	268.63	286.65	268.06	286.86	229.89
(10H) Surgeons and doctors	200.92	343.00	645.40	520.29	475.47	265.39	272.75
(11H) Schoolmasters	81.11	93.76	97.02	120.80	133.90	147.50	176.15
(12H) Engineers and surveyors	479.00	529.15	579.13	312.97	380.61	333.99	287.37

Sources and Notes: Williamson (1982d, Appendix Table 4). See also notes to Table 2.4.

Table 2.12   *Trends in nominal full-time earnings, compared with Wood and Bowley, 1851–1911 (1901 = 100)*

Year	(1) Blue-collar	(2) All workers	(3) Wood (1909)	(4) Bowley (1937)
1851	55.4	58.9	55.9	n.a.
1861	63.2	65.2	63.7	62.4
1871	72.6	75.0	77.1	71.0
1881	76.4	79.4	82.1	77.4
1891	87.0	87.2	91.1	89.2
1901	100.0	100.0	100.0	100.0
1911	101.7	94.4	104.5	102.2

Sources and Notes: Cols (1) and (2) are derived from Table 2.11 using census employment weights reported in Williamson (1982d, Appendix A).

Col. (3) – Wood's (1909) series, reproduced in Mitchell and Deane (1962, p. 343), 'not allowing for unemployment', and 1911 = 1910.

Col. (4) – Bowley's series (1937), reproduced in Mitchell and Deane (1962, pp. 344–5), where 1861 = 1860 and 1871 = 1870.

Table 2.13   *Trends in real full-time earnings: adult male workers, 1851–1911 (1901 = 100)*

Year	(1) Cost of living (1900 = 100)	(2) Real earnings Blue-collar	(3) Real earnings All workers
1851	108.7	51.1	54.3
1861	142.3	44.5	45.9
1871	134.1	54.2	56.0
1881	115.5	66.3	68.8
1891	99.6	87.5	87.8
1901	100.2	100.0	100.0
1911	106.1	96.0	89.2

Sources and Notes: Col. (1) – from Appendix Table A.8.
Cols (2) and (3) – use col. (1) to deflate nominal earnings in Table 2.12.

(8) Could Britain have done better for her poor?

Real wages grew much faster after 1850 than before. Furthermore, the social reforms did not begin to hit the British scene until the 1840s, and they increased in importance as the late nineteenth century progressed. This correlation has encouraged the inference that British capitalism could have done better for her poor if the reforms had come earlier and if they had contained a more revolutionary bite. The chronology of reform suggests a set of feasible policy instruments that, if introduced early in the century, would have accelerated 'trickle-down' during the first industrial revolution. The pessimists have always thought that these counterfactual inferences were warranted. They have thus contributed to British capitalism's bad press and supported a benign view of the welfare state.

I am hardly the first to stress the importance of a *counterfactual* assessment of British capitalism's ability to deliver basic needs to her poor and improved living standards to the working class as a whole. Almost a decade ago, Max Hartwell and Stanley Engerman (1975, p. 193) made the same plea. They urged that we turn away from the questions of this chapter – did the standard of living of the working class rise during the first industrial revolution – and focus instead on two new counterfactual questions:

> [Were] the working classes . . . better off than they would have been in the absence of industrialization?

> [Would it] have been possible for there to have been some set of policies which would have permitted the working classes to have been better off than they actually were?

Indeed, in a recent application of dynamic programming to an optimal growth model, Nick von Tunzelmann (1982, p. 218) concludes:

> [In] these computations I have indicated some of the possibilities for both higher living standards and faster growth. A suitably enlightened and more interventionist government could have brought about both objectives: the Hammond thesis is thereby vindicated.

It may well be that von Tunzelmann's computations will hold up in subsequent debate, but it seems to me that his assessment is premature. One needs to know much more about the underlying *causes* of the actual real wage performance during the British industrial revolution before one can explore the feasible alternatives available to a more enlightened government. So it is that Part III of this book will dwell at length on underlying causes.

Notes

1 The historical literature is too vast to cite here. Readers who want a full bibliography might begin with Flinn (1974), Taylor (1975), Engerman and O'Brien (1981), and the sources cited below.

2 Since Robert McNamara made his eloquent Nairobi speech in 1972, the World Bank and development economists in general have been interested in the Third World's 'bottom 40 per cent'. See Chenery, *et al.* (1974), Cline (1975), Ahluwalia (1976) and Kuznets (1979).

3 Asa Briggs (1967) offers an excellent treatment of the changing nuances of the term 'working class' in Britain.

4 Like past authors, I treat earnings as though they represented all 'pre-fisc' income. This simplification is valid for English workers before this century, since only a tiny proportion of blue-collar employees owned their own homes or other property, and only a tiny proportion paid any direct taxes (US Commissioner of Labor, 1890). The heavier indirect taxes – excises, import duties, and the local rates on property – were reflected in the prices and rents workers paid, which are measured below.

5 The choice of weeks per year is arbitrary and matters little to what follows in this chapter. Arthur Bowley (1900a, p. 68) thought that six weeks was the average 'lost time' per year. The choice matters only if the number of weeks 'lost' varied greatly over time due to movements in involuntary unemployment. This issue is considered in section 4.

6   For details on these nominal wage series, see Williamson (1982d).

7   At the very top of the government pay structure, a truly baroque payments system prevailed. For example, department heads and high titled clerks were part of a patronage system. Extremely high reported salaries were often gross salaries out of which the recipient had to maintain his staff of clerks. I have ignored the pay of all officials for whom this seemed to be the practice. Customs officials who received a portion of the taxes collected and thus had low reported incomes are also excluded. So too are individuals for whom public payment clearly reflects political side-payments and heraldic requisites.

8   Phelps-Brown and Hopkins (1956) also used budget weights from Eden (1797), though without house rents.

9   Five urban budgets for 1795–1845 are presented in Burnett (1969). Neale (1966, pp. 597–9) supplies a laborer's household budget for Bath in 1831. Tucker (1936, p. 75) ventured two non-farm household budgets as averages of other underlying budget studies.

10 There would be clearer signs of deterioration between about 1800 and 1820 if the earnings of weavers and other non-spinning cotton workers were added to the overall averages. Such information is available from about the turn of the century onwards, although the underlying piece rate data are overly pessimistic about trends since they ignore productivity change. Using the 'best guess' deflator in Table 2.6, the Bowley–Wood wage rates for *all* cotton textile workers (Mitchell and Deane, 1962, pp. 348–9) yield the following real wage trends: 1806, 78.62; 1810, 66.57; 1815, 75.43; 1819, 54.67; 1827, 66.96; 1835, 78.62; and 1851, 100.00. Compared with blue-collar earnings, these real earnings of cotton workers fell sharply from 1806 to about 1819. They gain as fast as others thereafter, however.

11 Flinn's dating of the real wage upturn has also been questioned by von Tunzelmann (1979, p. 48).

12 While real wages surged over this quarter century, workers' fortunes *did* vary in the short run. *All* of that variability appears to be due to movements in the workers' cost of living. While the variability of the cost-of-living index is clearly evident in Table 2.6, it might be even clearer when combined with nominal earnings data. Consider, for example, the earnings trends in the following four occupations:

Occupation	Nominal earnings index (1851 = 100)					Real earnings index (1851 = 100)				
	1827	1835	1839	1843	1851	1827	1835	1839	1843	1851
(1L) Farm laborers	106.9	103.4	110.3	110.3	100.0	75.9	91.7	77.5	100.6	100.0
(2L) Laborers: building trades	86.0	91.2	101.3	104.2	100.0	61.0	80.9	71.2	95.1	100.0
(4H) Skilled: building trades	100.0	90.0	100.0	100.0	100.0	71.0	79.8	70.3	91.2	100.0
(5H) Spinners: cotton textiles	99.8	110.1	103.5	100.0	100.0	70.8	97.6	72.7	91.2	100.0
'Best guess' cost-of-living index	140.9	112.8	142.3	109.6	100.0					

Sources: (1L) – bottom 40%; (2L) – Bowley's figures, laborers in the building trades, using linear interpolation; (4H) – skilled in London's building trades, from Bowley; (5H) – Wood's spinners in cotton textiles during 'ordinary' weeks, using linear interpolation.

Thus, the real wage 'surge' between the late 1820s and mid-century was seriously interrupted in the late 1830s.

Of course, these real earnings trends are for full-time workers. While section 4 below will deal with the unemployment during the late 1830s and the 'hungry forties' in far greater detail, it would do little to change the real earnings indices' configuration estimated above.

13 The closest approach to the present estimates is the guarded conjecture offered by Deane and Cole (1962, pp. 25–6) that 'real wages [improved by] about 25 per cent between 1800 and 1824 and over 40 per cent between 1824 and 1850'. This implies a total increase of about 75 per cent (1800–50), compared with my estimate of 86.5 per cent for blue-collar and 135.4 for all workers (1797–1851). Recall that Clapham (1926, pp. 128 and 561) estimated a 60 per cent real wage increase for the 'average' workers (1790–1850).

14   'Migration' is defined as changes in the labor force distribution across regions. There is, of course, an extensive literature that debates the demographic source of the population and labor shift to high-wage areas over the period that bounds the standard-of-living debate. This section is not concerned with whether the observed shift can be attributed to natural increase (and whether to birth or death rate differences) or to actual migration.

15   But hardly of the size suggested by the qualitative literature. See, for example, Deane and Cole (1962, Ch. III).

16   This result contrasts sharply with American nineteenth-century experience. Vedder and Gallaway (1980) have recently estimated that regional migration accounted for a 0.2 per cent per annum gain in per capita income after the Civil War. The only period in British history that comes close to this is the decade 1841–51, when the regional migration gains contributed to 0.28–0.36 per cent per annum growth in real wages economy-wide (Lindert and Williamson, 1980, p. 74).

17   The regression results on annual data for the United Kingdom are:

$$U_{EMS} = 32.96 - 16.15 \text{ (GNP ratio)} - 168.02 \, (I/GNP) - 71.37 \, \overset{*}{w}$$
$$\phantom{U_{EMS} = 32.96} (7.85) \phantom{- 16.15 \text{ (GNP ratio)}} (63.81) (21.83)$$
$$- 288.45 (\overset{*}{w})^2 - 0.0032 \text{ (Time)} + 0.148 \text{ (Time)}^2$$
$$(121.80) (0.0036) \phantom{- 0.0032 \text{ (Time)}} (0.151)$$
$$\bar{U}_{EMS} = 5.78, \; SEE = 2.50, \; R^2 = 0.543, \; F = 9.11, \; d.f. = 35$$

where standard errors are in parentheses. (See Lindert and Williamson, 1983a, Section 3.4, for details.) The variables are

U_{EMS} = the EMS unemployment rate (a 1 per cent rate measured as '1.0');
GNP ratio = the ratio of current nominal gross national product at factor cost to its average level over the immediately preceding five years;
I/GNP = the share of gross domestic capital formation in gross national product at factor cost;
$\overset{*}{w}$ = the rate of change from the previous year in the wage rate for shipbuilding and engineering (a 1 per cent rise is '.01'); and
Time = the year minus 1851.

3

Earnings Inequality, Skill Scarcity and the Structure of Pay

(1) The classical legacy and modern distribution theories

The classical economist viewed labor as homogeneous. As a result, the structure of pay and the distribution of earnings do not receive much attention by those British economic historians who are still influenced by the classical legacy. Sir Henry Phelps-Brown reminds us of this legacy in his introduction to the *Inequality of Pay* (1977) and Harold Lydall makes a related point in the introduction to *The Structure of Earnings* (1968, p. 2):

> Adam Smith, Ricardo and Malthus took it for granted that landlords were rich, labourers were poor, and capitalists somewhere in the middle. If this were so, it was possible to discuss the problem [of inequality] in terms of the distribution of the total product between wages, rent and profit . . .

In contrast, recent analysis of twentieth-century evidence has shown that conventional property income distribution and its share in total income explains very little of the variance in incomes in today's industrialized societies. What is true of cross-sections also seems to be true of time series. Indeed, while it has long been appreciated that the wage share in Britain has been 'miraculously stable' since the 1860s (Keynes, 1939), this chapter and the next will show that both the earnings and the income distribution leveled over the same period.

Modern distribution theories have tried to accommodate these new stylized facts – most notably with the application of the human capital model – although there have been a number of 'unorthodox' competitors to this current neoclassical orthodoxy. While the economics profession has shifted its attention to the distribution of earnings as a major source of inequality, economic historians have been slow to follow suit. For example, Hartwell and Engerman (1975) devote hardly a word to the distribution of earnings and the same is true of the recent O'Brien and Engerman (1981) review of income distribution during the industrial revolution. Perhaps the dominance of earnings inequalities in accounting for mid-twentieth-century income inequality can be explained in part by the rise in the human capital income share, but were nineteenth-century conditions really so different?

It seems a pity that so many British economic historians have tended to slight nineteenth-century experience with the distribution of earnings. Certainly the requisite data – as we have seen in Chapter 2 – are relatively abundant. This is in sharp contrast with what is known about trends in the distribution of property income and self-employed income. Indeed, given the scarcity of distributional data on property and self-employed incomes, what little is known about *total* income distribution trends is based almost exclusively on very imperfect and highly truncated tax returns data.[1] As Chapter 4 will show, that information suggests that income inequality was on the rise from the 1820s to the 1860s, after which incomes leveled modestly up to World War I. Trends such as these have come to be called the 'Kuznets curve', after its original discoverer (Simon Kuznets, 1955). The first goal of this chapter, therefore, is to establish whether the distribution of earnings in Britain also traces out a Kuznets curve across the nineteenth century.

(2) The historians' maintained hypothesis

Arthur Bowley's (1937) pathbreaking efforts to measure earnings inequality through the late nineteenth century has produced the historians' maintained hypothesis, at least for British capitalism's mature phases. Based in large measure on Bowley's impressive research, Routh (1965), Thatcher (1968), Lydall (1968) and Phelps-Brown (1977) have all concluded that the distribution of earnings has changed but little since the 1880s, although all have noted the short-run rise in inequality up to World War I that is apparent in Bowley's data. Sir Henry Phelps-Brown, for example, states (1977, p. 319):

> In this span of nearly seventy years there have been big changes in the distribution of manual workers between different occupations, industries, and regions, and in the relative pay of different grades and groups: yet not only has the form of the distribution of earnings been lognormal throughout, but the dispersion has varied little at any time, and in 1974 was almost exactly what it had been in 1886.

While important research on twentieth-century earnings distributions has been pursued by many others, the pre-World War I trends are based solely on Bowley's original analysis of the 1886 and 1906 *Wage Censuses*. Since conventional wisdom has been guided for some time by Bowley's unique effort, we had best examine his contribution in some detail.

In *Wages and Income in the United Kingdom since 1860*, Bowley constructed earnings distributions from the 1886 and 1906 wage inquiries, restricting wage earners to 'adult male manual workers'. Using weekly earnings of these manual workers, Bowley found evidence that suggested a modest, late nineteenth-century inequality drift.[2] But how is one to infer *economy-wide* earnings inequality trends from Bowley's data? After all, the 1886 *Wage Census* excluded agricultural laborers as well as almost all workers employed in the service sectors. Even among those employments included in the wage inquiries, it is not clear whether Bowley made use of reported figures on (i) the building and printing trades, or (ii) police, public utilities and the railways. He does tell us that he excludes miners. If Bowley excluded (i) and (ii), then his 'manual workers' comprised less than one-third of the total wage and salary earners reported in the 1881 population census.[3]

It would appear that the maintained hypothesis of long-term stability in the British earnings distribution and the short-run rise in inequality in the late nineteenth century is based on very limited coverage of the total employed labor force. The exclusion of farm laborers clearly truncates the total size distribution of earnings from the bottom, and this group declines in importance over time. Perhaps even more importantly, Bowley excludes service sector employment, where the distribution of earnings is known to be most skewed.[4]

This chapter will expand Bowley's effort. First, I shall augment his coverage to include the remaining two-thirds of the adult male labor force, thereby improving our knowledge of late nineteenth-century earnings inequality. Second, I shall extend the series backwards to include two earlier benchmarks, 1827 and 1851.[5] These earlier nineteenth-century dates are far more critical to the inequality debate initiated by Marx and Engels. Chapter 2 threw some modest support behind the view that capitalism breeds earnings inequality, since skilled workers appeared to be gaining relative to unskilled workers. This chapter will offer far more evidence consistent with that view.

(3) Estimating earnings distributions, 1827–1901

Three sets of data are required to reconstruct the distribution of earnings at each of the four benchmark dates (1827, 1851, 1881/6 and 1901/6).[6] First, one needs estimates of the distribution of earnings among male workers within occupational/industrial groups. That is, one needs estimates of *intra*-occupation earnings distributions. Second, one needs estimates of *inter*-occupational earnings differentials, or what might be called pay ratios. Third, one needs estimates of the distribution of employment across occupational/industrial groups. The census figures used to derive employment distributions are reported in detail elsewhere (Williamson, 1980a, Appendix Table 2; 1979b, Appendix C) and need little elaboration here. The other two components, however, do require more discussion.

Intra-occupational earnings distributions
Estimated earnings distributions for sixteen occupational/industrial groups are summarized in Table 3.1 by means of three generally accepted measures of inequality. These sixteen groups come very close to exhausting all wage and salary earners, although some industries and/or occupations have been excluded owing to data limitations (for example, the clothing trades and shop assistants). All sixteen groups have intra-occupational distribution estimates for 1881. The same is true for 1901, with the exception of male domestics, miners and local government employees. I assume that the 1881

Table 3.1 *Adult male earnings inequality statistics within industry/occupation, 1827–1901*

Occupational/industrial class	Gini coefficient				Percentage share held by top 5 per cent				Atkinson Index, ε = 2.5			
	1827	1851	1881	1901	1827	1851	1881	1901	1827	1851	1881	1901
Agricultural labor	0.091	0.098	0.073	0.039	6.62	7.49	6.48	5.81	0.030	0.036	0.020	0.004
Professionals	0.488	0.516	0.350	0.384	23.69	25.46	15.98	25.43	0.554	0.546	0.383	0.402
Clerks	0.322	0.347	0.331	0.358	17.99	19.20	12.06	15.56	0.284	0.310	0.336	0.360
Messengers and porters	0.164	0.180	0.215	0.210	8.31	12.19	14.79	11.66	0.104	0.119	0.166	0.151
All national government employees	0.418	0.416	0.447	0.353	21.34	24.01	20.96	21.14	0.464	0.438	0.466	0.316
Clergy	0.408	0.392	0.337	0.337	16.43	16.74	18.21	18.21	0.521	0.492	0.390	0.390
Printing trades			0.142	0.188			8.62	9.59			0.007	0.148
Teachers			0.216	0.239			11.42	11.95			0.177	0.203
Building trades (summer)			0.125	0.171			7.48	7.54			0.064	0.150
Male domestics			0.179				11.62				0.119	
All local government employees			0.103				8.53				0.045	
Miners			0.095				6.67				0.042	
Public utilities			0.166	0.181			8.77	9.01			0.109	0.154
Railways			0.154	0.179			9.48	9.87			0.089	0.114
Manual workers in commodity production			0.163	0.204			9.23	9.76			0.104	0.155
General non-agricultural labor			0.060	0.127			6.91	7.77			0.020	0.091

Sources and Notes: From Williamson (1980a, Table 1, p. 464). The Atkinson Index is estimated by

$$I = 1 - \left\{\sum_j \left[(\bar{y}_j/\bar{y})^{1-\epsilon} f(y_j)\right]\right\}^{1/1-\epsilon}$$

where $\bar{y}_j$ is mean earnings in the jth class, $\bar{y}$ is overall mean earnings and $f(y_j)$ is the percent of male employees in the jth class. The values of ϵ are arbitrary, but $\epsilon = 2.5$ is commonly used in the literature. See Atkinson (1970).

intra-occupational distributions apply to 1901 for those three groups. The intra-occupational distribution data are much skimpier for the early nineteenth century: estimates for 1827 and 1851 are available for only six of the groups. Here, again, I have assumed that the 1881 intra-occupational distribution estimates apply to the two earlier dates for the remaining ten groups.

Table 3.1 shows a wide range in the dispersion of earnings within each of these groups: the Gini coefficient, for example, rises from a low of 0.060 for general non-agricultural laborers to a high of 0.447 for all national government employees. One should also note the hint of a positive correlation between average earnings and earnings inequality among these sixteen groups, which suggests that high average earnings and greater dispersion are related to skill level. This positive correlation is confirmed by regression on both the 1881 and 1901 data,[7] and it is consistent with modern British evidence. Sir Henry Phelps-Brown (1977, p. 257), for example, reports that 'the dispersion is wider the higher are average earnings in Great Britain', based on full-time adult men in 1973. No doubt there are many potential explanations for this phenomenon, but surely the steeper age–earnings profile in higher-skilled occupations would explain much of the higher dispersion among the high-skilled occupations (given identical age distribution). In any case, it is comforting to know that the nineteenth-century British intra-occupational distribution estimates replicate the more reliable mid-twentieth-century evidence for Britain and America.[8]

Inter-occupational earnings differentials and the structure of pay
The estimates of average annual earnings for each of these groups, at each of the four years, are discussed at greater length in section 5 below, where I show that, contrary to the standard view, British pay differentials between occupations of various skill were *not* stable across the nineteenth century, but rather rose sharply after the 1820s, peaked between 1851 and 1871, and declined subsequently up to World War I. As it turns out, the view that the structure of pay was stable across the century has been based on the building trades (Phelps-Brown, 1977; Phelps-Brown and Browne, 1968; Phelps-Brown and Hopkins, 1955) and on 'manual workers in commodity production' (Knowles and Robertson, 1951). This view is not supported when the evidence is expanded to include agriculture, mining and the service sectors.

Likely bias in the intra-occupational distributions
There is reason to believe that the 1886 *Wage Census* understated the true level of intra-occupational distributional inequality (Bowley, 1937, pp. 41–2). As Bowley points out, the 1886 inquiry was voluntary and the returns selective. Since it seems likely that the response rate was much higher among the larger firms, and given abundant twentieth-century evidence that small firms pay lower wages, it seems reasonable to infer that the 1886 earnings distributions are truncated from below. This was apparently less true of the 1906 *Wage Census*. Furthermore, 1886 census interviewers and tabulators 'often assumed that operatives doing the same kind of work were paid at the same rate, [and] that the variation of wages

from the average in each occupation in the district observed was insignificant' (Bowley, 1937, p. 41). This tendency to minimize regional wage variance[9] in the 1886 inquiry, while not true of the 1906 inquiry, also imparts an upward bias in intra-occupational distribution trends over the late nineteenth century.

What is true of the intra-occupational distribution bias is also likely to be true of aggregate earnings distribution trends between 1881 and 1901. Thus, if a measured decline in earnings inequality across the late nineteenth century is observed, it seems likely that the extent of the decline is understated.

I have been forced to assume that the 1881 intra-occupational distributions apply to 1827 and 1851 for the ten occupational–industrial groups where the data are lacking. This procedure probably produces a downward bias in aggregate earnings distribution trends over the first three-quarters of the nineteenth century. This inference is based on the observation that skills scarcity was on the rise from the 1820s to the 1860s, in large part owing to the fact that sectoral output mix was shifting towards those activities that used skilled labor more intensively. These labor market forces were likely to have yielded rising intra-occupational earnings inequality, as indeed was the case between 1827 and 1851 in four of the six occupations for which there are data (Table 3.1). Since the assumption of intra-occupational earnings stability for ten of the sixteen groups minimized such trends, it seems likely that the actual rise in economy-wide earnings inequality is understated.

(4) Trends in earnings inequality

The Kuznets curve revealed

Regardless of the inequality statistic preferred, Table 3.2 confirms that earnings inequality passed through a Kuznets curve during the nineteenth century. Inequality rose sharply from the 1820s to the 1850s. This trend reversed in the last half of the century, but 1901 inequality did not return to its 1827 level. Furthermore, the discussion above suggests that the statistics in Table 3.2 probably understate the true extent of these trends; the direction of bias implies that the early nineteenth-century inequality surge and the late nineteenth-century leveling are both understated. Nor do these earnings inequality trends simply reflect the relative fortunes of farm laborers since the non-farm earnings distributions exhibit exactly the same trends.

The finding of a late nineteenth-century leveling may appear to contradict Bowley's (1937) estimates for 'manual workers', but it is in fact confirmed by the detailed estimates in Table 3.1. Although I have already indicated some reasons to expect an upward bias in the intra-occupational earnings distribution trends, earnings inequality among 'manual workers in commodity production' did indeed rise between 1881 and 1901 (the Gini coefficient, for example, rose from 0.163 to 0.204 over these two decades). It appears, however, that these post-1881 trends among 'manual workers in

Table 3.2   *Male earnings inequality statistics, economy-wide and non-agricultural, 1827–1901*

Inequality Statistics	1827	1851	1881	1901
Economy-wide:				
Gini coefficient	0.293	0.358	0.328	0.331
Atkinson Index				
$\epsilon = 1.5$	0.183	0.255	0.221	0.221
$\epsilon = 2.5$	0.235	0.308	0.271	0.288
$\epsilon = 4.0$	0.288	0.359	0.317	0.356
Top 5 per cent	20.46%	27.40%	25.34%	22.65%
Top 10 per cent	27.93%	34.31%	32.63%	30.66%
Non-agricultural:				
Gini coefficient:	0.294	0.357	0.330	0.325
Atkinson Index				
$\epsilon = 1.5$	0.189	0.259	0.225	0.218
$\epsilon = 2.5$	0.243	0.308	0.274	0.286
$\epsilon = 4.0$	0.302	0.358	0.319	0.362
Top 5 per cent	21.42%	28.80%	25.72%	22.86%
Top 10 per cent	28.91%	35.75%	33.58%	30.75%

Source: Williamson (1980a, Table 2, p. 467).

commodity production' were not typical of more fundamental forces at work in Britain, since the economy-wide Gini coefficient was quite stable over the same period and in fact *fell* among non-agricultural wage and salary earners. That is, other occupational/industrial groups were undergoing intra-occupational distribution leveling. Two of these are conspicuous: farm laborers and national government employees. The former has been discussed at length in the literature on regional convergence of farm wages (Hunt, 1973), and the latter in the literature on Civil Service reform (Routh, 1954). In addition, wage differentials across occupations were declining steadily over the period. These offsetting forces will be estimated explicitly and reported below.

It is apparent from Table 3.2 that the 1880s were preceded by three decades of pronounced leveling in the earnings distribution. Indeed, most of the leveling in earnings from mid-century to 1901 took place between 1851 and 1881. It appears, therefore, that the 'maintained hypothesis' of stability in the earnings distribution has been based on two unfortunate limitations in Bowley's original data base: first, it was limited to the manual trades and thus excluded urban services where the variance of earnings has always been greatest (Table 3.1); second, it excluded the period of more dramatic leveling in the size distribution of earnings, 1851–81.

Decomposing the 'sources' of earnings inequality trends
These trends can be decomposed into three components by appealing to the well-known theorem that aggregate variance can be separated into variance within and between groups. Table 3.3 applies that theorem to aggregate earnings inequality changes. Thus, trends in nineteenth-century earnings

Table 3.3   *Sources of nineteenth-century earnings inequality trends,*
1827–1901

| | | Inequality changes due to: | | | |
	Employment shifts (A)	Changing intra-occupational inequality (B)	Changing inter-occupational inequality (C)	Total inequality change	Ratio of (C) to total
Period					
Economy-wide:					
1827–51	+.363	+.740	+3.749	+4.852	0.77
1851–81	+.305	−.943	−1.980	−2.618	0.76
1881–1901	+.134	+.363	−1.096	−.599	1.83
1851–1901	+.324	−.206	−3.925	−3.807	1.03
Non-agriculture:					
1827–51	+.204	+.980	+4.935	+6.118	0.81
1851–81	+.211	−1.133	−2.373	−3.295	0.72
1881–1901	+.051	+.406	−1.229	−.773	1.59
1851–1901	+.163	−.229	−4.383	−4.449	0.99

Source and Notes: Williamson (1980a, Table 4, p. 470). The inequality statistic used here is the square of the coefficient of variation. The coefficient of variation is used for convenience in manipulation, but it traces out the same inequality trends as the alternative statistics presented in Table 3.2. Thus, total inequality change between two benchmark years is simply

$$dI = A + B + C$$
$$A = \Sigma\{(\bar{y}_j/\bar{y})^2 I_j + [(\bar{y}_j - \bar{y})/\bar{y}]^2\}d\omega_j$$
$$B = \Sigma[\omega_j(\bar{y}_j/\bar{y})^2]dI_j$$
$$C = \Sigma\{(\omega_j I_j)d(\bar{y}_j/\bar{y})^2 + \omega_j d[(\bar{y}_j - \bar{y})/\bar{y}]^2\}$$

and $\bar{y}_j$ = mean earnings in the jth occupational/industrial group, $\bar{y}$ = mean earnings economy-wide, and ω_j = the employment share in the jth group. End period (Paasche) weights are used throughout. Use of Laspeyres weights matters little to the key results reported in the text.

inequality in Britain can be traced to three factors: shifting employment weights, intra-occupational inequality trends, and inter-occupational inequality trends. Table 3.3 presents this decomposition for both economy-wide and non-agricultural trends between 1827 and 1901.

Since the underlying data are more complete for the 1881–1901 episode, consider those results first. Total inequality (as measured by the coefficient of variation) declined over the late nineteenth century both in the total labor force (−0.599) and in non-agricultural employments (−0.773), a result consistent with most of the statistics presented in Table 3.2. The source of this modest leveling was certainly *not* intra-occupational. Rather, it appears that a drift towards inequality *within* industries and occupations characterized the late nineteenth century. This finding confirms the standard view based on Bowley's analysis of 'manual workers in commodity production'. Yet, Table 3.3 shows how misleading such evidence has been to interpretations of late nineteenth-century British economic history. In spite of that modest intra-occupational inequality drift, inequality in the labor force as a whole *decreased*! The explanation for the apparent conflict lies with the overwhelming and offsetting importance of trends in occupational pay ratios, that is, the leveling of inter-occupational inequality. In fact, all of the leveling in British earnings across the late nineteenth century can be attributed to the steady contraction of the wage structure, pay ratio convergence, and the decline in skill premia, since even employment shifts increased aggregate inequality.

The latter result is hardly surprising given what is now known about the nineteenth-century correlation between occupational/industrial average earnings and the relative dispersion of earnings. Table 3.1 suggests high positive correlation between mean occupational earnings and intra-occupational inequality: high-skill occupations exhibit high earnings variance. Thus, as successful development and skill accumulation took place throughout the economy, this skill accumulation was accommodated by a rising skill endowment within each occupation (and thus rising occupation-specific mean earnings) and shifts in employment to those occupations requiring higher skill. This 'employment mix effect' has been noted by Simon Kuznets (1955) and others as one likely cause of the rise in aggregate inequality over time. The 1881–1901 evidence would appear to confirm that view, although Table 3.3 also indicates that this effect was relatively unimportant in late nineteenth-century Britain. No doubt the upward bias on the intra-occupational inequality trends between 1881 and 1901 offers some spurious support to that conclusion, but it seems unlikely that my main findings are affected by the bias.

The 1881–1901 findings are more or less replicated for the longer episode of aggregate earnings leveling following 1851. Once again, aggregate earnings inequality trends over this half-century were augmented by employment shifts to occupations and industries that tended to have higher earnings dispersion. Most of this employment mix effect is explained by the rise in the service sector in general, and high-skill service sector activities in particular. This is certainly manifested most dramatically by the relative demise of farm employment, an influence apparent in Table 3.3 where the employment shift effect is more pronounced for the economy as a whole than for non-agricultural employment alone. But the influence can also be seen within the non-agricultural labor force. The source of the employment mix effect outside agriculture was the massive decline in 'manual workers in commodity production' and general non-agricultural laborers combined. Both of these groups (accounting for about 62 per cent of non-agricultural employment in 1851) exhibited relatively equal earnings distribution in 1881 and 1901, but they declined relative to all other urban employment. Those service employments that had the highest 1881 intra-occupational earnings inequality and also enjoyed relative expansion over the half-century were the printing trades, clerks and national government employees.

In any case, the key finding for the half-century following 1851 is the unambiguous dominance of declining pay ratios.

The 1827–51 evidence presented in Table 3.3 must be treated with more caution. Total earnings inequality as measured in Table 3.3 rose sharply from the 1820s to mid-century, a result consistent with the alternative inequality statistics presented in Table 3.2. Recall, however, that these estimates are likely to understate the extent of the rise since I have assumed stability in intra-occupational distributions for ten of the sixteen groups involved. For that reason, Table 3.3 may understate the contribution of rising intra-occupational inequality to total earnings inequality trends following the 1820s.

Subject to these qualifications, note that all three sources of inequality were working in cooperation between 1827 and 1851: employment shifted towards occupations with high intra-occupational inequality, intra-occupational inequality rose, and pay ratios surged upward. Consistent with late nineteenth-century evidence, the employment mix effect had only a very modest influence – especially in non-farm employment activities; pay ratio behavior was by far the dominant force, accounting for about three-quarters of the rise in total earnings inequality both in the economy as a whole and in non-agricultural employment.

(5) Occupational pay ratios over longer periods

Some prominent British wage historians may be stunned by the finding that occupational pay ratios seem to have driven earnings inequality across the nineteenth century. After all, what about the tradition of rigid wage structure that has dominated wage histories for so long? How is it that my findings clash so sharply with that tradition? This section will suggest that the wage historian has been a victim of limited quantitative vision.

Custom and rigid wage structure?
As I point out in Chapter 7, the concept of non-competing groups was coined by Mill (1852) and Cairnes (1874) to deal with the nineteenth-century reality of class immobility. Since labor was burdened by 'class', occupation migration was constrained, and labor supply to a given occupation tended to be wage-inelastic. If one accepts some version of the theory of non-competing groups – and I do in Chapter 7 – must one then believe that wages in labor markets of various skills were controlled by non-market forces? Tocqueville thought this was true of early nineteenth-century public employment:

> . . . an aristocracy tends barely to allow a subsistence minimum to office messengers but to vote high salaries for the high offices of State, positions which they or their children might occupy and benefit from . . . (Cited in Scitovsky, 1966, pp. 25–6)

The tradition prevails to the present. For example, Peter Wiles (1974, p. 80) finds conventional economics of little use in accounting for historical trends in pay ratios:

> It is history, i.e., war and inflation, that governs the relations between noncompeting groups. Orthodox microtheory has little to say, and large shifts [in income distribution] take place that it cannot explain.

Some wage historians have gone even further. Not only have they felt that the wage structure was determined by forces exogenous to the conventional economic model of labor market behavior, but they have been persuaded by the view that the wage structure has been stable over time and that this stability can be explained by 'custom'. This group will certainly resist the findings of this chapter, so I must take care to show how they might have been misled by their evidence.

British experience in the building trades has done more to support the rigid wage structure thesis than any other evidence, and Sir Henry Phelps-Brown and Sheila Hopkins have done more in supplying those data than any other wage historians (Phelps-Brown and Hopkins, 1955, 1956, 1959; Phelps-Brown and Browne, 1968; Phelps-Brown, 1977; and the collection of essays in Phelps-Brown and Hopkins, 1981):

> In Great Britain . . . down to 1914, differentials were largely ruled by custom . . . A conspicuous instance of the stability of differentials has been traced to the building trade: from about 1410 until 1914 one and the same differential between the craftsman and the labourer persisted in the South of England. (Phelps-Brown, 1977, p. 6)

These findings are still cited extensively by some labor economists as evidence rejecting neoclassical theory of the market wage in favor of custom. (See the review in Cain, 1976.)

The building trades have not been the sole source of data supporting the rigid wage structure view, since the manual trades in the key export staple sectors have offered similar evidence for the late nineteenth century and beyond. For example, J. W. Rowe (1928) found stability in the wage structure in engineering and Knowles and Robertson (1951) found the same for manual workers in shipbuilding and the railways, as well as engineering and the building trades, concluding that there was 'considerable stability in all industries up to 1914' (Knowles and Robertson, 1951, p. 110). Until very recently, these findings by Knowles and Robertson have been accepted by Turner (1952), Lydall (1968, pp. 182–5) and other students of the problem. Thus, in Phelps-Brown's words, '. . . it may be said that there was no disturbance in the structure of differential rates during this period of nearly thirty years down to 1914' (1977, p. 72).

Those who still hold to the wage-rigidity view of nineteenth-century British labor markets find that these 'customs' were exploded by exogenous events of the twentieth century (Phelps-Brown, 1977, p. 7):

> . . . with the First World War came changes of the kind that would break up the role of custom . . . The doubling of money wages in five years carried men away from old landmarks, especially insofar as the rise in the general level was brought about by flat-rate cost-of-living allowances that narrowed differentials.

According to Turner (1952) and Douty (1953, 1961), unions were at the heart of this episodic shift in the wage structure from its nineteenth-century rigidity.

This traditional view has come under attack in the postwar period, led in large measure by a critique of the underlying data base. After all, the building trades employed less than a tenth of the male labor force in 1851, and now there is doubt that the building trades were even representative of historical trends in the pay structure. Harold Lydall (1968, p. 171) has cautioned that '. . . we cannot be sure that the building skill differential is a reliable indicator of changes in wage dispersion generally'. After a masterful review of the eighteenth-century evidence on wage flexibility, T. S. Ashton (1955, p. 224) concludes without qualification that 'The inelasticity of rates of pay in the building trades was not representative of wages in the industry as a whole' and in any case, while Gilboy's (1934) evidence confirms the rigidity of laborers' wages, 'the wages of skilled workers were less rigid' (Ashton, 1955, p. 220) even in the building trades. Perhaps comments such as these help explain Phelps-Brown's recent retreat from his custom–rigid-wages position, for in his 1977 book (p. 69) he considers that the building trades may have offered too limited a view and that the alleged stability in the wage structure

> may well owe much to the exceptional technical stability of building [where] there can have been little change in the relative number of craftsmen and labourers required. Where technical change impinges, it affects the differential for skill along with other differentials.

A word about the data
With very few exceptions, then, research on British pay ratios has focused on commodity-producing sectors generally, and manufacturing and the building trades in particular. As we have seen, Knowles and Robertson (1951) are frequently cited for evidence to reject conventional neoclassical theories of wage determination in favor of non-market influences. But their evidence of pay ratio stability from 1880 to World War I is based exclusively on the building trades and four manufacturing sectors, activities that even in 1871 accounted for only 17.5 per cent of the occupied male labor force and 34.5 per cent of the non-agricultural labor force (Mitchell and Deane, 1962, p. 60). Sir Henry Phelps-Brown (1977; Phelps-Brown and Browne, 1968; Phelps-Brown and Hopkins, 1955) is cited for the pre-1880 period even more frequently and his series, as I have stressed above, are restricted to the building trades of southern England. The building trades accounted for only 7.3 per cent of the male labor force in 1851 and 10.3 per cent of the non-agricultural labor force. The largest commodity-producing sector – agriculture – is ignored throughout; so, too, is mining.

In an effort to improve the trail blazed by these pioneers, two earlier papers of mine processed earnings data on a much wider sample of nineteenth-century occupations (Williamson, 1979b, 1980a). I began with the famous series of articles by Arthur L. Bowley in the *Journal of the Royal Statistical Society* (1898, 1900b, 1901; Bowley and Wood, 1899, 1905, 1906), where he reports earnings estimates by occupation and sector. Bowley's data, together with unpublished Board of Trade wage time series and other sources, made it possible to document the structure of pay in agriculture, industry, mining and construction in great detail from the 1850s onwards. While less abundant, there was sufficient information to construct similar time series for the 1790–1850 period.

But what about services? In 1841, 30.5 per cent of the British labor force was employed in the service sector (Mitchell and Deane, 1962, p. 60). The figure was even higher (39.3 per cent) in 1871. As we have seen, traditional scholarship has tended to slight this employment, presumably because of the difficulty in securing consistent time series on service sector pay. This neglect is doubly unfortunate, since not only did the large service sector contain the majority of the high-wage occupations, but, as we have seen above, it contained the widest dispersion in the wage structure.

Although the service sector is not well documented for the nineteenth century, there *are* sources of earnings data that I have mined extensively and that I discussed at length in Chapter 2. These sources have produced long time series on annual earnings for eighteen male occupations, six of which are unskilled and twelve of which are skilled:

Unskilled	*Skilled*
Farm laborers	Skilled labor in manual trades:
Non-farm, unskilled laborers:	Skilled in shipbuilding
Common laborers	engineering
Messengers and porters	building trades
Government low-wage, e.g.	textiles
police, messengers,	printing trades
porters, letter	Skilled labor in services:
carriers	Government high-wage, e.g.
Guards and watchmen	clerks, doctors, barristers,
Coal miners	engineers
	Clergymen
	Solicitors and barristers,
	non-government
	Clerks, non-government
	Surgeons, medical officers and
	doctors
	Teachers
	Engineers and surveyors, non-
	government

Given relevant employment weights, these data can then be used to construct pay trends for farm workers, unskilled non-farm workers and skilled workers, for the period 1781–1911. These wage series can be used to construct pay ratios of skilled to unskilled (Tables 3.4–3.7), as well as 'wage gaps' between farm and non-farm employment (Table 3.8).

Trends in pay ratios, 1781–1911
A glance at Tables 3.6 and 3.7 confirms my findings on earnings distribution trends reported earlier in this chapter. A Kuznets curve is apparent in both non-farm and economy-wide pay ratios, and their timing conforms to the earnings inequality trends in Table 3.2. In addition, while the earnings distribution data were available for only four benchmarks between 1827 and

Table 3.4   *Non-farm pay ratios during early industrialization: conjectures using various fixed employment weights, 1781–1819*

	Weighting year		
Year	1755 (Lindert)	1755–1811 (interpolated)	1811 (Lindert)
1781	1.535	1.494	1.547
1797	1.448	1.387	1.329
1805	1.413	1.379	1.322
1810	1.444	1.428	1.419
1815	1.486	1.448	1.454
1819	1.519	1.477	1.516

Sources and Notes: Seventeen occupations underlie the calculations – five unskilled and twelve skilled. See text for occupations, and Table 2.4 and Williamson (1982d, Table 1) for their nominal earnings. Average skilled and average unskilled wages are derived employing the employment weights in Lindert (1980a,b), with some adjustments (as in Williamson, 1982d, Appendix C). The pay ratios are simply the ratios of average skilled to average unskilled wages.

1901, the pay ratio time series supply additional information for 1781–1827 and 1901–11, as well as more frequent observations between 1827 and 1901.

Since I have already concluded from the decomposition analysis in Table 3.3 that inter-occupational inequality (pay ratios) did most of the work in driving earnings inequality between 1827 and 1901, it seems reasonable to use Tables 3.4–3.7 to infer earnings inequality trends for the period 1781–1911 more generally. First, judging by Tables 3.4 and 3.5, it would appear that the Napoleonic Wars may have interrupted a long-run trend towards wage inequality and relative skills scarcity. (For more details, see Williamson, 1982d.) Furthermore, there is very little evidence of a secular resumption of 'wage stretching' until the 1820s. In addition, it appears that the surge in earnings inequality had pretty much ceased by the 1850s, and most of that surge took place in the 1820s and 1830s. T. S. Ashton's (1955)

Table 3.5   *Economy-wide pay ratios during early industrialization: conjectures using various fixed employment weights, 1781–1819*

	Weighting year		
Year	1755 (Lindert)	1755–1811 (interpolated)	1811 (Lindert)
1781	2.009	1.832	1.763
1797	1.762	1.628	1.501
1805	1.648	1.567	1.467
1810	1.770	1.675	1.596
1815	1.886	1.739	1.653
1819	1.919	1.768	1.711

Sources and Notes: Williamson (1982d, Table 4). See notes to Table 3.4. Eighteen occupations underlie the calculation – six unskilled (five non-farm plus farm labor) and twelve skilled.

Table 3.6 *Nineteenth-century non-farm pay ratios: trends using various employment weights, 1815–1911*

	Fixed weights			Census weighting year			Variable
Year	1821	1831	1851	1871	1891	1911	weights
1815	2.035	2.077	2.082	2.238	2.318	2.282	2.035
1819	2.245	2.286	2.291	2.482	2.602	2.604	2.286
1827	2.133	2.164	2.169	2.382	2.509	2.527	2.164
1835	2.619	2.618	2.628	2.820	2.943	2.883	2.618
1851	2.737	2.719	2.734	2.796	2.876	2.780	2.734
1861	2.775	2.758	2.772	2.869	2.950	2.824	2.818
1871	2.817	2.790	2.804	2.884	2.954	2.884	2.884
1881	2.697	2.701	2.712	2.801	2.881	2.884	2.861
1891	2.312	2.333	2.343	2.427	2.491	2.433	2.491
1901	2.106	2.090	2.098	2.193	2.269	2.234	2.221
1911	2.086	2.080	2.088	2.115	2.173	2.162	2.162

Sources and Notes: Williamson (1982d, Table 2). See notes to Table 3.4. The 'variable weight' calculations use census year observations for both wages and weights over the period 1851–1911. For the remaining years, the correspondence is not exact, viz.:

Wage year	Weight year
1815	1821
1819	1821
1827	1831
1835	1831

Table 3.7 *Nineteenth-century economy-wide pay ratios: trends using various employment weights, 1815–1911*

	Fixed weights			Census weighting year			Variable
Year	1821	1831	1851	1871	1891	1911	weights
1815	2.452	2.488	2.462	2.564	2.571	2.524	2.452
1819	2.637	2.672	2.649	2.796	2.853	2.851	2.686
1827	2.921	2.932	2.871	3.002	2.967	2.944	2.932
1835	3.611	3.570	3.499	3.560	3.492	3.378	3.570
1851	3.922	3.849	3.675	3.641	3.476	3.297	3.765
1861	3.609	3.557	3.507	3.473	3.397	3.229	3.486
1871	3.587	3.525	3.481	3.441	3.364	3.255	3.441
1881	3.461	3.439	3.391	3.378	3.303	3.263	3.326
1891	3.198	3.192	3.128	3.075	2.950	2.835	2.950
1901	2.926	2.871	2.811	2.787	2.695	2.607	2.583
1911	2.821	2.784	2.732	2.643	2.544	2.483	2.483

Sources and Notes: Williamson (1982d, Table 5). See notes to Table 3.5.

thesis that rising wage inequality was characteristic of early modern economic growth appears to be confirmed (a position that is shared by Eric Hobsbawm, 1964, p. 276, Harold Perkin, 1969, and even John Stuart Mill, 1848). British experience also appears to conform with similar wage stretching during early modern growth in America following 1820 (Williamson and Lindert, 1980, Ch. 4). Finally, the late nineteenth-century leveling that was apparent in earnings distributions is also apparent in the pay ratios. The narrowing in wage differentials was quite pronounced, contrary to Hobsbawm's (1964, p. 293) allegations of rising relative income of the 'labor aristocracy' and contrary to Phelps-Brown, Knowles and Robertson, and so many others who have emphasized the stability of the pay structure during the forty years prior to World War I.

It appears, therefore, that conclusions based on the building and the manual trades have misled British historians for some time. When properly measured, there *is* a Kuznets curve in British nineteenth-century history. This result is not the product of my revising the two conventional pay ratio indicators that support the rigid wage structure view.[10] Nor is it the product of my including farm laborers in the unskilled wage calculation, since the same trends appear in the non-farm series (Tables 3.4 and 3.6). Furthermore, the 'wage gap' between unskilled farm and non-farm employment is remarkably stable between 1827 and 1911, although there is evidence of lagging farm wages throughout the inequality surge of 1819–51 (Table 3.8).

Table 3.8 *Trends in nineteenth-century 'wage gaps': the percentage differential between unskilled non-farm and farm wages*

Year	Weighting year	Percentage 'wage gap' (variable weights)
1781	Lindert, 1755–1811	36.82
1797	Lindert, 1811	31.69
1805	Lindert, 1811	27.45
1810	Lindert, 1811	30.65
1815	Lindert, 1811	33.31
1819	Lindert, 1811	31.58
1827	Census, 1831	41.95
1835	Census, 1831	42.69
1851	Census, 1851	46.99
1861	Census, 1861	35.32
1871	Census, 1871	32.32
1881	Census, 1881	33.02
1891	Census, 1891	43.04
1901	Census, 1901	44.58
1911	Census, 1911	41.02

Sources and Notes: Williamson (1982d, Table 3). The wage gaps are based on nominal annual earnings and thus contain no cost-of-living adjustments. The gap is calculated as the difference between the (weighted) average non-farm unskilled earnings rate and the farm earnings rate, divided by the farm earnings rate. Thus, it is the percentage differential by which urban unskilled wages exceeded farm wages, the common measure used in the development literature.

(6) The task ahead

The findings in this chapter present a formidable challenge to both the economist and the historian. There appear to have been three epochs of earnings inequality experience in Britain since the late eighteenth century: a period of stability in the earnings distribution through the Napoleonic conflict and postwar stabilization; a period of surging wage and earnings inequality up to mid-century; and a period of leveling in the distribution of earnings during the late nineteenth century up to World War I. What forces account for these epochs? Why the stability during the Napoleonic Wars? What were the underlying forces driving the Kuznets curve across the nineteenth century?

The successful explanation will have to account for the simultaneous occurrence of *both* an impressive rise in real wages and surging inequality from the 1820s to mid-century. As if that were not enough, the model will also have to explain the coincidence of stable real wages with a stable earnings distribution during the Napoleonic period. To complicate matters further, the model must then explain why real wages surged during a period of leveling of earnings distributions in the late nineteenth century. A tough challenge indeed.

Most important, perhaps, this chapter has shown that earnings inequality was being driven by the relative scarcity of skills and by the premium that skills commanded. That finding will motivate much of what follows in the remainder of this book.

What about the more conventional class conflicts? What about the distribution of income between workers, landlords and capitalists? While the earnings distribution was passing through a Kuznets curve in the nineteenth century, what was happening to the distribution of income?

Notes

1   The details can be found in Williamson (1979a), and Chapter 4 below. The social arithmetic offered by Colquhoun, Baxter and Bowley would appear to suggest the same. See Soltow (1968, pp. 17–19), and Lindert and Williamson (1982, 1983b).

2   Bowley's (1937, p. 42) key estimates follow (note the larger percentage increase in the upper quartile and highest decile):

	1886		1906		% change
Lowest decile	16s	7d	19s	6d	18
Lowest quartile	20	0	23	4	16
Median	24	2	29	4	21
Upper quartile	29	5	37	2	26
Highest decile	34	7	46	0	33

3   The text relies on the following data drawn from Williamson (1980a, p. 462):

Group	Percentage share of group in total 1881 wage and salary earners
Included in Wage Census:	
(1) Bowley's 'manual workers in commodity production'	31.1
(2) Row (1) plus printing and building trades	42.6

(3)	Row (2) plus police, public utilities and railways	49.7
(4)	Row (3) plus miners	57.9

Excluded from Wage Census:

(5)	Farm laborers	16.6
(6)	All service sector employment (not mentioned above)	25.5

4   On this issue, see the excellent discussion in Phelps-Brown (1977, pp. 256–7), and section 3 below.

5   Bowley also offered estimates for 1860. In addition, he expanded the figures to include mining and agriculture. This procedure still fails to capture the service sector, but in any case, since Bowley felt that the resulting 'deciles were subject to great error' (1937, p. 45), I have ignored them in the text discussion. The same is true of his 'bold attempt' (p. 46) to expand the exercise to include *all* incomes, although this effort is included in Chapter 4 where the 'social arithmetic' estimates are discussed.

6   The notation '1881/86' simply indicates that the vast majority of the intra-occupation distribution estimates are based on 1886 data, while the employment weights and mean occupational earnings are based on 1881 data. Similarly for '1901/6'. For simplicity, throughout this chapter 1881 = 1881/6 and 1901 = 1901/6.

7   The form of the regression is simply

$$I_j^k(t) = a_0 + a_1 \bar{W}_j(t)$$

where I_j^k is the inequality statistic for the jth group, $\bar{W}_j$ is the group's mean annual earnings, and $t = 1881/1886$ and 1901/6. The results are as follows (Williamson, 1980a, p. 465):

Inequality statistic	1901/6			1881/6		
	$\hat{a}_1$	t-statistic	R^2	$\hat{a}_1$	t-statistic	R^2
Gini	0.000697	4.51689	0.6711	0.000588	3.45750	0.4990
Top 5 per cent	0.042730	5.49323	0.7511	0.018130	2.56473	0.3541
Atkinson Index ($\epsilon = 2.5$)	0.000858	5.87129	0.7751	0.000793	4.04709	0.5772

Male domestics are excluded throughout since income in kind is such a large share of their true income, and the nominal estimates of $\bar{W}$ thus greatly understate true income.

8   See Jacob Mincer (1974) for a summary of the American twentieth-century evidence and Phelps-Brown (1977, Ch. 8) for a summary of the British twentieth-century evidence.

9   As E. H. Hunt (1973) has shown, regional wage variance was high even in the late nineteenth century.

10   Williamson (1982d, Tables 6 and 7). That paper also shows that it is wage effects within occupations that account for the vast majority of the pay ratio trends across the nineteenth century, not some quirk in the employment weights used. For example, between 1819 and 1851 *all* of the wage stretching is attributable to the behavior of occupational wages themselves and *none* to employment mix changes. That statement relates to the ratio of average skilled and average unskilled wages. As it turns out, employment did shift to higher-wage (skill) occupations over time in both 'unskilled' and 'skilled' categories, but apparently at the same rate.

4

Income Inequality

(1) A battle without weapons?

Most of the controversy over English inequality has been confined to the 'first' industrial revolution, but the late-Victorian era is not well understood either. The controversy certainly seems justified. Willford King (1915) was astonished by the concentration of British wealth before World War I, at least compared with America and other countries in Western Europe. Income inequality also appears to have been higher in Britain between 1880 and 1926, and greater wealth concentration was still an attribute in the 1950s (Lydall and Lansing, 1959). Was inequality always so great in England, or did it rise across the industrial revolution? Since Britain is relatively egalitarian by the mid-twentieth century, when did the leveling take place?

Contemporaries strongly suspected that inequality was on the rise from the late eighteenth century, but such suspicions were rarely guided by data. While their theories differed, Marx, Malthus, Ricardo and others all developed models designed to explain why the rich got richer and the poor got poorer. It would be striking indeed if it could be shown that income inequality was *not* on the rise in a period when suspicions of widening inequalities ran so deep, especially given the findings in Chapter 3 of rising earnings inequality to mid-century. Yet, the data have never been plentiful enough to offer an unambiguous victory to anyone who sought evidence rather than anecdote. For example, Engels and Marx thought inequality was on the rise in nineteenth-century England and they felt there was abundant evidence to support the position (Engels, 1974; Marx and Engels, 1930). Victorian apologists for capitalism denied it, Porter (1851) and Giffen (1889) countering the radical critique by using tax return data to document an *egalitarian* trend across the nineteenth century. Modern contributions have generated more conflicting assertions and evidence. In 1940, Colin Clark used income tax returns to document a *decline* in the inverse Pareto inequality slope between 1812 and 1845. Harold Perkin (1969, pp. 135–6) countered with other income tax return estimates that showed the top percentile of taxed income recipients *increasing* their share between 1801 and 1848. Perkin concluded that the first half of the nineteenth century witnessed a 'considerable shift in income distributions towards the rich and well-to-do', while Clark stated that 'the distribution of income in

England in 1850 was less unequal than it had been in 1800'. Perkin's evidence confirms, and Clark's evidence refutes, Simon Kuznets' conjecture on the British industrial revolution: 'I would place the early phase in which income inequality might be widening, from about 1780 to 1850 . . .' (Kuznets, 1955, p. 19).

Contradictions over early nineteenth-century trends have not abated. In an ambitious and pathbreaking article, which appeared over fifteen years ago, Lee Soltow (1968) offered rough measures of English inequality for the years 1436–1962/3. On the basis in large measure of the social arithmetic of Gray, King and Colquhoun, Soltow concluded that inequality dropped before 1688 and again after 1913, but he saw no clear trends in between, implying that the inequality that seemed so acute at the turn of the present century had always been characteristic of English society. It implied no increase in inequality across the nineteenth century, a position that Marx, Engels and the political left would find outrageous.

Two data sets have guided the debate over British inequality up to World War I, while a third has been ignored. First, there are the income tax data that became available in response to the crushing financial needs of the Napoleonic Wars. While the earnings distributions in Chapter 3 inform us about inequality 'from the middle to the bottom', the tax data inform us about distributions only 'at the very top', since the vast majority of the population fell below minimum taxable incomes until well into the twentieth century. These data must be treated with great care, not only because they describe a very limited component of total incomes but also because they lack comparability over time. A detailed critical evaluation is offered in section 3 before analysis of the data is presented in section 4. Second, there are the guesstimates offered by social arithmeticians from Massie in the mid-eighteenth century to Bowley in the early twentieth. These, too, are beset with serious problems of comparability. With the aid of recent efforts by Peter Lindert and myself (1982, 1983b), however, section 5 examines the inequality evidence embedded in the political arithmetic. Third, the chapter also offers some new permanent income distribution evidence – annual dwelling rents – which the debate has ignored. It may be the best evidence we have, but recent research by Peter Lindert (1982, 1984 forthcoming) on trends in the concentration of English wealth is about to change all that.

Before wading into this empirical thicket, section 2 raises some essential preliminaries: under what conditions might *income* and *earnings* inequality have behaved differently across the nineteenth century? Why is the evidence of a Kuznets curve in earnings inequality – found in Chapter 3 – not enough to imply similar trends in income inequality?

(2) Some inequality algebra guided by Occam's Razor

Rising pay ratios do not guarantee rising income inequality. Nor, for that matter, does rising earnings inequality guarantee rising income inequality. Nor is rising income inequality guaranteed by increasing wealth concentration or by greater inequality in schooling attainment, health and other indices of human capital endowment. That these assertions can be seen more clearly, some 'inequality algebra' is essential. The going is tedious for a few pages, and some readers may wish to skip to the end of the section for the punch line. But the accounting turns out to be very useful in suggesting the sources of conflicting inequality trends offered as evidence in the debate, as well as to guide my attempts to model British inequality history in later chapters.

Let us begin with the classic trilogy, defining an individual's income as the sum of wage earnings, profits, and rents:

$$Y_i = E_i + P_i + R_i. \tag{4.1}$$

This expression can be decomposed further into products of the individual's assets and the return on those assets:

$$Y_i = w_i + q_i S_i + r_i K_i + d_i \mathcal{J}_i \tag{4.2}$$

where

w = the unskilled common laborer's wage,
q = the premium paid for skills,
S = the stock of skills,
r = the rate of return on (conventional) capital,
K = the stock of (conventional) capital assets,
d = land rents per acre, and
$\mathcal{J}$ = total land holdings.

The British inequality debate centers on income gaps across social class, but more general inequality measures can be devised by examining the variance of incomes across *all* individuals, within and between classes. Applying well-known properties of variance to equation (4.2), suppressing the subscript i, we get

$$\begin{aligned} \text{Var}(Y) = {}& \text{var}(w) + \bar{q}^2\text{var}(S) + \bar{S}^2\text{var}(q) + \text{var}(S)\text{var}(q) \\ & + \bar{r}^2\text{var}(K) + \bar{K}^2\text{var}(r) + \text{var}(r)\text{var}(K) \\ & + \bar{d}^2\text{var}(\mathcal{J}) + \bar{\mathcal{J}}^2\text{var}(d) + \text{var}(d)\text{var}(\mathcal{J}) \\ & + 2\text{COV}(E,P) + 2\text{COV}(E,R) + 2\text{COV}(P,R). \end{aligned} \tag{4.3}$$

However, all participants in the inequality debate have *relative* dispersion in mind (Atkinson, 1970), not *absolute* variance as in (4.3). One such index of relative dispersion is the coefficient of variation, which, for any variable X, can be written as

$$C_X = \text{Var}(X_i)/\bar{X}^2.$$

One needs only define per capita income as $\bar{y}$, and write factor shares in national income as

unskilled labor's share $\theta_L = \bar{w}/\bar{y}$
skilled labor's share $\theta_S = \bar{q}\bar{S}/\bar{y}$
capital's share $\theta_K = \bar{r}\bar{K}/\bar{y}$
land's share $\theta_{\mathcal{J}} = \bar{d}\bar{\mathcal{J}}/\bar{y}$

to convert equation (4.3) into expression (4.4):

$$Cy = \theta_L^2 C_w + \theta_S^2 C_S + \theta_S^2 C_q + \theta_S^2 C_S C_q +$$
$$+ \theta_K^2 C_K + \theta_K^2 C_r + \theta_K^2 C_r C_K +$$
$$+ \theta_{\tilde{J}}^2 C_{\tilde{J}} + \theta_{\tilde{J}}^2 C_d + \theta_{\tilde{J}}^2 C_d C_{\tilde{J}} +$$
$$+ 2/\bar{y}^2[\text{COV}(E,P) + \text{COV}(E,R) + \text{COV}(P,R)]. \tag{4.4}$$

One final step remains. Our interest is in inequality *trends*, so we simply take the total differential of (4.4) to get the change in inequality over time:

$$dCy = d\theta_L(2\theta_L C_w) + d\theta_S[2\theta_S(C_S + C_q + C_S \cdot C_q)] +$$
$$+ d\theta_K[2\theta_K(C_K + C_r + C_r \cdot C_K)] + d\theta_{\tilde{J}}[2\theta_{\tilde{J}}(C_{\tilde{J}} + C_d + C_d \cdot C_{\tilde{J}})] +$$
$$\text{`FACTOR SHARE EFFECTS'}$$
$$+ dC_w(\theta_L^2) + dC_q[\theta_S^2(1 + C_S)] + dC_r[\theta_K^2(1 + C_K)] +$$
$$+ dC_d[\theta_{\tilde{J}}^2(1 + C_{\tilde{J}})] +$$
$$\text{`ALLOCATIVE DISEQUILIBRIUM EFFECTS'}$$
$$+ dC_S[\theta_S^2(1 + C_q)] + dC_K[\theta_K^2(1 + C_r)] +$$
$$+ dC_{\tilde{J}}[\theta_{\tilde{J}}^2(1 + C_d)] +$$
$$\text{`WEALTH DISTRIBUTION EFFECTS'}$$
$$+ d\bar{y}\{-4/\bar{y}^3[\text{COV}(E,P) + \text{COV}(E,R) + \text{COV}(P,R)]\} +$$
$$+ [d\text{COV}(E,P) + d\text{COV}(E,R) + d\text{COV}(P,R)]2/\bar{y}^2$$
$$\text{`RESIDUAL EFFECTS'} \tag{4.5}$$

By the application of Occam's Razor, expression (4.5) can be made even more useful for the discussion that follows. Suppose the 'residual effects' are sufficiently small to ignore – a reasonable assumption since the weights, $-4/\bar{y}^3$ and $2/\bar{y}^2$, are both extremely small. Suppose further that capital and land markets are sufficiently competitive in the long run that rates of return and rents are roughly equalized throughout Britain, e.g. $C_r = C_d \approx 0$. Then we emerge with expression (4.6):

$$dC_y \cong d\theta_L(2\theta_L C_w) + d\theta_S[2\theta_S(C_S + C_q + C_S \cdot C_q)] +$$
$$+ d\theta_K(2\theta_K C_K) + d\theta_{\tilde{J}}(2\theta_{\tilde{J}} C_{\tilde{J}}) +$$
$$\text{`FACTOR SHARE EFFECTS'}$$
$$+ dC_w(\theta_L^2) + dC_q[\theta_S^2[1 + C_S]] +$$
$$\text{`PAY RATIO AND PAY GAP EFFECTS'}$$
$$+ dC_s[\theta_S^2(1 + C_q)] +$$
$$\text{`HUMAN CAPITAL DISTRIBUTION EFFECTS'}$$
$$+ dC_K(\theta_K^2) + dC_{\tilde{J}}(\theta_{\tilde{J}}^2)$$
$$\text{`CONVENTIONAL WEALTH DISTRIBUTION EFFECTS'} \tag{4.6}$$

We are now equipped to confront the debate over British nineteenth-century inequality experience.

The classical economists had a three-factor model in mind, and only three actors appear on their stage – workers, capitalists and landlords. For them, income inequality was driven by only two forces. First, what we have called 'conventional wealth distribution effects', consisting of increased concentration of landholdings (dC_J) or capital (dC_K), may play a role in generating rising inequality over time. Traditional scholarship has focused on (agricultural) landownership trends, and the general consensus seems to be that C_J rose from the mid-eighteenth to the late nineteenth century, landownership becoming more concentrated in the hands of large landowners while the yeomen and small farmers vanished. The new view plays down enclosures and highlights 1815–30 as a key period of land concentration (Chambers, 1940; Grigg, 1963; Hunt, 1958; Martin, 1966; Mingay, 1964, 1968, 1976; Yelling, 1977). The importance of the rise in land concentration to income inequality trends, however, depends on the size of θ_J^2 and, since land's share was only 0.147 in 1801 and 0.065 in 1861 (Reich, 1980, Table 1, p. 5), that weight could not have exceeded .02. The moral here seems to be that 'gradualist' changes in the concentration of landholdings contributed very little to *income* inequality trends across the nineteenth century. While no comparable literature exists to guide our impressions of trends in C_K, it seems to me unlikely that total 'conventional wealth distribution effects' mattered much in driving British inequality across the nineteenth century.

Is the same true of 'human capital distribution effects'? Perhaps so. Appendix C supplies information to yield estimates on the skills share, which vary around 0.12 for much of the nineteenth century. Since the coefficient of variation must lie between 0 and 1, this implies that $\theta_S^2(1 + C_q) < 0.03$, not a very large weight either. However, there seems to be strong evidence supporting the view that C_S rose very sharply throughout much of the nineteenth century, especially up to mid-century, perhaps peaking in the 1870s. Two quite different pieces of evidence would suggest that inference. First, it seems that mortality became increasingly class-specific as the century progressed (Preston, Haines and Pamuk, 1981; Titmuss, 1943; Hollingsworth, 1977; Williamson, 1982c). Assuming a high correlation between mortality and sickness (Farr's mid-nineteenth-century rule was that two persons were 'seriously ill' for each one that died; in Wall, 1974, p. iv), then the dispersion of human capital in the form of health may well have risen sharply across much of the nineteenth century, sufficient to drive income inequality upwards. Second, schooling may have had the same effect. Even E. G. West's revisionist attack on educational history (West, 1965, 1970, 1975a,b) has failed to shake the traditional view that education 'gaps' actually widened across income class until the late nineteenth century and the advent of public schooling. Both of these forces – inequality in the distribution of health and schooling – would have contributed to rising C_S, positive 'human capital distribution effects' and thus rising income inequality.

Chapter 3 focused on 'pay ratio and pay gap effects'. The surge in wage inequality was certainly serving to raise income inequality up to mid-century. Wage inequality took two forms, and expression (4.6) captures both. The first 'pay gap effect' deals with wage variation for unskilled labor,

dC_w. There have been two important contributions to British wage history with this focus: Gilboy's (1934) emphasis on the appearance and persistence of a North–South wage gap from the late eighteenth century, and Hunt's (1973) emphasis on the convergence of regional wages in Britain in the late nineteenth century. In addition, Chapter 3 (Table 3.8) offered evidence of a rise in the urban–rural 'wage gap' from the Napoleonic Wars to mid-century. The second 'pay gap' effect deals with the influence of pay ratios across skills, industries and occupations. As we have seen in Chapter 3, these rose very sharply after the Napoleonic Era until mid-century.

Finally, there are 'factor share effects' to consider. Here the ground is probably most familiar. All of us share the intuition that land was the most concentrated asset in nineteenth-century Britain, unskilled 'raw' labor had the least dispersion, while skills and capital must have lain somewhere in between. That intuition suggests the following inequality.

$$2\theta_L C_w < 2\theta_K C_K, \quad 2\theta_S(C_S + C_q + C_S \cdot C_q) < 2\theta_J C_J.$$

The possibilities for conflict between various inequality indicators, especially during wartime, are immediately clear. The French Wars served to create land scarcity (by driving up the price of grain) *and* unskilled labor scarcity (by mobilization). Chapter 3 has already reported the tendency for pay ratios and thus earnings distributions to level across the Napoleonic Era. If the land rental share rose enough, income inequality may well have taken place while earnings distributions were leveling. Even if it did not, one would expect the top 5 and 10 per cent (rich landlords) to find their share in national income increasing at the same time that the bottom 40 per cent were improving their share, thus squeezing the middle.

This exercise should suffice to point out that a Kuznets curve in earnings inequality should hardly guarantee similar trends in income inequality. If they fail to coincide, we know where to look for the source of conflict.

(3) Soft data for a hard problem: tax assessments

Income and property taxes: distribution at the top
From Henry Pelham's tax reforms and the early experiments of Lord North, to the fiscal innovations of William Pitt the Younger, Britain developed a system of taxes on income, assets and expenditures that produced income distribution data by size that stretch back to the late eighteenth century. At first Pitt experimented with a true income tax imposed on upper-income groups – the top third in the size distribution. The tax was used to finance the crushing expense of the Napoleonic conflict. It lasted over the short period 1799–1802 before being replaced by a more efficient tax 'at the source' – misnamed the property tax. The property (or income) tax survived with one interruption (1816–42) throughout the nineteenth century and well into the twentieth. The tax was not imposed on total income, but rather on income by type and source. There were five types of income and five schedules, of which the most revealing are

Schedules D and E, reporting assessed income from wages, salaries and profits from trade.

The knottiest problem associated with the use of these tax assessment data has been the inability to infer anything about households from data on filers. For most years before World War I, one cannot identify household income from the tax returns. Since individuals paid separate taxes on separate kinds of incomes under Schedules A–E, a given household's income might have been spread across several schedules, giving few clues about their income from all sources. The result is that the distributions of income among filers of separate schedules are questionable proxies for the distributions of total household incomes. To complicate matters further, there are nation-wide size distributions for Schedules D and E incomes only.

In spite of their shortcomings, I propose to re-examine the prewar estimates from Schedules D and E more carefully than previous scholars have done. Perhaps they are not quite as bad as they seem. For example, previous work has shown that the 'filers versus householders' problem may be less serious than has been thought. On the basis of the only manuscript returns that have survived the bonfires and mash tubs of tax authorities following the Napoleonic Era – for Edinburgh – I was able to show that 'the inequality trends in taxable Schedule D income . . . are good proxies for inequality trends in total taxable income' (Williamson, 1979a, p. 37). True, the Schedule D data are limited to the top groups taxed – the top fifth of incomes in 1815/16 and the top quarter of incomes in 1860/1. Thus, the inequality statistics must be limited to measures of inequality *among* high-income groups only, and section 2 has already shown that trends in inequality among high-income groups may move in directions opposite to those measuring inequality *between* rich and poor. The tax assessment data have other flaws, discussed in detail by Josiah Stamp in his classic *British Incomes and Property* (1920). In spite of these reservations, the value of the Schedule D tax assessments would be greatly enhanced if they implied the same inequality trends documented by other sources.

We *do* have tax assessment data describing the distribution of *total* incomes for five dates that may prove valuable for time series analysis. The first observation is based on the published size distributions for 1800/1, the last year for which Pitt's income tax was imposed before being replaced by the property tax and Schedules A–E. As Deane and Cole (1962, Appendix 2) and others have pointed out, these Napoleonic assessments must be treated with great caution since the taxes were at first widely evaded. The second observation is 1814. A tax official, Benjamin Sayer (1833), supplied an estimate of the size distribution of *total* incomes taxed for that year. While the taxes were despised, there is some evidence of increased compliance. There is no way of knowing how extensive evasion might still have been, but surely Sayer would have known if anyone did. The Inland Revenue offered another estimate almost a century later for 1918/19, and in between there are G. R. Porter's (1851) estimates for 1848 and Arthur Bowley's (1914) for 1910. While each of these five observations deals with total household income and from all sources, they *still* apply only to the top of the distribution where the taxes were imposed. In 1801, they cover the top 33 per cent of total British income (based on Colquhoun's national income estimate), in 1819 the top 29 per cent (based on either Sayer's or Colquhoun's national income estimate), and in 1919 the top 27 per cent (based on Bowley's national income estimate).

My own judgment is that income inequality trends based on the tax assessment data are of limited use, even when treated with caution. Given changes in the distribution of taxable income across schedules, given changes in tax compliance rates, and given changes in the share of total incomes reached by tax, I suspect the evidence is completely ineffective in shedding much light on changing inequality over periods as long as a half-century. It may be more effective in telling us what happened to the distribution of income *among* the rich, but not *between* the rich and poor. What evidence there is is summarized below in Table 4.4 and discussed in section 4.

Reconstructing permanent incomes from house taxes
In an effort to finance the American War, Lord North increased Britain's taxable capacity in many directions, the most important of which for the student of British inequality was the inhabited house duty (IHD). The IHD, introduced in 1778, was a tax on the annual rental value of dwellings. The tax was imposed on the occupant. If a renter, he was assumed to pass the burden back onto the landlord by reducing future rental payments accordingly. If an owner-occupier, he simply paid the tax on the imputed rent according to the tax assessor's valuation. The tax was clearly an attempt to place the burden of war financing on those who could best afford it, since it was never imposed on the vast majority of laboring poor. Indeed, equity was clearly the motive as espoused by Adam Smith in the *Wealth of Nations* written two years prior to Lord North's introduction of the IHD:

> You should distribute the weight of taxation so as to effect a more equal pressure upon the whole people, and, as regards dwellinghouses, impose a more equal tax calculated by reference to the rent or annual value of the house, a much more fair and intelligible basis for taxation than the number of windows. (Quoted in Stephen Dowell, 1893, pp. vi–vii)

As it turns out, the IHD did not reach as far down in the income distribution as did the income and property tax introduced by William Pitt some two decades later: in 1830, the IHD caught only the top sixth or so. Nevertheless, it offers a number of distinct advantages over the income/property tax assessment data. First, the compliance rate was higher, in part because it was a lighter tax. Second, since rental expenditures and income are highly correlated, the IHD data reflect *total* incomes, not just Schedules D and E incomes. Third, house rents yield insights into *permanent* incomes, not current incomes, and the former is a far better measure of inequality. Fourth, the IHD fills in a crucial period (1823–34) when the income/property tax was repealed. Finally, the IHD data offer an independent observation.

British experience with the IHD has left behind nation-wide size distributions of households by rental value for the period starting 1823, the 1778–1822 period apparently leaving no published traces. The tax was repealed in 1834 as part of peacetime tax reform, but it was reintroduced in 1851. The Inland Revenue ceased reporting such size distributions in 1915, but the reluctant past has still left behind a consistent time series stretching from the 1820s to World War I.

The window tax has an even older history, and reached far lower in the income distribution than did any of the other taxes: in 1781, it reached more than half of England's households. If an empirical correspondence between the number of windows assessed and the dwelling's assessed annual rental value can be established, then size distributions of households by windows can be converted into size distributions of households by annual rental value, and the latter, of course, can be converted into size distributions of permanent income.

The early window tax data appear to be of high quality but their quality diminished as resistance to the tax grew and government collection atrophied over the first half of the eighteenth century. This deterioration was reversed by Henry Pelham's reforms of 1747 and by Lord North's efforts to improve the tax system in response to the financial needs of the American conflict (Ward, 1952). Thus, I feel confident about the quality of the data on the size distribution of households by number of dwelling windows from 1777 to 1849. This is especially true after 1812 when the tax was too small to make it profitable to avoid.[1] Not only do these data supply valuable information on the course of inequality during the eighteenth century, but they can also be used to test the veracity of the IHD data by comparing size distribution trends for overlapping years, 1823–49.[2]

As it turns out, both the window tax and the inhabited house duty data can be used to construct estimates of the size distribution of household income in Britain from 1777 to 1915. The next section reports the results of this rich harvest, along with an analysis of the better-known income and property tax data. Appendix B explains how the permanent income distributions have been derived from the house tax assessments.

(4) What do the tax data tell us?

The income distribution estimates built up from these three tax assessment sources are summarized in Tables 4.1–4.4. Each offers a set of inequality statistics that measure distribution 'at the top': the richest 5 per cent's share in total income, the top 10 per cent's share, the Pareto coefficient, and the inverse of the Pareto coefficient. In addition, where the source supplies the *total* income distribution – as in the case of the window and house assessment tax sources in Tables 4.1–4.3 – inequality indices are reported that measure overall inequality. These include the Gini coefficient and the less well-known Atkinson Index (see Atkinson, 1970) under three widely divergent parameter assumptions. Since each of these inequality indices places different weight on various parts of the income distribution, they need not generate the same trends. Indeed, section 2 has already suggested reasons why these indices might vary, and evidence of such non-conformity will be important in motivating the modeling in the remainder of the book.

Table 4.1   *Trends in permanent income inequality based on window tax assessment data: England and Wales, 1777–1849*

Year	Share in income of top		Gini coefficient	Pareto coefficient (b)	Inverse of Pareto coefficient (−1/b)	Atkinson indices		
	5%	10%				$\epsilon = 1.5$	$\epsilon = 2.5$	$\epsilon = 4.0$
1777	42.61	52.32	0.524	−1.773	0.564	0.468	0.517	0.543
1781	42.91	52.59	0.532	−1.771	0.565	0.476	0.527	0.553
1823	43.80	52.50	0.457	−1.246	0.803	0.412	0.440	0.454
1830	47.07	55.18	0.515	−1.110	0.901	0.466	0.497	0.513
1849	48.38	56.53	0.528	−1.114	0.898	0.480	0.511	0.527

Sources and Notes: Williamson (1979a, Table 8). See Appendix B. Evidence is also available for 1708 and 1760, but the number of size classes is much too small to warrant confidence in the inequality statistics compiled for those two years.

Table 4.2   *Trends in permanent income inequality based on inhabited house duty tax assessment data: England and Wales, 1823–1915*

Year	Share in income of top		Gini coefficient	Pareto coefficient (b)	Inverse of Pareto coefficient (−1/b)	Atkinson indices		
	5%	10%				$\epsilon = 1.5$	$\epsilon = 2.5$	$\epsilon = 4.0$
1823	39.51	47.51	0.400	−1.708	0.585	0.357	0.387	0.401
1830	39.44	49.95	0.451	−1.533	0.552	0.391	0.431	0.453
1871	49.35	62.29	0.627	−1.715	0.583	0.596	0.641	0.660
1891	45.71	57.50	0.550	−1.513	0.561	0.504	0.546	0.566
1901	37.25	47.41	0.443	−1.527	0.555	0.112	0.420	0.445
1911	29.65	36.43	0.328	−1.546	0.547	0.071	0.290	0.314
1915	29.71	36.46	0.333	−1.565	0.539	0.072	0.295	0.320

Source and Notes: Williamson (1979a, Table 9). See Appendix B.

Table 4.3 Trends in permanent income inequality based on inhabited house duty tax assessment data: Scotland 1830–1915

| Year | Share in income of top | | Gini coefficient | Pareto coefficient (b) | Inverse of Pareto coefficient (−1/b) | Atkinson indices | | |
	5%	10%				$\epsilon = 1.5$	$\epsilon = 2.5$	$\epsilon = 4.0$
1830	26.72	33.50	0.251	−2.155	0.464	0.199	0.224	0.239
1871	42.31	55.67	0.498	−2.028	0.493	0.454	0.493	0.511
1891	37.04	46.76	0.389	−1.921	0.521	0.342	0.374	0.390
1901	27.38	36.66	0.287	−1.894	0.528	0.227	0.259	0.278
1911	22.82	30.94	0.242	−1.852	0.540	0.178	0.207	0.227
1915	21.29	28.97	0.224	−1.928	0.519	0.159	0.187	0.207

Source and Notes: Williamson (1979a, Table 10). See Appendix B.

Table 4.4 Trends in income inequality among the top income earners based on tax assessments, 1800–1919

A. Schedule D income taxed

Year	Regions covered	Type of income	Number of size classes	Lowest income class taxed included in the estimate £	Pareto coefficient (b)	Inverse of Pareto coefficient (−1/b)
1806/7	GB	Sch D, Gross	13	100	−1.196	0.836
1808/9	GB	Sch D, Gross	13	100	−1.220	0.820
1810/11	GB	Sch D, Gross	16	50	−1.171	0.854
1812/13	GB	Sch D, Gross	16	50	−1.180	0.847
1814/15	GB	Sch D, Gross	16	50	−1.155	0.866

Year	Region	Schedule				
1815/16	GB	Sch D, Gross	15	100	−1.138	0.879
1842/3	E&W	Sch D, Gross	16	150	−1.556	0.643
1845/6	GB	Sch D, Gross	16	150	−1.447	0.691
1850/1	GB	Sch D, Gross	16	150	−1.401	0.714
1855/6	GB	Sch D, Gross	16	100	−1.340	0.746
1860/1	GB	Sch D, Gross	16	100	−1.301	0.769
1865/6	GB	Sch D, Gross	16	100	−1.197	0.835
1870/1	GB	Sch D, Net	16	100	−1.324	0.755
1879/80	GB	Sch D, Gross	17	100	−1.373	0.728
	GB	Sch D, Net	16	150	−1.387	0.721
1880/1	GB	Sch D, Net	16	150	−1.385	0.722
	UK	Sch D, Net	16	150	−1.387	0.721
1883/4	GB	Sch D, Net	16	150	−1.347	0.742
1890/1	GB	Sch D, Net	16	150	−1.348	0.742
1900/1	GB	Sch D, Gross	16	160	−1.711	0.584
1910/11	UK	Sch D, Gross	16	160	−1.614	0.620

B. Total income taxed

Year	Region					
1800/1	GB	Total	33	60	−1.235	.810
1813/14	GB	Total	9	20	−1.121	.892
1847/8	GB	Total	7	150	−1.441	.694
1909/10	UK	Total	11	5000	−1.727	.579
1918/19	UK	Total	25	130	−1.469	.681

Sources: Panel A: Williamson (1979a, Table 11). All data are taken from Inland Revenue *Annual Reports* except 1890/1 (which were collected at the Kew Public Record Office, IR 16/84) and 1870/1–1883/4 (which were supplemented by Levi, 1885, p. 58).

Panel B: 1800/1 – Stamp (1920, p. 514); 813/14 – Sayer (1833, Appendix, p. 45); 1847/8 – Porter (1851, p. 197); 1909/10 – Bowley (1914, p. 264); 1918/19 – *Parliamentary Papers* (1920, XVIII, pp. 706–8). I have excluded Porter's (1851, p. 197) estimate for 1811/12 since the number of classes is too limited. See Williamson (1979a, Table 11).

The window tax data supply insight into the late eighteenth century so I shall begin there. Table 4.1 suggests that inequality drifted downwards between the early 1780s and the 1820s. According to both the Atkinson indices and the Gini coefficient, this leveling in the income distribution was marked, but the recovery of the old inequality levels was even more dramatic. That is, the forty-two-year leveling up to 1823 was reversed only twenty-six years later, by 1849. In short, Table 4.1 supports the earnings inequality trends documented in Chapter 3. It replicates the leveling around the Napoleonic period, an attractive result since wartime conditions almost always tend to breed egalitarian trends, at least based on abundant twentieth-century evidence (Williamson and Lindert, 1980, Part I). Table 4.1 also captures the 'inequality surge' associated with modern economic growth.

Interestingly enough, these trends in the full size distribution are *not* reproduced in measures of inequality 'at the top'. While incomes were leveling among the bottom 95 per cent of English and Welsh households between 1781 and 1823, they were becoming *more* concentrated among those at the top, and the top 5 per cent was *increasing* its share of the total. Furthermore, there is abundant evidence that these four decades were characterized by rising income inequality *among the rich*. This is certainly apparent in the sharp rise in the inverse of the Pareto coefficient, but it is also supported by the coexistence of stable shares for the top 10 per cent with rising shares for the top 5 per cent. Those historians who judge inequality trends by looking only at the top of the distribution would have been misled by such evidence since, as we have seen, rising inequality at the top was more than offset by a leveling in the distribution among the vast majority of British households from the American Revolution to post-Napoleonic stabilization.

Between 1823 and 1849, in contrast, *all* inequality indicators are on the rise: the top 5 and 10 per cent increase their shares, the distribution of income among the rich becomes more unequal, the Gini coefficient rises, and all the Atkinson indices rise.

Tables 4.2 and 4.3 report the inhabited house duty data for England and Wales and for Scotland, respectively. Since they move alike over the nineteenth century, I can discuss the results in terms of overall British income inequality trends. The early nineteenth-century surge in inequality suggested by the window tax data is repeated in these IHD data. With one exception, every inequality indicator rises sharply from 1823 to 1871, drifting downwards thereafter. The exception is the inverse of the Pareto coefficient, a result suggesting once again that distributions *among* the rich have little to do with overall inequality trends.

It appears that the nineteenth-century Kuznets curve in earnings inequality is repeated in the income inequality data. While Tables 4.2 and 4.3 do not supply the intervening observations to date just when inequality peaks between 1830 and 1871, the window tax data in Table 4.1 suggest that the peak was reached sometime after 1849, while the earnings distribution and pay ratio data in Chapter 3 suggest a peak in the 1860s.

Finally, what about the property income tax assessment data based on taxable incomes only? Table 4.4 displays this evidence for the century following Pitt's Napoleonic tax innovations. Panel A in that table is restricted to Schedule D incomes while Panel B offers estimates based on total taxable incomes. The late nineteenth-century leveling is captured in these data too, Panel A suggesting a peak in the mid-1860s, almost exactly the turning point dated in Chapter 3. A much more modest leveling 'at the top' can be seen among total taxable incomes in Panel B, but a leveling took place there too.

The only contrast between Table 4.4 and the previous three tables is over the industrial revolution period. Panel A documents a rise in inequality 'at the top' between the early 1840s and the mid-1860s, but there is no evidence of rising inequality 'at the top' from Waterloo to mid-century. I have already given reasons that lead me to believe instead the overwhelming contrary evidence presented in Chapter 3 and in Tables 4.1–4.3 above, but this contrasting movement in the taxable income data from the repeal of the 'property tax' in 1816 to its revival in 1842 is there to support the avid revisionist.

A working hypothesis is now well established: incomes leveled across the late eighteenth century and the French Wars; inequality surged from Waterloo to mid-century; and incomes leveled again during the late nineteenth century. While that inequality tale is compelling, one certainly could use more evidence to convert the Kuznets curve hypothesis into an established stylized fact of British industrialization from 1780 to World War I.

(5) How did the 'social arithmeticians' see it?

Using the social tables to look at inequality
In 1968, Lee Soltow published an article on long-term trends in British income inequality. On the basis primarily of the social arithmetic of contemporary observers like Gregory King, Patrick Colquhoun, R. Dudley Baxter and Arthur Bowley, Soltow formed the tentative hypothesis that inequality changed but little between 1688 and 1913 (Soltow, 1968, p. 22). Beneath this stability, Soltow saw an egalitarian undercurrent implicit in the industrialization process, an undercurrent that began to tug British income inequality downwards only after World War I (Soltow, 1968, pp. 27–9).

Soltow's hypothesis is inconsistent with the Kuznets curve that this and the previous chapter uncovered. Is stability in the distribution of income over two and a half centuries *really* what the social arithmeticians were suggesting? Apparently not. *When properly reconstructed*, the social arithmeticians' observations trace out a Kuznets curve too.

Soltow was misled. It appears, for example, that he used Colquhoun's error-ridden reproduction of King's original data for 1688. Furthermore, Soltow used post-fisc data (that is, *after* including the impact of poor relief) for both 1688 and 1801/3, while he relied on pre-fisc data (that is, *prior* to tax and transfers) for the remainder of the nineteenth century. Certainly one can insist on a more consistent measure of inequality, and it is the pre-fisc attributes of long-run inequality that are at the heart of the distribution debate. In addition, Soltow failed to take account of Joseph Massie's social tables, and Massie's mid-eighteenth-century estimates appear to match in quality Gregory King's more famous seventeenth-century estimates (Mathias, 1957). To cloud the issue further, Soltow did not account for the criticisms by Stamp (1920) and others of the Baxter (1868) estimates for 1867, nor did he pay adequate attention to changing geographic definitions as the reported inequality data expanded to include Ireland and Scotland over the nineteenth century. Nor did he recognize the problem of pauperism lurking in the social tables.

There is, of course, no substitute for hard facts and it should be apparent already that – while imaginative and impressive – the information left behind by King, Massie, Colquhoun and Baxter is conjecture by perceptive observers and no more. Furthermore, the social arithmetic in King, Massie and Colquhoun offers income distributions constructed from class averages; income variance *within* occupational and social class is typically ignored. Thus, the social tables do not offer full size distributions in the modern sense. On the basis of late nineteenth-century evidence on earnings, for example, we know that there was considerable variance of incomes even within well-defined occupational classes like male domestics, male operatives in the cotton manufactures, or the clergy (Chapter 3 above, Table 3.1). Nevertheless, the variance of mean incomes between socioeconomic classes has always been at the heart of the distributional debate. Moreover, the historical evidence supports this view, at least for earnings: changes in the distribution of earnings seem to have been driven by changes in gaps in average pay between British socioeconomic classes in the nineteenth century (Chapter 3, Table 3.3).

The modern analyst might well be critical of the social arithmetic from King to Colquhoun for yet another reason: it is presented without the modern advantages of income and expenditure surveys, wage returns, industrial censuses, or tax returns. While Colquhoun could practice social arithmetic on a somewhat richer data base – the Napoleonic income tax assessments – none the less he could appeal only to information on taxable incomes, which, as we have seen, represented a small proportion of total British incomes. Thus, even Colquhoun had to rely on guesses in constructing his estimates of the distribution of income for the Napoleonic era. Baxter and Bowley, on the other hand, had the advantage of far more abundant wage and earnings data, which spill out of government offices after the mid-nineteenth century.

In spite of all these well-known weaknesses in the social arithmetic from King onwards, there are three excellent reasons for dwelling at length on their long-run inequality implications. First, these men were, after all, the most perceptive social observers of their time, and their estimates have survived the critical evaluations of a century or two of scholarship. Second, this social arithmetic offers additional evidence against which the 'harder' inequality time series can be gauged. No single data base is likely to establish with certainty the behavior of British inequality since the late eighteenth century. The social arithmetic must be used in conjunction with tax assessment data, occupational pay ratios, earnings distributions, and probated wealth. Third, and at the very least, the social arithmetic from King to Bowley reflects how intelligent observers felt about the inequality around them, and these *subjective* judgments are useful if we are to appreciate political responses to inequality trends as they were perceived by contemporaries.

Inequality trends from the revised social tables
Peter Lindert and I (Lindert and Williamson, 1982, 1983b) recently reported a collaborative effort to revise the social tables from King to Colquhoun. This effort entailed a complete revision of the distribution of income recipients by occupation (based on Lindert's early work – 1980a, b – with sampled probates from the eighteenth and early nineteenth centuries) as well as revisions in the occupational income estimates themselves (based on my own work with occupational earnings discussed in Chapters 2 and 3). A few years ago, I made an independent effort to amend the estimates for the modern era from Baxter to Bowley (Williamson, 1978), and the most polished revision has now been published as part of a larger effort (Lindert and Williamson, 1983b). The results of this research are summarized in Tables 4.5 and 4.6.[3]

Income inequality trends among non-paupers. Our view of inequality based on the social tables is impaired by the difficulty of counting paupers and their incomes. Unfortunately, King, Massie, Colquhoun and Baxter did not treat pauperism the same way, so this tough issue is set aside until inequality trends among the non-paupers are clearly understood.

English and British inequality trends without the pauper host are summarized in Table 4.5. The main result is unmistakable: 1867 looks like a watershed in the social tables too. Sometime around this mid-Victorian benchmark an episodic shift took place. It now appears that both income and earnings inequality declined for at least a century after 1867. Table 4.5 also suggests that the 1860s were preceded by at least a century of rising inequality, supporting the Kuznets curve hypothesis that has emerged from other data examined thus far in this book.

The early rise in inequality seems to have permeated the full size distribution. From 1688 to 1801/3, the richest 35 per cent gained larger shares of the pie at the expense of both the bottom and the middle. Between 1801/3 and 1867 the widening continued, but with a different twist: the top 5 and 10 per cent gained enormously, the unskilled bottom 40 per cent gained slightly, while those in between got squeezed. Of course, the 40–90 per cent 'middle class' was a mixed bag. According to Massie's and Colquhoun's social tables, they would have included the skilled and white-collar workers, but Chapter 3 has shown that these high-paid wage and salary earners *gained* relative to the bottom 40 per cent. It follows that those in the middle class who got squeezed must have been small and large capitalists (tradesmen, innkeepers, ale-sellers, and manufacturers of all kinds) and farmers plus freeholders, not those at the top of the *earnings* distribution.

Table 4.5 *Conjectures on British income inequality trends from the revised social tables, 1688–1913, 'without paupers'*

Date of original observation	Income recipients and number of income classes	Gini coefficient	Income shares (%)					Atkinson index		
			Bottom 40% group	40–65% group	65–90% group	Top 10%	Top 5%	ε = 1.5	ε = 2.5	ε = 4.0
		England and Wales								
King (1688)	Households and single individuals, 13 classes	0.468	15.4	16.7	26.0	42.0	27.6	0.393	0.491	0.569
Massie (1759)	"	0.487	15.8	14.1	25.8	44.4	31.2	0.399	0.474	0.531
Colquhoun (1801/3)	"	0.519	13.4	13.3	28.0	45.4	29.8	0.450	0.542	0.607
Baxter (1867)	"	0.551	14.8	11.7	20.8	52.7	45.1	0.473	0.523	0.562
		United Kingdom								
Baxter (1867)	All income recipients, 8 classes	0.538	15.2	32.4		52.4	46.8	0.464	0.510	0.547
Bowley (1880)	All income recipients, 6 classes	0.520	17.0	28.8		54.2	49.4	0.462	0.502	0.532
Bowley–Stamp (1913)	All income recipients, 12 classes	0.502	17.2	33.0		49.8	43.8	0.427	0.475	0.522

Sources: Lindert and Williamson (1983b, Table 2). The Atkinson Index is explained in Atkinson (1970).

These inequality trends from Colquhoun to Baxter suggest subtler hypotheses about the early and mid-nineteenth century than have yet been offered in traditional accounts of the first industrial revolution. They contrast with the pervasive inequality march posited by Marx (1947, Chs XXV, XXXII, esp. pp. 659, 660) and Perkin (1969, Chs V and X). They also contrast with the egalitarian triumph posited by Greg (1853), Giffen (1883, as cited in Perkin, 1969, p. 410), Clark (1940) and Hartwell (1961). Nor is it clear just how much of the 1801/3–1867 long-run trends are a peculiar result of offsetting shorter-run Napoleonic and post-Napoleonic events, offsetting movements apparent in pay ratios among wage and salary earners as well as in the window tax assessment and inhabited house duty data.

Alfred Marshall (1910, p. 687) thought a leveling trend had appeared in the late nineteenth century, suggesting a 'trickling-down' triumph for Victorian capitalism. As we have seen, the data on the distribution of earnings, on pay ratios, on income tax assessments and on house tax returns appear to confirm Marshall's benign view of Victorian capitalism on the far side of the nineteenth-century Kuznets curve. The social arithmetic summarized in Table 4.5 now adds further confirmation. From the 1860s to World War I, an egalitarian leveling is unambiguous, pronounced and pervasive across the full income distribution. The bottom 40 per cent increased their share of late-Victorian national income, while the top 5 and 10 per cent suffered a very sharp erosion. The 'middle-class' share rose modestly. Thus, the Gini coefficient declines over the half-century, and all the Atkinson indices drift downwards too. When the period is broken into two parts, however, some interesting and more complex patterns reappear. From 1880 to 1913, the inequality trends in Table 4.5 are exactly as I have described them for the longer late-Victorian era starting with the 1860s. Differences appear for the 1867–80 period. While an egalitarian leveling *was* at work during this transitional period following the 'watershed' of the 1860s – signaling the longer-term leveling up to World War I – the leveling has some of the peculiar attributes of the preceding Colquhoun–Baxter trends. That is, the Lorenz curve continued the rotation it had begun at the start of the century: both the bottom 40 per cent *and* the top 15 per cent gained further ground relative to groups in the middle, but the bottom 40 per cent had large enough gains to produce the modest leveling in the aggregate inequality statistics. After 1880, the gains for the bottom 40 per cent were more modest, while the shares going to the top 5 and 10 per cent dropped off very sharply. As we have seen, overall inequality declined unambiguously over the half-century as a whole.

What to do about the pauper host? Mapping the rise in income inequality up to the mid-nineteenth century is complicated by the problem of how to count the 'non-working' poor who, at best, were only marginal members of the primary labor force. The original social tables took very different approaches to pauperism, and Chapter 2 has already discussed those problems that arise when pauperism estimates are introduced into the standard-of-living debate (Table 2.8). But what about their use in the *inequality* debate? Extreme caution is the wise course of action, but let us see what the revised estimates imply about inequality trends. Then possible biases in these estimates of the pauper host and their pre-transfer incomes can be explored.

What happened to the pauper host? To repeat Table 2.8, the revised social tables imply the following trends:

Year	'Pauperism' or percentage in poverty	Original source of 'guesstimate'
1759	12.5	Joseph Massie (1760; Mathias, 1957)
1801/3	19.9	Patrick Colquhoun (1806)
1812	14.8	Patrick Colquhoun (1815)
1850	(10.0)	(Adelman and Morris, 1978, p. 265)
1867	6.2	R. Dudley Baxter (1868)

Given the massive fall in pauperism from Colquhoun to Baxter, it would be remarkable if any rise in inequality still persisted in the estimates. After all, what happens to the bottom 40 per cent determines in large measure what happens to the Gini coefficient. And what happens to the rate of pauperism clearly must have had a major influence on conditions at the bottom. Thus, can one *really* believe these measured rates of pauperism?

Ignoring their flaws, how do the pauperism estimates affect inequality trends over the century 1759–1867? With the pauper host included, the implications for inequality of the revised social tables are summarized in Table 4.6. Here it seems that the cause of equality suffered a major defeat sometime between 1759 and 1801/3 when the top third of the income distribution gained at the expense of the lower two-thirds. From 1801/3 to 1867, both the bottom and the top groups gained at the expense of the middle, with no net change in the overall Gini coefficient. Taken at face value, then, the 'with pauper' estimates confirm the drift toward more unequal incomes up to 1867, although they suggest a somewhat different timing. Here the rise of inequality seems to have come in the late eighteenth century, followed by mixed trends (e.g., rising fortunes at both the bottom and the top of the distribution) that produced a plateau of high inequality across seven decades of the nineteenth century.

As I argued in Chapter 2 (section 4), the 'with pauper' inequality trends cannot be accepted at face value since the underlying estimates of pauperism are shaky at best. The poor have always had varying levels of pre-transfer income. Perhaps more to the point, social observers changed their view of what constituted the poverty threshold over time, and changing the poverty income threshold from period to period surely affects trends in the pauper counts. My sources clearly had differing propensities to count the poor. I suspect that the Colquhoun pauper counts are too high and the Massie and Baxter counts are too low, even after the revisions that Peter Lindert and I have introduced. Colquhoun seems to have defined poverty too broadly in 1801/3 to make his figures comparable with those from other dates. Lindert and I have pruned Colquhoun's estimates but, as the discussion in Chapter

Table 4.6 Conjectures on income inequality trends in England and Wales from the revised social tables, 1759–1867, 'with paupers'

Observation	Income recipients and number of income classes	Average nominal income £	Gini coefficient	Income shares (%)					Atkinson index		
				Bottom 40%	40–65% group	65–90% group	Top 10%	Top 5%	ε = 1.5	ε = 2.5	ε = 4.0
1759	Households and single individuals, 13 classes	46.37	0.509	13.7	15.3	26.7	44.4	31.2	0.457	0.577	0.683
1801/3	"	91.00	0.577	10.3	12.5	29.4	47.9	32.7	0.571	0.700	0.781
1867	All income recipients, 'with paupers', 13 classes	72.03	0.577	13.2	12.1	21.3	53.4	46.0	1.000	1.000	1.000

Sources: Lindert and Williamson (1983b, Table 3). The Atkinson Index equals unity whenever any class has zero income, as do the 1867 paupers following Baxter's assumptions. See the discussion of Baxter's estimates in Lindert and Williamson (1983b, Section I).

2 points out, even the revised 1801/3 pauperism estimates may be too high. The poor relief returns for 1802/3 show 'only' 11 per cent on relief, so Colquhoun was obviously assuming that a very large share of the true pauper total went unrelieved. Colquhoun himself was apparently uneasy with his 1801/3 estimates, since for 1814 they are quite a bit lower (14.8 versus 19.9 per cent in the revised estimates). Moreover, as I pointed out in Chapter 2 (section 4), Colquhoun's estimates for 1801/3 far exceed those of the Webbs (1909, 8.6 per cent of the population) or of J. D. Marshall (1968, Table 2, 11 per cent of the total population). Colquhoun probably overstated the pauper count, thus overstating inequality in 1801/3. Furthermore, we *know* that Baxter's assumptions tend to minimize pauperism.

Counting the poor has always presented problems to social observers, whether they are looking at the late eighteenth century or the mid-twentieth century. That these pauper counts have flaws is not the issue. The issue is whether the flaws introduce a bias in the measured 'with pauper' income inequality trends over time. My own guess is that the revised pauper counts still exaggerate the rise in pauperism in the late eighteenth century and the subsequent fall from Colquhoun to Baxter. Thus, the 'with paupers' inequality estimates in Table 4.6 probably introduce a spurious leveling tendency between 1801/3 and 1867, understating the true rise in inequality from 1801 to 1867.

(6) Tentative findings and controlled conjectures

The income distribution evidence for the pre-twentieth century is fragile at best. But at least there is evidence from widely divergent sources, and for the most part these sources have similar stories to tell.

First, there was a leveling in incomes across the late nineteenth century. The egalitarian drift was universal, since the income shares at the top fell, the shares at the bottom rose, the relative pay of the unskilled improved, pauperism fell and the earnings distribution narrowed.

Second, there was a rise in inequality across the century following 1760. The inequality drift was universal, since the income shares at the top rose, the shares at the bottom fell, the relative pay of the unskilled deteriorated, and the earnings distribution widened.

Third, it follows that the inequality evidence traces out a Kuznets curve over the century and a half from 1760 to World War I.

Fourth, it appears that the upswing of the Kuznets curve was interrupted by the French Wars. The pay ratio and earnings distribution data clearly document an egalitarian leveling across the Napoleonic period, perhaps starting as early as the 1780s. These trends are reversed following the Wars, with a surge in wage inequality from the 1820s to mid-century. These trends are also apparent in the tax assessment data. In addition, the tax assessment data suggest that the wartime trends from the 1780s to the 1820s reflect offsetting movements: improvements took place at *both* the bottom *and* the top of the distribution – the middle being squeezed – but net egalitarian trends are apparent in all the summary statistics. The post-Waterloo period, in contrast, was one of consistent inequality movements. There is some evidence, however, that conflicts with this pre-Waterloo and post-Waterloo inequality characterization. The conflicting evidence is of two sorts: the distribution of taxable incomes between the 1800s and the 1840s; and the distribution of income implied by the social tables from Colquhoun to Baxter when pauperism is included.

These inequality facts support Simon Kuznets' (1955) conjecture that income inequality is likely to show an early rise and late decline as economic development proceeds. This and the previous chapter suggest an earlier inequality watershed than folklore has implied, however, since British inequality seems to have stopped rising by the middle of the nineteenth century. The timing is intriguing: apparently the corner was turned soon after 1867 – the year when Volume 1 of *Das Kapital* was published, well before the rise of trade union power, the introduction of Lloyd George's progressive taxes, and the rise of government spending as a share of national product.

True, caution suggests that the British Kuznets curve should be viewed as a working hypothesis only. Far more evidence must be accumulated before it can be converted into a true 'stylized fact' of British history. One source of evidence, of course, would lie with trends in the distribution of wealth. Peter Lindert's recent effort to determine who owned England in 1875 (Lindert, 1982) certainly suggests confirmation of my 'watershed' view, since the distribution of wealth was apparently at its apex in 1875 and declined over the century since. Lindert's work with sampled seventeenth, eighteenth- and early nineteenth-century probates also suggests evidence of a marked surge in British inequality from 1810 to 1875 (Lindert, 1984 forthcoming).

The evidence for a British Kuznets curve certainly seems compelling enough to warrant a search for explanations.

Notes

1   The window tax was repealed shortly after 1849 because it was a 'nuisance tax' that yielded trivial revenue.
2   This effort to utilize the window tax data to infer trends in the distribution of income was encouraged by Lee Soltow's (1971) success in reconstructing trends in Scottish inequality. Soltow utilized Scottish census data on households distributed by number of rooms, 1861–1961.
3   The remainder of this chapter draws heavily on Lindert and Williamson (1983b, Section II).

Part II

5

What Drives Inequality?

Part I has established that the first industrial revolution generated inequality trends that appear to confirm the Kuznets curve, a stylized fact that has characterized so many countries that have followed the British example in the nineteenth and twentieth centuries. In the British case, inequality seems to have risen from the Napoleonic Wars to mid-century, after which the distribution leveled up to World War I. Not only are these inequality trends apparent in rates of pay and in the earnings distribution, they also appear in size distributions of income.

What drove this inequality experience? What were the sources of the Kuznets curve? Why the turning-point in mid-century?

(1) How to think about inequality: a strategy[1]

Like my previous research with Peter Lindert on America (Williamson and Lindert, 1980), the initial theorizing in Part II is directed towards occupational pay ratios, skill premia, earnings distributions, and the share of unskilled labor in national income. This is because the evidence in Part I suggests that an understanding of the forces driving the earnings distribution will take us a long way towards understanding trends in more complex full size distributions of income by household. Indeed, Chapter 3 suggests that an effective explanation of the relative surplus and scarcity of unskilled labor lies at the heart of any theory of the Kuznets curve. Such explanations will serve to account for the initial fall and subsequent rise in the relative price of common labor, for the initial rise and subsequent fall in earnings inequality, for the initial fall and subsequent rise in *unskilled* labor's share in national income, and thus for the nineteenth-century British Kuznets curve more generally. Certainly this wasn't the only force at work: the behavior of land rents was surely a crucial determinant of income distribution among those at the top, as well as of their relative share in total incomes; and surely changes in the concentration of landholdings and changes in the distribution of human capital mattered as well. But understanding why common labor fared as it did certainly has high priority in any explanation of the Kuznets curve.

Second, my interest is primarily in rates of pay by skill and average income by class. I shall have far less to say about income shares accruing to various classes. My own feeling is that the central issue in the Great Inequality Debate has always been *rates of pay* by class, rather than the *numbers* in any given class. This certainly was the focus of all the classical models from Ricardo to Marx, who thought it enough to explain the behavior of wages, rents and profits where the numbers of capitalists and landlords were usually ignored. The remainder of this book falls into the classical tradition.

Third, I follow another well-established tradition shared by economic theorists, historians and sociologists alike: 'class' is the unit of observation that I have found most helpful in analyzing the Kuznets curve. This view is, of course, quite consistent with any approach that focuses on factor incomes, especially in nineteenth-century Britain. As Chapters 7 and 8 make clear, this book takes the position that class mobility was sufficiently limited in the short run and medium term that class distinctions are justifiable simplifications. Furthermore, since occupational/skill rankings by earnings level changed so little in nineteenth-century Britain (see Chapter 2) and given the striking symmetry in changes in earnings by skill – i.e. a general stretching in the wage structure was always characterized by the most pronounced wage improvement among the most skilled, and a general leveling in the wage structure was always characterized by the most pronounced wage improvement among the least skilled – little is lost by adopting a simple dichotomy between the 'unskilled' and the 'skilled'.

In effect, I augment the classic growth and distribution model to include the distribution of earnings, thus expanding the conventional class trio to a quartet – landlords, capitalists, common laborers and skilled workers. While a four-class model is certainly an improvement over the economist's more conventional three-class model, the social historian is still likely to find my approach too aggregative. The social historian simply finds English society too complex for such simplifications. Writing in 1847, William Dodd thought eight classes was about right (Floud and McCloskey, 1981, p. 260). More recently, R. S. Neale (1968) suggests that a five-class model may be of more value. While the social historian is certainly right, the economists' models cannot admit such class pluralism very effectively. Thus, I strike the middle ground in what follows and stick with the four-class model.

Fourth, what follows is motivated by the belief that wealth and its distribution is the tail wagged by the current income dog. It will be helpful to take the existing distribution of human and conventional wealth as given; then to explore the impact of macroeconomic events on the streams of income accruing to those assets; and, finally, to infer inequality implications as a result. This does not mean that I reject the view that independently changing wealth distributions can have an impact on trends in income distributions. I just do not believe that history yields very many relevant examples of such causal chains (e.g. emancipation, land reform, and revolution). Rather, I believe that wealth distributions are driven by, or are determined simultaneously with, rates of pay and returns on assets.

For example, the first-order effect of any macroeconomic event that raises the relative rent on farmland is to create additional inequality as landlords at the top of the distribution find their incomes augmented. Rising wealth concentration would be observed simultaneously since land *values* would also rise in response to improved future rental expectations. Since British landowners were at the top of the wealth and income distribution, rising income and wealth inequality would be closely correlated in the historical time series. As another example, suppose some macroeconomic event serves to increase the output of skill-intensive sectors, generating a strong demand for skilled labor, and thus increasing the relative scarcity of skills. Such an event would eventually tend to produce a rise in the premium on skills and a 'stretching' in the occupational wage structure, the top of the earnings distribution would benefit, and earnings inequality would result. The rise in earnings inequality would also produce increased wealth concentration, partly because the more affluent skilled worker would save more, but mostly because of the impact on human capital – an important component of total wealth among the working classes. After all, the rise in returns to skills implies that the capitalized value of those skills rises too. Thus, improved earnings on skills imparts an additional skew to the distribution of human capital *values*, as the 'labor aristocracy' and white-collar families at the top of the earnings distribution increase their share of total human capital. One final example will serve to illustrate the point. Suppose some macro-economic event serves to raise profit rates on conventional capital, augmenting capitalists' incomes and fostering a first-order rise in income inequality as a consequence. Wealth would become more concentrated as well, since the *value* of capital assets held by those near the top of the wealth distribution would increase as expectations of continued higher profit rates on existing plant and equipment served to inflate the value of those assets.

In addition, there are the more conventional accumulation responses to consider. In each of the three examples just considered, accumulation responses are likely to reinforce the wealth inequality trends already initiated. Landlords would be encouraged by the higher rents to invest in land improvements, thus augmenting wealth inequality still further. Capitalists would be encouraged to reinvest profits and accumulate given the higher rates of return to plant and equipment, thus augmenting wealth inequality still further. And skill scarcity would encourage more on-the-job training, formal education, and occupational migration. Since it is the skilled laboring classes that are more likely and more able to engage in that kind of human capital creation, wealth inequality would increase on this score too. Thus, second-order wealth inequality effects – the accumulation responses – should serve to augment the first-order income inequality effects.

But what about the long run? The increased stock of skills should eventually serve to lower the skill premium, the increased stock of conventional capital should eventually drive down profit rates, and land improvements may eventually serve to lower rents per acre. Thus, the relative scarcity of labor rises in the long run as various forms of capital accumulate in response to the rise in rates of return to land, capital and skills. What happens to factor income *shares* depends on various substitution elasticities that characterize the macro-economy, but it is clear that the structure of pay and factor rents will be leveled by the long-run accumulation response. Indeed, the tension between factor demand disequilibrium and the equilibrating factor supply response will be apparent in the analysis of the Kuznets curve for the remainder of this book.

Finally, and perhaps most important, it should be stressed that any theory of the Kuznets curve must also be capable of explaining other economic events that were closely correlated with the inequality trends. General equilibrium theory alerts us that any competing explanation of the British Kuznets curve must also offer a consistent explanation of British experience with international trade, industrialization, urbanization and growth. While the Kuznets curve from the 1820s to mid-century is associated with export-led growth, an industrialization surge, rapid urbanization and trend acceleration in overall national income growth, the late nineteenth century has been traditionally characterized by trade woes, 'failure' in manufacturing, agricultural 'depression' and overall growth retardation. Any model purporting to account for the Kuznets curve must also be consistent with these other important macro-events that characterized nineteenth-century Britain.

(2) The critics and defenders of capitalism: looking at inequality through factor markets

The previous section should have made it clear that this book has found it helpful to distinguish disequilibrating factor demand forces, which often – though not always – tend to augment inequality during early industrialization, from equilibrating factor supply responses, which often – though not always – tend to produce egalitarian trends during late industrialization. After all, while rising inequality can be viewed as an unsightly blemish on early capitalist growth, it can also be viewed as a set of price signals that eventually trigger health supply responses. If one views rising British inequality up to mid-century as a set of price signals that were flashing factor scarcities and bottlenecks, then the Kuznets curve may have a more salubrious interpretation than the critics of British capitalism have allowed. Perhaps rising earnings and income inequality were simply a reflection of some powerful disequilibrating forces unleashed by rapid early nineteenth-century industrialization? Perhaps the egalitarian trends following the mid-century were simply a reflection of equilibrating factor supply responses generated by the earlier price signals?

According to this view, capitalist inequality is seen as a necessary condition for successful industrialization. Indeed, this has always been the position of apologists for capitalism: rising inequality was induced by capital and skill shortages; those shortages were eventually alleviated because the incentives to accumulate skills and capital were there, illuminated by price signals; and the means to accumulate was also made available by the growing potential surplus implied by rising inequality.

The critics of capitalism have always been impatient with this view. The fact that inequality persisted for so long suggests that the unfettered capitalist economy was not generating the promised accumulation response and skill creation that would have reduced the scarcity of capital and skills, that would have reduced profit rates and skilled wage differentials, and thus would have leveled earnings and income. The critics, therefore, stress the leveling influence of the state later in the nineteenth century – through, for example, the Factory Acts and education reform – and the more dramatic leveling in the twentieth century when the state gets even more activist.

Critics and defenders of capitalism both seem to be willing to make interpretations of factor market behavior the main battlefield in assessing British inequality experience across the nineteenth century. I shall do the same in the remainder of this book. In terms of the Kuznets curve, the issues are clear. What were the disequilibrating factor demand forces that created the rise in inequality sometime after Waterloo? Did those disequilibrating forces eventually die out late in the century, thus initiating a leveling in earnings and incomes? What role did factor supplies play in the process? Was the rate of skills-deepening and capital-deepening fairly slow early in the century, thus allowing inequality to persist and even worsen? Did those conditions change late in the century, thus contributing to the leveling?

(3) The industrialization bias and disequilibrating factor demand

Why would the industrial revolution tend to create inequality? What are the forces that tend to favor those at the top of the distribution – with skills and capital – while by-passing those at the bottom with little endowment beyond raw labor power?

One explanation was offered first by Kuznets himself (Kuznets, 1955; see also Robinson, 1976). He thought that the Kuznets curve could be explained merely by diffusion of high-wage jobs. Imagine that a society begins with a perfectly egalitarian distribution, everyone earning £50. Let some modernizing influence introduce a single job earning £100, which is first enjoyed by one lucky individual, but is then rapidly diffused over time until everybody is earning the £100. Any conventional inequality measure will rise from the initial perfect equality toward increasing inequality before returning to perfect equality at the higher income level. Table 5.1 offers one such example of this process, where I have supposed that the rate at which these high-wage jobs are created starts slowly at first, then accelerates, and then slows down again until the diffusion is complete, in this case seven decades later. This example traces out a pattern of the proportion of those with the favored job much like time series of urbanization or of the proportion employed in manufacturing. And, sure enough, Table 5.1 shows the richest 20 per cent increasing their share of national income from 20 to 30.8 per cent by the end of the third decade of 'industrialization' and declining thereafter, while the poorest 40 per cent undergo an erosion in their share of national income from 40 to 25 per cent by the end of the fourth decade before the trend is reversed.

Like all simple explanations with a core of truth, this 'statistical diffusion'

Table 5.1   *A simple model of 'job diffusion' and the Kuznets curve*

Income and income class		Decade 1	2	3	4	5	6	7
£50:	Number	100	90	70	40	20	10	0
	Income (£s)	5,000	4,500	3,500	2,000	1,000	500	0
£100:	Number	0	10	30	60	80	90	100
	Income (£s)	0	1,000	3,000	6,000	8,000	9,000	10,000
Total:	Number	100	100	100	100	100	100	100
	Income (£s)	5,000	5,500	6,500	8,000	9,000	9,500	10,000
Top 20% share		20%	27.3%	30.8%	25%	22.2%	21.1%	20%
Bottom 40% share		40%	36.4%	30.8%	25%	33.3%	36.8%	40%

model is seductive. First, the model does indeed generate a Kuznets curve. Second, it makes the assessment of distribution issues for this society very simple. If every poor person has an equal chance of getting the good job, then one could hardly say that this society lacks equal opportunity and economic justice. Furthermore, none of the poor suffers (except from envy) as the diffusion continues over the seven decades. As a result, the society might be judged only on its ability to create those jobs efficiently and perhaps on the willingness of the favored rich to insure the 'basic needs' of the poor by some tax transfer scheme.

Unfortunately, the statistical diffusion model has its flaws. Consider two of these.

The first flaw is theoretical. The diffusion argument does not really offer a true explanation of the Kuznets curve, since the spread of the high-paying jobs should itself be an endogenous event in any satisfactory theory of growth and distribution.

The second flaw is empirical. It is not true that the inequality history of Britain can be characterized by fixed relative incomes (for example, 2:1 in Table 5.1). Chapter 3 has shown that the pay advantages of high-skill jobs themselves rose and fell across the nineteenth century. Indeed, that chapter showed that changes in pay ratios did most of the work in driving earnings inequality across the nineteenth century. In short, the structure of pay and earnings inequality is one critical aspect of the growth–distribution connection that simply cannot be ignored. The statistical diffusion model could, however, be augmented to deal with changing pay ratios over the Kuznets curve. In its present form, the model assumes that the supply of skilled workers facing the favored jobs is perfectly elastic. Suppose instead one introduced lags in regional migration, occupational immobility, class restrictions on entry, costs of training, and other labor market forces that would serve to make skill supplies *in*elastic. Then the society characterized in Table 5.1 would find it difficult to fill those high-paying jobs in the short run, skill bottlenecks would appear, and the structure of pay would be 'stretched' to reveal those excess demands.

Thus, the statistical diffusion model can be amended to make it a more attractive candidate to explain the British Kuznets curve. Its most compelling attribute, it seems to me, is that it focuses on the *industrialization bias*. The thesis is simple enough. Early industrialization tends to be very capital and skill intensive, bidding up the rewards on those jobs and assets that are held at the top of the distribution. As the rate of industrialization slows down late in the process, so too does the rate of increase in the demand for skills and machines. Thus, early industrialization generates disequilibrating factor demand, a bias that tends to create greater inequality. These disequilibrating forces settle down later in the growth process as the rate of industrialization itself settles down.

(4) What about unskilled labor supplies?

Industrialization may create a bias that favors the demand for skills and other assets, but, to make matters worse, the unskilled may glut the labor market from below.

Unskilled labor supplies grew quite a bit faster early in the nineteenth century than late. Part of those trends can be attributable to immigration from Ireland into the North of England, but perhaps a larger part can be explained by the forces of 'demographic transition'. Population and labor supply accelerated from the mid-eighteenth century, reaching peak levels sometime early in the nineteenth century, levels that did not begin to decline until almost at the tail end of the upward swing in the Kuznets curve.

Correlations like these have contributed to the durability of the 'labor surplus' hypothesis in both the historical and the Third World development literature. Obviously, accelerating unskilled labor supply growth associated with demographic transition and immigration serve to reinforce the industrialization bias. But the issue can be put more sharply: how much of the observed Kuznets curve can be traced to these demographic forces?

(5) The sources of equilibrating factor supply

The industrialization bias would have initiated factor supply bottlenecks and scarcities that would have had inequality implications. What about factor supply responses? Would they not have served to eliminate those scarcities and thus to have leveled incomes? There are three class-specific assets to consider – land, capital and skills. The accumulation of any of these offered a potential long-run leveling influence.

First – and in the absence of foreign trade – would not farmland scarcities, rising rents and booming land values have encouraged a land supply response? Since land was a factor of production in most inelastic supply, one would hardly expect to observe anything but the most marginal extension of Britain's land stock by improvements. Yet Britain's land stock could have been and was *indirectly* augmented by other forces. The most famous of these was the flood of foreign grains into British markets, a process that effectively augmented the stock of British land by the importation of land-intensive agricultural commodities. Obviously, these imports were purchased by the simultaneous expansion of manufactures exports, but the latter can be viewed as the result of investment in machines and skills to augment the supply of land through trade. Now this indirect land accumulation through trade was influenced greatly by free trade forces, conventionally dated by the repeal of the Corn Laws in the 1840s, long after the inequality forces on the upswing of the Kuznets curve had been set in motion. This indirect land accumulation through trade was also influenced greatly by investment in transportation improvements, both in the newly settled surplus grain producing areas as well as in international waterborne transportation. Since this book makes no effort to endogenize tariff policy and foreign investment in social overhead abroad, these indirect land supply responses will be viewed as a set of fortuitous exogenous events conditioned by world markets.

Second, what about 'machine scarcity' and capital accumulation responses? In the classical model, industrialization breeds rising profit shares, and the higher saving rates out of profits insures that the share of saving in national income will rise during early stages of modern economic growth. Chapter 7 will, in fact, confirm that rising rates of capital accumulation seem to have been an attribute of the *upswing* of the Kuznets curve. Yet, rates of accumulation do *not* rise later in the century, so one would be hard pressed to establish evidence of a capital supply response that offers an explanation for the leveling of incomes on the downside of the Kuznets curve. For that matter, we have yet to establish that rising profit shares and profit rates were an important part of the inequality experience from the Napoleonic Wars to mid-century. Finally, it might be argued that the correlation between rising saving rates, rising rates of accumulation and rising inequality on the upswing of the Kuznets curve is a spurious one, or at least that the causation may have gone from rapid accumulation to *more* inequality, not less.

Third, what about the accumulation of skills as a response to the industrialization bias? Here we may be on more fertile ground. While the literature on nineteenth-century education and the Victorian reforms is extensive, quantitative evidence of education's impact on skills accumulation is almost non-existent. Chapter 7 will measure the human capital accumulation response so that the issue of skills supply, and its potential contribution to the late nineteenth-century leveling, can be confronted. The prospects appear promising.

(6) Missing 'institutional' ingredients: Inflation, unions and social reform

Nowhere in this brief account on what drives inequality has there been any mention of inflation and 'wage-lag', or of unions and the replacement of the Old Poor Law with the New, and little on Victorian educational reform.

With regard to inflation and wage-lag, the hypothesis hardly seems very promising. DeCanio and Mokyr (1977) have attempted to resuscitate Wesley C. Mitchell's (1903, 1908) version of the hypothesis for America, and Mokyr and Savin (1976) tried to do the same for Britain, by applying a stagflationist's view of wage-lag to the Napoleonic Era. The wage-lag thesis cannot possibly survive the test on British history since the inflation–inequality correlation is *inverse*! As we have seen in Part I, there is evidence of *leveling* trends between 1790 and 1820, followed by an inequality surge to mid-century. Yet, the former was a period of spectacular inflation while the latter was, of course, deflationary. To confound the correlation further, the deflation during the late nineteenth century coincides with a modest leveling on the downside of the Kuznets curve. These gross correlations do not offer much promise for the thesis that inflation and wage-lag were a major driving force behind inequality, especially over periods as long as a half-century.

What about institutional forces like unions or social reforms? There are at least two reasons for placing such events at the bottom of the research agenda. First, it seems wise to begin by searching for underlying forces that are more likely to be common among all countries, past and present, that embark on the path to industrialization and modern economic growth. Policies, institutions and cultural norms vary across countries, but technological, demand and accumulation experience tend to be similar. Second, it has yet to be established that unions matter much, that the Poor Laws had a significant impact on labor supplies, that the Factory Acts had much bite, that Victorian education reforms really influenced the rate and spread of schooling, and so on. In any case, even if it is eventually shown that they *did* matter (and the revisionist trend in the literature makes that appear highly unlikely[2]), a persuasive argument can be made that such institutional events are nothing more than political manifestations of market forces already at work.

(7) The agenda

We are now armed with an overview of the task, my biases have been exposed, and I hope the reader has been motivated. Chapter 6 will list all the potential influences that might have served to create the factor markets disequilibria associated with the rising inequality up to mid-century – what I have called the industrialization bias. It will also confront those same forces in the late nineteenth century to see if their abatement may have served to contribute to the leveling on the downside of the Kuznets curve. Chapter 7 will explore the issue of factor supply response. We shall then be equipped in Part III of the book to disentangle the quantitative contribution of these derived factor demand and equilibrating factor supply forces to the British Kuznets curve from the Napoleonic Wars to World War I. I hope that I shall then be in a position to elevate and sharpen the debate over capitalism's success or failure.

Notes

1 This section draws freely on Williamson and Lindert (1980, pp. 135–6 and 143–6). In addition, section 3 also draws heavily on Lindert and Williamson (1984, forthcoming).
2 The revisionist view of the Poor Laws begins, of course, with Blaug (1963), although both he and McCloskey (1973) have focused primarily on the short-run impact of relief on labor supply. The longer-run Malthusian labor supply forces have been confronted by Huzel (1969, 1980), and a recent endogenous treatment of the Poor Laws as implicit labor contracts can be found in Boyer (1982). The revisionist view of the Factory Acts and schooling can be found in West (1965, 1970, 1975a,b), Nardinelli (1980) and, for American analogies, in Landes and Solomon (1972).

6

Disequilibrating Factor Demand: The Industrialization Bias

(1) An unskilled labor-saving bias?

Was the industrial revolution labor saving? If modern technological progress tends to economize on some factors of production and to favor the intensive use of others, then income distribution may be significantly influenced as a result. Unskilled-labor-saving technological change can widen income gaps by worsening job prospects and relative earnings for the unskilled. Capital-using and skills-using technological progress may have the same effect, bidding up the return to skills and machines relative to common labor. These complex technological forces will be abbreviated by the term 'labor-saving' technological change, but it is *unskilled* labor saving that matters most to earnings inequality trends, and perhaps even to income inequality trends as well.

If the industrial revolution tends to save on unskilled labor relative to skills and machines, then it follows that, as technical progress quickens, the pace of labor saving will rise as well. The relative displacement of unskilled labor may accelerate over time, fostering rising inequality on the upswing of the Kuznets curve.

Labor saving has long been part of the lexicon of growth theorists, economic historians, political economists and development analysts. Yet surprisingly little has been done by economic historians to isolate its impact on the derived demand for factor inputs, on the skills and assets traditionally supplied by each social class, and more generally on earnings and income inequality. Certainly there have been many anecdotal accounts of how certain craftsmen with occupation-specific skills were displaced by modern technology (e.g. the handloom weavers), but a comprehensive assessment of the social impact of these disequilibrating technological forces on economy-wide skill demands and earnings inequality has yet to be made.

(2) Accounting for the labor-saving bias and its turning points[1]

If one can find a mechanism that insures a labor-saving bias during early industrialization, then one would have a plausible explanation for the upswing of the Kuznets curve. But what about the downswing? What would account for the switch from high and rising aggregate rates of unskilled labor saving early in the industrial revolution to neutrality or even unskilled labor using at more advanced stages of development?

To understand the impact of the factor-saving bias on inequality trends, one must take care to identify which part is truly exogenous, and which part is an endogenous part of development and thus simply a result of other forces measured independently. An aggregate labor-saving bias can be decomposed into the following four component parts:

(i)   an aggregate bias owing to *endogenous* labor saving within industries in response to the secular rise in labor's relative scarcity;

(ii)   an aggregate bias owing to *endogenous* shifts in industrial activity, induced by shifts in the structure of domestic demand or some supply-side forces;

(iii) an aggregate bias owing to *exogenous* differences in the rate of technological advance between industries with different labor intensities; and

(iv)   an aggregate bias owing to *exogenous* labor saving within industries in response to the introduction of new technologies.

The first source of labor saving is no bias at all. That is, an apparent bias toward labor saving that is simply a response to rising labor scarcities induced by long-run development can hardly be counted as an exogenous technological force influencing the rate of job creation, wage rates and other factor incomes. On the contrary, this kind of labor saving is no more than conventional factor substitution, which serves to minimize any leveling in earnings and income that the initial labor scarcity generated in the first place.

The second source might appear more promising. Development economists agree that changes in output mix have been a critical determinant of aggregate labor saving and rising inequality in the Third World since 1950 (Kelley, Williamson and Cheetham, 1972; Morawetz, 1974; Cline, 1975; Kelley and Williamson, 1984, Chs 4–6). The same appears to have been the case in America since 1820 (Williamson and Lindert, 1980, Ch. 7). While statistically important, this second source of aggregate labor saving may, nevertheless, fail to offer an independent explanation of the Kuznets curve. The expansion of manufacturing at agriculture's expense may look like aggregate unskilled-labor-saving technological change, since the favored sector uses unskilled labor far less intensively than does agriculture, but one may have to dig deeper for causes.

This point deserves stress, especially when confronting the British evidence. It is certainly true that one of the best-documented 'stylized facts' of development is the non-linear shift in output mix as economies undergo long-run development from an agrarian base to advanced industrialization (Chenery and Syrquin, 1975; Morris and Adelman, 1980). Thus, the rate at which agriculture declines as a share of aggregate output begins slowly, then quickens, reaches a peak as the industrial revolution hits full stride, and then drops off as the transformation nears completion at late stages of

Table 6.1   *Unbalanced output growth and the Kuznets curve (per annum growth rates)*

	(1) Early industrialization 1770–1815 %	(2) On the upswing of the Kuznets curve 1821–61 %	(3) On the downswing of the Kuznets curve 1861–1911 %
Sector			
Agriculture	0.78	1.49	0.01
Manufacturing	1.55	3.70	2.01
Services	1.51	2.32	2.05
Mining	—	2.62	2.34
Unbalanced output growth proxy: manufacturing minus agriculture	0.77	2.21	2.00

Sources: Col. (1) – Harley (1982, Table 9).
Col. (2) – Table 9.2.
Col. (3) – Table 9.1.

development. Table 6.1 suggests that the same was true of Britain from the late eighteenth century to World War I. The gap between growth rates in manufacturing and agriculture did indeed rise from a modest 0.77 per cent per annum in the period 1770–1815, to an enormous 2.21 per cent per annum 1821–61, and eased off to 2 per cent per annum 1861–1911. To the extent that traditional agriculture was unskilled labor intensive while modern industry was more skilled labor intensive, high and rising aggregate unskilled labor saving from 1770 to the mid-nineteenth century and a decline in that rate thereafter are assured.

Convenient and elegant, this 'explanation' does not go quite far enough. How much of the impressive acceleration in the rate of industrialization between 1770 and 1861 can be explained by the changing structure of domestic demand as British households responded to higher incomes – that is, by Engel effects? In contrast, how much of it was owing to the rapid rates of technical progress outside of unskilled-labor-intensive agriculture ((iii) above)? How much of the acceleration is to be explained by the shift from wartime conditions prior to the 1820s, when foreign trade was suppressed, to *Pax Britannica*, when foreign trade boomed? That is, how much of the acceleration in the rate of industrialization can be accounted for by changing world market conditions? These are important questions and we need some answers. The key point being made here is simply that the sectoral shift itself may not be an independent influence driving unskilled labor saving and inequality across the British Kuznets curve unless it can be shown that it comes from exogenous forces, like world market conditions, or what I shall call below unbalanced productivity advance.

What about the third and fourth items listed above? While economists have worked hard to derive adequate explanations of labor saving at the firm and industry level (Hicks, 1932; Binswanger, 1974; David, 1975, Ch. 1), the results have not been very useful. This judgment holds with special force when the apparent switch to unskilled labor saving around the 1820s and the apparent retardation in that rate after mid-century are both confronted. While Ephraim Asher (1972) found abundant evidence of labor saving in British cotton textiles, 1820–80, and in wool textiles, 1850–1900, for example, he made no effort to explain any *variety* in the rate of labor saving across the nineteenth century. Furthermore, efforts to explain the variety in industry factor saving have met with limited success when applied to British nineteenth-century history. For example, William Phillips (1982, p. 102) applied the induced innovation hypothesis to account for factor saving in British cotton textiles 1854–1907 and found 'that induced innovation was a rare phenomenon for British entrepreneurs'. All of this suggests to me that unbalanced productivity advance – item (iii) above – is likely to offer a more promising explanation for the changes in the aggregate rates of labor saving in Britain than will the more conventional focus on labor saving at the firm or industry level – item (iv) above.

Unbalanced total factor productivity advance has always played an important supply-side role in qualitative economic histories and in dualistic models of growth. Marx made the claim in Chapter XXV of *Capital* that capitalist development is uneven across sectors, and that unbalanced technological advance tends to breed an increasing concentration of production and capital in the modern sectors. Simon Kuznets (1966) has argued that the more rapid technological progress in modern sectors explains the shift in output mix observed with economic growth. Herbert Simon (1947) showed exactly how that process works in a two-sector model where urbanization was the issue, and so did William Baumol (1967) in his examination of 'the anatomy of the urban crisis'. Peter Lindert and I (Williamson and Lindert, 1980) showed how unbalanced productivity advance accounts for structural change in America since the early nineteenth century.

Unbalanced productivity advance has always been viewed as the primary supply-side force driving industrialization and urbanization. Since the rate of technological change has always been viewed as far higher in modern than in traditional sectors, industry 'leads' and agriculture 'lags' in capital formation, output expansion and job creation. So said the qualitative accounts of the British industrial revolution, and now there are some tentative numbers documenting the process. Table 6.2 summarizes that evidence. True enough, unbalanced productivity advance was very much an attribute of British growth after 1780. Furthermore, unbalanced productivity growth was no longer an attribute of the British economy in the late nineteenth century. Given that agriculture was relatively unskilled labor intensive and that industry was relatively skilled labor intensive, it would appear from Table 6.2 that unbalanced rates of total factor productivity advance are leading candidates as supply-side forces driving British inequality since the late eighteenth century.

If demand conditions were right in commodity markets,[2] unbalanced productivity advance supplies an exogenous source of industrialization, urbanization and structural change; and it supplies an exogenous source of

Table 6.2   *Unbalanced productivity advance and the Kuznets curve*

Sector	(1) Labor productivity growth (per annum) 1780–1860 %	(2) Total factor productivity growth (per annum) On the upswing of Kuznets curve 1821–61 %	(3) On the downswing of Kuznets curve 1861–1911 %
Agriculture	(0.45)	0.30	0.60
Manufacturing	(1.80)	1.05	0.26
Services	(0.65)	0.37	0.37
Mining	—	0.50	0.37
Unbalanced productivity growth proxy: manufacturing minus agriculture	+1.35	+0.75	−0.34

Sources: Col. (1) – McCloskey in Floud and McCloskey (1981, Table 6.2, p. 114).
Cols (2) and (3) – Appendix Tables E.1 and E.2 below.

aggregate unskilled labor saving. Perhaps in combination with world market conditions, it may provide an adequate explanation for the disequilibrating factor demand forces tending to produce rising inequality in nineteenth-century Britain.

(3)   An added possibility: capital–skills complementarity

The industrialization bias is not limited to the unskilled labor saving generated by unbalanced productivity advance between 'modern' and 'traditional' sectors. It may also be true that the rate of total factor productivity growth is *most* rapid in the capital goods sector, at least in the producer durables sector. And rapid technological advance in the producer durables sector should tend to lower the relative (quality-adjusted) price of such items, thereby encouraging their purchase, fostering the adoption of more mechanized processes and thus displacing unskilled operatives. Skilled labor, in contrast, may be required to produce the machines and maintain them once in place, further augmenting the demand for skills and reinforcing the industrialization bias.

Indeed, one of the classic attributes of modern economic growth is the shift of investment out of plant and into equipment. Feinstein (1978a, Table 6, p. 40) documents that shift between the 1760s and the 1860s, when the share of machinery and equipment investment in total capital formation rose from 19.4 per cent to 44.3 per cent over the century.[3] This shift in the final demand structure of investment will tend to reinforce the industrialization bias if machines and skills are complements in production (see Chapter 8 below), or if the construction of producer durables is a very skill-intensive activity. Perhaps the best example of the construction effects associated with changes in the structure of investment was the shift out of farm-formed land improvements – a very unskilled-labor-intensive investment activity – into steam engines and other equipment production (used in modern transportation, coal extraction and textile manufacturing) – a very skilled-labor-intensive investment activity.

Urban social overhead and sophisticated urban services should be added to the industrialization bias. These activities may not be direct inputs into industry, but they are indirect and 'facilitating'. To the extent that the urbanization associated with the industrial revolution requires skill- and machine-intensive inputs, the unskilled-labor-saving industrialization bias is reinforced.

(4) World market conditions

World market conditions may serve to reinforce or offset the disequilibrating factor demand forces set in motion by the industrialization bias.

First, to the extent that Britain was able to vent her manufacturing staples on to world markets along fairly elastic export demand functions, export staples could continue their growth without creating a glut on world markets and a collapse in prices. As it turns out, the relative price of manufactures *did* decline markedly over the period, but not nearly so much as productivity rose. If the price decline had matched British manufacturing's rate of technological progress, then the industrialization bias would have been severely blunted. That is, industrialization would have been forestalled, since the rising marginal *physical* product of all factors favored by technical change in manufacturing would have been offset by the commodity price decline. The net result would have been stable marginal *value* products, no encouragement for factors to migrate to manufacturing, no unbalanced growth favoring industry, and thus no rise in the modern sector's share in national income. The inequality induced by unskilled labor saving would have been limited to the labor displacement at the firm level as the new technologies were adopted all over Britain.

Second, to the extent that raw materials were falling in price in world markets, the industrialization bias was reinforced still further, since these raw materials, along with domestically produced coal, were used very heavily in manufacturing and the urban facilitating industries.

Third, to the extent that the relative price of agricultural commodities was driven down in Britain by expanding supplies in the New World and elsewhere, British agriculture would have tended to contract, unskilled farm labor would have been displaced, and the low-wage urban labor market would have been glutted. Of course, landlords would have suffered the windfall losses of falling land rents, so rising *earnings* inequality generated by displaced farm labor would not necessarily have implied rising *income* inequality. In any event, the Corn Laws would have postponed all of these influences, and their repeal would have accelerated them.

How do these world market conditions correlate with the Kuznets curve?

Prior to Waterloo, British foreign trade was suppressed, domestic agriculture was given a stimulus, and industrialization was blunted. Chapter 12 will explore the implications of those events in forestalling the upswing of the Kuznets curve. After Waterloo, foreign trade boomed under *Pax Britannica* (conditions that would have reinforced the industrialization bias), thus helping account for the upswing of the Kuznets curve after the Napoleonic Wars. Finally, rising protection in America and the Continent in the late nineteenth century would have blunted the bias by slowing industrialization down, but the flood of grains from America would have augmented the bias. Chapter 10 will offer an assessment of the net effect of these offsetting world market conditions on British experience with unskilled labor saving, the industrialization bias, and inequality across the nineteenth century.

(5) Disequilibrating factor demand: testing the hypothesis

Speculation and anecdotal correlations are one thing. Hypothesis testing is quite another. It remains to assess the importance of the industrialization bias and world market conditions in accounting for the British Kuznets curve. But before I do, what about the factor supply side? Even if the industrialization bias was quantitatively important in creating disequilibrating factor demand conditions, would not an elastic supply of capital and skills have served quickly to eliminate those excess demands and thus have served quickly to erode any long-run inequality drift?

Notes

1 This section draws heavily on Williamson and Lindert (1980, Ch. 7) as well as Lindert and Williamson (1984, forthcoming).
2 Price elasticities of demand play an important role here. The unbalanced productivity advance favoring manufacturing must not be faced with problems of absorption on the demand side, otherwise the relative price of manufactures will fall. If demand is inelastic, then obviously the decline in price will exceed the improved marginal physical productivities of factors used in manufacturing. In other words, to the extent that output demand is inelastic, productivity gains in the favored sector will be shifted to consumers, there will be no excess demand for skills and machines used intensively in the favored sector, and no rising inequality. However, the evidence seems to support overwhelmingly the high elasticity characterization, especially when the possibilities for foreign trade are considered.
3 Investment in machinery and equipment includes industrial machinery and equipment, railways, carriages and coaches, and ships. Total capital formation excludes investment in dwellings. Both are in constant 1851–60 prices.

7
Equilibrating Supply: Men, Machines and Skills

(1) Labor surplus and demographic transition

It has become commonplace in the historical literature to associate demographic transition with labor surplus and inequality. The argument develops along the following lines. Modern economic growth begins on a traditional agrarian base, which is characterized by elastic labor supplies, or what has come to be known as 'surplus' unskilled labor. Accelerating rates of capital accumulation associated with early industrialization fail to generate rising real wages among the unskilled until this 'surplus' labor pool is exhausted. The turning point can be postponed for some time if demographic forces are right and Malthusian population pressures or immigration continually replenish the initial surplus labor pool (Fei and Ranis, 1964; Kindleberger, 1967; Minami, 1973; Kelley and Williamson, 1974; Williamson and Lindert, 1980). Under such conditions, stable real wages for unskilled labor could coincide with rising average real wages and per capita incomes, tending to create more inequality as early industrialization unfolds.

This classical model of capitalist growth with inequality was built by English economists surrounded by the poverty and pauperism of early nineteenth-century Britain. W. Arthur Lewis (1954) carried the classical labor surplus model into the twentieth century, where it has become the dominant paradigm used by Third World observers to analyze exactly the same set of problems. To the extent that the application of the labor surplus model to Britain was encouraged in part by the forces of demographic transition there – rising rates of population growth driven primarily by rising fertility (Wrigley and Schofield, 1981), but aided by declining child mortality and further augmented by Irish immigration into the industrializing North – then its application to the contemporary Third World has even more to defend it, since the population growth there has been almost double that of early nineteenth-century Britain.

Time series correlations would appear to support the labor surplus hypothesis. The real wage *was* stable from the late eighteenth century to the 1820s (Chapter 2). Inequality *did* rise across the industrial revolution

Table 7.1   *Factor supply growth, 1821–1911 (% per annum)*

Factor	1821–61	1861–1911	Difference
Capital: $\overset{*}{K}$	2.50	1.97	−0.53
Labor: $\overset{*}{L}$	1.40	0.90	−0.50
Skills: $\overset{*}{S}$	1.46	1.74	+0.28
Land: $\overset{*}{\jmath}$	0.03	0.18	+0.15
Capital–labor ratio: $\overset{**}{K-L}$	1.10	1.07	−0.03
Skills per laborer: $\overset{**}{S-L}$	0.06	0.84	+0.78
Land per laborer: $\overset{**}{\jmath-L}$	−1.37	−0.72	+0.65

Source and Notes: Appendix E. The skills per laborer figure for 1861–1911 (0.84) is a bit higher than that reported in Appendix Table C.4 and Table 7.2 below (0.69). See the discussion in Appendix C, section 1, and Appendix Table E.2.

before reaching a peak sometime around the 1860s (Chapters 3 and 4). And have we not been told that population growth rates underwent trend acceleration from the mid-eighteenth century to the 1820s, not declining significantly from that plateau until after the 1860s (Deane and Cole, 1962; Habakkuk, 1972; Drake, 1969; Wrigley and Schofield, 1981)? Furthermore, we also know that the population was considerably younger in 1815 than in 1750, implying a glut of unskilled labor in the 1820s and afterwards (Floud and McCloskey, 1981, p. 23).

Table 7.1 documents the sympathetic correlation between labor force growth and the Kuznets curve – the higher labor force growth rate of 1.4 per cent per annum prior to 1861 and the lower rate of 0.90 per cent per annum after. Surely the high rates of labor force growth early in the century fostered labor surplus and inequality? Surely the decline in labor supply growth tended to breed the labor scarcity and income leveling observed during the late nineteenth century? Even the decadal rates of labor force growth seem to conform well with the timing of inequality trends. According to Mitchell and Deane (1962, Table 31), while labor force growth rates peaked in the 1830s, they did not decline sharply and permanently to lower levels until the 1850s:

1821–31	1.50%	1851–61	1.07%	1881–91	1.15%
1831–41	1.54	1861–71	1.05	1891–1901	1.28
1841–51	1.44	1871–81	0.88	1901–11	1.08

Before the case seems clinched, however, recall that it is the *relative* scarcity or surplus of labor that matters. So, what happened to the rate of accumulation during the early nineteenth century when labor supplies were expanding more rapidly? Was Britain equipping her workers slower early in the century? Table 7.1 suggests to the contrary. The rate of capital accumulation ($\overset{*}{K}$) was *also* higher early in the century, so much higher in fact that the capital–labor ratio ($\overset{**}{K-L}$) grew no faster after 1861 than before.

This evidence on the capital–labor ratio should tend to unsettle the labor supply advocate. How can he argue that relatively rapid labor force growth accounts for cheap labor, stable real wages and inequality early in the century when in fact the labor force was being equipped with machines at a rate that was no slower early in the nineteenth century than it was later?

(2) Rising accumulation on the upswing of the Kuznets curve: A growth–inequality trade-off?

Accumulation and capital-deepening cannot explain the turning point of the Kuznets curve in mid-century. But what about the upswing of the Kuznets curve? As we shall see in a moment, saving rates were higher after 1820 than before, rates of accumulation were also higher and, of course, inequality was on the rise after 1820 as well. This correlation might encourage support for the view developed in Chapter 6 that rising rates of accumulation create *earnings* inequality since they tend to generate a booming complementary demand for skills. The correlation might also encourage support for the classic trade-off view – that more inequality made for larger surpluses available for accumulation during the early industrial revolution.

First, what is the evidence? While the early work of Deane and Cole (1962) seemed to refute the view that saving rates rose from 1760 to 1860, Charles Feinstein (1978a, p. 90) has shown more recently that 'the investment ratio did rise . . . and by quite a substantial margin', from 9.08 to 13.68 per cent of national income (Table 11.3 below). Nick Crafts (1983, Table 6, p. 195) suggests that the savings ratio may have risen by even more than Feinstein estimated, so the rise in the saving rate from the late eighteenth century to the mid-nineteenth century seems destined to become the new conventional wisdom. As it turns out, the rate of accumulation rose even more sharply, from 0.8 per cent per annum in 1760–80 to 2 per cent per annum in 1831–60 (Feinstein, 1978a, p. 86). Ignoring depreciation, the rate of capital accumulation ($\overset{*}{K}$) can be written as the product of the investment ratio in national income (I/Y) and the average productivity of capital (Y/K):

$$\overset{*}{K} = \Delta K/K = (I/Y)(Y/K).$$

Thus, a rise in the investment share is not essential for a rise in accumulation rates, but it certainly helps.

Now then, suppose for the sake of argument that technological and demographic forces were somehow generating the rise in inequality up to mid-century. Could these forces also explain the high and rising rates of accumulation observed over the same period? The classical economists certainly thought so, and their models were constructed to help explain that accumulation response. The response is also the central hypothesis embedded in both W. Arthur Lewis' (1954) 'labour surplus' model and W. W. Rostow's (1961) characterization of 'take-off'. Let the investment ratio in the expression above be determined by the rate of return to capital (r), inequality (INEQ), thrift (THRIFT), and other forces (OTHER), so that

$$\overset{*}{K} = (I/Y)(Y/K) = s(r,\text{INEQ},\text{THRIFT},\text{OTHER})(Y/K).$$

It follows that $\overset{*}{K}$ should have risen in response to a quickening in the rate of technological change and of labor force growth – both of which were associated with the early industrial revolution – and for three reasons: (i) capital's productivity would have risen (which it most certainly did – Feinstein, 1978a, Table 25, p. 84); (ii) the rise in the rate of return encouraged higher saving rates, $s'(r) > 0$ (about which we know very little – see Chapter 11 below); and (iii), increasing inequality shifted income to those who saved, inducing a further rise in the aggregate saving rate, $s'(\text{INEQ}) > 0$. Accumulation of machines can thus be seen as a response to disequilibrium, in this case induced by the demographic and technological forces associated with the industrial revolution as it quickened its pace after Waterloo.

This explanation for the correlation between rising inequality and rising accumulation up to 1860 is certainly worth pursuing, but, to repeat, it cannot help us understand why the Kuznets curve turns down *after* mid-century.

(3) Skills shortage: price signals and inequality

Table 7.1 suggests that experience with the growth in skills may offer a more promising factor supply explanation for the Kuznets curve. Chapter 3 has already documented a sharp rise in the premium on skills from the 1820s to mid-century. Rising inequality was therefore manifested in part by rising pay ratios, increasing skill premia and skill shortage. The price changes signaling this disequilibrium were dramatic, since the premium on skills rose very fast in real terms (Table 9.2, +1.65 per cent per annum, 1821–61). Skill accumulation rose across the nineteenth century, from 1.46 per cent per annum prior to 1861, to 1.74 per cent after 1861, just as one would have predicted. Furthermore, skill accumulation *per worker* rose at even more impressive rates, from practically no growth at all prior to 1861, to 0.84 per cent per annum afterwards.

Skill-deepening may go a long way towards explaining the turning point of the Kuznets curve. And was it the lagging skill supply response to the industrialization bias that made inequality persist at high levels for so long before the mid-century downturn?

(4) Skill supply response: did Britain fail?

The short run: immobility and non-competing groups
Sociologists contend that relative pay by occupation and skill depends more on 'social structure' than on pure market forces. Historians influenced by this view have taken the sensible position that occupational mobility was extremely limited in nineteenth-century Britain, and thus that labor supply by skill was highly wage-inelastic – at least in the short run. The orthodox

economist, in contrast, tends to stress elastic supplies by skill, as well as high substitution elasticities among skills. The assumption of elastic skill supply is supported by the belief that inter-occupational mobility was and is a powerful competitive force that augments the stock of skills when derived demands create scarcity. The orthodox economist feels that a demand-distorted pay structure could not persist for a half-century, and thus, I presume, that associated earnings inequality could not have persisted for long either. Chapter 3 has shown the orthodox view to be incorrect, at least on the basis of British nineteenth-century experience. Skill supplies must have been sufficiently inelastic to make skill scarcity persist for very long periods.

There are, of course, some unorthodox economists who have joined the sociologists. They, too, stress limited mobility between classes and low substitution elasticities between skills. Furthermore, the unorthodox modern economist would find good company among nineteenth-century economists. Indeed, the concept of non-competing groups can be found in John Stuart Mill (1848). J. E. Cairnes (1874, pp. 64–8), was even more explicit and his work laid the foundations for modern stratification and occupational mobility studies:

> What we find, in effect, is not a whole population competing indiscriminately for all occupations, but a series of industrial layers, superimposed on one another . . . [The] average workman, from whatever rank he is taken, finds his power of competition limited . . . to a certain range of occupations, so that, *however high the rates of remuneration in those which lie beyond may rise, he is excluded from sharing them. We are thus compelled to recognize the existence of non-competing industrial groups* as a feature of our social economy. (Emphasis added)

The tradition of non-competing groups may be a century old, but current debate among labor economists is extremely active on precisely the same issue (Cain, 1976). The more recent assault on the conventional neoclassical orthodoxy may go by different names – theories of segmented labor markets, the job competition model, and the dual labor market theory – but the issues appear to be the same.

The more labor markets were segmented in nineteenth-century Britain, the greater would have been the impact of derived-demand shocks on skill scarcity and inequality. To the extent that occupational mobility was very limited in the short run, skill supplies must have been highly inelastic, and it could indeed be alleged that Britain 'failed' to cope effectively with the disequilibria induced by the new technologies initiated by the industrial revolution.

The long run: education, Victorian reforms and the revisionists
As early as 1848, John Stuart Mill predicted that industrialization's skill-scarcity bias on the upswing of the British Kuznets curve would eventually be eliminated by the operation of long-run human capital accumulation responses and skill-deepening:

The general relaxation of barriers, and the increased facilities of education which are already . . . within the reach of all, tend to . . . bring down the wages of skilled labour. (Mill, 1848, II, xiv, p. 2)

Both immigration and education effect the qualitative composition of the stock of labour, but we should hardly expect to notice an immediate response [except] in the long run. (Mill cited in Lydall, 1968, p. 172)

Writing on pay ratios in 1954, Guy Routh had the advantage of a century's hindsight over Mill, but Routh (1954, p. 210) also stressed the influence of education on the long-run supply of skills:

The decisive influence, no doubt, was that series of measures, beginning with the Elementary Education Act of 1870, which made literacy the right of all instead of the privilege of a few.

While few would doubt the importance of education in augmenting the supply of skilled labor, the role of the state, public schooling and the impact of the Victorian reforms *has* been challenged. E. G. West (1970, 1975a,b) has argued that, as early as the 1820s and 1830s, the private schooling sector was very responsive to the needs generated by the industrial revolution. In any case, West has stressed that public and private schooling served to augment the supply of skills long before the educational reforms of the 1870s, and that Britain invested at least as much if not more in educational capital before mid-century than did her competitors in North America and on the Continent.

Back to the basics: what happened?
Did nineteenth-century Britain fail? That is, were the social restrictions on class mobility sufficiently severe, and was formal and informal schooling sufficiently inaccessible to common labor, to have made the supply of skills sufficiently inelastic to warrant the judgment that Britain failed? While there is certainly no shortage of speculation in an enormous historical literature that has accumulated since the early 1800s, the question cannot be answered in the absence of two critical pieces of information. First, one needs measures of skills scarcity. Second, one needs measures of the growth in skills. The pay ratios summarized in Chapter 3 supply the first item. The second item is derived in the next section.

(5) Measuring the accumulation of skills

Some feasible alternatives
After Gary Becker (1962, 1964) and Theodore Schultz (1960, 1961) got us thinking about human capital in the 1960s, there was a veritable flood of empirical work estimating trends in labor force quality. With the exception of some guesses that Peter Lindert and I offered recently for nineteenth-century America (Williamson and Lindert, 1980, Ch. 9), these labor force quality estimates dealt with twentieth-century trends only (Denison, 1962, 1967, 1974; Christensen, Cummings and Jorgenson, 1980; Denison and Chung, 1976; Gollop and Jorgenson, 1980). There is really no reason why

the same cannot be done for nineteenth-century Britain. Certainly the methodology has been well enough established over the past two decades, since each of these past studies used pretty much the same procedure. What follows is an exposition of two feasible alternatives that the extant British nineteenth-century data make possible.

Why do some people work for higher wages than others? Human capital theorists argue that people get paid what their skills are worth and that differences in wages across occupation, age and education reflect true differences in labor quality – differentials that reflect an investment in human capital that the market compensates. Critics reply that earnings differentials reflect instead artificial restrictions on entrance into high-paying jobs, not skills or quality differentials as such. Without committing myself to a position in the debate, my purpose here is only to develop measures of the growth in the aggregate stock of the higher-paid stuff called 'skills' from the 1820s to World War I. Given the nature of the historical data, there is only one operational concept that can be applied to nineteenth-century Britain: 'skills' are those attributes that give a worker higher pay than 'common' labor. These attributes tend to be occupation specific and they may range from formal education, on-the-job training, sex, race, age, health, speech, good grooming, or luck. Two skill-stock measures might be considered.

One way to define skills and their compensation is to divide total employment into two wage-earning groups, those receiving high and those receiving low rates of pay. Here, the stock of skills is simply the total employed in the high-wage occupations, the residual being the unskilled. The division is arbitrary, but the approach is reasonable if it cuts at a well-defined break in the earnings distribution. For example, unskilled labor might include farm workers, messengers and porters, dock laborers, watchmen, and other common laborers, with all remaining occupations thrown into the skilled labor class. This measure corresponds to the usual definition of skills offered in the sociological literature on occupational mobility and class structure.

An alternative is to view skills as those advantages that command pay above that of common labor, in which case an occupation is skilled to the extent that it pays wages above the unskilled (common laborer's) wage. The greater the pay advantage over the common laborer's wage, the greater is the share of a given occupation's earnings that is returned to skilled labor, and the larger is the stock of skills per employee in that occupation. According to this measure, the relevant skilled wage is a premium, a gap or a markup, not the ratio of skilled to unskilled wage rates. This second measure is more consistent with the economist's view of human capital and it is used in Appendix C in constructing estimates of the rate of skills-deepening ($\overset{*}{s}$) in nineteenth-century Britain.

Nineteenth-century estimates

Appendix C estimates that growth in skills per worker was very slow between 1821 and 1861, 0.06 per cent per annum. It accelerated throughout the century, however, achieving an impressive 0.69 per cent per annum between 1861 and 1911, a figure that coincides almost exactly with a recent estimate for 1856–1913 offered by Matthews *et al*. (1982, Table 4.7, p. 113, 0.7 per cent per annum).

What can we conclude from these skill accumulation estimates? First, these estimates appear to conform with skill accumulation rates taking place at the same time on the other side of the Atlantic. Peter Lindert and I (Williamson and Lindert, 1980) have estimated the rate of skills-deepening for nineteenth-century America and a comparison with Great Britain can be found in Table 7.2. True, it appears that America began her skills-deepening a bit later in the century than did Britain, no doubt as a result of America's absorption of unskilled European migrants from the 1830s onwards, including the Irish host that was deflected from the North of England to America during the famine and after. Britain also shows signs of an Edwardian retardation at the end of the period, while America does not. Nonetheless, the similarities are more striking than the differences. Between 1839 and 1909, the rate of skills-deepening ($\overset{*}{s}$) in America was 0.35 per cent per annum. Between 1841 and 1911, the rate of skills-deepening in Britain was 0.32 per cent per annum. From 1869/71 to the turn of the century, the rates were 0.54 and 0.50 for Britain and America, respectively. The close correspondence is reassuring since the two estimates were constructed very differently. They also conform with figures documenting investment in education.[1]

Second, Table 7.2 suggests that late nineteenth-century rates of skills-deepening in Britain were quite adequate when compared with twentieth-century experience. Indeed, apart from three exceptions – fast-growing Japan and Korea in the post-World War II era, and America between 1929 and 1948 – late nineteenth-century Britain seems to have achieved rates of skills-deepening equal to or greater than the twentieth-century cases listed in Table 7.2.

Third, there is abundant evidence of trend acceleration in the rate of skills-deepening in Britain (and America). Not only is the rate of skills-deepening far higher after 1861 than before (0.69 versus 0.06 per cent per annum), but the rate of skills-deepening rises in the early nineteenth century: from 1821 to 1841, it appears that the skill–labor ratio actually fell ($\overset{*}{s} = -0.05$ per cent per annum); while from 1841 to 1861, the rate of skills-deepening began a rise (+0.10 per cent per annum) that was to persist through the remainder of the century.

Fourth, note how skill accumulation rates respond to apparent shortages only very slowly and with a long lag. Part of this may be simply demographic: the rise in schooling rates in the 1820s and 1830s (West, 1970, 1975a,b), for example, could hardly have had an impact on $\overset{*}{s}$ until a decade or so beyond. But the fact remains that high and rising skill shortages persisted for some time before skill accumulation rates began to respond.

Fifth, the evidence would appear to support those revisionists who reject the view that the Victorian school reforms of the 1870s had an important positive impact on the rate of human capital accumulation in Britain. Indeed, it may well be that the 'failure' of British industry in the late nineteenth century can be laid at the doorstep of inadequate investment in

Table 7.2 *The rate of skills-deepening: nineteenth-century Britain compared with others (% per annum)*

Country	Period	$\overset{*}{s}$	Source
Nineteenth century:			
Great Britain	1821–41	−0.05	Appendix C tables
	1841–61	0.10	Appendix Table C.4, Case B
	1821–61	0.06	*ibid.*
	1871–1901	0.54	Appendix Table C.4, Case A
	1901–11	0.30	Appendix C tables
	1861–1911	0.69	Appendix Table C.4, Case A
United States	1839–59	0	Williamson and Lindert (1980, pp. 218, 240)
	1869–99	0.50	*ibid.*
	1899–1909	0.57	*ibid.*
	1839–1909	0.35	*ibid.*
Twentieth century:			
United States	1909–29	0.68	Denison (1962, p. 85)
	1929–48	1.08	Denison (1974, p. 32)
	1948–69	0.66	*ibid.*
	1947–73	0.80	Christensen, *et al.* (1980, Table 11.A.3US)
	1947–73	0.69	Gollop and Jorgenson (1980, p. 55)
United Kingdom	1955–73	0.60	Christensen, *et al.* (1980, Table 11.A.3UK)
Netherlands	1951–73	0.50	Christensen, *et al.* (1980, Table 11.A.3N)
Korea	1960–73	1.21	Christensen, *et al.* (1980, Table 11.A.3K)
Japan	1952–71	1.06	Denison and Chung (1976, p. 31)
Italy	1952–73	0.20	Christensen, *et al.* (1980, Table 11.A.3I)
Germany	1950–73	0.40	Christensen, *et al.* (1980, Table 11.A.3G)
France	1950–73	0.47	Christensen, *et al.* (1980, Table 11.A.3F)
Canada	1947–73	0.53	Christensen, *et al.* (1980, Table 11.A.3C)

human capital (even with the reforms) compared to her main competitors. Skills per worker growth in the UK *did* slow down after the turn of the century; $\overset{*}{s}$ in the UK *did* fall below the American rate after 1900; and UK educational expenditure shares in GNP fell far below those of America and Germany by 1900 too.

(6) Failure relative to what? A comparative evaluation of nineteenth-century Britain

While it is true that a skills shortage persisted throughout much of the nineteenth century, and while it is also true that the rate of skills-deepening

Table 7.3. *Long-run skill supply elasticities: America and Britain compared*

Variable and period	Britain	America
Growth in the relative price of skilled labor: $\overset{*}{q} - \overset{*}{w}$, in % per annum		
1821–41 (a)	2.18	2.96
1821–61 (b)	1.65	2.22
Growth in skills per worker: $\overset{*}{s}$, in % per annum		
1841–1911 (a)	0.32	0.35
1861–1911 (b)	0.69	0.52
Ex post skills per worker supply elasticity, lagged:		
ϵ(a)	0.15	0.12
ϵ(b)	0.42	0.23

Sources and Notes: The '*ex post*' supply elasticity is calculated simply as

$$\epsilon = \overset{*}{s}/(\overset{*}{q} - \overset{*}{w})$$

where lags are introduced by combining the periods (*a*), where 1841–1911 supplies are viewed as responses to 1821–41 shocks, and (*b*), where 1861–1911 supplies are viewed as responses to 1821–61 shocks. The entries for America under $\overset{*}{s}$ actually refer to 1839–1909 and 1869–1909. The growth in the relative price of skilled labor is calculated on the pay ratio minus 1, that is, on the premium over and above common labor. The data for Britain are taken from Appendix C, and for America from Williamson and Lindert (1980, Appendix D, p. 307).

up to the 1860s tended to be low by standards of the twentieth century, it does not necessarily follow that Britain failed to invest in human capital at a rate that high and rising skill premia appeared to warrant. It may, after all, reflect a lower benefit stream on that investment rather than inadequate human capital supply (i.e., formal education facilities, clean cities), or that class immobility pushed private returns to schooling and on-the-job training below social returns. Surely one proper yardstick for evaluating British accumulation performance is her response to incentive compared to her competitors.

Was Britain so burdened with the institutional trappings of 'social class' that skill accumulation was significantly suppressed? Did this result in a far lower skill supply response than in Germany or America? The American evidence is readily available and it is exploited in Table 7.3. The calculation is primitive[2] but the results are suggestive to say the least. There I have calculated what might be called an *ex post* supply elasticity that compares the skills per worker growth rate response late in the century with the relative price of skilled labor 'shock' early in the century. If anything, the

American elasticities are *lower*, a surprising result given the folklore on social mobility and the American Dream![3]

(7) Inequality and inelastic skill supplies: testing the hypothesis

The moral of the story appears to be that derived labor demand shocks can have very long-lasting effects on both the structure of pay as well as the distribution of income. That is, skilled labor responses were sufficiently slow to allow the derived-demand influences of the industrial revolution to persist for some time. This by no means a quaint, class immobility attribute that characterized Britain alone. It appears that American skilled labor supplies were equally inelastic, and that Britain's human capital accumulation 'failure' was hardly a fault that she alone carried through the nineteenth century.

This chapter has served to motivate a hypothesis that a good share of the nineteenth-century Kuznets curve is attributable on the upswing to the derived factor demand shocks associated with industrialization, and on the downswing to the lagged skilled-labor accumulation response late in the century. The acid test will appear in Part III of this book where a general equilibrium model attempts to sort out the 'sources of nineteenth-century inequality'.

Notes

1 The proportion of GNP committed to formal education (public and private) in America and Britain would appear to be consistent with these skill per worker trends. Albert Fishlow (1966, Tables 3 and 4) and E. G. West (1975a, Table 4) estimate the following:

Country	Date	Share of direct educational expenditure in GNP (%)
England and Wales	1833	1.00
	1858	1.10
	1882	1.06
United Kingdom	1880	0.90
	1900	1.30
United States	1840	0.60
	1860	0.80
	1880	1.10
	1900	1.70

US educational expenditures were relatively low early in the century. Both US and UK expenditure shares rose sharply across the nineteenth century, mirroring the trends in skills-deepening. Richard Easterlin (1981) shows similar trends in enrollment rates.

The figures for other countries show the following range for the late nineteenth century:

France	1860–1900	0.4–1.9%
Germany	1860–1900	1.0–1.9%
Italy	1883–98	0.98–1.39%

2   I have characterized supply and demand in the skills market as

$$S_s = Z_S \, (q/w)^\epsilon \text{ or } \overset{*}{S_s} = \overset{*}{Z_S} + \epsilon(\overset{*}{q} - \overset{*}{w})$$
$$D_s = Z_D \, (q/w)^\eta \text{ or } \overset{*}{D_s} = \overset{*}{Z_D} + \eta(\overset{*}{q} - \overset{*}{w})$$
$$S_s = D_s \qquad \text{ or } \overset{*}{S_s} = \overset{*}{D_s}$$

where q/w is the relative price of skilled labor, asterisks refer to rates of change per annum, and ϵ and η are elasticities.

Assumptions about the derived demand for skills do not matter for the calculations in the text on ϵ. The only assumption that does matter is that $\overset{*}{Z_S} = 0$. If in fact $\overset{*}{Z_S} > 0$, and the supply schedule shifted to the right, then ϵ is overestimated. If instead $\overset{*}{Z_S} < 0$, then ϵ is underestimated. I see no compelling reason to favor either of these views, and thus feel at ease with the $\overset{*}{Z_S} = 0$ assumption. In any case, the critical issue in Table 7.3 is $\overset{*}{Z_S}$ in Britain relative to America, since it is the *relative* bias that matters in the elasticity comparison. The point may be seen more clearly in the following diagram:

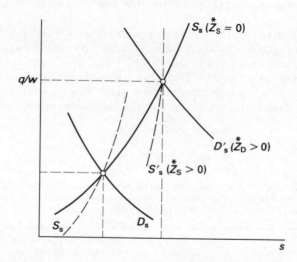

The reference to the 'primitive' character of the estimate of ϵ refers to the complete absence of econometrics in deriving it.

3   This conclusion is, of course, overdrawn since I have not factored out the net reduction in average US skills per worker levels caused by immigration of the lower skilled. It should be pointed out that some economic historians believe that Britain had an *abundance* of skills compared with Germany and America just prior to World War I (Harley, 1974).

Part III

8

Modeling Inequality in a Resource-scarce Open Economy

(1) Inequality history: modeling the Kuznets curve

Having documented a British Kuznets curve in Part I, how do I account for it?

Certainly the earnings inequality trends cannot be explained by the simple 'statistical models' originally offered by Simon Kuznets (1955) and extended by others (Robinson, 1976). These statistical models have two main components. In the first place, Kuznets suggested that the rise in inequality during early modern growth could be explained by employment shifts to those sectors and occupations that traditionally exhibit greater inequality. Thus, the rise of urban industry and modern service employment at rural agriculture's expense was thought to account for rising aggregate earnings inequality since earnings inequality was far greater within the former than the latter. Chapter 3 has shown that such influences had a modest impact on the measured earnings inequality surge to the 1850s, and they fail to account for any of the leveling thereafter. It was inequality trends *within* cities and towns that mattered most, not the shift to the more inegalitarian cities.

In addition, Kuznets suggested a second statistical mechanism that might have accounted for the trends in earnings inequality. Consider an agrarian economy embarking on early industrialization and assume for argument's sake that earnings are equally distributed within both sectors. It is known that such economies exhibit far higher average earnings in non-farm than in farm employment. Accumulation in the industrial sector creates a rapid expansion in urban job vacancies, and rural–urban migration takes place to fill them. Obviously, the initial migration implies earnings inequality where there was none before since the migrants are now at the top of the earnings distribution, leaving the non-migrants at the bottom. When the demise of agriculture is virtually complete a century later, the vast majority of wage earners are now in urban employment and the earnings distribution has returned to its initial egalitarian level, but at the higher average earnings. While Kuznets' second statistical mechanism seems plausible, Chapter 3 has shown that it accounts for little of the earnings inequality trends observed in nineteenth-century Britain. Instead, it was changes in pay differentials by sector, occupation and skill that contributed most to those inequality trends.

In short, these simple statistical models simply won't suffice as explanations for the British Kuznets curve. Since the driving force behind the aggregate trends was inter-occupational inequality, one needs explicit explanations of the structure of pay across industries, occupations and skills. Thus, any explanation for nineteenth-century inequality trends must deal explicitly with the determinants of the structure of pay and skill scarcity, as well as with the more conventional factor shares that were the focus of Mill, Malthus, Ricardo and Marx.

What explanations do I have in mind? Part II of this book offered some hypotheses, and the time has come to embed those hypotheses into an explicit general equilibrium model of industrialization and inequality.

(2) Establishing some guidelines

In the absence of explicit models, one has only historical description. Surely the cliometrician and the 'conventional' historian would both agree that simplification, abstraction and generalization are essential ingredients to good history. But which ingredients are essential to the explanation and which can be dispensed with?

To begin with, if ever there was an economy that obeyed the theorist's competitive assumptions, nineteenth-century Britain was surely as close as one will ever get. In addition, since I shall be analyzing very long periods – leaping over five decades on the upswing of the Kuznets curve from 1821 to 1861 and over four decades on the downside from 1861 to 1911 – the assumption of flexible wages and prices seems defensible. I shall therefore develop a model in which all prices, wages and rents have sufficient time to clear factor and product markets. Excess factor supply and unemployment will not be an attribute of the model.

While it also seems reasonable to assume a high degree of factor mobility across sectors and regions over periods defined by decades, what should one assume about 'class mobility'? Here I am persuaded by the sociologists, the Marxists and the unorthodox economists.

As Chapter 7 pointed out, sociologists – and British labor historians of like mind – have long maintained that nineteenth-century British labor markets were 'stratified' and 'segmented'. It is a simple matter to translate the sociologists' jargon into the economists' jargon: mobility across occupations of different skill was extremely limited in nineteenth-century Britain, which implies that labor supplies by skill were highly wage-inelastic. A number of economists support this view. Indeed, John Stuart Mill (1852) dealt explicitly with class immobility, and Cairnes (1874) coined a word for it – non-competing groups. Thus, Cairnes viewed occupational labor supplies as class-specific and mobility between them unresponsive to wage differentials and excess demands.

It seems to me that whatever model is selected to account for nineteenth-century British experience with inequality, it must take account of class immobility and non-competing groups. In essence, therefore, the model must be consistent with highly limited labor mobility between skill and occupational class. In more technical terms, the macro-model that follows will draw on Cairnes' notion of non-competing groups by assuming that labor supplies by skill were highly wage-inelastic in nineteenth-century Britain.

(3) A macro-model of British industrialization and inequality

Research on American inequality (Williamson, 1976a, 1979c; Williamson and Lindert, 1980; following Jones, 1965) suggests the usefulness of applying general equilibrium models to growth and distribution history. Can one use the *same* models that have worked so well in American history? I think not, since the American models embody some key assumptions that cannot be maintained for Britain. While nineteenth-century America can be viewed as a relatively closed, resource-abundant economy, Britain must be viewed as open and resource scarce. The model that follows has been motivated by an interest in capturing key differences between these two industrializing, capitalistic systems.[1]

First, the British model that follows will stress the distinction between internationally tradeable commodities and non-tradeable ('home') services. Its structure will make it possible to explore the impact of important external economic events like the repeal of the Corn Laws, the role of foreign demand for key British export staples, the loss of export markets to foreign competition, the impact of sharply declining international transport costs, and, of course, the interruption of trade induced by international conflict. Second, one can hardly ignore manufacturing's raw material requirements in any model of British industrialization. With the exception of fuel (e.g. coal), British raw material requirements were satisfied by net importation and the model must allow for the influence of the relative scarcity or abundance of these imported intermediate inputs. Third, the primary sector must be disaggregated. While British farming was clearly competitive with foreign imports, the same was not true – at least not to the same degree – of raw materials. The raw materials producing sector was a heterogeneous aggregate, and most of British raw material imports were non-competitive (e.g. cotton, timber) since they were not produced at home. Coal mining was an obvious exception to that rule, but, for simplicity, I shall treat all outputs of the home sector (primarily mining and quarrying) as non-tradeable.

The model is characterized by five 'domestic' factors of production, four of which are primary inputs and one of which is an intermediate input ($i = J, K, L, S, B$):

- *farm land* (J), excluding improvements other than initial clearing for cultivation or pasture;
- *capital* (K), consisting of all non-human asset services in the business and government sector, other than farm lands, and excluding dwellings;
- *unskilled labor* (L), or total manhours, compensated at the unskilled wage rate, including 'own labor time' utilized in owner-occupied farms and in non-farm proprietorships;

- *skills* (*S*), or all attributes of labor inputs generating earnings in excess of the unskilled wage; and
- *intermediate resource inputs* (*B*), used directly in the manufacturing sector or indirectly in the urban sectors 'facilitating' manufacturing production.

In addition, there is one imported intermediate input:

- *imported raw material inputs* (*F*), processed by manufacturing and unavailable at home.

It should be emphasized that the first four primary factor stocks listed above are 'givens' in the model: that is, I invoke the traditional assumption of comparative static analysis – factor endowments are determined exogenously. The flow of both intermediate inputs (*F* and *B*), however, will be determined endogenously in response to domestic demand and supply as well as to foreign trade.

These factor inputs are used in the production of four sectoral outputs (*j = A, M, C, B*):

- *agriculture* (*A*), or all national income originating in agriculture, forestry and fisheries;
- *manufacturing* (*M*), or all national income originating in manufacturing, building and construction;
- *the tertiary sector* (*C*), or all national income originating in finance, trade, gas, electricity and water, private services, local and national government, transport and communications; and
- *intermediate resources* (*B*), or all national income originating in mining and quarrying.

The empirical counterparts to the model's sectors have been listed above with a pragmatic eye on existing national accounts (see Appendices C–E).

I assume that the economy is open to trade in all final consumption and investment goods, save the tertiary sector, which produces non-tradeable 'home' services. The home-produced intermediate good *B* cannot be traded internationally (e.g. coal[2]), while the foreign-produced intermediate good *F* cannot be produced at home (e.g. cotton). Furthermore, the model conforms to the reality that Britain was a net importer of the agricultural good, while a net exporter of the manufactured good. I shall also invoke the 'small country' assumption and allow prices of all tradeables to be determined exogenously by the combined influences of British commercial policy, world market conditions and international transport costs. That is, I assume that demands for exportables and supplies of importables were both highly price-elastic in nineteenth-century Britain.[3]

Production relationships can be summarized as:

$$A = A(L, K, \mathcal{J}),$$
$$M = M(L, K, S, B, F),$$
$$C = C(L, K, S, B),$$
$$B = B(L, K).$$

Capital and unskilled labor are assumed to move freely among all sectors, skilled labor is mobile between the industrial and tertiary sectors to which its use is restricted, land is specific to agricultural production, the imported intermediate resource is an input to manufacturing only, while the home-produced intermediate resource (coal) is used in manufacturing and the service sector (primarily in transportation and public utilities). Skill inputs are ignored in the resource sector (i.e. coal mining) partly for empirical reasons – I have been unable to document the skill labor content of mining activity in nineteenth-century Britain – and partly in the belief that coal mining and other extractive activities were extremely unskilled labor intensive.

The assumption of complete mobility of unskilled labor across regions and sectors may appear to violate a tradition among wage historians that nineteenth-century British labor markets were segmented, that regional wage differentials were commonplace and that 'wage gaps' between farm and city employment persisted well into the twentieth century. The assumption of complete mobility need not be inconsistent with that tradition, however, since my specification would also be consistent with roughly constant percentage wage differentials over time. This assumption of relatively stable wage differentials between unskilled farm and urban common labor is, in fact, confirmed with the British wage evidence (Hunt, 1973; Chapter 3, above, Table 3.8).

The assumption of complete capital mobility across sectors implies, of course, that average net rates of return were everywhere the same (or at least that they moved alike over time). While this surely was not likely to have been the case in the short run or even the medium term, the reader should be reminded that my model will be applied to very long epochs – the Kuznets curve itself stretching over a century – when the assumption has far more to recommend it.

Given six inputs and four produced outputs, there are nine prices (and/or rents) in the model, since one of the produced outputs is also an input. By invoking the small country assumption, P_A, P_M and P_F are taken as exogenous. The remaining six prices will be determined endogenously:

d = rent earned on an acre of cleared farm land under crop or pasturage;
r = rent (or rate of return) earned on reproducible non-human capital (and the return on equity $i = r/P_K$, where P_K = price of capital);
w = the wage rate (or annual earnings) for unskilled labor;
q = the wage premium for skilled labor;
P_C = the price of tertiary services; and
P_B = the price of home-produced resources.

The first four of these prices are the factor rents that are central to the inequality trends documented in Part I. For example, in my model the total wages share is simply the ratio of $(wL + qS)$ to national income. Pay ratios are measured by q/w, and the distribution of earnings is approximated by unskilled labor's share, $wL/(wL + qS)$. Furthermore, the distribution of income among property income recipients can also be explored, at least in part, by the behavior of rents $(d\mathcal{J})$ and profits (rK), offsetting and competing factor shares whose owners were in abrasive public debate throughout the century.

This class-ridden general equilibrium model is quite capable, therefore, of telling explicit stories about the determinants of inequality trends in nineteenth-century Britain, although the *quality* of those stories has yet to be assessed. Is the model pure fiction? The evaluation hinges on the model's effectiveness in capturing British experience with growth, industrialization and distribution (Chapter 9). Finally, while all six endogenous prices are nominal values, it is a trivial matter to convert any of them into real or relative prices. For example, the standard-of-living debate can be confronted simply by deflating the nominal wage of common labor by some cost-of-living index, the latter constructed by taking a weighted average of the model's P_j where the weights are supplied by the budget shares implied by the demand system elaborated below.

In addition to these six endogenous prices, the model will also predict the historical behavior of the following seven quantities:

A = the quantity of the agricultural good that is home-produced;
M = the quantity of the manufactured good that is home-produced;
C = the quantity of tertiary services that are home-produced and consumed;
B = the quantity of the home-produced resource that is extracted;
A_M = the quantity of the agricultural good that is imported;
M_X = the quantity of the manufactured good that is exported;
F = the quantity of the foreign-produced intermediate good that is imported.

With these seven quantities determined, two remaining quantities can be derived residually:

A_D = home demand for the agricultural good; and
M_D = home demand for the manufactured good.

Note that industrial output mix is determined endogenously in the model. For example, the relative demise of agriculture is measured by the endogenous behavior of $P_A A$ as a share in national income, while industrialization is measured by the behavior of $P_M M$ as a share in national income. We have, then, a model of industrialization where world market conditions and domestic supply can both play a critical role as 'engines of growth'.

Under competitive assumptions, the equality of price and average costs yields four cost equations:

$$P_A = a_{\mathcal{J}A}d + a_{KA}r + a_{LA}w \tag{8.1}$$

$$P_M = \quad a_{KM}r + a_{LM}w + a_{SM}q + a_{BM}P_B + a_{FM}P_F \tag{8.2}$$

$$P_C = \quad a_{KC}r + a_{LC}w + a_{SC}q + a_{BC}P_B \tag{8.3}$$

$$P_B = \quad a_{KB}r + a_{LB}w \tag{8.4}$$

where the a_{ij}'s are physical input–output ratios. Each of these a_{ij}'s is an endogenous variable, and their determinants will be discussed at greater length below. These cost equations take on an extremely convenient form when they are converted into rate-of-change equations involving sectoral factor cost shares, θ_{ij}, for the ith factor in the jth sector. These factor shares add up to unity in each sector, since costs are assumed to exhaust the value of product. To explore linear approximations involving rates of change, I use the asterisk notation for rates of change per annum: $\overset{*}{X} = (dX/dt)/X$. Differentiating the cost equations and converting them into rates of change yields:

$$\overset{*}{P}_A = \overset{*}{d}\theta_{jA} + \overset{*}{r}\theta_{KA} + \overset{*}{w}\theta_{LA} \hspace{5cm} + \Sigma_i\overset{*}{a}_{iA}\theta_{iA} \quad (8.5)$$

$$\overset{*}{P}_M = \hspace{1.5cm} \overset{*}{r}\theta_{KM} + \overset{*}{w}\theta_{LM} + \overset{*}{q}\theta_{SM} + \overset{*}{P}_B\theta_{BM} + \overset{*}{P}_F\theta_{FM} + \Sigma_i\overset{*}{a}_{iM}\theta_{iM} \quad (8.6)$$

$$\overset{*}{P}_C = \hspace{1.5cm} \overset{*}{r}\theta_{KC} + \overset{*}{w}\theta_{LC} + \overset{*}{q}\theta_{SC} + \overset{*}{P}_B\theta_{BC} \hspace{2cm} + \Sigma_i\overset{*}{a}_{iC}\theta_{iC} \quad (8.7)$$

$$\overset{*}{P}_B = \hspace{1.5cm} \overset{*}{r}\theta_{KB} + \overset{*}{w}\theta_{LB} \hspace{5cm} + \Sigma_i\overset{*}{a}_{iB}\theta_{iB} \quad (8.8)$$

The $\Sigma_i\overset{*}{a}_{ij}\theta_{ij}$ terms are weighted sums of increases in physical input–output ratios. These may look more familiar if they are rewritten as *minus* the weighted sum of increases in output–input ratios, where the input cost shares serve as weights. In other words, each of these expressions is simply the negative value of the rate of exogenous total factor productivity growth ($\overset{*}{T}_j$) measured in nominal prices. Regrouping so as to put all terms involving endogenous variables on the right-hand side and exogenous on the left, the cost equations simply become 'price dual' expressions for sectoral total factor productivity growth:

$$\overset{*}{P}_A + \overset{*}{T}_A = \overset{*}{d}\theta_{jA} + \overset{*}{r}\theta_{KA} + \overset{*}{w}\theta_{LA} \hspace{5cm} (8.9)$$

$$\overset{*}{P}_M - \overset{*}{P}_F\theta_{FM} + \overset{*}{T}_M = \overset{*}{r}\theta_{KM} + \overset{*}{w}\theta_{LM} + \overset{*}{q}\theta_{SM} + \overset{*}{P}_B\theta_{BM} \hspace{2cm} (8.10)$$

$$\overset{*}{T}_C = \overset{*}{r}\theta_{KC} + \overset{*}{w}\theta_{LC} + \overset{*}{q}\theta_{SC} + \overset{*}{P}_B\theta_{BC} - \overset{*}{P}_C \hspace{1cm} (8.11)$$

$$\overset{*}{T}_B = \overset{*}{r}\theta_{KB} + \overset{*}{w}\theta_{LB} \hspace{2cm} - \overset{*}{P}_B \hspace{2cm} (8.12)$$

The next six equations describe full-employment equilibrium conditions in each factor market, where factor prices are assumed to clear each market so that excess supplies are zero. Total aggregate demand for each factor is the sum over all sector uses, and these are equated to exogenous factor supplies (with the exception of B and F, which are endogenously determined):

$$J = a_{JA}A \hspace{5cm} (8.13)$$

$$K = a_{KA}A + a_{KM}M + a_{KC}C + a_{KB}B \hspace{2cm} (8.14)$$

$$L = a_{LA}A + a_{LM}M + a_{LC}C + a_{LB}B \hspace{2cm} (8.15)$$

$$S = \hspace{1.5cm} a_{SM}M + a_{SC}C \hspace{2.5cm} (8.16)$$

$$B = \hspace{1.5cm} a_{BM}M + a_{BC}C \hspace{2.5cm} (8.17)$$

$$F = \hspace{1.5cm} a_{FM}M \hspace{4cm} (8.18)$$

As I have already pointed out, the stock of land, capital, unskilled labor and skills are exogenously given, while the home production and the quantity imported of the resource goods are both determined endogenously. Equations (8.13)–(8.18) can be converted into rate-of-change form by introducing λ_{ij}'s (the share of the ith factor used in the jth sector). Again putting endogenous variables on the right-hand side and exogenous on the left, differentiation yields:

$$\overset{*}{y} = \overset{*}{A} + \overset{*}{a}_{yA} \tag{8.19}$$

$$\overset{*}{K} = \lambda_{KA}(\overset{*}{A} + \overset{*}{a}_{KA}) + \lambda_{KM}(\overset{*}{M} + \overset{*}{a}_{KM}) + \lambda_{KC}(\overset{*}{C} + \overset{*}{a}_{KC}) + \lambda_{KB}(\overset{*}{B} + \overset{*}{a}_{KB}) \tag{8.20}$$

$$\overset{*}{L} = \lambda_{LA}(\overset{*}{A} + \overset{*}{a}_{LA}) + \lambda_{LM}(\overset{*}{M} + \overset{*}{a}_{LM}) + \lambda_{LC}(\overset{*}{C} + \overset{*}{a}_{LC}) + \lambda_{LB}(\overset{*}{B} + \overset{*}{a}_{LB}) \tag{8.21}$$

$$\overset{*}{S} = \qquad\qquad \lambda_{SM}(\overset{*}{M} + \overset{*}{a}_{SM}) + \lambda_{SC}(\overset{*}{C} + \overset{*}{a}_{SC}) \tag{8.22}$$

$$0 = \qquad\qquad \lambda_{BM}(\overset{*}{M} + \overset{*}{a}_{BM}) + \lambda_{BC}(\overset{*}{C} + \overset{*}{a}_{BC}) - \overset{*}{B} \tag{8.23}$$

$$0 = \qquad\qquad (\overset{*}{M} + \overset{*}{a}_{FM}) \qquad\qquad - \overset{*}{F} \tag{8.24}$$

Each of the rate of change in input–output ratios $(\overset{*}{a}_{ij})$ consists of two parts: one is exogenous $(\overset{*}{b}_{ij})$ while the other is an endogenous response to factor prices $(\overset{*}{c}_{ij})$: i.e. $\overset{*}{a}_{ij} = \overset{*}{b}_{ij} + \overset{*}{c}_{ij}$. In what follows, I shall pull the $\overset{*}{b}_{ij}$ terms together into summary measures of the factor saving resulting from exogenous productivity change. These factor-saving measures, $\pi_i = -\sum \lambda_{ij} \overset{*}{b}_{ij}$, quantify the economy-wide savings on the use of each ith factor. The exceptions involve B and F, as I assume that the intermediate resource is used in fixed proportions in manufacturing and services. This implies that $\overset{*}{a}_{FM} = \pi_F$ and that $\pi_B = \lambda_{BM} a_{BM} + \lambda_{BC} a_{BC}$, and that all other $\overset{*}{a}_{ij}$ will not be affected by substitution between that factor and B or F.

The induced part of each change in an input–output ratio is determined by firm optimizing behavior (with the exception of $\overset{*}{c}_{BM} = \overset{*}{c}_{BC} = \overset{*}{c}_{FM} = 0$, which obey Leontief fixed-coefficient assumptions). Thus, $\overset{*}{c}_{ij}$ is defined in terms of elasticities of factor substitution and factor price movements $(\overset{*}{V}_i)$:

$$\overset{*}{c}_{ij} = \sum_k \theta_{kj} \sigma^j_{ik} (\overset{*}{V}_k - \overset{*}{V}_i).$$

The key parameter in these expressions for $\overset{*}{c}_{ij}$ is the elasticity of factor substitution, σ^j_{ik}. A large empirical literature tends to place capital–labor elasticities close to unity for long-run analysis, a finding supported by von Tunzelmann's (1982, p. 214) analysis of British industry between 1760 and 1850. There is also some evidence that capital and skills tend to be less substitutable, and closer to being complements, than either of them is with unskilled labor (Griliches, 1969; Fallon and Layard, 1975; Kesselman, Williamson and Berndt, 1977; Hamermesh and Grant, 1979); I shall assume this to be the case when the model is applied to nineteenth-century

Britain. In addition, the literature continues to debate the substitution possibilities between labor of various skills. Participants in the debate have divided into two camps: the manpower structuralists, who stress limited substitution possibilities; and the neoclassicists, who stress high substitution possibilities. On the basis of the survey of the econometric literature provided by Hamermesh and Grant (1979), it seems wisest to adopt the middle ground. Namely, I shall assume that elasticities of substitution between capital and labor are the same as those between 'raw' labor and skills.

Final product demands are endogenous. The budget constraint serves to eliminate the demand equation for tertiary services, and the remaining two final demand equations take the form:

$$A + A_M = D_A(y/P)^{\eta_A}(P_A/P)^{\epsilon_A}(P_M/P)^{\epsilon_{AM}}(P_C/P)^{\epsilon_{AC}}Pop \qquad (8.25)$$

$$M - M_X = D_M(y/P)^{\eta_M}(P_A/P)^{\epsilon_{AM}}(P_M/P)^{\epsilon_M}(P_C/P)^{\epsilon_{MC}}Pop \qquad (8.26)$$

where I have imposed in addition the market clearing condition that sectoral supplies equal final aggregate demand. D_j is an exogenous shift term, y is nominal gross national product per capita, P is a general price (or cost-of-living) index, Pop is total population, η_j is the income elasticity of demand for j, and ϵ_j and ϵ_{jk} are own-price and cross-price elasticities of demand for j. Nominal income is defined as:

$$Y = P_A A + P_M M + P_C C + D,$$

where resource output, $P_B B$, is excluded since it is an intermediate good, and D is the net trade deficit in nominal terms. Differentiating the nominal income expression yields:

$$\overset{*}{Y} = \phi_A(\overset{*}{P_A} + \overset{*}{A}) + \phi_M(\overset{*}{P_M} + \overset{*}{M}) + \phi_C(\overset{*}{P_C} + \overset{*}{C}) + \phi_D \overset{*}{D}, \qquad (8.27)$$

where the ϕ_j's are the shares of total nominal income attributable to each component of income. Using (8.27), we can differentiate the demand equations, putting exogenous variables on the left-hand side:

$$\overset{*}{D_A} + \overset{*}{P_A}(\epsilon_A + \eta_A\phi_A) + \overset{*}{P_M}(\epsilon_{AM} + \eta_A\phi_M) + (1 - \eta_A)\overset{*}{Pop} + \eta_A\phi_D\overset{*}{D}$$
$$= (\alpha_A - \eta_A\phi_A)\overset{*}{A} + \alpha_{A_M}\overset{*}{A_M} - \eta_A\phi_M\overset{*}{M} - \eta_A\phi_C\overset{*}{C} - \overset{*}{P_C}(\epsilon_{AC} + \phi_C\eta_A) \qquad (8.28)$$

$$\overset{*}{D_M} + \overset{*}{P_A}(\epsilon_{AM} + \eta_M\phi_A) + \overset{*}{P_M}(\epsilon_M + \eta_M\phi_M) + (1 - \eta_M)\overset{*}{Pop} + \eta_M\phi_D\overset{*}{D}$$
$$= (\alpha_M - \eta_M\phi_M)\overset{*}{M} - \alpha_{M_X}\overset{*}{M_X}\eta_M(\phi_A\overset{*}{A} + \phi_C\overset{*}{C}) - \overset{*}{P_C}(\epsilon_{MC} + \phi_C\eta_M) \qquad (8.29)$$

where α_A and α_{A_M} represent the shares in the final demand for agricultural goods home produced and imported respectively, α_M represents the ratio of home-produced manufactured goods to home final demand for manufactured goods, and α_{M_X} represents the ratio of exports of the manufactured good to home final demand for the manufactured good.

A final equation insures that the trade account is in balance:

$$P_A A_M + P_F F = P_M M_X + D. \tag{8.30}$$

Putting this equation in rate-of-change form yields:

$$\overset{*}{P_A} z_A + \overset{*}{P_F} z_F - \overset{*}{P_M} z_M - \overset{*}{D} z_D = \overset{*}{M_X} z_M - \overset{*}{A_M} z_A - \overset{*}{F} z_F, \tag{8.31}$$

where z_A and z_F represent the share of the agricultural and the resource good in the nominal value of total imports, and z_M and z_D represent the share of the manufactured good exports and the nominal trade deficit in the nominal value of total imports.

The complete system is summarized in Table 8.1, where there are thirteen rate-of-change equations and thirteen unknowns. The thirteen endogenous variables include four factor price changes – $\overset{*}{d}$, $\overset{*}{w}$, $\overset{*}{q}$ and $\overset{*}{r}$ (or $\overset{*}{i} = \overset{*}{r} - \overset{*}{P_K}$); two product price changes – $\overset{*}{P_C}$ and $\overset{*}{P_B}$; and seven output or trade volume changes – $\overset{*}{A}$, $\overset{*}{M}$, $\overset{*}{C}$, $\overset{*}{B}$, $\overset{*}{A_M}$, $\overset{*}{M_X}$ and $\overset{*}{F}$. The exogenous variables are the sectoral rates of total factor productivity growth ($\overset{*}{T_j}$), the rates of factor saving produced by technological change (π_i), three prices in rates of change ($\overset{*}{P_A}$, $\overset{*}{P_M}$, $\overset{*}{P_F}$), the factor supply growth rates ($\overset{*}{J}$, $\overset{*}{K}$, $\overset{*}{L}$, $\overset{*}{S}$), the population growth rate ($\overset{*}{Pop}$), and the demand and trade balance shift terms ($\overset{*}{D_j}$, $\overset{*}{D}$).

(4) The sources of inequality and industrialization

How can the model be used? First we must be assured that the model can replicate, at least roughly, nineteenth-century British economic history, especially the inequality history documented in Part I. In terms of Table 8.1, that historical exercise involves four steps: first, measuring all exogenous shift terms over the two long epochs 1821–61 and 1861–1911 (Appendix E); second, estimating (or guessing at) each parameter (Appendix D); third, documenting all initial conditions for benchmark years, 1821, 1861, 1891 and 1911 (Appendix D); and then, fourth, using these to generate predictions on various industrialization and inequality indicators. These predictions can then be compared with historical fact. If the model is successful in accounting for nineteenth-century British trends – including the Kuznets curve – then I shall be in a position to decompose the sources of the Kuznets curve into the various component parts that have been debated for the past century and a half since Marx and Engels fired their first salvo against capitalism.

While the final inequality accounting in Chapters 10 and 11 will be far more complex, it might be useful to motivate that analysis by focusing here on factors influencing the relative scarcity of unskilled labor. That is, the inequality evidence reviewed in Part I leads one to suspect that the key to

British inequality experience will be found once one understands the forces driving the income share of the bottom 40 per cent of households, and the income share of the bottom 40 per cent is clearly determined by the relative behavior of the real earnings of the common unskilled laborer. What follows, then, is a menu of potential forces that might account for the relative scarcity or surplus of unskilled labor, and thus ultimately the distribution of earnings and income. Each of these forces – or hypotheses – was discussed in Chapters 5, 6 and 7 so they will be reviewed here only briefly. At this point, my purpose is simply to show how the model has captured those forces, making tests of these hypotheses now possible.

First, there is a role for derived factor demand in the model, although it is not a Keynesian sort, of course, since this is a full-employment model. The most popular demand-side forces in the literature are Engel effects and external trade influences. It is alleged that both of these forces served to lower the derived demand for common labor. The most celebrated influence, of course, was the relative demise of unskilled-labor-intensive agriculture and the expansion of what were to become the key manufacturing export staples – activities that tended to be more skill intensive. Engel effects would have insured such results in a closed economy, but they were hastened in Britain by the move to free trade as well as by the trade-creating decline in international transport costs. In addition, the development of urban service infrastructure served to generate unbalanced output growth favoring the more skill-intensive sectors. These forces should have served to create an excess demand for skills (Chapter 6), a disequilibrating influence that should have persisted given the absence of an elastic skill-supply response (Chapter 7). Unbalanced rates of technological progress must have served to reinforce these influences. Technological progress appears to have been most dramatic in the modern industrial sectors (Chapter 6). While such forces surely account for the nineteenth-century drift in dynamic comparative advantage in Britain, they would also account for the relative increase in the demand for skills, since those commodity-producing sectors thus favored also appear to have been more skill intensive, certainly compared with agriculture, and certainly when the derived input–output demands for the urban service infrastructure are included. Given late-Victorian England's alleged 'entrepreneurial failure', productivity slowdown and loss of world market shares, it seems likely that these unbalanced rates of total factor productivity growth were more pronounced in the early nineteenth century than late, corresponding to the earnings inequality trends observed.

The model quantifies derived factor demand influences through the total factor productivity growth rates $(\overset{*}{T}_j)$, world market conditions $(\overset{*}{P}_j)$, and exogenous final demand shifts $(\overset{*}{D}_j)$, as well as through the endogenous Engel effects embodied in the model's demand parameters. While there is no way of isolating exogenous domestic demand shifts $(\overset{*}{D}_j)$, one *can* estimate $\overset{*}{T}_j$ and $\overset{*}{P}_j$, thus making it possible to assess the relative importance of supply-side unbalanced productivity advance against the demand-side influences of world market conditions.

Table 8.1 *The British nineteenth-century general equilibrium model in rate-of-change form*

Eqn	d^*	r^*	w^*	q^*	P_B^*	P_C^*	A^*	A_M^*	M^*	M_X^*	C^*	B^*	F^*	Endogenous variables	Exogenous variables
Eqn (8.9)	θ_{JA}	θ_{KA}	θ_{LA}											d^*	$P_A^* + T_A^*$
Eqn (8.10)	θ_{JM}	θ_{KM}	θ_{LM}	θ_{SM}	θ_{BM}									r^*	$P_M^* + T_M^* - P_F^*\theta_{FM}$
Eqn (8.11)		θ_{KC}	θ_{LC}	θ_{SC}	θ_{BC}	-1								w^*	T_C^*
Eqn (8.12)		θ_{KB}	θ_{LB}		-1									q^*	T_B^*
Eqn (8.19)	g_{51}	g_{52}	g_{53}											P_B^*	$\hat{J} + \pi_J$
Eqn (8.20)	g_{61}	g_{62}	g_{63}	g_{64}			λ_{KA}		λ_{KM}		λ_{KC}	λ_{KB}		P_C^*	$K^* + \pi_K$
Eqn (8.21)	g_{71}	g_{72}	g_{73}	g_{74}			λ_{LA}		λ_{LM}		λ_{LC}	λ_{LB}		A^*	$L^* + \pi_L$
Eqn (8.22)	g_{81}	g_{82}	g_{83}	g_{84}					λ_{SM}		λ_{SC}			A_M^*	$S^* + \pi_S$
Eqn (8.23)									λ_{BM}		λ_{BC}			M^*	π_B
Eqn (8.24)									1			-1	-1	M_X^*	π_F
Eqn (8.28)						$(-\epsilon_{AC} - \eta_A\phi_C)$	$(\alpha_A - \eta_A\phi_A)$	$\alpha_{A_M} - \eta_A\phi_M$			$-\eta_A\phi_C$			C^*	$D_A^* + P_A^*(\epsilon_A + \eta_A\phi_A) + P_M^*(\epsilon_{AM} + \eta_A\phi_M) + (1-\eta_A)P_O\rho^* + \eta_A\phi_D D^*$

Eqn (8.29)

$$(-\epsilon_{MC} - \eta_M\phi_C) \quad (\alpha_M - \eta_M\phi_M) \quad -\alpha_{MN} \quad -\eta_M\phi_C \quad B^* = \begin{aligned} &D_M + P_A^*(\epsilon_{AM} \\ &+ \eta_M\phi_A) + \\ &P_M(\epsilon_M + \\ &\eta_M\phi_M) + (1 - \\ &\eta_M)Pop + \\ &\eta_M\phi_D D^* \end{aligned}$$

Eqn (8.31)

$$-z_A \qquad z_M \qquad -z_F \qquad F^* = \begin{aligned} &P_A^* z_A + P_F^* z_F - \\ &P_M z_M - D z_D \end{aligned}$$

Definition of symbols

$$g_{51} = -\underbrace{(\theta_{KA}\sigma^A_{JK}}_{g_{52}} + \underbrace{\theta_{LA}\sigma^A_{JL})}_{g_{53}}$$

$$g_{62} = -(\underbrace{\lambda_{KA}\theta_{JA}\sigma^A_{JK}}_{g_{61}} + \underbrace{\lambda_{KA}\theta_{LA}\sigma^A_{KL} + \lambda_{KM}\theta_{LM}\sigma^M_{KL} + \lambda_{KT}\theta_{LT}\sigma^C_{KL} + \lambda_{KB}\theta_{LB}\sigma^B_{KL}}_{g_{63}} + \underbrace{\lambda_{KM}\theta_{SM}\sigma^M_{KS} + \lambda_{KT}\theta_{ST}\sigma^C_{KS}}_{g_{64}})$$

$$g_{73} = -(\underbrace{\lambda_{LA}\theta_{JA}\sigma^A_{JL}}_{g_{71}} + \underbrace{\lambda_{LA}\theta_{KA}\sigma^A_{KL} + \lambda_{LM}\theta_{KM}\sigma^M_{KL} + \lambda_{LT}\theta_{KT}\sigma^C_{KL} + \lambda_{LB}\theta_{KB}\sigma^B_{KL}}_{g_{72}} + \underbrace{\lambda_{LM}\theta_{SM}\sigma^M_{LS} + \lambda_{LT}\theta_{ST}\sigma^C_{LS}}_{g_{74}})$$

$$g_{84} = -(\underbrace{\lambda_{SM}\theta_{KM}\sigma^M_{KS} + \lambda_{SL}\theta_{KT}\sigma^C_{KS}}_{g_{82}} + \underbrace{\lambda_{SM}\theta_{LM}\sigma^M_{LS} + \lambda_{ST}\theta_{LT}\sigma^C_{LS}}_{g_{83}})$$

As an aside, I should point out that my review of derived factor demand forces suggests that the model is equipped to confront those episodes when the components of inequality exhibit offsetting trends. For example, the invasion of grains from the New World and the rapid technological advance in manufacturing relative to agriculture would both serve to raise the relative scarcity of those factors used intensively in manufacturing. At the macro level, this implies unskilled labor saving and skilled labor using, a labor glut and a skills scarcity, wage stretching, and earnings inequality. Whether the profits share would rise, thus reinforcing the earnings inequality trends already set in motion, depends on whether or not the favored 'export staple' sectors were relatively capital intensive, an unlikely event given the high capital-intensity of British agriculture. In any case, the earnings inequality trend might be fully offset by the decline in rents[4] associated with the relative demise of agriculture. It is quite possible, therefore, that for some historical episodes the model will predict rising pay ratios and increasing earnings inequality, but stability or leveling in the distribution of income. This possibility is comforting since Part I has suggested some episodes in British history when such offsetting trends were apparent.

Second, one has to consider the factor supply side. How much of the trends in occupational pay ratios, the economy-wide skill premium, earnings and income inequality can be accounted for by skills per worker accumulation? Mill, Marshall and economists since have stressed subsidized schooling as a great leveling device, and it is true that these schooling effects are primarily a late nineteenth-century phenomenon, precisely the period when earnings distributions were leveling. Certainly the skills per worker growth rates documented in Chapter 7 are consistent with that view. Furthermore, many historians have viewed 1861 as a benchmark: the earlier years being ones when Britain was a net importer of unskilled labor, primarily from Ireland; the later years being ones when Britain was a net exporter of labor to the New World. Finally, there are the long-run forces of demographic transition, which tended to produce higher population and labor force growth rates early in the century when the inequality was on the rise (Chapter 7). The model is equipped to sort out these influences by estimating the independent impact of $\overset{*}{L}$, $\overset{*}{S}$ and $\overset{*}{Pop}$.

Third, capital accumulation ($\overset{*}{K}$) must play a role in the accounting. If skills and physical capital are viewed as complements, then rapid rates of capital accumulation would imply relatively rapid rightward shifts in the derived demand for skills, while displacing unskilled labor as capital–labor ratios were raised economy-wide. The model is, of course, quite capable of tracing out the influence of $\overset{*}{K}$ on inequality. Indeed, it may offer an explanation for periods in British history when the distribution of earnings moved in a different direction from the 'profits share' or the share of the top 5 or 10 per cent. Of course, no one really believes that capital accumulation, emigration and skill augmentation are independent of the structure of pay and the distribution of income, but it may be necessary to begin by assuming as much before moving on to more elaborate dynamic models of distribution, accumulation and growth. In any case, according to recent research on America, the assumption that capital accumulation can be treated as independent of the distribution of income may have far more to recommend it than the classical models of Marx and Ricardo would suggest (see Williamson, 1979c). Furthermore, the assumption that short-run skill supplies are approximately independent of the structure of pay is consistent with Cairnes' theory of non-competing groups, a theory for which I have already expressed an attraction. Even long-run skill-supply elasticities were low in nineteenth-century Britain (Chapter 7).

Fourth, the factor-saving bias in technological progress must be considered. While economic historians have long emphasized labor saving as a source of poverty, unemployment and inequality in early Britain, Chapter 6 stressed that it is far more difficult to secure quantitative estimates of its magnitude. And when we *are* offered estimates, either at the aggregate level (Floud and McCloskey, 1981, Ch. 8) or at the industry level (Asher, 1972), these estimates fail to distinguish between *unskilled* and *total* labor saving. For the present, therefore, I am compelled to assume that these factor-saving forces are captured by the π_i alone.

Nowhere in this list have I considered the role of inflation, unionization, civil service reform, Poor Law reform, government expenditures and tax incidence, and other important aspects of institutional change. Yet, it seems reasonable to start with the simpler competitive-factor-markets approach and see what it tells us about the forces that were primary in driving distribution and industrialization across the nineteenth century. We may well find that these institutional forces have been exaggerated in the conventional literature, an appealing conclusion if we find that the model accurately replicates British inequality trends.

Finally, note that the model generates predictions about a wide range of endogenous outputs and prices, each of which can be used to derive predictions about all manner of variables central to debates in British economic history. Thus, the model will allow us to confront *simultaneously* the standard-of-living debate, the debate over the sources of industrialization, *and* the debate over British experience with inequality since the late eighteenth century.

We are now equipped to confront the Big Question: what was driving British inequality and industrialization across the nineteenth century? Inherent aspects of capitalist development, demographic forces, or chance?

Notes

1   The non-economist and/or the non-modeling economist may wish to skip this section and turn immediately to section 4 where the verbal punch lines are offered.
2   In fact, of course, coal was exported increasingly in the late nineteenth century and a large share of final demand was to become foreign. The no-trade simplification is retained for convenience but it will present us with problems in Chapter 9.
3   This 'standard view' of British trade has been challenged recently by Donald McCloskey (1980), but it appears to remain conventional wisdom. The issue of price elasticities in export demand is central to many debates regarding Victorian development. It has yet to be resolved empirically.
4   The model does not treat urban land use explicitly and thus is not equipped to confront 'Ricardo's paradox' and the rise in land scarcity generated by non-farm land requirements (see Offer, 1980; Lindert, 1974). Non-farm land is embodied in capital in the model, so urban rents are included in r, the rate of return.

9

Fact or Fiction?

(1) An overview

British inequality from the late eighteenth century to World War I seems to be correlated with a number of variables. Each of these has a place in the qualitative literature, and each could – in theory – have contributed to the inequality experience. Moving from qualitative narratives to quantitative decomposition of the sources of that inequality history requires the explicit model of Chapter 8 and some very laborious processing of nineteenth-century British national income accounts, industry data, trade figures, prices and factor costs. The effort pays off since the next two chapters will actually quantify the impact of technological change, labor force growth, skill accumulation, capital accumulation and world market conditions on inequality and industrialization across the nineteenth century.

The first step, however, is to assure ourselves that the simple model in Chapter 8 is more than pure fiction. All models are, of course, fiction, for their purpose is to simplify and to isolate the important from the unimportant. The advantage that explicit modeling offers is that the historian can then be quite precise in his causal historical narrative. The disadvantages, however, are many. Many models may be equally plausible, and each model may well suggest a different interpretation of history. This is not a problem unique to cliometrics and theory: *any* historian faces the same problem, whether he uses qualitative, implicit theorizing or quantitative, explicit modeling (Fogel, 1967; Williamson, 1974a, Ch. 4; Williamson and Lindert, 1980, Part III). At least critics of my explanation of British nineteenth-century inequality will know exactly why they disagree and will be able to make revisions they think appropriate in formulating their own explanations. An additional disadvantage, however, is that explicit modeling places heavy demands on the historical data. As Appendices D and E should reveal, even a simple general equilibrium model has a voracious quantitative appetite.

Having made apologies for theoretical simplification, does the model account for nineteenth-century British inequality history? The model not only explains pay ratios, earnings inequality and income distribution; it also makes predictions about the rate of industrialization, the rate of migration to the cities, prices of non-traded services, the volume of trade, and the rate of economic growth. For the model to be credible, therefore, it must also account for the wide variety of British industrialization and growth experience across the nineteenth century. The evaluation is often difficult since in many cases the historical facts simply are not known! We have already seen in Chapters 2, 3 and 4 that documentation of nineteenth-century inequality is less than ideal, and is especially inadequate for the Napoleonic period and the postwar stabilization to the 1820s. The same is true of industrialization and output growth. Generally, the quality of the data improves as the nineteenth century progresses, and, with the appearance of Charles Feinstein's (1972) work, the 1861–1911 era is documented fairly well. In spite of the pioneering efforts of Feinstein (1978a) and Deane and Cole (1962), however, the early nineteenth century is less adequately documented, and early industrialization prior to 1821 is very poorly documented indeed. The eighteenth- and early nineteenth-century output figures have been considerably improved of late, making adequate documentation more nearly possible even for these epochs (Crafts, 1980, 1983; Hanley, 1982; Lindert and Williamson, 1982, 1983b).

In short, for some periods and for some variables, one simply cannot distinguish a good prediction from a bad one. That is, the historical 'facts' are often sufficiently vague to make a full test of the model's veracity impossible. That confession suggests the organization that follows in this chapter and in the next two.

Section 2 evaluates the model against the late nineteenth-century evidence. The tests here are extensive since the data are relatively abundant. Fact and prediction are compared for land rents, unskilled wages, the skill premium pay ratios, the rate of return on capital, and income shares of all sorts; for the price of services, products of the mines and quarries, and the cost of living; for output in manufacturing, agriculture, services, mining and aggregate income; and for trade. The exercise is important since one's confidence in any analysis of the sources of nineteenth-century British inequality is conditional on the model's ability first to replicate what happened to inequality, industrialization and growth. The model appears to pass the test with flying colors.

Section 3 then moves on to a 'darker statistical age', 1821–61. Here the data base is weaker and thus some predictions cannot be confronted with fact since we do not know what the facts are. Where there is *qualitative* evidence – the direction of change and rough orders of magnitude – I insist that the model replicate that history. In a few cases, however, even the direction of change is uncertain. Given these qualifications, the model appears to pass the test on 1821–61 too, perhaps even better.

The historical data base for 1797–1821 is almost totally absent, at least for the kind of analysis embodied in my model of inequality and industrialization. As a result, Chapter 11 will deal separately with conjectures on this more distant past.

(2) Assessing the model on the late nineteenth century, 1861–1911

Table 9.1 summarizes the model's performance over the late nineteenth century. The 'actual' per annum growth rates of a variable in question are

Table 9.1   *The model's performance: actual and predicted, 1861–1911*

Endogenous variable	Per annum rates Actual %	Per annum rates Predicted %	Source of actual rates
*d Land rents per acre	−0.40	−0.46	Linked series: 1860–70 from R. J. Thompson (1907); 1870–1909/13 from Rhee (1949, App. Table 2, pp. 44–5).
*r Gross rental rate on capital	n.a.	−0.47	Not available.
*i Rate of return on 'equity' = *r − *P_{COL}	−0.13	−0.16	The Consol rate was stable at 3.2% between 1858/62 and 1908/12 (Mitchell and Deane, 1962, p. 455), but Edelstein (1982, Table 6.1, p. 142, 'total U.K. domestic financial assets') estimates the price-deflated, realized rate of return on home portfolio capital to have declined at 0.13% per annum, 1870–1914.
$\hat{w}$ Unskilled wage	+0.83	+0.77	From worksheets and computer output underlying Williamson (1982d). An employment-weighted average of six low-wage occupations, including farm labor. See Chapter 2.
$\hat{q}$ Wage on skills	−0.14	+0.23	Williamson (1982d). Here, *$\hat{q}$ is measured as the growth in $w_H - w_L$, where w_H is an employment-weighted average of eleven 'high-wage' occupations, from clergy to doctors to skilled craftsmen, while w_L is simply the unskilled wage as defined above in *$\hat{w}$. See Chapters 2 and 3.
*P_C Price of services	n.a.	−0.33	Not available.
*A Agricultural output	+0.01	+0.09	Feinstein (1972, T-8), output index for 'agriculture, forestry and fishing', 1859/63–1909/13.
*A_M Net import of A-goods	n.a.	+2.28	Not available.
*P_A + *A_M Net import values of A-goods	+2.09	+1.91	Imports less re-exports of agricultural commodities in current prices, from Mitchell and Deane (1962, pp. 298–308) for 1861–1911.
*M Industrial output	+2.01	+2.13	Feinstein (1972, T-51, cols (3) and (10)), output indices for 'total manufacturing' and 'building and construction', 1858–1909/13.
*C Service output	+2.05	+2.12	Weighted average of utilities, transportation, communications, distribution and other services, 1861–1911. 1907 GDP weights are applied to output indices, all in Feinstein (1972, Table 8 and p. 208).

$\overset{*}{F}$	Net imports of foreign-produced intermediate inputs	n.a.	+1.87	Not available.
$\overset{*}{P_F} + \overset{*}{F}$	Net import value of intermediate inputs	+1.37	+1.16	Net imports of raw materials in current prices from Mitchell and Deane (1962, pp. 298–309) for 1861–1911.
$\overset{*}{P_B}$	Price of home-produced intermediate input	-0.09	+0.01	Linked Sauerbeck–Statist–Board of Trade price indices for 'minerals' and 'coal and metals' 1859/63–1909/13, in Mitchell and Deane (1962, pp. 474–6).
$\overset{*}{P_{\mathrm{COL}}}$	Cost-of-living index	-0.43	-0.31	Urban working-class families' cost-of-living index, Appendix Table A.8.
$w - P_{\mathrm{COL}}$	Real unskilled wage	+1.26	+1.08	See above.
$d - P_{\mathrm{COL}}$	Real land rent per acre	+0.03	-0.16	See above.
$q - P_{\mathrm{COL}}$	Real wage on skills	+0.29	+0.54	See above.
$\overset{*}{q} - \overset{*}{w}$	Skilled wage differential	-0.97	-0.54	See above, and Chapter 3.
$\overset{*}{Y}$	Real income	+1.82	+1.91	Gross domestic product at constant factor cost, 1859/63–1909/13 from Feinstein (1972, Table 8).
$\overset{*}{y_P}$	Real income per capita	+0.92	+1.01	Y minus population growth rate of 0.9% per annum over 1861–1911 (Mitchell and Deane, 1962, pp. 8–10).
$\overset{*}{y_L}$	Real income per worker	+0.92	+1.01	Y minus labor force growth rate of 0.9% per annum over 1861–1911 (total working population less those in armed forces, Feinstein, 1972, Table 57).
	Average real wage for all workers	+1.19	+1.24	Real full-time earnings, all workers, 1861–1911, Table 2.12.
$d\theta_{L+S}$	Change in labor's share, economy-wide, % per annum	+0.11	+0.07	Income from employment as a share in total domestic income, from Feinstein (1972, Table 1).
$d\theta_J$	Change in (farm)land's share, economy-wide, % per annum	-0.10	-0.09	Farm rent share in total domestic income, from Feinstein (1972, Table 23, col. (3) divided by Table 1, col. (7)) 1859/63–1909/13. Differs only slightly from Offer's (1980, Fig. 1) 'agricultural rents' share based on England and Wales 'lands'.

Note: All predicted values reported in this table use parameters and initial conditions from 1891 (see Appendix D). Results using 1861 and 1907/11 year initial conditions and parameters have also been calculated and they produce somewhat different results for some endogenous variables, although most are only slightly affected. For clarity, this table is restricted to the 1891 'mid-period weights' only. See Appendix D.

given in the first column. For example, the growth in nominal rents per acre of farmland, $\overset{*}{d}$, was -0.40 per cent per annum during this period of 'grain invasion' from the New World. The source of the historical documentation of the actual performance is also given in the table. For example, the nominal farmland rental series is taken from R. J. Thompson (1907) for 1860–70 and from H. A. Rhee (1949) for 1870–1909/13. While the reader may wish to debate the quality of any given 'actual' estimate, it is my judgment that the estimates in Table 9.1 are the best that economic historians have to offer and in most cases are the conventional estimates most often used in the literature. When the estimate is not from a conventional source, and when I have adjusted or rejected the estimate, a comment to that effect can be found in the table. In the second column of the table, the reader can find the model's prediction. For example, nominal farmland rents are predicted to have declined at -0.46 per cent per annum, about as close a conformity with historical fact that one could wish.

Recall that these predictions are the results of two pieces of information: the impact multipliers, in this case those for 1891 listed in Table 10.1, and the per annum rates of change in all exogenous variables, in this case the 1861–1911 rates reported in Appendix E. I have been able to document all of the exogenous variables except the demand shift terms $(\overset{*}{D}_j)$, so any discrepancy between the model's prediction and fact can be due to any one or combination of the following:

(i)   the model is in error;
(ii)   the estimated historical 'facts' are in error;
(iii)   the underlying structural estimates of the model are in error (see Appendix D);
(iv)   the estimated rates of change in the exogenous variables are in error (see Appendix E); or
(v)   my inability to estimate exogenous demand shifts $(\overset{*}{D}_j)$ creates an error of omission.

On the basis of extensive sensitivity analysis, my own judgment is that (iii), (iv) and (v) are never significant sources of poor prediction. Poor predictions are almost always due to (i) flaws in the model, or (ii) flaws in the historical 'facts'. The commentary that follows will make that judgment clear where relevant and useful.

Inequality and factor rewards
I shall start with the model's prediction on land rents. We have already seen that the model predicts almost exactly the true fall in nominal rents after 1861. It also predicts the decline in land's share in total national income, documented by Charles Feinstein and Avner Offer (-0.09 versus -0.10 per cent per annum). Thus, the model seems to track British agriculture's late nineteenth-century Great Depression with remarkable precision.

In spite of the extensive literature on British 'failure' and the productivity slowdown in the late nineteenth century, only recently have the trends in the rate of return to capital been established. While the yield on Consols was stable at 3.2 per cent over the five decades following 1861, recent work by Michael Edelstein (1982, Table 6.1, p. 142, 'total U.K. domestic financial assets') suggests a modest decline in the price-deflated, realized rate of return on the home portfolio after 1870 (-0.13 per cent per annum), a result that the model closely predicts (-0.16 per cent per annum).

What about aspects of wage structure and earnings inequality? Most important, the surge in unskilled wages is closely replicated by the model, although there is a slight tendency for the model to underpredict real wage growth for the unskilled ($+1.08$ versus $+1.26$ per cent per annum). Predicted *average* real wages, on the other hand, seem to replicate historic rates more closely ($+1.24$ versus $+1.19$ per cent per annum). This rate is far in excess of real income per worker growth, implying a rise in the wage share, a result that the historical facts confirm ($+0.11$) and that the model predicts ($+0.07$). The model also faithfully replicates the collapse in pay ratios over the late nineteenth century, although not quite at the enormous rate of compression documented in Chapter 3 ($\overset{*}{q} - \overset{*}{w}$: -0.54 versus -0.97 per cent per annum). The reason for the discrepancy lies mainly in the fact that the nominal wage on skills actually fell a bit over the period (-0.14 per cent per annum) while the best the model can do is predict a very modest rise ($+0.23$ per cent per annum), far below the rise in unskilled wages. Consistent with the collapse in pay ratios, the model also predicts a greater rise in unskilled labor's share than in skilled labor's share (not reported in Table 9.1). This implies the leveling in the distribution of earnings documented in Chapter 3.

In short, the model appears to account for all the complex attributes of the leveling portion of the Kuznets curve documented in Chapters 2, 3 and 4. It captures the surge in the real wage, the modest decline in yields on equity, the decline in pay gaps between high- and low-skill occupations, the leveling in the distribution of income and earnings, the sharp rise in the wage–rental ratio, and the dramatic erosion in land's share in national income.

Unbalanced output growth
The model closely replicates Feinstein's aggregate output growth performance ($+1.91$ versus $+1.82$ per cent per annum). Indeed, given the quality of the data, one wonders whether a discrepancy of 0.09 per cent per annum between fact and fiction is worth worrying about. In any case, aggregate growth rates are relatively easy to predict with any comparative static model that takes total factor productivity growth and accumulation rates as exogenous. The tougher task is to predict sectoral growth. Nineteenth-century growth was, after all, very unbalanced, and industrialization was the century's prime attribute.

How well does the model account for unbalanced output growth and industrialization? The relative demise of agriculture is effectively captured since predicted real output growth departs hardly a whit from Feinstein's index ($+0.01$ versus $+0.09$ per cent per annum). Thus, the model appears to reproduce agriculture's stagnancy. Rapid industrial output growth ($+2.13$ versus $+2.01$ per cent per annum) and service sector growth ($+2.12$

versus +2.05 per cent per annum) are both predicted extremely well, too. In short, the model appears to capture the demise of agriculture, rapid industrialization and the rise of the service sector, all key attributes of late nineteenth-century growth.

Trade and intermediate outputs
The model in Chapter 8 was not designed to confront trade issues. As a result, I have introduced simplifications that make it difficult for the model to do more than yield only the roughest replication of late nineteenth-century experience. For example, the price of manufactured goods is taken as exogenous when we know in fact that Britain's export volumes were likely to have had an impact on world market conditions. Furthermore, I do not allow the economy to export home-produced intermediate inputs, B, when in fact Britain was a major exporter of coal over the period. Finally, the domestic demand parameters discussed in Appendix D are only 'stylized facts', since the data are not available for more precise estimation, and the size of those parameters can have a significant impact on the volume of manufactures vented on to world markets and on the volume of imported foodstuffs that satisfied British excess demands. The model could be revised to improve these predictive dimensions of the model, but the revisions would be mostly cosmetic. They would have little impact on industrialization, growth and inequality.

Having made these confessions, note that the composition and level of imports predicted by the model are roughly correct, if not precisely accurate. Net imports of agricultural goods in value are slightly underpredicted (+1.91 versus +2.09 per cent per annum) and the same is true of net imports of intermediate inputs in value (+1.16 versus +1.37 per cent per annum). Exports are not reported, since they consist of manufactures only and can be derived by the weighted sum of imports by type.

(3) Assessing the model on a darker statistical age, 1821–61

Table 9.2 reports my success in replicating growth, inequality and industrialization between 1821 and 1861. The model and the method underlying Table 9.2 are exactly the same as with Table 9.1, although the former uses the initial conditions prevailing in 1821 and trends in exogenous variables from 1821 to 1861, while the latter uses 1891 initial conditions and trends in exogenous variables from 1861 to 1911. Much to my surprise, the model performs even better on the upswing of the Kuznets curve.

Inequality and factor rewards
The model captures nominal wage behavior almost exactly, although the predicted decline in the cost of living is a bit more than the estimates in Appendix A suggest (−0.85 versus −0.70 per cent per annum), so that real wage growth predictions are not quite so close to fact. Yet, the conformity between fact and fiction is remarkable for both the real unskilled wage (+0.68 versus +0.92 per cent per annum) and the real wage on skills (+1.65

versus +1.71 per cent per annum). It follows that the surge in the skilled wage differential is faithfully captured by the model (+0.78 versus +0.97 per cent per annum). The model has captured a key attribute of the early nineteenth century uncovered in Chapters 2 and 3: significant improvement in common labor's standard of living during a period of rising earnings inequality and wage stretching. Indeed, earnings inequality trends can be seen quite clearly in Table 9.2: the model predicts that unskilled labor's share in total *labor* income should have declined very sharply, conforming to the decline in the bottom 90 per cent share in total earnings between 1827 and 1851 documented in Chapter 3 (−0.11 versus −0.27 per cent per annum). The model also predicts average real wage growth very closely (+1.23 versus +1.06 per cent per annum), a rate sufficiently in excess of real income per worker growth that total labor's share rises – although it is the middle-class 'white-collar' and blue-collar labor aristocracy who are enjoying most of those gains.

Property income variables also appear to be tracked fairly well by the model. Land rents per acre rise in nominal terms (+0.98 versus +0.63 per cent per annum), and the improvement is even greater in real terms (+1.82 versus +1.33 per cent per annum). The boom in rents was not enough, of course, to stave off the gradual decline in the rental share in national income (−0.03 versus −0.09 per cent per annum). A decline in the rate of return to capital and equity is also predicted by the model (−0.47 per cent per annum), a result consistent with historical trends in either the rate of return on foreign investment or the yield on Consols (−0.31 and −0.58 per cent per annum, respectively).

Unbalanced output growth
Although national accounts data for this period are almost non-existent, Charles Feinstein (1978a) has added to the pioneering Deane and Cole (1962) estimates to give us sharper guesses on overall growth performance from 1821 to 1861. In addition, Harley (1982) has improved the industrial output indices for 1815–41, and Crafts (1980, 1983) has added to the 1801–31 estimates for all sectors. Pollard's (1980) recent effort to improve coal output indices up to 1859 has inspired the attempt reported in Table 9.2 (under $\overset{*}{B}$) to estimate output growth in mining and quarrying up to 1861. These and other contributions make it possible at least to assess the overall ability of the model to predict both aggregate as well as sectoral performance.

The Deane and Cole economy-wide growth estimates are somewhat lower than Feinstein's, so these two sources serve to supply upper and lower bounds to measured real income growth, 2.3–2.6 per cent per annum. The model's prediction (+2.35) is much closer to the Deane and Cole estimate, a result no doubt influenced by the fact that the Deane and Cole data were used extensively to establish the model's 1821 initial conditions. In a like fashion, the real income per capita growth prediction (+1.12) lies within the range of 'fact' offered by Feinstein and Deane and Cole (1.07 to 1.37). The same is true for real income per worker growth.

Table 9.2 *The model's performance: actual and predicted, 1821–61*

Endogenous variable	Per annum rates Actual %	Predicted %	Source of actual rates
$\hat{d}$ Land rents per acre	+0.63	+0.98	From estate books, 1819/23–1859/63, based on c. 120,000 acres in Lincoln, Hereford, Bucks, Beds, Cambridge, Essex and North Wales reported in R. J. Thompson (1907, p. 613).
$\hat{r}$ Gross rental rate on capital	n.a.	−1.32	Not available.
$\hat{i}$ Rate of return on 'equity', $= \hat{r} - \hat{P}_{COL}$	−0.31 to −0.58	−0.47	Imlah's (1958, p. 180) average rate of return on UK foreign investment fell by 0.31% per annum over 1822–62 while the yield on Consols fell by 0.58% over 1819/23–1859/63 (Mitchell and Deane, 1962, p. 455).
$\hat{w}$ Unskilled wage	−0.02	+0.08	From worksheets and computer output underlying Williamson (1982d). An employment-weighted average of six low-wage occupations, including farm labor. See Chapter 2 and note on average real wage below.
$\hat{q}$ Wage on skills	+0.95	+0.86	See $\hat{w}$ above. Here, $\hat{q}$ is measured as the growth in $w_H - w_L$, where w_H is a weighted average of eleven 'high-wage' occupations, from clergy to doctors to skilled craftsmen, while w_L is simply the unskilled wage as defined under '$\hat{w}$'. See Chapters 2 and 3.
$\hat{P}_C$ Price of services	n.a.	−0.85	Not available; but the imperfect index used to deflate Deane and Cole's current price estimate of P_C (see below under C) suggests a figure of −0.18.
$\hat{A}$ Agricultural output	+1.49	+1.37	Calculated from Deane and Cole (1962, Table 37, pp. 166–7), deflated by Rousseaux's 'total agricultural products' price index (Mitchell and Deane, 1962, pp. 471–2), following Deane and Cole (Table 38, source note), 1821–61 (prices derived by 5-year moving averages centered on 1821 and 1861). The 1.49% per annum growth rate is also favored by Harley (1982, Table 9, p. 286), while for the period 1801–31 is estimated at 1.18% by Crafts (1983, Table 5, p. 187).
$\hat{A}_M$ Net imports of A-goods	n.a.	+2.67	Not available.
$\hat{P}_A + \hat{A}_M$ Net import values of A-goods	+2.35	+2.31	Imports less re-exports of agricultural commodities in current prices, 1830–55, UK (Mitchell and Deane, 1962, pp. 291 and 297).

M	Industrial output	+2.45, 3.21, 3.70	+3.17	The low figure of 2.45% per annum is calculated from Deane and Cole, deflating current output (1962, Table 37, pp. 166–7) by the Rousseaux 'principal industrial products' price deflator following their lead in the source notes to Table 38 (1962, p. 170). The Rousseaux deflator is clearly inappropriate, however. The high figure of 3.7% per annum results from applying a new deflator to the Deane and Cole current output figures. The new P_M deflator is discussed in Appendix E, where the 'shift parameter' estimates are presented. Both price deflators cover 1819/23–1859/63. The 2.45 figure is much too low, based on Feinstein's (1978a, Table 26, p. 86) estimate of *total* national product growth of 2.6% per annum, compared with Deane and Cole's estimate (p. 170) of 2.3%. Crafts (1980) agrees. The 3.21% per annum estimate comes from Harley (1982, Table 9, p. 13) but covers the period 1815–41.
*C	Service output	+2.32	+2.38	Deane and Cole (1962, Table 37, pp. 166–7), deflated by the Rousseaux 'overall index' of prices (Mitchell and Deane, 1962, pp. 471–2), following Deane and Cole (Table 38, source note), for 1821–61 (5-year moving averages centered on 1821 and 1861). By modifying Deane and Cole, Harley (1982, Table 9, p. 286) estimates a 2.04% per annum rate for the 1815–41 period.
*B	Output of home-produced intermediate inputs	+2.62	+2.11	B covers mining and quarrying. Deane and Cole (1962, p. 220) tell us that in 1858 the value shares in that aggregate were coal (60%), iron ore (9%), copper, lead and tin (12.5%), and stone and clay (18.5%). Using the growth rate estimates that follow, these share weights can be projected back to 1840. Applying the 1840 weights to the four sub-sector growth rate estimates yields the 2.62% per annum figure. The sub-sector growth rates come from: coal – 1821/4–1854, Pollard (1980, Table 14, p. 229); iron ore – 1820/4–1860/4, based on pig iron output, Mitchell and Deane (1962, p. 225); copper, lead and tin – copper ore, 1821–60, Mitchell and Deane (1962, pp. 158–9); stone and clay – based on gross domestic fixed capital formation (constant prices) in dwellings, public buildings and works, roads and bridges, estimated in Feinstein (1978a, Table 6, p. 40). The sub-sector growth rates are: coal, 3.7% per annum; iron ore, 5.85%; copper, lead and tin, 1.59%; and stone and clay, 0.60%.

Table 9.2 *The model's performance: actual and predicted, 1821–61 (continued)*

Endogenous variable	Per annum rates		Source of actual rates
	Actual %	Predicted %	
$\overset{*}{F}$	n.a.	+2.12	Not available.
$\overset{*}{P_F} + \overset{*}{F}$	+3.22	+1.58	See discussion of $\overset{*}{P_A} + A_M$ above.
$\overset{*}{P_B}$	−1.10	−0.86	'Best coals at the ships' side in London' 1819/23–1831/5 and 'All coal exports' 1831/5–1859/63, from Mitchell and Deane (1962, pp. 482–3). Presumably, the fall in coal prices was dramatic compared with some of the other components of mining and quarrying. Thus, the −1.10% per annum figure may be too high.
$\overset{*}{P}_{COL}$	−0.70	−0.85	Urban working-class families' cost-of-living index, using 'export' series for clothing, 1819/23–1859/63, Appendix Tables A.5 and A.8.
$\overset{*}{w} - \overset{*}{P}_{COL}$	+0.68	+0.92	See above.
$d - \overset{*}{P}_{COL}$	+1.33	+1.82	See above.
$\overset{*}{q} - \overset{*}{P}_{COL}$	+1.65	+1.71	See above.
$\overset{*}{q} - \overset{*}{w}$	+0.97	+0.78	See above, and Chapter 3.
$\overset{*}{Y}$	+2.3–2.6	+2.35	Deane and Cole's estimate (1962, Table 38, p. 170) for Britain 1821/31–1851/61 is somewhat lower than Feinstein's (1978a, Table 26, p. 86) for 1801–60 or 1831–60, 2.6 and 2.5% per annum respectively. These new estimates appear to be consistent with Deane's own attempts at revision (1968, Table 2, p. 98). My model has been estimated using much of Deane and Cole's sectoral output and input data for this period, so the predicted value of 2.35% per annum should perhaps be judged by the 'actual' 2.3, rather than the newer estimates. Harley's (1982, Table 9, p. 286) estimate for 1815–41, 2.26% per annum, is certainly closer to Deane and Cole's.

y_P^*	Real income per capita	+1.07–1.37	+1.12	*Y minus population growth rate of 1.23% per annum, the latter from Mitchell and Deane (1962, pp. 8–9, Great Britain only).
y_L^*	Real income per worker	+0.90–1.20	+0.95	*Y minus labor force growth rate of 1.4% per annum, the latter from Deane and Cole (1962, Table 31, p. 143, 'total occupied' British labor force).
	Average real wage for all workers	+1.06	+1.23	Real full-time earnings, all workers, 1827–61, Tables 2.7 and 2.12.
$d\theta_L$	Change in unskilled labor's share, economy-wide, % per annum	n.a.	+0.01	Not available.
$d\theta_S$	Change in skilled labor's share, economy-wide, % per annum	n.a.	+0.10	Not available.
$d\theta_{S+L}$	Change in labor's share, economy-wide, % per annum	n.a.	+0.11	Not available.
$d\left(\dfrac{\theta_L}{\theta_L+\theta_S}\right)$	Change in unskilled labor's share of total labor income, economy-wide, % per annum	−0.27	−0.11	Change in bottom 90% share of total male earnings, 1827–51, from Chapter 3.
$d\theta_J$	Change in (farm)land's rent share, economy-wide, % per annum	−0.09	−0.03	Share of net rent on land in national income, 1801–1860/9, from Deane and Cole (1962, Table 80, p. 301).

Note: All predicted values reported in this table use parameters and initial conditions from 1821 (see Appendix D). Results using 1861 parameters and initial conditions have also been calculated, and these produce somewhat different results for some endogenous variables, although the differences are usually quite small. See Appendix D.

Once again, while most macro-models find it easy to replicate aggregate growth rates in the long run, accounting for unbalanced rates of sectoral output advance is a much tougher challenge. Britain up to mid-century has long been viewed as the classic case of rapid early industrialization where manufacturing is the 'leading' sector, where services follow close behind, but where agriculture – though hardly stagnant – lags far behind. The model tells the same tale. The predicted rapid growth of manufacturing falls mid-way between the 2.45 per cent per annum estimated by Deane and Cole (using the Rousseaux price deflator) and the 3.7 per cent per annum that I offer as a revision (using a newly constructed manufacturing output price deflator). Furthermore, predicted manufacturing growth almost exactly replicates Harley's estimate for 1815–41 (+3.17 versus +3.21 per cent per annum). Agricultural output growth is closely replicated by the model (+1.49 versus +1.37 per cent per annum), a strong performance by eighteenth-century standards but falling far behind industry's boom up to 1861. The growth of services falls between agriculture and industry, and the model predicts that growth almost exactly (+2.38 versus +2.32 per cent per annum). While the model tends to underpredict the growth in mining and quarrying ($\overset{*}{B}$), the correspondence is still fairly close (+2.11 versus +2.62 per cent per annum).

In short, the model has little difficulty replicating the industrialization and distributional attributes of early nineteenth-century British growth.

Trade and intermediate inputs
For much the same reasons as those offered for the 1861–1911 period, the model does not do as well explaining foreign trade. This statement does *not* hold for agricultural imports since the model replicates that experience extremely well (+2.31 versus +2.35). The problem lies with the import values of foreign-produced intermediates, which the model underpredicts (+1.58 versus +3.22).

(4) A final nineteenth-century assessment

No simple general equilibrium model can be expected to explain all economic events with equal precision. The model in Chapter 8 was devised to account for British long-run inequality and industrialization experience from Waterloo to World War I. How well has it done?

As far as inequality is concerned, the critical historical event was the Kuznets curve. The model reproduces that inequality history quite well: it predicts wage stretching, widening pay gaps and rising earnings inequality on the upswing of the Kuznets curve prior to 1861. It also predicts the improvement in workers' living standards, the rise in land rents and the falling yield on equity, all trends apparent up to mid-century. In the late nineteenth century, Britain underwent aspects of leveling in the distribution tracing out the downswing of the Kuznets curve. The model predicts those changes too: the collapse in pay gaps and the premium on skills, the rise in unskilled labor's share, falling earnings inequality and the accelerated decline in land's share in national income. Furthermore, the model's *quantitative* predictions of British inequality history over the Kuznets curve are usually very close.

As far as growth and industrialization are concerned, the model predicts the continued relative demise of agriculture across the nineteenth century, accelerating in the late nineteenth century with the invasion of New World grains. It also predicts the very rapid growth of the leading sector, manufacturing, and its marked retardation from the 1821–61 export-led success to the late nineteenth-century 'failure'. The model also captures the service sector's impressive growth, which was not far behind manufacturing in the early nineteenth century and became a leading sector late in the century. Once again, the *quantitative* predictions of British industrialization experience across the nineteenth century are usually quite close.

The model captures the retardation in British growth across the century – in total real income, in per capita real income, and in average labor productivity. While the magnitude of the retardation depends on whose estimates of the early nineteenth-century growth one accepts, the model's quantitative predictions are pretty close to the modest decline suggested by Deane and Cole's (1962) estimates: a predicted decline in per capita income growth of 0.11 per cent per annum compared with the 'facts' of the decline, 0.15 per cent ($\overset{*}{\hat{y}}_P$), Table 9.2 less Table 9.1).

The main conclusion would appear to be that the model developed in Chapter 8 is quite effective in accounting for nineteenth-century British inequality and industrialization. What, then, were the forces responsible for that experience?

10

Accounting for the Kuznets Curve, 1821–1911

(1) Looking for sources

What were the major forces driving British inequality across the nineteenth century? The answer will depend both on the magnitude of the exogenous influence thought to be important and on the sensitivity of inequality to that influence. I begin in sections 2 and 3 with the second issue. How sensitive *was* the British economy to unbalanced rates of technical progress by sector, to the rates of factor saving produced by the new technologies, to world market prices, to unskilled labor scarcity, to skill bottlenecks, to capital formation, and to overall population growth? Section 2 estimates impact multipliers for 1891: the exercise documents what *might* have mattered by measuring the full general equilibrium impact of each exogenous variable viewed by the traditional literature to have been a 'key' source of British inequality trends and industrialization rates. To what forces was the late nineteenth-century British economy most sensitive? Section 3 raises a related but somewhat different issue: was the British economy more or less vulnerable to those forces in 1821?

The core of the chapter lies in sections 4 and 5. While the earlier sections of the chapter ask 'To what forces was the British economy most sensitive?', the later sections ask 'What forces actually mattered most?' The distinction is important because historical patterns may reflect the result of a modest shock to an economy that was very sensitive to that particular shock, or they may reflect the result of a major shock to an economy that was relatively insensitive to that particular shock. Finally, I turn to an accounting of the Kuznets curve. What were the most important forces accounting for the mid-century turning point (section 5)?

(2) How the model works: 1891 impact multipliers

How does the model work? Rather than dwell on the tidy elegance of qualitative theory, I shall leap back directly to 1891 and see what forces would have had the greatest potential impact on industrialization and inequality at that time. It is, of course, essential to dwell on the determinants of industrialization along the way since changes in the output mix imply changes in the mix of input demands, and these in turn can have a potent influence on factor incomes and inequality.

Table 10.1 summarizes the sensitivity of the 1891 British economy to four kinds of shocks: the impact of technological change in any one of the four sectors[1]; the impact of world market conditions through prices of traded commodities; the impact of land expansion, capital accumulation, labor force growth, and skill augmentation; and the impact of exogenous changes in domestic demand. To simplify, only the thirteen endogenous variables will be examined, although one should have little difficulty inferring the derivative effects on inequality and industrialization from the behavior of these endogenous variables.

Without a doubt the forces that had the greatest potential influence on Britain in 1891 appear to have been unbalanced technological advance and world market conditions. Changing domestic demand conditions appear to have been least important. I shall begin with unbalanced technological advance.

The first result to note in Table 10.1 is that output in both agriculture and manufacturing increases by more than the rate of total factor productivity growth itself. For example, a 1 per cent improvement in total factor productivity in agriculture would have served to raise output there almost 1.7 per cent. While this result would be impossible in partial equilibrium analysis, it certainly makes sense in the real world, where general equilibrium responses are a fact of life: the technological improvement would raise the marginal productivity of all factors used in agriculture, and, with time, farming would attract resources from the remainder of the economy until marginal value products were again equated. Thus, agricultural output growth would be doubly favored – from the initial productivity gain *and* from the subsequent factor migration response. The same narrative holds for technological advance in manufacturing: it too would expand by more than the initial productivity advance, as labor, capital and skills would migrate to the sector of high marginal productivity until rising economy-wide factor scarcities would choke off the added supply response. In short, one would expect the impact multipliers of $\overset{*}{T}_j$ on A and $\overset{*}{M}$ to exceed unity; but why is the impact multiplier lower for agriculture, 1.6758, than for manufacturing, 1.9675? Once again the answer is obvious, at least after a moment's reflection: in response to the temporary excess demand created by the technological advance, *all* factors of production used in manufacturing (capital, labor and skills) can be attracted from some other sector where they are used as well, while agriculture, in contrast, faces the constraint of *fixed* land endowments, a factor of production specific to farming and constant.

The reader will also note that the multiplier on $\overset{*}{T}_j$ is close to zero for mining, 0.0452, and even negative for home services, −0.1945. No net output growth in mining from technological progress there, and a contraction in net service output from technological progress there? How could this have been so? The answer must lie with demand conditions at home and

Table 10.1 *Impact multipliers for the 1891 British economy*

Endogenous variable	Impact of technological change: total				Impact of prices		$\hat{j}$*	Impact of factor stocks			Demand impact	
	T_A*	T_M*	T_C*	T_B*	P_A	$P_M - \theta_{FM}P_F$*		K*	L	S*	D_A*	D_M*
Land rents: d*	3.6755	−3.6656	0.2260	−0.2716	3.6971	−3.5290	−0.1525	−0.0474	1.1202	−0.9278	−0.1088	−0.1642
Rate of return to capital: r*	0.1744	0.5095	0.3961	0.0483	0.2123	0.7489	0.0570	−0.8616	0.5359	0.2553	−0.1907	−0.2879
Nominal unskilled wage: w*	0.2235	1.2940	−0.2382	0.0920	0.2008	1.1500	0.0406	0.3385	−0.6517	0.2807	0.1147	0.1731
Nominal skilled wage: q*	−1.1669	2.9864	−0.1964	0.1051	−1.1857	2.8677	−0.2745	1.0181	0.8180	−1.5551	0.0945	0.1427
Service prices: P_C*	−0.0288	1.1685	−0.9064	0.0413	−0.0199	1.2257	−0.0025	−0.1654	0.1970	−0.0323	−0.0451	−0.0681
Agricultural goods output: A*	1.6758	−3.6660	0.2260	−0.2717	2.6974	−3.5294	0.8475	−0.0474	1.1203	−0.9279	−0.1088	−0.1642
Agricultural goods imports: A_M*	−1.5117	3.5315	−1.1098	0.2260	−2.2422	3.6512	−0.6774	0.2355	−0.5094	0.8463	1.9018	0.1924
Manufacturing goods output: M*	−0.8185	1.9675	−1.4530	0.0783	−0.9575	2.0893	−0.2499	0.4766	0.3282	0.4938	0.6994	1.0559
Manufacturing goods exports: M_X*	−1.7305	4.7195	−1.8170	0.2304	−2.4021	4.2516	−0.7004	0.4935	−0.1957	0.9916	1.9651	0.8307
Services output: C*	−0.2752	−0.7285	−0.1945	−0.0306	−0.1982	−0.2417	−0.0276	0.5038	0.2686	0.2282	−0.3878	−0.5854
Intermediate goods output: B*	−0.6537	1.8461	−0.7677	0.0452	−0.7271	1.3821	−0.1824	0.4848	0.3101	0.4132	0.3696	0.5579
Intermediate goods imports: F*	−0.8185	2.9675	−1.4530	0.0783	−0.9575	2.0893	−0.2499	0.4766	0.3282	0.4938	0.6994	1.0559
Intermediate goods prices: P_B*	0.2081	1.0467	−0.0383	−0.9218	0.2044	1.0235	0.0457	−0.0398	−0.2774	0.2727	0.0184	0.0278

Sources and Notes: Inverse of 13 × 13 matrix in Table 8.1, where 1891 initial conditions are used (Appendix D). The T_j impacts include the *total* effects listed in Table 8.1; namely, that due π_i, as well as T_i.

problems of absorption of the now-augmented supplies in B and C. Table 10.1 shows this quite clearly by the impact multiplier of $\overset{*}{T}_C$ on $\overset{*}{P}_C$, -0.9064, and of $\overset{*}{T}_B$ on $\overset{*}{P}_B$, -0.9218. In contrast with agriculture and manufacturing, C and B are both non-tradeables for which domestic demand elasticities matter a great deal. I have assumed unitary price elasticity of demand for services, which guarantees the large negative impact on P_C, apparently completely offsetting the rise in marginal *physical* product generated by technological advance. That is, the decline in service output can only have taken place by the out-migration of resources from C, and that can only happen if the marginal *value* products of capital, labor and skills used there initially diminish. The mining case is similar. Here, rapid total factor productivity growth serves to glut a goods market whose demand is very unresponsive to price: after all, B is an intermediate input in manufacturing and services, used there in fixed coefficients. While productivity advance in coal mining might serve to improve the competitive position of British manufactures in world markets (and the impact multiplier on $\overset{*}{M}_X$ of 0.2304 certainly supports this view), thus serving to augment manufacturing output and the derived intermediate demand for B, these second-order effects apparently would not have been important enough to stave off the dissipation of productivity advance in coal mining through price decline. In short, coal mining and services serve as classic examples of 'immiserizing growth'. Economic agents in B and C are able to capture little or none of the rents from productivity advance in their own sector: most if not all of the productivity advance becomes a windfall gain to consumers elsewhere in the economy.

To continue the narrative on the impact of technological advance in agriculture, note that the induced output expansion attracts mobile resources to agriculture, thereby raising the ratio of labor and capital to immobile land. Land rents are 'magnified' by the technological change effects (R. W. Jones, 1965), and the impact multiplier is very large, 3.6755. If magnification effects like this were associated with the introduction of new husbandry in the late eighteenth century, one can readily imagine the incentive behind enclosures to release landlords from fixed-rent contracts with farmers (Allen, 1982)! The impact on other factor prices is predictable: the unskilled wage is raised, and by more than the rate of return to capital since agriculture in 1891 was more unskilled labor intensive than was non-agriculture. All three non-agriculture sectors contract as resources migrate to farming, but the only factors of production that suffer an absolute loss are skills, the reason being that, since skills are not used in farming, they cannot share in the boom spilling over from agriculture's productivity gains. In short, relatively rapid technological advance in agriculture would have fostered an output shift towards agriculture, a contraction in trade as British farming became more competitive with foreign imports, and a collapse in skill differentials and earnings inequality as unskilled labor gained and skilled labor lost from the shift in output mix.

However, relatively rapid technological advance favoring agriculture was most certainly *not* an attribute of nineteenth-century Britain. On the contrary, agriculture lagged behind. Fair enough, one needs only reverse the argument in the previous paragraph: a technologically stagnant agriculture would have insured lower growth rates in national income, but it also would have insured greater inequality, industrialization and trade expansion – a moral worth remembering.

'Leading' technological advance in industry would have had the same effect as lagging technological progress in agriculture. Output would have been augmented by more than the $\overset{*}{T}_M$ influence itself since resources would have migrated into manufacturing in response to the improved marginal factor productivities there. Given sufficient time, labor in-migration would continue until real wages were equated again and capital would tend to flow towards manufacturing until rates of return were again equal to those prevailing elsewhere. Given domestic demand limitations, however, this augmented manufacturing output had to be vented on to world markets.

Indeed, the impact multiplier of $\overset{*}{T}_M$ on $\overset{*}{M}_X$, 4.7195, is by far the largest in Table 10.1. Since there was a backward linkage from manufacturing to coal mining, the derived demand for B rises, its price rises, and the output of B expands sharply, 1.8461. The other sectors contract to accommodate manufacturing's growth, agriculture suffering the greatest injury (with an impact multiplier of -3.6660), and land – the immobile factor – absorbs *all* of the windfall losses since it cannot migrate to share in any of the leading sector's boom. Who gains? First and foremost, skilled labor gains and gains handsomely. After all, skills are used intensively in manufacturing and they are not used at all in agriculture. Capital gains the least since manufacturing is not very capital intensive compared with the *average* of the two contracting sectors, agriculture and home services. Unskilled labor's gains lie in between.

Thus, while unskilled wages rise in response to technological advance in manufacturing, skilled wages rise by far more, wage gaps are fostered, and earnings inequality is generated. The behavior of $\overset{*}{T}_C$ and $\overset{*}{T}_B$ seems to matter far less. In short, technological advance favoring manufacturing produces the classic correlates of early modern growth: rapid industrialization, even more rapid trade expansion (encouraging some economic historians to label this 'export-led' growth), a rise in the workers' living standards, but increased pay gaps and earnings inequality. On the basis of these 1891 impact multipliers, one key to nineteenth-century British industrialization and inequality must clearly have been the gap between $\overset{*}{T}_M$ and $\overset{*}{T}_A$, or what I called in Chapters 5 and 6 unbalanced technological advance. Furthermore, the more rapid was the unbalanced technological advance, the more potent would the inequality influence have been – an attractive conclusion since the early nineteenth century included years of both more rapid technological advance and rising inequality.

What about the impact of world market conditions? One need not dwell here for long since the effects of prices are symmetric to the technological change effects just discussed. The impact of agricultural price changes of the same magnitude as $\overset{*}{T}_A$ have exactly the same qualitative impact throughout the economy, and almost exactly the same quantitative impact. The statement holds for changes in the net price of manufactures too (the net price being the 'value added price', since the influence of imported raw materials' prices is subtracted). In short, world market conditions could have had a very potent impact on British experience with inequality in the nineteenth century. Whether they did or not depends on the magnitude of changes in those world market conditions as reflected in relative prices: any rise in the relative price of manufactured export staples would have fostered earnings inequality; and any fall in the relative price of imported raw materials would have had the same effect.

Of the four factor stock effects that must be considered, land expansion has the most predictable qualitative impact. It is also the least relevant force reported in Table 10.1, since British land endowments changed hardly at all across the nineteenth century. Nevertheless, the size of some of the multipliers is sufficiently surprising to warrant a moment's diversion. For example, since land's factor payments share in agriculture was about 0.23 in 1891 (Appendix Table D.3), simple partial equilibrium analysis would have predicted output expansion $\overset{*}{A} = 0.23 \times \overset{*}{J} = 0.23$, which is far below the actual figure of 0.8475. As with technological advance, the explanation for the discrepancy lies with second-order general equilibrium effects: any exogenous increase in farm acreage serves to raise the marginal productivity of capital and labor used there, thus encouraging the influx of both factors from the rest of the economy and creating a far larger general equilibrium impact on farm output. More important for our purposes, however, is the wage leveling that land expansion breeds. As has been learned from research on America (Williamson and Lindert, 1980), abundant land may have quite a different influence on the distribution of earnings than on the distribution of income. While it is true that land rents per acre fall, they do not fall as much as the acreage increase itself, so that total rental income expands. On the other hand, since agricultural capital intensities were far less than non-agricultural capital intensities in 1891, the rate of return to capital hardly changes at all in response to the rise in farm output induced by the acreage expansion. Since land wealth appears to have been far more concentrated than non-land wealth in Victorian England, property income would have become *more* unequally distributed under conditions of greater land abundance. In short, land expansion would have served to equalize labor earnings but to concentrate property incomes, leaving an ambiguous impact on the distribution of income. Since land expansion was never significant in nineteenth-century Britain, however, the key factor stock effects on industrialization and inequality must lie elsewhere.

Consider capital accumulation ($\overset{*}{K}$) first. The sectors using capital most intensively in 1891 were, in descending order, services, mining and manufacturing – with agriculture falling far behind (Appendix Table D.3). The impact of capital accumulation on output expansion is therefore predictable: the non-agricultural sectors grow roughly apace, agriculture stagnates, and trade expands. Who gains and who loses? Landlords certainly suffer an unambiguous loss, but the effect on their total rental incomes is very small,

-0.0474. Capitalists grapple with the law of diminishing returns, but note that the rate of return falls by slightly less than the rise in $\overset{*}{K}$, a result that implies that total profits rise. Here, too, the impact is very small, since total profits rise by only $\overset{*}{K} + \overset{*}{r} = 1 - 0.8616 \cong 0.14$ per cent. Landlords hardly lose anything and capitalists gain very little from accumulation, but what about the workers? While the labor scarcity induced by accumulation produces significant wage gains for unskilled labor, 0.3385, it is the *skilled* worker who gains the most by far, 1.0181. There are two reasons for this result. First, the major capital-intensive sectors – C and M – are also the only sectors employing skills. Since these two sectors are favored most by capital accumulation, their relatively rapid growth spills over into buoyant demands for skills. Second, skills are relative complements to capital within each of the two sectors, while unskilled labor is everywhere a relative substitute. Firms can more effectively substitute away from labor when it gets scarce than they can from skills. Both of these forces serve to raise the skill premium and breed wage inequality, although the unskilled worker *is* enjoying standard-of-living improvements in response to capital accumulation. The moral of the story is that capital accumulation breeds industrialization, trade expansion *and* wage inequality.

Unskilled labor force growth tends to offset many of the influences set in motion by accumulation, but certainly not all. While all sectors expand in response to an augmented labor supply, labor-intensive agriculture expands far more rapidly, which implies de-industrialization and a trade contraction. That moral bears repeating: unskilled labor force growth and elastic labor supplies generate a relative rise in agricultural output and a diminution in trade. Who gains and who loses? The landlords gain mightily, the capitalists gain more modestly and the now more abundant unskilled laborers lose heavily – distributional consequences upon which Malthus and his colleagues dwelt at length. In addition, note that the skilled wage rises sharply, generating wage inequality. It follows that expanding unskilled labor supplies in late nineteenth-century Britain would have served to forestall industrialization, suppress trade and foster wage and income inequality. In contrast, a retardation in unskilled labor supply growth in the late nineteenth century would have served to foster industrialization and trade expansion as well as equality. Since the unskilled labor force *did* grow more slowly late in the nineteenth century than early, here is another prime candidate for explaining the Kuznets curve.

What about the impact of growth in skills? Skill accumulation appears to have all the influences on industrialization and trade expansion that capital accumulation does, and more. It tends to erode the property income share more drastically, at least on the basis of the larger decline in land rents induced by skill expansion (-0.9278 versus -0.0474). It also has the opposite effect on earnings inequality. That is, the wage gap declines in the face of a skills glut and earnings equality is fostered. This is another moral worth repeating: an industrialization strategy that favors conventional capital accumulation tends to foster earnings inequality, while one that favors skills accumulation tends to foster a leveling of incomes. Since there is considerable evidence that Britain in fact underwent a switch from capital-favored to skill-favored accumulation across the nineteenth century, we do indeed have a promising explanation of the Kuznets curve.

Finally, what about the impact of domestic demand? The issue here is not the price elasticity of demand for non-tradeable home services and products of the mines and quarries; we have already seen that these price elasticities matter, especially in distributing the gains from total factor productivity improvements in B and C across the economy as a whole. But what about *shifts* in domestic demand? While British economic historians have debated this issue in the literature at length – especially regarding eighteenth-century experience (see the summaries in Floud and McCloskey, 1981, vol. I, Chs 1 and 3) – Table 10.1 shows those demand forces ($\overset{*}{D}_A$ and $\overset{*}{D}_M$) to be trivial in all cases but trade volumes. There is no evidence to support the view that dramatic changes in British domestic demand occurred during the nineteenth century, and Table 10.1 shows that such unlikely changes would not have mattered much for inequality and industrialization trends anyway.

What have we learned from the 1891 impact multipliers in Table 10.1? First, unbalanced technological progress favoring industry should have helped to generate the key stylized facts of nineteenth-century British growth: the relative demise of agriculture, the relative expansion of industry and mining, an even more dramatic growth in export staples, improved workers' living standards, rising skill scarcity, widening pay gaps and earnings inequality. Whether unbalanced technological progress can also account for *income* inequality is less clear, since a modest rise in capitalists' incomes would have been offset by a sharper decline in landlords' incomes. Landlords' and capitalists' relative shares in national income would influence the result: since the latter exceeded the former in 1891, a net income inequality impact appears to be assured. Second, any increase in capital per worker, through accumulation, should have reinforced the effects of unbalanced productivity advance: industrialization and trade expansion would have been fostered, although the impact would have been less powerful than that of unbalanced productivity advance; and earnings inequality would have been fostered by the creation of skills scarcity, although the workers' standard of living would have been augmented. Third, any rise in skills per worker should have had the opposite effect on earnings inequality, although the impact on industrialization and exports would have been the same.

Unbalanced productivity advance and conventional capital accumulation would have served to contribute to earnings inequality, industrialization and trade expansion, following the favored hypotheses of Part II. To account for the observed nineteenth-century inequality trends, therefore, one needs to know whether these two forces were in fact offset by world market conditions and/or skill accumulation, and whether these two forces were in fact operative throughout the century with equal force.

(3) Structural change, 1821–91

What is meant by the phrase 'structural change'? Most economic historians and development economists use the term to describe the change over time in an economy's final demand shares, output mix, employment distribution and other aspects of resource use. That is exactly the way the term is used here. At any point in time, the structure of the British economy can be described by the following 'initial conditions' (see Appendix D), all of which appear in the matrix on the left-hand side of Table 8.1:

- *Sectoral factor cost shares:* fourteen factor payment shares describing the relative importance of inputs by sector, of which

    three in agriculture, θ_{JA}, θ_{KA}, θ_{LA}
    five in industry, θ_{KM}, θ_{LM}, θ_{SM}, θ_{BM}, θ_{FM},
    four in services, θ_{KC}, θ_{LC}, θ_{SC}, θ_{BC}
    two in mining, θ_{KB}, θ_{LB};

- *Factor employment distribution across sectors:* twelve shares describing the distribution of a given factor's employment across the economy for those factors of production (K, L, S, B) that are used in more than one sector, of which

    four for capital, λ_{KA}, λ_{KM}, λ_{KC}, λ_{KB}
    four for labor, λ_{LA}, λ_{LM}, λ_{LC}, λ_{LB}
    two for skills, λ_{SM}, λ_{SC}
    two for 'coal', λ_{BM}, λ_{BC};

- *Output and final demand structure:* eleven shares describing the national accounts on both the output and the expenditure side, of which

    four sectoral output shares in national income, ϕ_A, ϕ_M, ϕ_C, ϕ_D
    four sectoral (net) income shares in national income, $\hat{\phi}_A$, $\hat{\phi}_M$, $\hat{\phi}_C$, $\hat{\phi}_B$
    three sectoral shares in final demand, $\bar{\phi}_A$, $\bar{\phi}_M$, $\bar{\phi}_C$

- *Patterns of trade:* eight shares describing the patterns and composition of trade, of which

    two import and home-production shares in agriculture's final demand, α_A, α_{A_M}
    two home-production shares of manufacturing in exports and home demand, α_M, α_{M_x}
    four trade shares accounting for the composition of trade, z_A, z_F, z_M, z_D.

It should be intuitively clear that these initial conditions will matter in assessing just what were the key forces that drove industrialization and inequality. The British economy in 1821 was vastly different in per capita income levels, relative prices, output mix, employment distribution, trade specialization patterns, the composition of final demand and factor endowment than it was in 1891. The difference must have mattered: surely the 1821 economy was more sensitive to some economic and demographic forces than was the 1891 economy. For example, a fall in the domestic price of grains induced by repeal of the Corn Laws, or railroad development in America, or improved port turnaround time might each have caused roughly the same economic injury to British farming, but they must have had a far different economy-wide impact, if for no other reason than the fact that agriculture was of far smaller relative size late in the century than early. The impact of some given rate of technological change in manufacturing might also imply a very different economy-wide impact if manufacturing was both larger and more skill-intensive late in the century than early: for example, under those conditions the same rate of technological change in manufacturing would have generated far more potent excess demand for skills and wage stretching in 1891 than in 1821. The same would be true if, relative to agriculture, manufacturing was more capital intensive late in the century but *less* capital intensive earlier – as indeed was the case! And technological change in coal mining might well have had different forward linkage effects on manufacturing and services if the relative fuel intensity of these two sectors changed across the century. These examples serve to make the point: the structure of the British economy changed over the nineteenth century, and those changes must have had a powerful impact on the economy's sensitivity to technological, price, accumulation and labor supply forces.

Table 10.2 presents impact multipliers for the 1821 British economy. Rarely do the *signs* in Table 10.1 and 10.2 differ, but the *size* of the impact multipliers is often very different. In fact, for most of the variables of interest to us, Table 10.2 offers the impression that the impact multipliers were far higher early in the nineteenth century than late. To simplify the comparison, Table 10.3 collects the impact multipliers for wage or earnings inequality $(\overset{*}{q} - \overset{*}{w})$, for an industrialization index $(\overset{*}{M} - \overset{*}{A})$, and for export growth $(\overset{*}{M}_X)$. To begin with, Table 10.3 confirms that earnings inequality, industrialization and export growth were far more sensitive to unbalanced productivity advance in 1821 than in 1891. It is known that the 'wave of gadgets' that swept through England in the late eighteenth and early nineteenth centuries fostered relatively high rates of total factor productivity growth in manufacturing $(\overset{*}{T}_M)$. It is also known that an agricultural depression beset British agriculture for much of the early nineteenth century following the Napoleonic boom in grain prices, implying low rates of total factor productivity growth in agriculture $(\overset{*}{T}_A)$. From section 2, we also know that unbalanced productivity advance of this sort tends to foster industrialization, export growth and wage inequality. Table 10.3 now tells us in addition that the British economy was *far* more sensitive to those technological forces in 1821 than in 1891! For example, a 1 per cent increase in British manufacturing's total factor productivity would have fostered a 16 per cent increase in exports in 1821 but 'only' about a 5 per cent increase seven decades later. This is a useful finding, given that export growth was far more dramatic early in the century than late. Consider another example. A 1 per cent increase in British manufacturing's total factor productivity would have fostered a 2.2 per cent increase in the 'wage gap' in 1821 but 'only' a 1.7 per cent increase seven decades later. This is another useful finding, given that increasing wage inequality was a pre-1860 phenomenon, while the late nineteenth century was a period of leveling in the distribution of earnings.

Table 10.2 *Impact multipliers for the 1821 British economy*

Endogenous variable	Impact of technological change: total				Impact of prices		Impact of factor stocks				Demand impact	
	$\overset{*}{T}_A$	$\overset{*}{T}_M$	$\overset{*}{T}_C$	$\overset{*}{T}_B$	$\overset{*}{P}_A$	$\overset{*}{P}_M - \theta_{FM}\overset{*}{P}_F$	$\overset{*}{\dot{y}}$	$\overset{*}{K}$	$\overset{*}{L}$	$\overset{*}{S}$	$\overset{*}{\dot{D}}_A$	$\overset{*}{\dot{D}}_M$
Land rents: $\overset{*}{d}$	3.0597	−3.3406	0.4147	−0.1468	3.1672	−3.1357	−0.2260	0.1674	0.8957	−0.8294	−0.3729	−0.3098
Rate of return to capital: $\overset{*}{r}$	1.0272	−0.2253	0.1313	−0.0139	1.0613	−0.1605	0.2591	−0.8503	0.6237	−0.0301	−0.1181	−0.0981
Nominal unskilled wage: $\overset{*}{w}$	0.0384	1.6503	−0.2553	0.0745	−0.0278	1.5241	−0.0223	0.3377	−0.7174	0.3971	0.2296	0.1907
Nominal skilled wage: $\overset{*}{q}$	−2.3461	3.8495	0.4180	0.1373	−2.2376	4.0561	−0.5037	0.9224	0.6192	−1.0301	−0.3759	−0.3122
Service prices: $\overset{*}{P}_C$	0.0758	1.1293	−0.9297	0.0319	0.0940	1.1640	0.0266	−0.1488	0.2186	−0.0950	−0.0632	−0.0525
Agricultural goods output: $\overset{*}{A}$	1.0575	−3.3383	0.4144	−0.1467	2.1650	−3.1335	0.7742	0.1673	0.8951	−0.8289	−0.3727	−0.3095
Agricultural goods imports: $\overset{*}{A}_M$	−4.2840	10.7836	−2.8037	0.4549	−6.8619	10.8476	−2.2332	0.2333	−1.6027	2.8540	5.0148	0.9707
Manufacturing goods output: $\overset{*}{M}$	−2.0083	4.2029	−1.7478	0.1577	−2.4618	4.3392	−0.6896	0.4714	0.0466	1.1392	1.5719	1.3057
Manufacturing goods exports: $\overset{*}{M}_X$	−6.2762	15.9265	−4.4834	0.6183	−9.3983	15.2452	−2.9619	0.6557	−1.6562	4.0089	6.6714	2.1597
Services output: $\overset{*}{C}$	−0.6772	−0.5539	0.0053	−0.0091	−0.4163	−0.0571	−0.0368	0.4673	0.2696	0.3185	−0.9041	−0.7510
Intermediate goods output: $\overset{*}{B}$	−1.9423	4.9174	−1.6113	0.1494	−2.3603	4.1211	−0.6573	0.4712	0.0576	1.0985	1.4491	1.2037
Intermediate goods imports: $\overset{*}{F}$	−2.0083	5.2029	−1.7478	0.1577	−2.4618	4.3392	−0.6896	0.4714	0.0466	1.1392	1.5719	1.3057
Intermediate goods prices: $\overset{*}{P}_B$	0.3501	1.0591	−0.1334	−0.9534	0.3155	0.9932	0.0664	−0.0367	−0.2947	0.2625	0.1200	0.0997

Sources and Notes: Inverse of 13 × 13 matrix in Table 8.1, where 1821 initial conditions are used (Appendix D).

Table 10.3   *Structural change, 1821–91: comparing impact multipliers on inequality, industrialization and exports*

Impact of:	Wage inequality $(\overset{*}{q} - \overset{*}{w})$		Industrialization $(\overset{*}{M} - \overset{*}{A})$		Export growth $(\overset{*}{M}_X)$	
	1821	1891	1821	1891	1821	1891
Technology:						
$\overset{*}{T}_A$	−2.3845	−1.3904	−3.0658	−2.4943	−6.2762	−1.7305
$\overset{*}{T}_M$	+2.1992	+1.6924	+7.5412	+5.6335	+15.9265	+4.7195
$\overset{*}{T}_C$	+0.6733	+0.0418	−2.1622	−1.6790	−4.4834	−1.8170
$\overset{*}{T}_B$	+0.0628	+0.0131	+0.3044	+0.3500	+0.6183	+0.2304
Prices:						
$\overset{*}{P}_A$	−2.2098	−1.3865	−4.6268	−3.6549	−9.3983	−2.4021
$\overset{*}{P}_M - \theta_{FM}\overset{*}{P}_F$	+2.5320	+1.7177	+7.4727	+5.6187	+15.2452	+4.2516
Factor stocks:						
$\overset{*}{J}$	−0.4814	−0.3151	−1.4638	1.0974	−2.9619	−0.7004
$\overset{*}{K}$	+0.5847	+0.6796	+0.3041	+0.5240	+0.6557	+0.4935
$\overset{*}{L}$	+1.3366	+1.4697	−0.8485	−0.7921	−1.6562	−0.1957
$\overset{*}{S}$	−1.4272	−1.8358	+1.9681	+1.4217	+4.0089	+0.9916

Source: See Tables 10.1 and 10.2.

Similar findings emerge for price changes and labor force growth. A 1 per cent rise in the 'net value added price' of manufactured goods in world markets would have fostered a 7.5 per cent growth in industry relative to agriculture $(\overset{*}{M} - \overset{*}{A})$ in 1821, but 'only' a 5.6 per cent increase in 1891. Equally intriguing are the comparisons involving skilled labor supplies. While a 1 per cent increase in skilled labor supply $(\overset{*}{S})$ would have fostered a 1.4 per cent reduction in wage inequality in 1821 $(\overset{*}{q} - \overset{*}{w} = -1.4272)$, the same increase in skills would have fostered a 1.8 per cent reduction in 1891 $(\overset{*}{q} - \overset{*}{w} = -1.8358)$. This is another useful finding, especially given that Britain achieved considerably higher rates of skilled labor force growth later in the century than early.

The implications of the changing impact multipliers across the nineteenth century are very important. If exogenous events associated with early industrialization tend to breed inequality, then the 1821 British economy was especially vulnerable to those events. Similarly, if technological advance, world market conditions and accumulation were all tending to favor industrialization and export growth early in the century, the British economy in 1821 was especially ripe for those forces to have had a massive impact. Most of the differences in the impact multipliers between 1821 and 1891 hinge quite simply on the relative size of the farm sector, its relatively low labor productivity and its relatively high unskilled labor intensity.

Table 10.4 *The sources of British inequality trends, 1861–1911*

Due to:	Growth in real factor incomes				Changes in the pay gap	Changes in factor shares Unskilled wages in national income	Unskilled wages in total wages
	$\overset{*}{w} - \overset{*}{P}_{\text{COL}}$	$\overset{*}{i} \cong \overset{*}{r} - \overset{*}{P}_{\text{COL}}$	$\overset{*}{q} - \overset{*}{P}_{\text{COL}}$	$\overset{*}{d} - \overset{*}{P}_{\text{COL}}$	$\overset{*}{q} - \overset{*}{w}$	$d\theta_L$	$d\theta_w$
Total factor productivity growth:							
All	0.398	0.434	0.096	1.299	−0.302	0.036	0.058
$\overset{*}{T}_A$	0.110	0.153	−0.720	2.234	−0.830	0.068	0.159
$\overset{*}{T}_M$	0.115	0.111	0.568	−1.028	0.453	−0.028	−0.087
$\overset{*}{T}_C$	0.166	0.158	0.165	0.160	−0.001	0.000	0.000
$\overset{*}{T}_B$	0.008	0.012	0.082	−0.068	0.074	−0.005	−0.014
Prices:							
All	0.022	0.070	0.373	−0.818	0.351	−0.013	−0.067
$\overset{*}{P}_A$	−0.011	0.021	0.505	−1.278	0.515	−0.044	−0.099
$\overset{*}{P}_M$	−0.013	−0.037	−0.433	1.022	−0.420	0.027	0.081
$\overset{*}{P}_F$	0.046	0.086	0.302	−0.562	0.256	0.005	−0.049

Factor stocks:

All	0.675	−0.681	0.084	−0.643	−0.591	−0.001	−0.048
*$\hat{y}$	0.008	0.011	−0.049	−0.027	−0.057	0.005	0.011
*K	0.810	−1.554	2.149	0.050	1.339	−0.013	−0.256
*L	−0.664	0.405	0.658	0.930	1.323	−0.041	−0.081
**S	0.513	0.469	−2.681	−1.590	−3.194	0.048	0.279
$P\overset{*}{o}p$	0.009	−0.011	0.007	−0.006	−0.001	0.001	0.000
Residual	−0.014	0.018	−0.012	0.009	0.002	−0.001	0.000
Total predicted	1.081	−0.159	0.541	−0.153	−0.540	0.021	−0.057
Total actual	1.26	−0.13	0.29	0.03	−0.97	n.a.	n.a.

Source: See text.

(4) The sources of inequality

1861–1911
What were the underlying forces leveling British earnings and incomes in the late nineteenth century?

Table 10.4 supplies an accounting using the exogenous rates of total factor productivity growth, price changes, and factor stock trends estimated for 1861–1911 in Appendix E. These exogenous forces confirm conventional wisdom: the relative price of agricultural products fell with the invasion of grains from the New World; total factor productivity growth in industry was sufficiently slow (reflecting the late nineteenth-century retardation and manufacturing's 'failure') that *balanced* technological advance was a characteristic of the period as a whole; labor force growth was quite a bit below the peak rates achieved earlier in the century as Britain passed through her demographic transition; skills growth was more rapid, having risen above the lower levels obtained early in the century; and capital formation rates were modest, much like those achieved in the first half of the century. When these forces are combined with the 1891 impact multipliers in Table 10.1, we emerge in Table 10.4 with the sources of the late nineteenth-century inequality trends.

The rise in common labor's real wage (1.081 per cent per annum, predicted) appears to be explained primarily by factor supply forces (0.675 per cent per annum), the rise in skills and capital per laborer doing all the work. Balanced total factor productivity growth had a somewhat smaller influence (0.398 per cent per annum), and world market conditions contributed nothing at all. The latter suggests that the cost-of-living gains from the import of cheaper foodstuffs served to balance the nominal wage losses as unskilled-labor-intensive agriculture collapsed in the face of foreign competition.

Real wages for skilled workers rose at a much slower rate (0.541 per cent per annum predicted), and the sources were more complex. Here, world market conditions were more favorable (0.373 per cent per annum) because the growth in skill-intensive export staples was fostered, tending to raise nominal skilled wages, to which were added the cost-of-living benefits from cheaper food. On the other hand, the combined influence of all factor supply forces had a trivial influence on skilled workers' incomes (0.084 per cent per annum): the negative impact from the rapid expansion in skills (−2.681 per cent per annum) served to offset the positive impact of capital accumulation (2.149 per cent per annum) and labor force growth (0.658 per cent per annum). The relatively balanced productivity advance favored the unskilled worker far more than the skilled worker (0.398 versus 0.096 per cent per annum).

As a result, the model predicts a collapse in pay ratios and skill differentials (−0.54 per cent per annum). The source of the leveling in pay across skills is partly the result of balanced technological progress (−0.302 per cent per annum), and partly the result of factor supply growth (−0.591 per cent per annum), the latter dominated by skills growth. World market conditions

– the fall in the relative price of agricultural products – served to offset these effects (0.351 per cent per annum). The rise in unskilled labor's share in national income is, according to the model, explained entirely by the more balanced productivity advance.

The real rate of return to capital (or the rate of return on equity) drifted down slowly over the period ($\overset{*}{r} - \overset{*}{P}_{COL}$, −0.159 per cent per annum predicted). This relative stability was due to the fact that diminishing returns to capital (−1.554 per cent per annum) were offset by the combined influence of labor force growth (0.405 per cent per annum), skills growth (0.469 per cent per annum), productivity advance (0.434 per cent per annum), and world market conditions (0.070 per cent per annum). Thus, productivity advance by itself was certainly not enough to offset diminishing returns as capital per worker rose across the late nineteenth century. It required the critical support of skills accumulation and, to a lesser extent, favorable world market conditions.

Finally, the model predicts the fall in land rents per acre. The fall in real rents (−0.153 per cent per annum) is accounted for almost entirely by world market conditions (−0.818 per cent per annum) and the rise in skills per worker ($\overset{*}{S}$ and $\overset{*}{L}$, −0.66 per cent per annum), a result that productivity advance in agriculture could not forestall.

1821–61

What explains rising inequality from Waterloo to mid-century?

Table 10.5 offers an assessment using the total factor productivity growth rates, price changes and factor stock trends estimated for 1821–61 in Appendix E. These estimates are more tentative than those for 1861–1911, but their qualitative attributes certainly conform to conventional wisdom: total factor productivity growth in manufacturing was far more rapid than in the late nineteenth century, producing rates of technological advance that were much more unbalanced across sectors; the relative price of manufactures fell, in sharp contrast with the late nineteenth century; the rate of labor force growth was higher; capital accumulation rates were about the same; and skill augmentation rates were more modest. These forces are then combined with the 1821 impact multipliers in Table 10.2 to produce the sources of early nineteenth-century inequality trends in Table 10.5.

The rise in common labor's real wage (0.923 per cent per annum predicted) is explained almost entirely by technological forces (1.137 per cent per annum), and the lion's share of that influence can be traced to rapid total factor productivity growth in manufacturing (1.024 per cent per annum). While factor stock growth adds to the productivity effect (0.525 per cent per annum), it is not conventional capital-deepening alone that accounts for that result. That is, capital-deepening by itself was insufficient to augment real wages ($\overset{*}{K}$ and $\overset{*}{L}$ effects = −0.137); so was skill-deepening by itself ($\overset{*}{S}$ and $\overset{*}{L}$ effects = −0.483); but together, capital-cum-skills-deepening ($\overset{*}{K}$, $\overset{*}{S}$ and $\overset{*}{L}$ effects = 0.492) *did* serve to raise real unskilled wages. These capital-cum-skills-deepening forces were completely offset by

Table 10.5 The sources of British inequality trends, 1821–1861

Due to:	Growth in real factor incomes				Changes in the pay gap	Changes in factor shares	
	$\overset{*}{w} - P_{COL}$	$i \cong \overset{*}{r} - P_{COL}$	$\overset{*}{q} - P_{COL}$	$\overset{*}{d} - P_{COL}$	$\overset{*}{q} - \overset{*}{w}$	Unskilled wages in national income $d\theta_L$	Unskilled wages in total wages $d\theta_w$
Total factor productivity growth:							
All	1.137	−0.104	3.577	−2.479	2.440	0.043	−0.431
$\overset{*}{T}_A$	−0.040	0.317	−0.651	0.971	−0.611	−0.005	0.108
$\overset{*}{T}_M$	1.024	−0.541	4.024	−3.511	3.001	0.047	−0.530
$\overset{*}{T}_C$	0.139	0.127	0.117	0.117	−0.022	0.003	0.004
$\overset{*}{T}_B$	0.015	−0.006	0.086	−0.056	0.072	−0.001	−0.013
Prices:							
All	−0.639	0.826	−3.689	3.684	−3.050	−0.027	0.539
$\overset{*}{P}_A$	0.137	−0.238	0.962	−0.984	0.825	−0.005	−0.146
$\overset{*}{P}_M$	−0.897	1.130	−5.184	5.104	−4.286	−0.042	0.758
$\overset{*}{P}_F$	0.121	−0.066	0.532	−0.437	0.411	0.020	−0.073

Factor stocks:							
All	0.525	−1.230	1.678	0.479	1.153	0.021	−0.214
*J	−0.001	0.008	−0.015	−0.007	−0.014	0.000	0.003
*K	0.975	−1.995	2.437	0.549	1.462	0.011	−0.258
*L	−1.112	0.766	0.759	1.147	1.871	−0.092	−0.083
*S	0.629	0.005	−1.455	−1.162	−2.084	0.093	0.110
Pop*	0.034	−0.013	−0.048	−0.047	−0.081	0.009	0.014
Residual	−0.100	0.038	0.140	0.139	0.239	−0.027	−0.008
Total predicted	0.923	−0.470	1.706	1.823	0.782	0.010	−0.114
Total actual	0.68	n.a.	1.65	1.33	0.97	n.a.	−0.27

Source: See text.

world market conditions (-0.639 per cent per annum), with the decline in manufacture's prices (-0.897 per cent per annum) doing all the work.[2]

Real wages for skilled workers rose at a much faster rate (1.706 per cent per annum predicted), and once again unbalanced productivity advance was the key contributing force, with total factor productivity growth in manufacturing doing all the work (4.024 per cent per annum). Factor stock changes reinforced the productivity effects (1.678 per cent per annum), but they were strongly offset by world market conditions (-3.689 per cent per annum).

The net effect, of course, was to generate wage stretching and a rise in pay ratios (0.782 per cent per annum predicted). Unbalanced productivity advance was the major force producing this rise in earnings inequality (2.440 per cent per annum), with factor stock growth having about half the positive impact (1.153 per cent per annum), and world market conditions serving as a potent offset (-3.050 per cent per annum).

The model predicts a rapid rise in real land rents over the four decades following 1821 (1.823 per cent per annum), and the sources of the boom appear to be conventional. Unbalanced productivity advance in manufacturing reinforced comparative advantages there, inducing the relative demise of agriculture, and a downward pressure on rents was one consequence (-2.479 per cent per annum). These productivity forces, however, were fully offset by others more favorable to the landlord. World market conditions and the Corn Laws strongly favored the farm sector, thus pushing land rents upwards (3.684 per cent per annum). Factor stock growth also favored land rents (0.479 per cent per annum), but for reasons that require some clarification. Capital and unskilled labor were both used in agriculture, so their expansion served to favor rents (0.549 and 1.147 per cent per annum, respectively). Skills, however, were not used in farming, so their accumulation served to expand non-farm sectors, forces that tended to cause a contraction in agriculture, a declining demand for relatively fixed land stocks and thus a fall in rents (-1.162 per cent per annum). In short, from 1821 to 1861, economic forces served to raise British land rents sharply, in spite·of the offsetting forces of technological progress associated with the industrial revolution *per se*. Nevertheless, the boom in land rents, when combined with an almost stable land stock, was not enough to forestall the decline in the rental share in national income.

The most surprising result involves the real rate of return to capital, or the rate of return on equity. While Chapter 9 offered some scraps of information confirming a decline, there is little hard evidence to verify the magnitude of the decline implied by the model (-0.470 per cent per annum). If that prediction approximates reality, how are we to explain it? Certainly the factor stock effect is hardly surprising (-1.230 per cent per annum) to the extent that capital accumulation exceeded labor force growth. This, after all, is a conventional manifestation of diminishing returns. What *is* surprising, at least at first glance, is that world market conditions were tending to *raise*, and technological changes *lower*, the return to equity. That is, the decline in P_M had a *positive* impact (1.130 per cent per annum), while the rise in T_M had a *negative* impact (-0.541 per cent per annum), a result puzzling only if one believes that manufacturing was more capital intensive than agriculture early in the century. In fact, Appendix D and the impact multipliers in Table 10.2 show that it was not! In contrast with the late nineteenth century, and compared with manufacturing, agriculture was relatively capital intensive in the early nineteenth century. With that added knowledge, these results now make perfect sense.

(5) Accounting for the Kuznets curve in earnings inequality

The two previous sections have shown that the model is quite capable of accounting for the sources of earnings inequality and factor price trends across the nineteenth century. In particular, the model identified the forces accounting for the surge in pay differentials by skill and for rising earnings inequality from 1821 to 1861. The model also identified the forces contributing to the leveling from 1861 to 1911. These two epochs of inequality experience constitute the nineteenth-century Kuznets curve, the turning point appearing in mid-century. While I have offered a detailed accounting of the sources of these inequality trends within each epoch, the underlying morals might be clearer if I list the changing economic and demographic conditions that account for the turning point itself.

First, consider the four candidates for the 'key driving forces' summarized in Table 10.6: unbalanced technological advance, world market conditions, the rate of capital-deepening and the rate of skills-deepening. It appears that the rate of capital-deepening can be dismissed right at the start since it was roughly stable across the century. The rate of skills-deepening, in contrast, accelerated sharply between these two epochs, offering one potential explanation for the Kuznets curve. Unbalanced productivity advance offers another potential explanation. While the early nineteenth century reveals the classic outlines of 'leading' technological progress in industry and 'lagging' technological progress in agriculture, the late nineteenth century

Table 10.6   *Four potential forces driving the Kuznets curve*

| | Per annum rates of change | | |
| | Early 19th century (1821–61) | Late 19th century (1861–1911) | Change |
Key driving force	(1)	(2)	(2) − (1)
Unbalanced technological advance $(\overset{*}{T}_M - \overset{*}{T}_A)$	+0.75	−0.34	−1.09
World market conditions $(\overset{*}{P}_M - \theta_{FM}\overset{*}{P}_F - \overset{*}{P}_A)$	−0.94	+0.28	−1.22
Rate of capital-deepening $(\overset{*}{K} - \overset{*}{L})$	+1.10	+1.07	−0.03
Rate of skills-deepening $(\overset{*}{S} - \overset{*}{L})$	+0.06	+0.84	+0.78

Sources: Appendix Tables E.1, E.2 and D.3.

Table 10.7   *Explaining the Kuznets curve in earnings inequality: changes between 1821–61 and 1861–1911*

| | Real wages | | Pay gap | Changes in unskilled labor share in total wages |
| | Unskilled workers | Skilled workers | | |
Decomposition	$d(\overset{*}{w} - \overset{*}{P}_{COL})$	$d(\overset{*}{q} - \overset{*}{P}_{COL})$	$d(\overset{*}{q} - \overset{*}{w})$	$d(d\theta_w)$
Actual change	0.58	−1.36	−1.94	n.a.
Predicted change, of which due to:	0.158	−1.165	−1.322	0.057
Productivity:	−0.739	−3.481	−2.742	0.489
$\overset{*}{T}_A$	0.150	−0.069	−0.219	0.051
$\overset{*}{T}_M$	−0.909	−3.456	−2.548	0.443
$\overset{*}{T}_C$	0.027	0.048	0.021	−0.004
$\overset{*}{T}_B$	−0.007	−0.004	0.002	−0.001
$(\overset{*}{T}_A + \overset{*}{T}_M)$	(−0.759)	(−3.525)	(−2.767)	(0.494)
Prices:	0.661	4.062	3.401	−0.606
$\overset{*}{P}_A$	−0.148	−0.457	−0.310	0.047
$\overset{*}{P}_M$	0.884	4.751	3.866	−0.677
$\overset{*}{P}_F$	−0.075	−0.230	−0.155	0.024
Factors:	0.150	−1.594	−1.744	0.166
$\overset{*}{\jmath}$	0.009	−0.034	−0.043	0.008
$\overset{*}{K}$	−0.165	−0.288	−0.123	0.002
$\overset{*}{L}$	0.448	−0.101	−0.548	0.002
$\overset{*}{S}$	−0.116	−1.226	−1.110	0.169
$\overset{*}{Pop}$	−0.025	0.055	0.080	−0.014
$(\overset{*}{K} + \overset{*}{L})$	(0.283)	(−0.389)	(−0.671)	(0.004)
$(\overset{*}{S} + \overset{*}{L})$	(0.332)	(−1.327)	(−1.658)	(0.171)
Residual forces	0.086	−0.152	−0.237	0.008

Sources: Tables 10.4 and 10.5. See text.

reveals just the opposite. Since we now know that unbalanced sectoral total factor productivity growth should have fostered inequality, the changing character of technological progress offers another potential explanation of the nineteenth-century British Kuznets curve. Finally, trends in world market conditions switched dramatically between the two epochs. While the relative (net value added) price of manufactures declined sharply early in the century, it *rose* late in the century, a relative price trend that in large measure reflected the invasion of British markets by New World grains. The

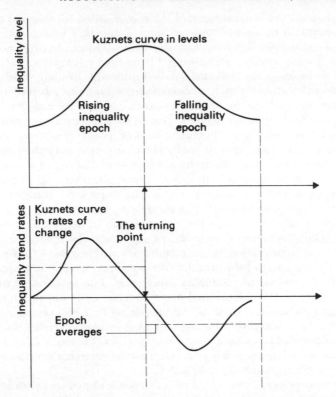

Figure 10.1   *The stylized Kuznets curve in levels and rates of change*

relative rise in the net value added price of manufactures was also aided by the accelerating decline in the relative price of imported raw materials. Based on what we now know, this switch in world market conditions should have served to offset the other forces driving the Kuznets curve across the century: in the absence of this change in trending world market conditions, Britain would have traced out a far more dramatic Kuznets curve than in fact was the case.

Table 10.7 focuses on three key aspects of inequality: the real wage itself, the skilled wage differential and unskilled labor's share in total earnings. The table reports *changes* in average inequality trends between the two epochs, following the lower panel in Figure 10.1. For example, $d(\overset{*}{q} - \overset{*}{w})$ computes the difference between pay ratio growth experience in 1861–1911 and 1821–61, the large negative number (-1.94 actual, -1.322 predicted) reflecting the mid-century watershed with rising and falling pay ratios on either side. Similarly, $d(d\theta_w)$ reports the switch in the behavior of unskilled labor's share in total earnings from the very sharp declines witnessed prior to the turning point. And the positive entry for $d(\overset{*}{w} - \overset{*}{P}_{COL}) - 0.158$ predicted – simply documents the trend acceleration in the per annum increase in unskilled labor's real wage.

What caused the Kuznets curve? What accounted for the mid-century turning point? The answers emerge from Table 10.7 with unambiguous clarity. Productivity advance was the central force driving inequality trends, a finding that has also emerged from research Peter Lindert and I recently completed on America (Williamson and Lindert, 1980). The switch from relatively rapid, unbalanced productivity advance favoring manufacturing early in the century to slower, more balanced productivity advance late in the century would appear to have accounted for most of the Kuznets curve and the mid-century turning point. This was *not* true, however, of real wage growth itself. Here, the drift over the century to slower, more balanced productivity advance served to retard growth in the common worker's standard of living. Thus, the rate and character of productivity advance had quite a different impact on common labor's *absolute* income gains than it did on his *relative* gains.

Second in importance was the accumulation of skills and capital per worker. While the acceleration in skills-cum-capital-deepening jointly contributed to an acceleration in common labor's real income – thus partially offsetting the impact of the productivity slowdown – separately each had a very different impact on inequality experience. The acceleration in skills-deepening across the century had more than twice the impact on pay gap trends than did conventional capital-deepening (-1.658 versus -0.671); the acceleration in skills-deepening had an even bigger relative impact on trends in unskilled labor's share in total wages (0.171 versus 0.004). In other words, the switch in the mode of accumulation – from conventional capital to skills – explains much of the British Kuznets curve.

Exogenous prices, commercial policy and world market conditions also played a critical role. The switch late in the century from rising to falling relative agricultural prices served to cause real wage growth to accelerate. In fact, the invasion of grains from the New World seems to account for almost all of the trend acceleration in common labor's real wages, which is a good thing since otherwise the productivity slowdown would have caused a late nineteenth-century retardation in real wage growth. World market conditions also served to generate earnings inequality, but since these price effects failed to dominate, earnings inequality declined, as we have seen.

Two morals emerge. First, it is very important to distinguish between the worker's *absolute* performance – which relates to standard-of-living debates – and his *relative* performance – which relates to inequality debates. Second, unbalanced productivity advance (a derived factor demand influence) and skills per worker growth (a factor supply influence) are at the heart of British earnings inequality trends across the nineteenth century.

(6) Reprise

One can view inequality and industrialization as disequilibrium phases through which all capitalist countries must pass as they emerge from a backward agrarian past. While the inequality that typically accompanies early experience with the industrial revolution has been documented for many contemporary Third World countries, one was never really sure about nineteenth-century capitalist development, in spite of the allegations by classical economists and other contemporaries of that time. Nor was one really sure how much of the alleged early inequality experience might have been purely demographic – associated with the demographic transition that swelled the ranks of the poor. It appears that America and Britain both experienced the Kuznets curve of first rising, then falling, inequality. What was not anticipated by Marx, Ricardo, Malthus and others, however, was that *earnings inequality* may have been the most systematic and striking attribute of the Kuznets curve. In any case, rarely has one been offered anything but speculations on the underlying sources of that curious inequality experience.

The model constructed in Chapter 8 and tested successfully in Chapter 9 offers a tool for decomposing the Kuznets curve into sharply defined component parts. The component parts are many, since, after all, the Kuznets curve is a complex social event. But one component part stands out as the key driving force: unbalanced productivity advance appears to have driven both industrialization and inequality experience across the nineteenth century. An acceleration in the rate of skills-deepening also played an important supporting part. Clearly, the wage gaps and earnings inequality set in motion by unbalanced productivity advance served to offer great and increasing incentive to investment in human capital. However, the slow and inelastic response of skills per worker made it possible for inequality to persist for many decades before the disequilibrium was rectified and earnings inequality settled back down. In contrast, capital-deepening in the conventional sense made no contribution at all to the Kuznets curve for the simple reason that the conventional capital–labor ratio grew at roughly the same rate on either side of the Kuznets curve. There is another, more provocative, way of stating this finding: demographic forces 'from below' played no role in accounting for British inequality trends in the nineteenth century since it appears that the rate of conventional capital accumulation fully accommodated any quickening or retardation in labor force growth induced by previous demographic events. Finally, world market conditions and British commercial policy served to mute the Kuznets curve. During the inequality surge up to mid-century, relative price trends for internationally traded commodities moved in a direction that partially offset the inequality forces set in motion by the industrial revolution. During the income leveling following the mid-century turning point, relative price trends served to inhibit the leveling. In short, the British Kuznets curve would have been far more pronounced had not relative prices of internationally traded commodities behaved as they did.

These morals hold for an economy enjoying the benefits of Victorian growth under *Pax Britannica*. What about a wartime economy struggling simultaneously with the resource requirements of the French Wars and of the industrial revolution during its earlier years, 1780 to the 1820s?

160   DID BRITISH CAPITALISM BREED INEQUALITY?

Notes

1 For simplicity, I have used the notation $\overset{*}{T_j}$ in Table 10.1 and in the tables following. The reader lingering over technical detail will have noted that Table 8.1 lists factor-saving effects among the exogenous variables, π_i, influences that clearly should be added to the $\overset{*}{T_j}$ effects. In fact, Table 10.1 and all others following include the 'total' effects of technological change, factor-saving too.

2 Some readers may argue that the model overstates the positive role of productivity advance and the negative role of 'world market conditions'. Those who believe that Britain faced a significantly downward sloping world demand for manufactures in general, and for cotton textiles in particular, will want to attribute some of the decline in P_M to supply expansion in industry due to $\overset{*}{K}$, $\overset{*}{S}$ and $\overset{*}{T_M}$. That position would do very little to change the interpretation in the text since the 'factor stock effects' and the 'productivity effects' would both be reduced. So too would the negative influence of world market conditions, since some of the decline in P_M would now be induced rather than fully exogenous. This argument applies throughout this chapter.

11

Why Was British Growth so Slow Before the 1820s?

(1) The problem: development during wartime

Watersheds, turning points and trend acceleration

The quantitative dimensions of the classic British industrial revolution are understood far better now than a century ago when debate over the causes and consequences of that social event began to heat up. Charles Feinstein (1978a) has pioneered estimates of accumulation rates from 1760 to 1860, and Tony Wrigley and Roger Schofield (1981) have offered a brilliant reconstruction of demographic events over the same period. The early national income estimates of Phyllis Deane and Arthur Cole (1962) have been slowly sharpened by a steady revisionist stream, most recently augmented by Nick Crafts (1976, 1980, 1983), Knick Harley (1982), and Peter Lindert and myself (Lindert and Williamson, 1982, 1983a). Informed guesses on the rate of total factor productivity growth are now available (Feinstein, 1976, p. 86; Floud and McCloskey, 1981, Chs 1 and 6; Crafts, 1983, p. 196), and, as we have seen in Chapter 2, even trends in workers' living standards have now been nailed down securely.

What does all this new evidence suggest? Without a doubt, the evidence confirms what has come to be called 'trend acceleration'. Somewhere around the 1820s Britain passed through a secular turning point. National income growth rates were much lower before than after: for example, Harley (1982, p. 286) estimates the growth in per capita income at 0.33 per cent per annum 1770–1815 and 0.86 per cent per annum 1815–41, while aggregate income growth rose from 1.31 to 2.33 per cent per annum. This growth rate doubling is repeated in the industrial production indices, which grew at 1.5 or 1.6 per cent per annum before 1815 and at 3.0 or 3.2 per cent per annum afterwards (Harley, 1982, p. 276, Divisia Index). Feinstein's capital formation rate also drifts upward during the period: in constant prices, the share of gross domestic investment in national income rose from about 9 per cent in the 1760s to almost 14 per cent in the 1850s (Table 11.3, col. 10); the rate of capital accumulation rose from 1 per cent per annum 1761–1800 to 1.7 per cent per annum 1801–60 (Feinstein, 1978a, p. 86); the capital per worker growth rate rose from 0.11 per cent per annum 1761–1830 to 0.88 per cent per annum 1830–60 (Feinstein, 1978a, p. 84).[1] As far as the standard of living is concerned, the turning point is even more dramatic: the adult male, blue-collar, average real wage failed to increase at all between 1755 and 1819, but then soared at the rate of 1.85 per cent per annum 1819–51 (Lindert and Williamson, 1983a, Table 5, p. 13; Table 2.8 above, 'all blue-collar' workers).

Some paradoxes

Trend acceleration there was, but British growth performance prior to the 1820s was modest at best. While one must be cautious with comparative history, per capita income growth of 0.33 per cent per annum is hardly very impressive by the standards of the many industrial revolutions that were to follow. Even during productivity slowdown, OPEC fuel-crunch, Malthusian burdens, and capital scarcity abroad, the Third World managed per capita income growth rates around 3.2 per cent per annum in the 1970s (IBRD, 1980, p. 372), ten times that of Britain prior to the 1820s!

In fact, British growth prior to the 1820s presents five puzzling paradoxes, some of which I have mentioned already, others of which I have not, and still others of which are derivatives.

- *Paradox 1:* there is no evidence of standard-of-living improvement among the working classes up to about 1820. This stability in the real wage during the early industrial revolution encouraged the English economist to construct what have come to be known as labor surplus models. These classical models are still popular today in the Third World (e.g. W. Arthur Lewis, 1954).
- *Paradox 2:* per capita income growth was very slow prior to the 1820s.
- *Paradox 3:* the rate of industrialization was unimpressive up to the 1820s. Industrial output grew at 1.5 or 1.6 per cent per annum, a rate that exceeded national income growth only modestly.
- *Paradox 4:* Britain was a low saver during the early industrial revolution. A gross domestic saving share of 9 or 10 per cent is certainly low compared with the contemporary Third World average of 20.1 per cent in 1977 (IBRD, 1980, p. 421), but it is also low by the standards of Meiji Japan (Kelley and Williamson, 1974, p. 233, 14.8 per cent, 1910–16) and late nineteenth-century America (Williamson, 1979c, p. 233, 28 per cent, 1890–1905). As a result, the rate of capital accumulation was so modest that hardly any capital-deepening took place at all.
- *Paradox 5:* the absence of capital-deepening has encouraged the speculation that the new technologies sweeping England were capital saving (von Tunzlemann, in Floud and McCloskey, 1981, Ch. 8), a paradoxical finding given the long historiography on labor saving in nineteenth-century America and the even longer empirical attention to the problem in the contemporary Third World.

Why was British growth so slow during those six decades prior to the 1820s? One answer is that the conventional dating of the first industrial revolution is just plain wrong. Another answer, however, is that Britain tried to do two things at once – industrialize *and* fight expensive wars – and she simply did not have the resources to do both effectively.

Can we factor out the wars?

During the sixty years following 1760, Britain was at war for thirty-six. Even more striking, in the three decades following the late 1780s Britain went from a peacetime economy to a level of wartime commitment that had no parallel until World War I. The war mobilized a good share of the civilian labor force – the unskilled labor force in particular – suggesting that labor scarcity might have been created in the civilian economy. The war debt grew to enormous size, suggesting that civilian capital accumulation might have been suppressed by crowding out. Tax revenues surged to become a fifth of national income (Table 11.2, col. 2), implying that post-fisc real private incomes were eroded. Meanwhile, hostilities, blockades and embargoes diminished international trade, inflating the relative prices of agricultural and raw material importables in the home market, while lowering the price of manufactured exportables deflected from world markets. Surely these war-related events had a profound impact on the rate and character of British growth while she struggled to become the Workshop of the World.

The coincidence of war with early industrialization has troubled economic historians ever since Britain began her experiment with modern economic growth. How much of the stability in real wages, the modest rate of industrialization, and the slow overall growth up to the 1820s can be explained by the wars, how much by Malthusian pressures of the demographic transition, and how much by forces endogenous to the industrial revolution itself?

Certainly there has been no shortage of speculation on these issues. While Hartwell and Engerman (1975, p. 193) feel that it still is not known 'what would have happened to living standards if there had been no wars', Ashton (1949, pp. 22–3) thought that the wars 'almost certainly worsened the economic status of labor'. Indeed, the view that wars can help account for real wage stability in early industrialization has been emulated in the literature on Meiji Japan:

> Professor Ashton . . . once suggested that the misery and unrest which attended the Industrial Revolution . . . were not so much the product of the factory system as of the Napoleonic Wars. Under more peaceful conditions it would have been far easier to raise living standards as productivity increased . . . Certainly this has been true of Japan. (Lockwood, 1954, p. 578)

Even the social historian has joined the ranks of the revisionists who find war rather than the emerging industrial revolution to have been the dominant factor in English life from the early 1790s to the early 1820s (Emsley, 1979).

Table 11.1 Civilian investment in reproducible capital and national income per annum, Great Britain, 1761–1860: based on Feinstein, Deane and Cole

	(1)	(2)	(3)	(4)	(5)	(6)	(7)	(8)	(9)	(10)
	National income		Investment and 'saving', current prices			Investment and 'saving', 1851–61 prices			Implicit price deflators (1851–60 = 1.0)	
	Current prices	Constant 1851–61 prices	Gross domestic fixed capital formation	Gross domestic capital formation	Gross domestic saving in reproducible capital	Gross domestic fixed capital formation	Gross domestic capital formation	Gross domestic saving in reproducible capital	P_I	P_Y
Decade	£m.	£m.	£m.	£m.	£m.	£m.	£m.	£m.		
1761–1770	74.60	89.55	3.68	4.68	5.18	6.64	7.64	8.14	0.554	0.833
1771–1780	88.75	96.04	3.99	5.99	6.49	7.05	9.05	10.05	0.566	0.924
1781–1790	107.10	110.18	6.80	8.80	10.30	11.12	13.12	14.62	0.612	0.972
1791–1800	174.25	139.73	11.41	14.91	16.41	14.31	17.31	18.81	0.797	1.247
1801–1810	266.55	172.07	20.38	21.88	18.88	16.57	17.57	15.57	1.230	1.549
1811–1820	296.05	212.22	26.54	29.54	37.04	20.51	22.51	27.51	1.294	1.395
1821–1830	315.50	291.58	31.33	35.83	44.33	28.29	32.29	39.79	1.107	1.082
1831–1840	396.15	396.94	40.48	43.98	48.48	38.59	42.09	46.59	1.049	0.998
1841–1850	487.80	495.73	50.47	54.97	61.47	49.43	54.43	60.93	1.021	0.984
1851–1860	595.65	595.65	57.99	61.49	81.49	57.99	61.49	81.49	1.000	1.000

Sources: Cols (1) and (2) – mid-decade averages, based on Deane and Cole (1962, Tables 19 and 37), where Table 19 is converted into current prices by applying Gilboy's price index reported in Mathias and O'Brien (1976, p. 605), and linking on 1801; Table 37 is converted into constant prices by applying Deane and Cole's (1962, Table 72, p. 282) implicit national product price deflator, which is, in fact, the Rousseaux index.

Cols (3) and (6) – decade averages, in Feinstein (1978a, Tables 6 and 7, pp. 40–1).

Cols (4) and (7) – cols (3) and (5) plus stockbuilding, in Feinstein (1978a, Table 16, p. 69).

Cols (5) and (8) – cols (4) and (7) plus net investment abroad, in Feinstein (1978a, Table 16, p. 69).

Col. (9) = col. (3) ÷ col. (6).

Col. (10) = col. (1) ÷ col. (2).

Table 11.2 *The tax burden in Great Britain, 1761–1860*

Decade	(1) Share of direct taxes in total tax revenues ϕ_t	(2) Share of net tax revenue in national income	(3) Share of direct taxes in national income
1761–1770	0.208	0.1278	0.0265
1771–1780	0.188	0.1294	0.0243
1781–1790	0.184	0.1404	0.0258
1791–1800	0.168	0.1392	0.0233
1801–1810	0.235	0.1800	0.0423
1811–1820	0.258	0.2024	0.0522
1821–1830	0.136	0.1651	0.0224
1831–1840	0.088	0.1220	0.0107
1841–1850	0.150	0.1023	0.0153
1851–1860	0.199	0.0968	0.0192

Sources: Col. (1) – calculated from Mitchell and Deane (1962, pp. 387–8, 392–3), where taxes on income and wealth include land and assessed taxes, property and income taxes. Central government only.
Col. (2) – takes current price national income from Table 11.1, col. 1. Net tax revenues for 1760–1800 are from Mathias and O'Brien (1976, Table 2, p. 605), five-year averages, central government only, and for Great Britain. For 1801–61, the UK gross tax revenues in Mitchell and Deane (1962, pp. 392–3) are adjusted downwards to get estimated net tax revenues for Great Britain, and refer to five-year averages.
Col. (3) = col. (1) × col. (2).

What is true of living standards may also be true of growth and industrialization. Was industrialization fostered by wartime final demand requirements (a position that has also been popular in accounting for American nineteenth-century industrialization following the Civil War and Japanese industrialization from the 1880s onward)? Or was it choked off by the sharp curtailment of trade and British inability to exploit international markets for her export staples? Which civilian expenditures suffered most from the rise in military needs – investment or consumption? Did the rate of capital formation slow down?

Until the influence of the wars have been sorted out for this period of early industrialization, surely the question 'did capitalism breed inequality?' cannot be answered. Chapter 2 showed that the growth in living standards passed through a turning point in the 1820s, being negligible before and fast thereafter. Chapter 3 established that earnings inequality surged upwards following the 1810s, after a long period of relative stability from the 1760s to the end of the Napoleonic Era. Chapter 4 suggested that even income inequality may have been deflected from its long-run Kuznets curve by the war. Each of these inequality issues will be confronted in Chapter 12, but only after I have identified whether the 1760–1820 epoch is a 'peculiar' historical example of the industrial revolution; and the central peculiarity lies with the question: why was British growth so slow before the 1820s?

This chapter offers some suggestions about how the wars might be factored out of the industrial revolution. Section 2 confronts the accumulation issue, leaning heavily on the crowding-out influence of the war debt. Section 3 offers some counterfactual conjectures on what civilian accumulation might have been like in the absence of war. Section 4 discusses some of the shortcomings underlying such counterfactual conjectures, but I am, nevertheless, confident of the chapter's main conclusion: most of Britain's slow growth prior to the 1820s seems to have been due to the impact of the wars on accumulation. Chapter 12 will use that finding to explore some implications for inequality, industrialization and the standard of living.

(2) War debt: crowding out civilian capital accumulation

Wasn't saving a constraint on British growth?
What is one to make of such evidence of 'modest' accumulation[2] during most of the first industrial revolution? Was it choked off by a saving constraint? Or was it simply that technological progress was both slow and capital saving, thus producing only modest growth in investment demand? The two views are offered in Figure 11.1, where the rate of return or interest rate (r) is on the vertical axis and the investment share in GNP (I/Y) is on the horizontal axis (see Williamson, 1979c; Williamson and Lindert, 1980, Ch. 12). To simplify, assume for the moment price stability, so that the nominal and the real interest rate are the same. If you believe – as most neo-Keynesians did in the 1950s and early 1960s – that investment demand was doing all the work, then you will feel most comfortable with the elastic saving function characterization ($\hat{S}$), along which investment demand shifts while saving responds passively. If you believe – as most neoclassicists in the 1980s do – that saving was an active constraint, then you will find the upward-sloping saving functions more to your liking. Here, investment demand and saving supply *both* play a role. Thus, the modest rise in the investment ratio from, say, 1760 ($t = 0$) to 1815 ($t = 1$, and under actual wartime conditions 'W') is driven both by the shift to S_1^W and by the shift to I_1^D. If you also believe that the rise in the war debt tended to compete with civilian accumulation, then S_1^W would be somewhere to the left of S_1^P, the counterfactual peacetime case where the war debt was kept constant. Clearly, the war debt helps explain the modest rate of accumulation up to 1815 if you believe that the saving function was inelastic. The war debt explains none of the modest rate of accumulation if, instead, you believe the function to have been elastic. Which belief dominates the literature on the British industrial revolution? My reading of Francois Crouzet's *Capital Formation in the Industrial Revolution* is that the active-investment-demand–passive-saving belief dominated as late as 1972.

While contemporaries living in or shortly after the French Wars had some strong hunches about forgone civilian accumulation and the cost of the wars, most modern economic historians seem to have forgotten these neoclassical messages from the past. Perhaps one needs to be reminded of the neoclassical view. Certainly Deane and Cole's chapter on 'Longterm

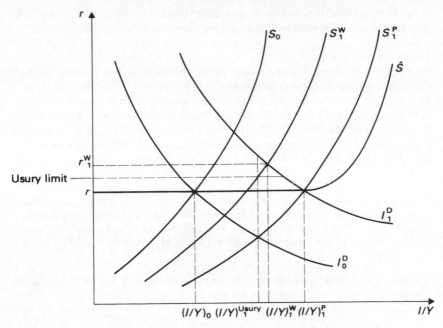

Figure 11.1 *Wasn't saving a constraint on growth during the first industrial revolution? The civilian sector*

Trends in Capital Formation' (1962, Ch. VIII, pp. 259–77) has no mention of the wars' impact, even though they are puzzled by the modest rates of accumulation during the early nineteenth century. The same is true in von Tunzlemann's (1982) recent paper on the standard-of-living debate. In his otherwise stimulating assessment of the question 'could an enlightened policy have done better for Britain's poor during the industrial revolution?', von Tunzlemann makes no mention of the resource commitment to military conflict during the better part of the epoch 1760–1850. Mokyr and Savin (1976, p. 209) add crowding out to their list of potential explanations of British economic performance between 1793 and 1815, but they choose to ignore these crowding-out influences when they offer their empirical assessment of Britain's slow growth (or 'stagflation'). Even Charles Feinstein's oft-cited 'Capital Accumulation and Economic Growth in Great Britain' (1976, p. 20) ignores the issue, save for suggestive references to a 'wartime dip' in the investment to GNP ratio. Although Mathias and O'Brien tell us that '. . . the ability of the British state to wage war effectively seems even more dependent upon the ability of governments to raise loans through the accumulation of a permanent National Debt than it was upon increasing revenues from taxation . . .' (Mathias and O'Brien, 1976, p. 623), their useful paper is devoted entirely to documenting the thesis that '. . . the main economic impact of taxation in Britain fell upon consumption and demand, rather than upon savings and investment' (p. 616).

So it is that modern economic historians tend to ignore the impact of the war debt on civilian accumulation during the first industrial revolution.

The Mill–Ashton hypothesis

Contemporary observers saw things quite differently. For them, new war debt crowded out private debt and the usury laws served to deflect saving to government borrowing, much as contemporary Third World financial markets are 'repressed' to favor state-backed projects and government borrowing (McKinnon, 1972). Writing on the state of the private capital market in the 1780s after the government borrowed £12 million in 1781, David Macpherson and George Chalmers saw the crowding out quite clearly:

> Such high interest with government security evidently makes it extremely difficult, if not quite impossible, for individuals to borrow any money, *upon legal interest*, either for the extension of commerce and manufacture, or the improvement of agriculture. (Macpherson, 1805, Vol. iii, p. 686)

> Every one must remember how impossible it was for individuals to borrow money on any security for any premium towards the end of 1784. (Chalmers, 1794, p. 186)

Writing after the French Wars had ended, but with the war debt still an enormous legacy, John Stuart Mill considered deflection and crowding out to be important ingredients of the relatively modest British progress he saw around him:

> England employed comparatively few additional soldiers and sailors of her own, while she diverted hundreds of millions of capital from productive employment, to supply munitions of war and support armies for her Continental allies. (Mill, 1909, I, pp. 111–12)

> Did the government, by its loan operations, augment the rate of interest? . . . When they do raise the rate of interest, as they did in a most extraordinary degree during the French War, this is positive proof that the government is a competitor for capital . . . (Mill, 1909, II, p. 481)

What was true of England was apparently also true of Scotland:

> A small amount of of government securities first appeared in the accounts of the Bank of Scotland in 1766, but they did not become a permanent feature until the American Revolution. Such investments, including Bank of England . . . stock, shot up dramatically after 1792, quickly overshadowing ordinary lending . . . [T]his policy, which was apparently also followed by the other Edinburgh banks, drew criticism on the grounds that it deprived Scottish industry of capital . . . (Cameron, 1967, pp. 81–2)

Mill had a view of crowding out where new war debt issues displaced private capital accumulation, one-for-one (Mill, 1909, II, pp. 481 and 483)

. . . the government by draining away a great part of the annual accumulations . . . subtracted just so much [capital] while the war lasted.

Mill thought the crowding-out influence was large enough to warrant the belief that the counterfactual peacetime rate of capital accumulation would have been 'enormous' (Mill, 1824, p. 40):

[While] the accumulation going on in the hands of individuals was sufficient to counteract the effect of that wasteful [military] expenditure, and to prevent capital from being diminished. The same accumulation would have sufficed, but for the government expenditure, to produce an enormous increase.

But then again, Mill was just a theorist, offering brilliant speculation. He did not offer evidence.

A century later, T. S. Ashton (1955, 1959) gave the crowding-out hypothesis more credibility by fleshing out Mill's thesis with eighteenth-century evidence on the operation of capital markets. Ashton believed that saving was an active constraint on British eighteenth-century growth; not to the exclusion of investment demand, of course, but in the sense of Figure 11.1, where saving functions are relatively inelastic and play a joint role with investment demand in dictating the pace of civilian accumulation.

The best statement of the Ashton thesis can be found in Chapter 3 ('War, Trade and Finance') and Chapter 4 ('Building and Construction') of his admirable *Economic Fluctuations in England*. To begin with, how did 'portfolio crowding out' work and who suffered the greatest crowding out (Ashton, 1959, p. 65)?

. . . much of the revenue needed for the prosecution of war had to be obtained from loans. The proportion was low at first, but mounted as the cost of maintaining the forces increased: in 1709–11, 1748, 1758–63, 1779–85, and 1795–1801 over 40 per cent of government expenditure was met by borrowing. Some of the money subscribed must have come out of idle balances, but . . . a good deal of it was deflected from other channels, and in particular from investment in building and construction. The production of capital goods was relatively low in most years of war.

Everyone appreciates the importance of the cost of borrowing to capital-intensive projects of long life, so no one should be surprised that construction is one of the first sectors to contract during wartime. As Ashton points out, however (1959, pp. 86 and 101), when the wars persist, construction (especially of dwellings) begins to cut corners on quality too – with deleterious effects on the workers' living standards:

In industries concerned with consumers' goods a rise of a half or of 1 per cent in the rate on loans makes little difference to the cost of the product. But in those concerned with buildings and the means of communication (where a long time must elapse between the beginning of an enterprise and the return of profits) it is of the greatest consequence. A rise in the rate of interest might not merely check new enterprise but bring projects already begun to a halt. Nor was it only the quantity of production that suffered: when rates of interest rose, builders would be tempted to economize in land, reduce the depths of foundations, and make use of inferior bricks and timber. Jerry-building was partly, at least, a consequence of dear money . . . It was not only industrialization that was responsible for overcrowding in slums at this time.

Although building and construction were the key losers to the crowding-out forces, were they large shares in total gross domestic fixed capital formation? Very important, it appears. Charles Feinstein (1978a, Table 7, p. 41) suggests that they were 60 per cent of the total in the 1760s and 68 per cent in 1801–10, even when farm buildings and agricultural improvements are excluded from the total.[3]

Ashton has far more to say about the operation of British capital markets during wartime, and about usury and credit rationing in particular. First, there is little evidence that the banking system expanded total credit when it purchased war debt, but plenty of evidence that it rationed what credit remained (Ashton, 1959, pp. 65–6):

> . . . when the Bank of England increased its advances to the state it usually curtailed its loans and discounts to other clients . . . Nor does the cautious policy of the Bank seem to have been offset by an expansion of credit elsewhere. There was no marked increase in the number of private banks, and there is evidence that the London banks, at least, reduced their loans to private customers when they lent to the state.

Second, the civilian loan market was constrained by usury (1959, p. 86):

> . . . in the eighteenth century the range of possible rates on mortgages and bonds was limited. No instance has been found of a rate below 3 per cent.; and the Usury Laws prohibited borrowers from offering, or lenders from receiving, more than 6 per cent. until 1714 and more than 5 per cent. during the rest of the century. The existence of this upper limit is of the utmost importance to an understanding of the fluctuations of the period. Once the critical point had been reached further borrowing might become impossible.

Of course, one need not appeal to the usury laws to get crowding out, but it helps Ashton explain (1959, pp. 86–7) eighteenth-century macro-instability, and it also helps one avoid the mistake of using 'the' interest rate as the sole index of scarcity in the civilian capital market:

> It was not, then, simply through a rise in the cost of borrowing, but through interruptions to the flow of funds, that depression came to [building and construction] . . . When the rate of 5 per cent. had been reached builders and contractors might be getting all the loans they wanted or, on the other hand, many of them might be in acute need of more. If we want to know the degree of scarcity we must look for other sources of information.

Figure 11.1 illustrates Ashton's point where the usury limit has been reached and the civilian loan market is cleared by rationing during periods of war debt issue.

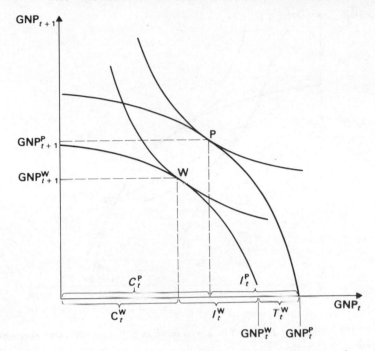

Figure 11.2   *The impact of war finance on civilian sector output: taxation only*

The Mill–Ashton hypothesis can also be dressed in more contemporary clothing for those readers who would find a more formal statement of the government debt burden appealing. But first note that the effect of the war debt on economic growth really involves two issues: first, the deflection of resources from civilian consumption and investment purposes to war uses and, second, the additional effect of the method of finance on the invest-ment–consumption mix, the rate of accumulation, and thus the economy's capacity in the future. Consider the simplest case first, where, as in Figure 11.2, the war is financed by current taxes only (T_t^W). Such taxes clearly deflect resources from civilian to war use, thus shifting the economy's capacity to produce civilian goods inwards. In the absence of war, civilian demands produce an equilibrium mix between consumption (C_t^P) and investment (I_t^P). The transformation curve indicates just how that invest-ment at time t would serve to increase future GNP (i.e. $\text{GNP}_{t+1}^P > \text{GNP}_t^P$). Now let war taxes of T_t^W be imposed, in which case the current standard of living falls (i.e. $C_t^W < C_t^P$). Note, however, that the figure has been drawn such that current investment levels remain unchanged (i.e. $I_t^W = I_t^P$). In this case, civilian output levels in $t + 1$ are lower only because taxation continues, *not* because less investment took place.

Now consider the added complexity of war debt. It should be emphasized at the start that, while civilian securities are claims on productive capital assets (i.e. past investments, I), public war debt is not. The war debt simply represents a claim on tax revenue streams. It follows that the presence of war

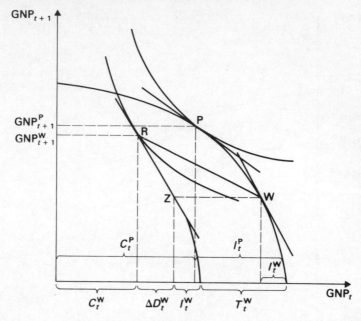

Figure 11.3   *The impact of war finance on civilian sector output: debt issue and taxation*

debt implies a burden on future generations since growth through civilian capital formation is forgone, and the amount of capital formation forgone will be greater than that under current taxation in Figure 11.2. Individual savers may be indifferent between public and private debt in satisfying their motives for wealth accumulation, providing, of course, that the war debt is offered at rates competitive with the more risky civilian debt, but the presence of additional war debt clearly implies lower levels of civilian accumulation and lower levels of future GNP.

In Figure 11.3, if the government is to float war debt successfully amounting to, say, ΔD_t^W, it must induce potential savers to diminish their new purchases of civilian debt and thus the real capital formation upon which that debt lays claim. Figure 11.3 illustrates one such result where the interest rate at W is driven upward, where capital formation contracts ($I_t^P > I_t^W$), where the current tax burden is T_t^W, where current consumption is diminished ($C_t^P > C_t^W$), and finally where future GNP levels are reduced ($\text{GNP}_{t+1}^P > \text{GNP}_{t+1}^W$). A new wartime equilibrium is reached at R where civilians add two types of assets to their previous stock: war debt (ΔD_t^W) and the investment (I_t^W). The rate of return on civilian capital is determined by the slope of the line at W, while the social return on (unproductive) war debt is zero – although the rate to an individual holder of war debt is the same as on civilian capital. The resulting net social rate of return is determined by the slope of the line RW and this, of course, is less than that at P – the magnitude depending, among other things, on the size of the war debt issue.

Table 11.3 *Public debt issue, gross domestic saving in reproducible capital, and gross private saving: levels and shares in national income, 1761–1860*

	(1) Government debt outstanding D (£m.)	(2) National income price deflator (1851–61 = 1.0) P_Y	(3) Real debt outstanding D/P_Y (£m.)	Decade	(4) P_Y	Per annum increase in government debt			Shares in national income			Gross private saving rate	
						(5) Nominal ΔD (£m.)	(6) Real (RAA) $\Delta(D/P_Y)$ (£m.)	(7) Real (NIA) $\Delta(D/P_Y)$ (£m.)	(8) RAA $\Delta(D/P_Y)$ %	(9) NIA $\Delta D/P_Y$ %	(10) S/P_I %	(11) RAA $(S/P_I + \Delta(D/P_Y))$ %	(12) NIA $(S/P_I + \Delta D/P_Y))$ %
Year													
1761	103.18	0.766	134.70										
1771	130.22	0.899	144.85	1761–1771	0.833	2.70	1.02	3.25	1.13	3.62	9.08	10.21	12.70
1781	173.68	0.948	183.21	1771–1781	0.924	4.35	3.84	4.70	3.99	4.90	10.46	14.45	15.36
1791	243.64	0.995	244.86	1781–1791	0.972	7.00	6.17	7.20	5.60	6.53	13.26	18.86	19.79
1801	443.12	1.499	295.61	1791–1801	1.247	19.95	5.08	16.00	3.63	11.45	13.46	17.09	24.91
1811	618.86	1.598	387.27	1801–1811	1.549	17.57	9.17	11.35	5.33	6.59	9.04	14.37	15.63
1821	837.98	1.191	703.59	1811–1821	1.395	21.91	31.63	15.71	14.91	7.40	12.96	27.87	20.36
1831	790.58	0.972	813.35	1821–1831	1.082	−4.74	10.98	−4.38	3.77	−1.50	13.64	17.41	12.14
1841	790.90	1.023	773.12	1831–1841	0.998	0.03	−4.02	0.03	−1.01	0.01	11.73	10.72	11.74
1851	789.10	0.945	835.03	1841–1851	0.984	−0.18	6.19	−0.18	1.25	−0.04	12.29	13.54	12.25
1861	805.82	1.054	764.54	1851–1861	1.000	1.67	−7.05	1.67	−1.18	0.28	13.68	12.50	13.96

Sources: Col. (1) – funded and unfunded government debt of the United Kingdom, where annual observations are five-year averages, centered, in Mitchell and Deane (1962, pp. 402–3).

Cols (2) and (4) – are described in the Sources to Table 11.1.

Cols (6) and (7) offer two alternative estimates of the *real* increase in the war debt: RAA refers to 'real accrual accounting' = $\Delta(D/P_Y)$; NIA refers to Department of Commerce 'national income accounting' = $\Delta D/P_Y$.

Cols (8) and (9) = cols. (6) and (7) divided by Table 11.1, col. 2.

Col. (10) – from Table 11.1, col. 8 ÷ col. 2.

Col. (11) = col. (8) + col. (10).

Col. (12) = col. (9) + col. (10).

The size of the war debt issue

Table 11.3 (col. 10) shows that domestic saving in reproducible capital rose from 9.08 to 13.68 per cent of national income over the century 1761–1860 as a whole. Feinstein (1978a, p. 90) views this rise as substantial:

> Contrary to the view tentatively advanced by Deane and Cole and now widely (and sometimes dogmatically) accepted, the [domestic saving] ratio did rise during the eighteenth century, and by quite a substantial margin.

I disagree. While the share certainly did rise, it does not seem very substantial to me. After all, it rose only enough to keep the rate of accumulation barely ahead of the rate of labor force growth. Furthermore, the share did not rise at all between the 1780s and the postwar decades. In addition, why is it that the share of domestic saving in reproducible capital fell during the first two decades of the nineteenth century? In any case, regardless of trends, a gross saving rate of 9 or 12 per cent must be considered very low by the standards of nineteenth-century America and Germany, of Meiji and Taisho Japan, and of the contemporary Third World.

Can the modest saving rate and its unspectacular rise be explained by war debt and crowding out?

The first step in testing the Mill–Ashton hypothesis is to compute the size of the war debt issue. The calculation requires two pieces of evidence: net additions to the war debt (ΔD) and national income. While ΔD was available even to Mill, national income estimates became available only with the appearance of Deane and Cole's (1962) pioneering contribution. Table 11.3 summarizes this information using two different concepts of the real impact of the war debt. One estimate follows most of the economics profession and uses the Department of Commerce 'national income accounts' (NIA) view, where the increase in nominal debt outstanding is deflated. Siegal (1979), Dewald (1983) and others have recently argued that one should use instead 'real accrual accounting' (RAA), where the real debt is computed at the beginning and the end of the period before the increase is calculated. While the RAA concept includes the impact of inflation on the stock of debt outstanding, the NIA concept does not. Since decades of British war debt issue were also ones of inflation, the two concepts may well suggest quite different inferences regarding the real crowding-out effects in civilian capital markets.

Whether one favors the NIA or the RAA concept, the size of the war debt issue was enormous. True, the two concepts imply somewhat different timing in the real impact of war debt. While the NIA concept in Table 11.3 (col. 9) suggests a peak share in national income of 11.45 per cent across the 1790s, the RAA concept (col. 8) reduces this figure to 3.63 per cent by taking account of the impact of rapid inflation on the outstanding stock of war debt. Symmetrically, the price deflation across the 1810s raises the RAA share above the NIA share (14.91 versus 7.4 per cent). Nevertheless, the estimates are comparable over the long run: for the 1760–1820 epoch, the RAA and NIA estimates averaged 5.77 and 6.75 per cent of national income. Since it is used so commonly in the economics literature, the remainder of this chapter will rely on the NIA concept.

Net additions to the war debt were already 3.62 per cent of national income in the 1760s (Table 11.3, col. 9), about the same as the 3.7 per cent that America achieved during 1980–2 when crowding out and capital scarcity attracted so much attention. The share had risen to 6.53 per cent by the 1780s, a near doubling in the burden. The share reached a peak of 11.45 per cent in the 1790s. This figure approximates that for America during the Civil War (15.5 per cent, average per annum 1861–6 – Williamson, 1974b, Table 3, p. 643). Yet, while America generated a similar war debt burden over five years or so of the Civil War decade, and while Japan did the same over the decade 1894–1905 during conflicts with China and Russia (Kelley and Williamson, 1974, Ch. 7; Williamson and DeBever, 1977), neither of these two newly industrializing countries maintained the burden over six decades! In contrast, net additions to the British war debt continued at high levels throughout the first two decades of the nineteenth century, holding at 6.59 per cent of national income in the 1800s and 7.40 per cent in the 1810s.

The average burden of these net additions to the war debt was 6.75 per cent between 1761 and 1820, and even higher (8.48 per cent) between 1791 and 1820. To get an estimate of the *gross private saving rate*, civilian reproducible capital formation and new public war debt should be added. When they are, Britain's private sector saving rates no longer seem so modest. Indeed, while domestic saving in reproducible capital averaged only around 11.4 per cent of national income from 1761 to 1820 (Table 11.3, col. 10), the gross private saving rate averaged 18.1 per cent (Table 11.3, col. 12).

It appears that Britain was not a 'modest' saver during the first industrial revolution after all. What appears to make Britain unusual is how much of that potential saving went into unproductive wartime finance.

Crowding out, tax incidence and the Ricardian non-equivalence theorem
Is the one-for-one crowding-out assumption a good one for this period of British growth? The answer hinges on whether the typical household viewed government debt issue as an increase in net wealth. Certainly this is the case for full employment models (e.g. Modigliani, 1961) where an increase in government debt implies an increase in perceived household wealth, inducing a decline in the share going to capital accumulation (Barro, 1974, p. 1096). While one-for-one crowding out survived Franco Modigliani's (1966, pp. 363–4) tests on twentieth-century American data, and while Paul David and John Scadding (1974, p. 239) thought that the 'invariance [of the gross private saving rate] to changes in the size of the government deficit suggests that private debt and public debt are close substitutes in private portfolios', the debate over crowding out has shown no signs of dying out.

In terms of its historical application to Britain, a critical assumption of these models is full employment. To the extent that Britain is better described by under-full employment, then the war debt issue may have crowded *in* private investment (Friedman, 1978). However, I believe the full employment assumption to be the best description of Britain during the industrial revolution, certainly when the focus covers a period as long as three–six decades.

Even granting full employment, there were always strong opponents to the one-for-one crowding-out view. James Tobin (1971, p. 91) thought such arguments implied 'fiscal illusion':

> How is it possible that society merely by the device of incurring a debt to itself can deceive itself into believing that it is wealthier? Do not the additional taxes which are necessary to carry the interest charges reduce the value of other components of wealth?

It was Barro's 1974 paper 'Are Government Bonds Net Wealth?' that attracted all the attention, however. Barro was able to show that taxes and debt issues are equivalent, but to get that result he made two assumptions that are likely to be grossly inconsistent with the environment of the British industrial revolution (Buchanan, 1976). First, were future tax liabilities fully capitalized or did bond-holders suffer fiscal illusion? While Barro assumed away fiscal illusion, Ricardo (1962, IV, pp. 186–7) thought it was the best characterization of bond-holders' behavior in late eighteenth- and early nineteenth-century Britain (see O'Driscoll, 1977):

> In [theory], there is no real difference [between taxes and debt issue] . . .; but [in fact] the people who pay the taxes never so estimate them, and therefore do not manage their private affairs accordingly. We are too apt to think that war is burdensome only in proportion to what we are at the moment called to pay for it in taxes, without reflecting on the probable duration of such taxes.

Apart from the fact that he was a brilliant theorist, why do we care about Ricardo's position? Because his analysis of the impact of the war debt was written in September of 1820 when crowding out and sinking funds were being publicly debated, at which point he could assess first-hand two decades of British accumulation under war finance.

Barro's second assumption has doubtful relevance for our period of interest:

> [He] is willing to make the severely restrictive assumption that the source for the ultimate purchase of the government bonds is identical to the source from which the alternative taxes would be drawn. (Buchanan, 1976, p. 339)

As it turns out, historians have always assumed exactly the opposite. Table 11.2 suggests that the historians have been right all along. The British central government tax system was highly regressive at this time, and direct taxes on income and wealth produced a very small share of the total tax take (Table 11.2, col. (1), ϕ_t). Furthermore, those temporary direct taxes that *had* been imposed in the late 1790s and afterwards were quickly dismantled after the war was over, leaving tariffs and excise taxes on necessities as the main source of revenue to finance charges on the outstanding war debt. 'Fiscal illusion' certainly made good sense *ex post*.

While the issue will be taken up again in section 4, I have argued here that the one-for-one crowding-out assumption may not be such a poor description of behavior during the British industrial revolution. The assumption may be good enough, at least, to warrant its use to assess what the rate of accumulation might have been like had the wars never been fought and had the debt never been issued.

(3) Civilian accumulation in the absence of wars: counterfactual conjectures

The next step is to explore the implications of the crowding out when it is posed in its strongest, one-for-one form. By far the trickiest part of the exercise involves the 'redistributive effect' of the war debt.

The redistributive effect is a simple enough notion, and it has a long tradition in British historiography (Hartwell and Engerman, 1975, pp. 208–9; Pollard and Crossley, 1968, p. 207; Thompson, 1963, p. 304). Since the war debt was held by high-income savers, and since an essentially regressive tax system fell primarily on low-income non-savers, then the tax revenue needed to pay interest charges on the debt implied a redistribution from non-savers to savers. The redistribution effect did not have very pleasant implications for workers' living standards, but it served to augment the gross private saving rate. Thus, the redistribution effect should have tended to offset the crowding-out effect.

How large was the offset during the first industrial revolution? The answer depends in part on the size of the debt charges. These were quite sizeable, exceeding the new debt issue itself in all but one decade, the 1790s. The answer also depends on the source of the tax revenue used to finance the debt charge payout. If the taxes fell on the non-saver entirely, then the total tax revenue figures would measure the extent of the income redistribution. Thanks to Pitt, however, an income tax was imposed on the rich from 1799 to 1816, and again from 1841 onwards. Of course, there were land and assessed taxes too, and here one has to deal with thorny problems of tax incidence. Third, it depends on the marginal saving rate differential between the taxed poor and the war-debt-holding rich.

The assumptions underlying Table 11.4 can be stated briefly. I assume that taxes on income and wealth fell to the top half of the income distribution, and that these rich bore the full incidence of those direct taxes. Symmetrically, I assume that all indirect taxes fell on the bottom half of the income distribution. These assumptions are likely to exaggerate the size of the redistribution effect: while *some* of the direct taxes on wealth must have been shifted back on the poor, my guess is that the shifting was trivial; more importantly, *some* of the regressive indirect taxes fell on the rich; on net, I think the latter bias dominated the former. If I am right, the offset is exaggerated and the impact of the war debt on civilian accumulation rates is understated.

What about the marginal saving rate differential between the taxed bottom half of the income distribution and the debt-holding top half? Here I can offer only informed guesses. Let the average saving rate out of incomes in the lower half of the distribution be zero, and define the average saving rate out of the top half to be s_H. Then, the economy-wide saving rate (including war debt) can be written as

$$s = (s_H Y_H)/Y, \quad \text{where by definition } Y_H/Y = 0.5.$$

The values for s (1760–1820) implied by Table 11.3 (cols 11 and 12) range between 17.1 and 18.1 per cent, implying that s_H ranged between 0.342 and 0.362.[4] The differential between *average* saving rates (δ) may, of course, exceed the true differential between *marginal* saving rates. If so, the assumption exaggerates the positive net saving associated with the redistribution effect and the impact of the war debt on civilian accumulation rates is, once again, understated.

By how much would the investment share have risen in the absence of the wars? To motivate the more complete assessment in Chapter 12, a counterfactual conjecture is reported in Table 11.4. Including the redistribution effect's offset, the counterfactual rise in I/Y is calculated as:

$$d(I/Y)_{CF} = [\Delta D - (\delta)(1 - \phi_t)(iD)]/Y,$$

where ϕ_t is the share of income and wealth taxes in total tax revenue. Using Harrod's identity, it is now a simple matter to compute the counterfactual rise in the accumulation rate:[5]

$$d(\overset{*}{K})_{CF} = (Y/K) \cdot d(I/Y)_{CF},$$

where Y/K is the output–capital ratio.

Table 11.4 reports these counterfactual conjectures. If my crowding-out assumptions are anywhere near correct, it appears that war debt issue explains much of the empirical peculiarities of the first industrial revolution. Between 1761 and 1820, the capital formation share would have been 3.96–4.84 per cent higher in the absence of war, and the rate of accumulation would have been 1.43–1.74 per cent per annum higher. Assuming an output elasticity (α_K) of 0.35, national income would have grown some 0.5–0.6 per cent per annum faster. If one focuses attention on those decades where the economic impact of the wars reached their peak (1791–1820), the counterfactual calculations are even more striking: the capital formation share would have been higher by 5.97–6.38 per cent, the rate of accumulation would have been higher by 2.27–2.42 per cent per annum, and the rate of output growth would have been some 0.8 per cent per annum faster. In contrast, the post-1820 growth rates would have been lower in the absence of the wars. Thus, most of the trend acceleration from the pre-1820 war-distorted decades to the post-1820 *Pax Britannica* may well be explained by exogenous war debt crowding out, rather than by some endogenous attribute of capitalist development.

Table 11.4   *Conjectures on the impact of war debt issue on civilian sector accumulation and growth, 1761–1860*

Period	(1) Counterfactual rise in I/Y RAA %	(2) Counterfactual rise in I/Y NIA %	(3) Capital's productivity Y/K	(4) Counterfactual rise in the rate of accumulation (dK̇) RAA %	(5) Counterfactual rise in the rate of accumulation (dK̇) NIA %	(6) Counterfactual rise in the aggregate growth rate (dẎ) RAA %	(7) Counterfactual rise in the aggregate growth rate (dẎ) NIA %
1761–1820	+3.96	+4.84	0.36	+1.43	+1.74	+0.50	+0.61
1791–1820	+5.97	+6.38	0.38	+2.27	+2.42	+0.79	+0.85
1821–60	−1.10	−2.22	0.53	−0.58	−1.18	−0.20	−0.41

Sources and Notes: Cols (1) and (2) are constant price estimates derived from $d(I/Y)_{CF} = [\Delta D - (\delta)(1 - \phi)(iD)] \div Y$. The RAA and NIA estimates of the real deficit (ΔD) are taken from Table 11.3, cols 6 and 7. The estimate of ϕ is taken from Table 11.2, col. 1, and the estimates for δ can be found in the text (0.342 and 0.362, RAA and NIA respectively). Average annual charges on the funded and unfunded government debt (iD) are taken from Mitchell and Deane (1962, pp. 390–1 and 396–7), Great Britain 1761–1800 and United Kingdom 1801–60, deflated by P_Y in Table 11.1, col. 10. The constant price national income figure (Y) is taken from Table 11.1, col. 2.
Col. (3) assumes that a *net* capital–output ratio of 2.5 applies to the 18th and early 19th centuries as a whole (1760–1830); from Deane (1961, p. 356), an estimate that Floud and McCloskey (1981, p. 8, fn. 2) also accept, and that Kuznets (1973, pp. 143 and 149) cites with favor. Feinstein reports *gross* capital–output ratios that are much higher, but his estimated *trends* in capital productivity (Feinstein, 1978a, Table 26, p. 87) are used here.
Col. (4) or (5) = col. (1) or (2) times col. (3).
Col. (6) or (7) = col. (4) or (5) times 0.35, the latter an estimate of capital's output elasticity (α_K) from Floud and McCloskey (1981, p. 8). See text.

(4) Have I exaggerated crowding out? Two possible problems

Could the revisionist findings reported in Table 11.4 be exaggerated? This section explores two possible sources of overstatement: foreign investment and less than one-for-one crowding out.

Net foreign investment
Did England evade 'the inherent trade-off between power and profit' (Neal, 1977, p. 35) by exporting the war debt abroad? While this was certainly the case up through the Seven Years War, thanks to Dutch investment, it apparently was not the case thereafter. Indeed, Feinstein's (1978a, pp. 68 and 71–2) summary of the evidence suggests that, with the exception of 1801–10, Britain was a net investor abroad for the whole period following 1761. Thus, critics cannot appeal to foreign investment in any effort to argue that the crowding-out effect on Britain's accumulation rates has been overstated in Table 11.4.

One-for-one crowding out
Table 11.4 assumes one-for-one crowding out. The size of that impact is exaggerated to the extent that domestic saving and firm reinvestment rates

were responsive to the rate of return. As civilian accumulation was choked off by war debt issue, the rate of return on the now-smaller capital stock would have been higher, thus encouraging more saving. How much more depends on the elasticity of saving to the rate of return. Since most economists believe that saving is inelastic with respect to the rate of return (but see Edelstein, 1982, p. 198, who estimates an elasticity of 0.65 for late nineteenth-century Britain), the capital scarcity created by crowding out is unlikely to have encouraged much more civilian saving. In addition, if usury laws were binding, then interest rates in private capital markets would have remained stable, encouraging no saving response as a consequence. If *both* of these assumptions – zero interest elasticity *and* binding usury laws – were violated, then Table 11.4 overstates the crowding-out influence of the war debt issue.

While the historical data for this period are simply too poor to make it possible to estimate the interest elasticity of saving directly, *indirect* evidence is available to guide one's judgment. Indeed, while the capital formation share tended to fall during decades of heaviest debt issue, the gross private saving rate rose. Some might argue that the gross private saving rate boomed during wartime precisely because the interest elasticity of private saving was high. How else is one to explain the extraordinary instability in the gross private saving rate over these six decades?

The puzzling instability in the gross private saving rate
When Charles Feinstein (1978a) offered his pioneering estimates of British saving in reproducible capital, he used the data primarily to confirm the hypothesis that the *national* saving rate rose across the industrial revolution, from 9.08 to 13.68 per cent (Table 11.3, col. 10, in constant prices). That secular rise was more or less completed by the 1790s. Had he looked at the *private* saving rate, Feinstein would have found that it rose far more dramatically over the same period (Table 11.3, cols 11 and 12). Indeed, the RAA gross private saving rate rose from 10.21 to 17.09 per cent between the 1760s and the 1790s. Yet, this episode was followed by a very sharp fall in the gross private saving rate to the 1800s, and then by an enormous jump to the 1810s (14.37 and 27.87 per cent). The instability continued through the postwar stabilization decades.

What explains this instability in the gross private saving rate? Is it explained by an interest-elastic private saving response and thus something less than one-for-one crowding out? Or is it explained by some other influence? The answers will be hard in coming since the data cannot support very rigorous hypothesis testing. After all, Table 11.3 offers only ten observations, and these are limited to decadal averages. Furthermore, one cannot explore many of the currently popular models of saving behavior since most explanatory variables cannot be documented for this century of British growth. This applies to the life-cycle model (which requires asset data), to dependency effects associated with the demographic transition (which requires saving parameters specific to stage of life-cycle), or, alas, even to the interest elasticity hypothesis (which requires time series on returns to non-government assets).

Yet one *can* use one simple model of saving behavior to confront this puzzling instability, one that is especially plausible under conditions of war-induced 'stop–go' growth, and one that has had considerable success when applied to currently industrializing nations in the Third World – the Wealth–Consumption (*WC*) model.

The *WC* model (e.g. Ball and Drake, 1964) expresses the individual wealth–consumption ratio as

$$W_{it} = k_i C_{it}.$$

Making conventional assumptions and aggregating yields a consumption function of the form

$$C_t = (1 - \sigma)Y_t + \sigma C_{t-1}, \quad \text{where } \sigma = k/(1 + k).$$

The *WC* model can also be written in terms of savings, or, for that matter, in terms of savings rates, s_t:

$$s_t = \sigma\left(\frac{\lambda_{t-1}}{\lambda_t}\right) + \sigma\left(\frac{1}{\lambda_t} \cdot s_{t-1}\right)$$

or

$$s_t = \sigma\left[\left(\frac{\lambda_{t-1}}{\lambda_t}\right) + \left(\frac{1}{\lambda_t} \cdot s_{t-1}\right)\right], \quad \text{where } \lambda_t = Y_t/Y_{t-1} \quad (11.1)$$

and λ_t is an income growth rate, here reflecting the stop–go performance of the British economy across the ten decades of the first industrial revolution. This stop–go performance can be seen clearly in Table 11.5, where the booming decades – like the 1790s – are followed by slumping decades – like the 1800s, at least based on Deane and Cole. The *WC* model is an attractive candidate since it explains the rise in s_t during booming decades by reference to growth rates above the trend, while low s_t during slumping decades are explained by poor growth rates. One could argue that the causation went from saving rates to growth via the rate of accumulation and capacity expansion, but there are two reasons for rejecting that view of causality. First, I have already pointed out that economy-wide rates of total factor productivity growth, not capital-deepening, seem to have driven British per capita income growth up to 1860. Second, gross private saving rates include government debt, and the latter laid no claim on productive accumulation of any sort.

In an attempt to estimate (11.1), the λ's were constructed from the constant price national income data in Table 11.1 divided by the Wrigley and Schofield (1981, Table A3.1, p. 529) estimates of population aged 15–59. The results were as follows:

RAA	NIA
$\hat{\sigma} = 0.633$ (*t*-statistic = 7.33)	$\hat{\sigma} = 0.641$ (*t*-statistic = 8.63)
$R^2 = 0.871$	$R^2 = 0.903$
DW = 2.37	DW = 2.01

Table 11.5 *Accounting for the instability in the gross private saving rate using the simple Wealth–Consumption model*

Decade	(1) Per annum growth in real income per capita %	(2) λ_t	Gross private saving rate (RAA)			Gross private saving rate (NIA)		
			(3) Actual s_t	(4) Predicted $\hat{s}_t$	(5) Equilibrium s_t^e	(6) Actual s_t	(7) Predicted $\hat{s}_t$	(8) Equilibrium s_t^e
1761–1770	−0.68	0.9341	0.1021	—	—	0.1270	—	—
1771–1780	0.85	1.0880	0.1445	0.1107	0.1224	0.1536	0.1267	0.0809
1781–1790	0.34	1.0346	0.1886	0.1096	0.0545	0.1979	0.1166	0.0563
1791–1800	1.87	1.2036	0.1709	0.2064	0.2259	0.2491	0.2139	0.2320
1801–1810	0.68	1.0702	0.1437	0.1427	0.1016	0.1563	0.1913	0.1048
1811–1820	1.30	1.1379	0.2787	0.1567	0.1729	0.2036	0.1658	0.1779
1821–1830	2.06	1.2256	0.1741	0.2606	0.2410	0.1214	0.2245	0.2474
1831–1840	0.74	1.0768	0.1072	0.1476	0.1095	0.1174	0.1180	0.1130
1841–1850	1.07	1.1126	0.1354	0.1251	0.1486	0.1225	0.1325	0.1530
1851–1860	0.17	1.0171	0.1250	0.0949	0.0282	0.1396	0.0880	0.0291

Sources and Notes: Cols (1) and (2) – from Table 11.1, col. (2), divided by population aged 15–59 (Wrigley and Schofield, 1981, Table A3.1, p. 529).
Cols (3) and (6) – from Table 11.3, cols (11) and (12).
Cols (4) and (7) – derived from the estimated *WC* models (see text).

$$\text{RAA: } \hat{s}_t = 0.633\left[\left(\frac{\lambda_{t-1}}{\lambda_t}\right) + \left(\frac{1}{\lambda_t} \cdot s_{t-1}\right)\right]; \quad \text{NIA: } \hat{s}_t = 0.641\left[\left(\frac{\lambda_{t-1}}{\lambda_t}\right) + \left(\frac{1}{\lambda_t} \cdot s_{t-1}\right)\right].$$

Cols (5) and (8) – derived under the assumption that the process is stable, so that

$$s_t^e = \frac{\sigma(\lambda_{t-1}^e)}{\lambda_t^e - \sigma}.$$

While these may seem like satisfying results,[6] predictions from these estimated models miss the timing of the gross private saving rate's turning points at some crucial decades (Table 11.5, cols 4 and 7).

While the saving rate instability from 1760 to 1860 can be explained in part by war-induced stop–go, there are some puzzles left in Table 11.5. What accounts for the very high saving rates in the 1780s and 1810? What accounts for the very low saving rates in the 1820s? Apparently not the growth performance of the economy over each of these decades as a whole. It could, of course, simply reflect flaws in the underlying Deane and Cole income estimates. It could also reflect a response to appeals to patriotism, appeals that coincided with the biggest debt issues. *Or*, it could reflect omitted variables, like the rate of return to capital. The latter explanation implies, of course, that the one-for-one crowding-out assumption is an inadequate characterization of this period. How poor depends in large part on the 'true' elasticity of the gross private saving rate to the rate of return. Even if the interest elasticity was fairly high, in late eighteenth- and early nineteenth-century Britain, what about the effect of the usury laws? If the usury laws were in fact binding, interest rates in private capital markets would have remained stable, encouraging credit rationing but no saving response as a consequence.

It certainly looks as if much more remains to be done to understand the determinants of saving and accumulation during the first industrial revolution. The critical issues for future research appear to be whether usury laws were binding through much of the years between 1761 and 1820, by how much, and the extent to which British gross private saving rates were responsive to rates of return, and by how much.

(5) Questions left unanswered

In spite of all the shouting about industrial revolutions, British growth was actually very slow before the 1820s. Furthermore, most of the increase in national income per worker was due to total factor productivity growth associated with technological advance, and little to accumulation and capital-deepening. This has always been the conventional wisdom, but now there is some hard evidence to support the colorful description of the 'wave of gadgets' that swept England. Charles Feinstein (1978a, Table 26, p. 86), for example, estimates that total factor productivity growth accounted for almost nine-tenths of output per worker growth from 1761 to 1860. Donald McCloskey finds much the same, encouraging the conclusion that 'ingenuity rather than absention governed the industrial revolution' (Floud and McCloskey, 1981, p. 108). Yet these findings seem inconsistent with everything else that is known about other economies passing through the early stages of the industrial revolution. In the contemporary Third World, total factor productivity growth 'explains' only about 10 per cent of growth (Maddison, 1970, Table 11.11, p. 53). Similarly, Moses Abramovitz and Paul David (1973, Table 1, p. 430) have shown that total factor productivity growth 'explains' very little of *ante bellum* US per capita output growth (about 27 per cent). Kazushi Ohkawa and Henry Rosovsky (1973, presented in Williamson and de Bever, 1977, Table 1, p. 128) suggest the same for Japan between 1908 and 1938, where total factor productivity growth 'explains' only one-third of labor productivity growth. Britain's first industrial revolution seems odd: whereas other nations passing through early industrialization record high contributions for conventional capital accumulation and low contributions for total factor productivity growth, Britain prior to 1820 suggests the opposite. In fact, the rate of accumulation was so slow that the capital–labor ratio hardly rose at all.

There is now an explanation for the low rates of accumulation, and it has nothing to do with Thrift. When civilians' saving is properly augmented to include their increased holdings of government war debt, the gross private saving rate turns out to have been as high as 18.1 per cent between 1761 and 1821 – not so low after all. Since private savers were accumulating central government debt issued to finance the wars, productive accumulation was crowded out and the first industrial revolution was slowed down.

What were the implications for inequality and the standard of living?

Notes

1   Crafts (1983, p. 195) also offers new estimates for aggregate output growth, industrial output growth, and the 'saving rate'. While his revisions may turn out to be superior, Crafts' choice of benchmark dates – 1760, 1780, 1801 and 1831 – is inconvenient for the analysis in this chapter, where wars are at issue and the 1815 or 1821 benchmark is critical.
2   Deane and Cole (1962, p. 276) call it a 'modest' increase and in Peter Mathias' words ('Preface' to Crouzet, 1972, p. viii) the 'modesty of rates of capital accumulation' is one profound difference between eighteenth-century England and contemporary Third World economies.
3   Building and construction includes: dwellings, public buildings, public works, industrial and commercial buildings, roads and bridges, canals and waterways, docks and harbors, and ships.
4   If these estimates seem large, recall that they cover business reinvestment rates in a pre-corporate era. These estimates are very close to those favored by Simon Kuznets (1950) for America, and that have been applied to Civil War crowding-out experience (Williamson, 1974b, p. 644).
5   The counterfactual assumes that all of the rise would be allocated to domestic accumulation. It should also be pointed out that I ignore the possibility that the rate of return to capital might have declined in response to the higher rates of accumulation. Unless capital rationing under usury continued to bind private capital markets, rates of return would have fallen with more rapid accumulation. Would gross private saving rates have fallen in response to declining rates of return, and if so, by how much? The answer hinges on the interest elasticity of saving, an issue raised again in section 4.
6   I also estimated an unconstrained version of the WC model where

$$s_t = \alpha_1 + \beta_1\left(\frac{\lambda_{t-1}}{\lambda_t}\right) + \lambda_1\left(\frac{1}{\lambda_t} \cdot s_{t-1}\right).$$

Since it turns out that $\hat{\alpha}_1$ is insignificantly different from zero, and that $\hat{\beta}_1$ is insignificantly different from $\hat{\gamma}_1$, I have kept to the constrained version of the WC model in the text and in Table 11.5.

12

Inequality, Industrialization and the Standard of Living during Wartime: Conjectures

(1) The issues

While the counterfactual conjectures reported in Table 11.4 are useful in uncovering the main causes of slow British growth prior to the 1820s, they are not enough. First, they offer insight into accumulation and output growth only at the most aggregate level. Can the wars also account for the poor performance of living standards up to the 1820s? Can they account for the relatively slow rate of industrialization prior to the 1820s? And what impact did the wars have on inequality in early nineteenth-century Britain? Did they serve to offset or reinforce inequality trends on the upswing of the British Kuznets curve? Second, the calculations in Table 11.4 ignore the potential impact of other war-induced economic influences. They fail to consider the impact of mobilization on labor scarcity, or the impact of blockades and embargoes on food and resource scarcity.

This chapter will pick up where the previous one left off: can one factor out the influence of war on inequality, industrialization and the standard of living prior to *Pax Britannica*?

(2) Accumulation, mobilization and world markets during wartime

Accumulation and crowding out: reprise
Chapter 11 argued that between 1761 and 1820 the rate of accumulation would have been 1.43–1.74 per cent per annum higher in the absence of the war debt issue and crowding out. For the shorter period 1791–1820, the figures range between 2.27 and 2.42 per cent per annum higher. These counterfactual estimates will be used in the analysis underlying sections 4 and 5 below.

Mobilization and labor scarcity at home

Major wars tend to create unskilled labor scarcity, and the French Wars were no exception. Ashton's (1959, Table 8, p. 187) compilation from the *Parliamentary Papers* shows the number of men in the armed forces rising from 98,000 in 1790 to 437,000 and 482,000 in 1795 and 1802. Colquhoun (1815, Table 1, p. 47) estimated that men under arms numbered 501,000 in 1812. By 1820, demobilization had reduced the figure back to a peacetime level of about 100,000. These figures suggest that the share of the total labor force mobilized for the French Wars rose from about 2 to 10 per cent,[1] a mobilization rate that begins to approximate twentieth-century wars.

Furthermore, mobilization had a predictable impact on the composition of the diminished civilian labor force: mobilization fell on the young, unskilled and rural male. Peter Lindert's data (from private correspondence) taken from Woodbridge, Suffolk, militia lists in 1814 supply an average age of $22\frac{1}{2}$; 63 per cent were laborers, servants or in menial service. Certainly there was no shortage of complaints from British farmers about the scarcity of farm labor for harvest and for farm capital-creating projects (John, 1967, pp. 32–3; Hueckel, 1973, p. 371). In Ashton's words: 'Many boys went into the forces before they had acquired knowledge of a trade: they left the navy and army totally unskilled . . .' (Ashton, 1959, p. 52).

These mobilization effects imply that the wars served to lower the growth of the civilian labor force from what it might have been (1.25 per cent per annum) to what it was (0.91 per cent per annum) between 1790 and 1815. That is, in the absence of war mobilization, the unskilled labor force might have grown some 0.34 per cent per annum faster after 1790. In contrast, the growth of skills can be assumed to have remained unchanged. For the longer period from the 1760s to the 1810s, the mobilization effects were more modest: the same analysis suggests that the unskilled labor force might have grown some 0.17 per cent per annum faster in the absence of war.

These late eighteenth- and early nineteenth-century mobilization effects on the size and composition of the civilian labor force should come as no surprise, since the same bias tended to produce unskilled labor scarcity in the twentieth-century civilian economy as well. Indeed, both world wars were times of very steeply rising relative costs of unskilled labor in America (Williamson and Lindert, 1980, Ch. 4) and Europe (Williamson, 1984, Figure 4), which helped to produce a collapse in pay gaps between the skilled and unskilled, and a leveling in the earnings distribution. Perhaps the collapse in pay gaps during the Napoleonic Wars (Chapter 3) can also be explained by these mobilization effects.

Food and imported resource scarcity

The economic impact of the French Wars can be separated into two parts: factor supplies and relative prices.[2] I have already dealt with factor supplies. What about prices?

The relative price of agricultural goods rose sharply across the period, implying a deterioration in Britain's terms of trade, an erosion in aggregate real income, and standard-of-living losses for the working classes. By re-working the Gayer–Rostow–Schwartz and Beveridge series, Glenn Hueckel

(1973, p. 369) estimates that, relative to manufactures, grain prices rose by 1.05 per cent per annum 1790–1815, and Appendix E estimates that the relative price of imported raw materials rose by even more, 2 per cent per annum. These relative price trends are somewhat less dramatic when the longer period from the 1760s to the 1810s is examined, but the drift towards food and imported resource scarcity is still apparent. How much of these price trends was due to wartime conditions and how much to other forces?

All observers agree that this relative price drift towards food and resource scarcity at home was induced by forces affecting total British supplies. Three supply-side forces have received special attention. First, relatively rapid technical progress in manufacturing tended to raise the relative price of non-manufactures. Second, some have argued that weather-related harvest failures can account for increased food scarcity (Chambers and Mingay, 1966, p. 113; Jones, 1964), although the evidence does not appear to support this view (Hueckel, 1973, pp. 367–8). Indeed, even the originator of the view, Thomas Tooke (1838), made far more of a third force than do subsequent writers who cite him (Hueckel, 1973, p. 368). The third force, of course, was the impact of the French Wars on trade (Mancur Olson, 1963; for a more recent survey, see Mokyr and Savin, 1976, pp. 223–31). Glenn Hueckel (1973, p. 369) has estimated that the hostilities and blockades served to inflate 1812 wheat prices by some 25–40 per cent owing solely to higher freight and insurance costs. For the 1790–1815 period as a whole, Hueckel (1973, p. 389) estimates that the wars raised the relative price of grains by 28 per cent.[3] Table 12.1 summarizes these conjectures.

Table 12.1   *Conjectures on the impact of war on Britain's relative price trends (per annum rate of change)*

	(1) Actual wartime 1790–1815 %	(2) The impact of war: based on Hueckel 1790–1815 %	(3) 1760s–1810s %
Price variable			
Grains: $\overset{*}{P}_A$	1.57	0.99	0.49
Manufactures: $\overset{*}{P}_M$	0.52	0	0
Imported raw materials: $\overset{*}{P}_F$	2.00	0.99	0.49
$\overset{*}{P}_A - \overset{*}{P}_M$	1.05	0.99	0.49
$\overset{*}{P}_F - \overset{*}{P}_M$	1.48	0.99	0.49

Sources and Notes: Col. (1) – P_M and P_A from Hueckel (1973, Table 3, p. 388), who reworked the Gayer–Rostow–Schwartz and Beveridge series: P_F is based on Gayer–Rostow–Schwartz, 'imported commodities', in Mitchell and Deane (1962, p. 470; sugar, tea, cotton, wool and raw silk).
Cols (2) and (3) are based on Hueckel's (1973, p. 389) estimate that the wars raised P_A/P_M by 28 per cent.

(3) Does one need a special 'wartime' model?

The arguments pro: economic response to war and peace
Why can one not apply the 'peacetime model' developed in Chapter 8, and tested in Chapter 9 on the 1820–60 period, to the war-distorted years of early industrialization prior to the 1820s? I believe one can. Indeed, general equilibrium models like that developed in Chapter 8 seem especially well designed to 'factor out the wars' from the industrial revolution, as an early effort by Glenn Hueckel (1973) has shown.[4] If the main impact of war on the British economy was through relative prices (a decline in trade, creating food and imported resource scarcities), capital accumulation (war debt crowding out, creating capital scarcities), and labor force growth (mobilization, creating unskilled labor scarcities), then there is no reason why the 'peacetime' model cannot be used to explore the British economy's response to these war-induced influences.

The arguments con: what about government expenditures and tax incidence?
The peacetime model in Chapter 8 failed to distinguish between private and public sector activities since the latter was so small after 1820. That was certainly *not* the case up to 1815, since net tax revenues rose to as much as 20 per cent of national income during the 1810s (Table 11.2, col. 2). The fact that the government sector was larger prior to the 1820s matters for two reasons. First, it may have induced important shifts in the composition of final demand. Second, the complex array of direct and indirect taxes that were developed to finance the war effort clearly had an unequal influence on real disposable incomes across social classes.

Did military expenditures have a very different sectoral expenditure pattern from civilian expenditures? If the military placed approximately the same mixture of demands on agriculture, manufacturing, mining and services as did civilian expenditures, then one would be justified in applying the peacetime model to the French Wars. While there is a very large literature that has dealt with the role of demand during the industrial revolution (see, for example, the survey in Floud and McCloskey, 1981, Chs 1, 3 and 6), no one has offered comprehensive evidence that makes it possible to compare civilian and military expenditure patterns by supplying sector. A recent paper by Patrick O'Brien (1983) makes an heroic effort to supply some scraps of evidence on this issue, however. On the basis of O'Brien's estimates, it appears that the military market basket favored agriculture strongly, favored manufacturing (which includes booming shipbuilding and slumping construction), and penalized urban services harshly.[5] Since this evidence is so tentative, I am forced to assume in what follows that military and civilian expenditures generated pretty much the same distribution of final demand for agriculture, manufacturing, mining and services.

The second simplification may prove to be more serious. Nowhere have I confronted the fact that Britain relied heavily on indirect taxes (78 per cent of total tax revenues between 1790 and 1820, Table 11.2), and that these taxes appear to have been very regressive. If they fell heavily on the working poor, as conventional wisdom suggests (Mathias and O'Brien, 1976), then it would appear that this chapter will understate the role of war finance in accounting for the dismal growth in workers' living standards up to the 1820s. However, while regressive indirect taxes inflated common labor's cost of living, progressive transfers to the poor under the Old Poor Law also augmented their nominal incomes. Is the *net* distributive impact so obvious?[6] In addition, nowhere does the model include the impact of the inhabited house duty – introduced in 1778 to help finance the American War. The inhabited house duty seems to have fallen on the top of the income distribution, but it is quite possible that some of this tax was shifted on to poor renters. Furthermore, nowhere does the model include the impact of the various direct taxes on assets and incomes introduced by William Pitt, which increased as a share of the total tax take from 17 per cent in 1803 to 33 per cent in 1812.

Distributional inferences ought to be based on 'post-fisc' measures whenever possible. This statement holds with special force during these wartime years of crushing tax burdens and rising transfers. It also holds with special force during an epoch when common labor's standard of living failed to rise, encouraging some to infer that British capitalism failed. Alas, post-fisc quantitative assessments have not yet been attempted for this period, and they are certainly far beyond the scope of this book. It seems wise, however, to keep these limitations in mind when interpreting the results that follow.

(4) How would Britain's growth and industrialization have differed in the absence of war?

One could imagine two counterfactuals, and both would serve to factor out the wars from the industrial revolution. First, one could ask how the British economy would have performed in the absence of the wars. Second, one could ask how Britain's performance *would have differed* in the absence of the wars. This chapter takes the second approach, and for a very simple reason: economic historians still do not agree on the exact quantitative dimensions of Britain's macro performance through the Napoleonic period. Thus, I shall focus on the differences between predicted actual wartime performance and a predicted counterfactual peacetime performance that the model suggests would have taken place. That is, I shall ask how Britain's growth would have differed if, for example, war mobilization had never occurred. Similarly, I shall ask the same questions of war-suppressed capital accumulation and war-distorted relative prices.

Table 12.2 reports the counterfactual. The last column supplies the total impact while the first three columns break that total into its three parts: crowding out and capital formation, $d\overset{*}{K}$; mobilization and civilian unskilled labor force growth, $d\overset{*}{L}$; and relative price distortion at home, $d\overset{*}{P}_j$. Furthermore, Table 12.2 reports the counterfactual for 1790–1815 and for the 1760s–1810s separately, the former containing the years when war effects

Table 12.2 *By how much would Britain's growth have changed under counterfactual peacetime conditions?*

Endogenous variable (per annum growth)	No war debt crowding-out effects (dK^*)		No mobilization effects dL_j^*	No war-distorted price effects dP_j^*	All effects combined	
	RAA	NIA			RAA	NIA
1790–1815:						
Real income: dY^*	0.87	0.93	0.13	0.46	1.46	1.51
Sector outputs: dA^*	0.38	0.40	0.34	−2.76	−2.08	−2.05
dM^*	1.07	1.14	0.02	2.93	4.02	4.09
dC^*	1.06	1.13	0.09	0.70	1.86	1.93
dB^*	1.07	1.14	0.02	2.82	3.91	3.98
Industrialization index: $dM^* - dA^*$	0.69	0.74	−0.32	5.69	6.10	6.14
Export of manufactures: dM_X^*	1.49	1.59	−0.56	11.92	12.85	12.95
1760s–1810s:						
Real income: dY^*	0.55	0.67	0.06	0.23	0.84	0.96
Sector outputs: dA^*	0.24	0.29	0.15	−1.38	−0.99	−0.94
dM^*	0.67	0.82	0.01	1.47	2.15	2.30
dC^*	0.67	0.81	0.05	0.35	1.07	1.21
dB^*	0.67	0.82	0.01	1.41	2.10	2.24
Industrialization index: $dM^* - dA^*$	0.43	0.53	−0.14	2.85	3.14	3.24
Export of manufactures: dM_X^*	0.94	1.14	−0.28	5.96	6.62	6.82

Notes: The counterfactual civilian capital stock assumptions are taken from Table 11.4 where

	$\overset{*}{\mathrm{d}K}$		
		1790–1815	*1760s–1810s*
RAA		2.27	1.43
NIA		2.42	1.74

The counterfactual civilian unskilled labor force assumptions are taken from the text in section 2: for the 1790–1815 period, $\overset{*}{\mathrm{d}L} = 0.17$, $\mathrm{d}\overset{*}{P_A} = -0.49$, $\mathrm{d}\overset{*}{P_F} = -0.99$, and $\mathrm{d}\overset{*}{P_M} = 0$;   for the 1760s–1810s period, $\overset{*}{\mathrm{d}L} = 0.34$, $\mathrm{d}\overset{*}{P_A} = -0.99$, $\mathrm{d}\overset{*}{P_F} = -0.99$, and the counterfactual civilian capital stock assumptions are taken from

The counterfactual price assumptions are taken from Table 12.1, and the counterfactual civilian unskilled labor force assumptions are taken from the text in section 2: for the 1790–1815 period, $\overset{*}{\mathrm{d}L} = 0.34$, $\mathrm{d}\overset{*}{P_A} = -0.99$, $\mathrm{d}\overset{*}{P_F} = -0.99$, $\mathrm{d}\overset{*}{P_A} = -0.49$, and $\mathrm{d}\overset{*}{P_M} = 0$.

were most severe. Each of the panels reports the impact on the per annum growth rates of seven variables: aggregate real income, output in four sectors, manufactures exports (in constant prices), and an industrialization index (the difference between industry and agriculture's output growth). Finally, Table 12.2 reports results using both the real accrual accounting (RAA) and the national income accounting (NIA) approach to assessing the impact of the war debt on crowding out. Since the differences between them are relatively small, the discussion that follows will focus on the RAA counterfactuals.

The results are certainly striking. First, consider aggregate growth performance. Chapter 11 (Table 11.4, Notes to cols 6 and 7) offered a very simple calculation

$$d(\overset{*}{Y}_{CF}) = \alpha_K \cdot (\overset{*}{K}_{CF})$$

based only on the impact of the wars on civilian accumulation. That (RAA) calculation predicted that growth would have been higher by 0.50 per cent per annum from the 1760s to the 1810s, and 0.79 per cent per annum higher from 1791 to 1820. Those crude estimates turn out to be fairly close to the full general equilibrium calculations reported in Table 12.2, 0.55 and 0.87 per cent per annum higher due solely to capital accumulation effects $(d\overset{*}{K})$. Table 12.2 informs us that these capital accumulation effects were the most important source of British slow growth prior to the 1820s (0.55/0.84 = 65 per cent of the combined effects of war for the 1760s–1810s epoch). Yet the war-induced decline in the terms of trade (the $d\overset{*}{P_j}$ effects) plus mobilization (the $d\overset{*}{L}$ effects) were both sufficiently important that *total* war effects exceeded the accumulation effects themselves. It appears that Britain's aggregate real income growth would have been higher by 1.46 per cent per annum from 1790 to 1815, and 0.84 per cent per annum higher from the 1760s to the 1810s, had peace prevailed. If these calculations are even close to the mark, they have very important implications for the debate over British growth during the industrial revolution. Harley (1982, p. 286) has estimated that aggregate income growth in Britain accelerated from 1.3 to 2.3 per cent per annum between 1770–1815 and 1815–41. Table 12.2 suggests that *all* of this 'trend acceleration' must have been due to the fact that Britain ceased hostilities after the late 1810s. In other words, the trend acceleration had little to do with the underlying forces of capitalist development.

Furthermore, the relatively slow rate of industrialization prior to 1820 appears to have been war-induced. Had peacetime conditions prevailed, manufacturing output would have grown 2.15 per cent per annum faster; that is, Harley's Divisia Index (Harley, 1982, Table 5, p. 276) would have grown 3 or 4 per cent per annum, rather than the modest 1.5 or 1.6 per cent actually achieved between 1770 and 1815. Once again, if these calculations are even close to the mark, they imply that Harley's measured doubling in industrial output growth can be explained entirely by the switch from war to peace.

Agriculture, in contrast, would have undergone far slower growth, almost 1 per cent per annum slower, had not the wartime food scarcity encouraged domestic production. Since British agriculture grew no faster than 0.8 percent per annum between 1770 and 1815, the counterfactual suggests that agricultural output might even have declined under peacetime conditions. So much for the 'agricultural revolution'.

Finally, what about exports as an 'engine of growth'? Table 12.2 informs us that the great surge in Britain's trade volumes and export of manufactured staples (dominated by cotton textiles) would have been much faster and occurred far sooner under peacetime conditions, faster by some 6.62 per cent per annum over the six decades as a whole, according to the model. Furthermore, prices and world markets were doing most of the work: $5.96/6.62 = 90$ per cent due to $d\overset{*}{P}_j$. It follows that exports were indeed an engine of British growth during the first industrial revolution, and the export engine was clearly sputtering during this period of war-distorted world markets. All of these conclusions hold with even greater force for the 1790–1815 epoch, when all of these world market conditions had even more dramatic impact.

(5) Inequality and living standards during war and peace

The standard of living
One of the strangest paradoxes to emerge from the British industrial revolution is that the standard of living of the working class rose hardly at all up to the 1820s. How was it that growth failed to 'trickle down' to the working poor, to the common laborer? Social reformers have argued for more than a century that British capitalism simply failed to deliver, while others have stressed elastic labor supplies.

Table 12.3 suggests instead that most of the dismal standard-of-living performance prior to the 1820s can be attributed to the wars and their financing, not to the failure of capitalism or Malthusian burdens. Peacetime conditions would have raised the growth in the workers' living standards by 0.73 per cent per annum over the 1760s–1810s epoch of slow growth, or by 54 per cent for the six decades as a whole. Once again, if this counterfactual result is even close to the mark, then it suggests that historical evidence

Table 12.3 *By how much would common labor's standard of living have changed under counterfactual peacetime conditions?*

Real wage (per annum growth) $d(\overset{*}{w} - \overset{*}{P})$	*No war debt crowding out effects* ($d\overset{*}{K}$)		*No mobilization effects* $d\overset{*}{L}$	*No war-distorted price effects* $d\overset{*}{P}_j$	*All effects combined*	
	RAA	NIA			RAA	NIA
	%	%	%	%	%	%
1790–1815	0.89	0.94	−0.27	0.59	1.21	1.27
1760s–1810s	0.56	0.68	−0.13	0.30	0.73	0.85

Notes: See notes to Table 12.2.

generated by the English standard-of-living debate is of doubtful relevance in testing whether capitalism's gains 'trickled down' to the working poor during early industrialization.

Which war effects were doing most of the work? Crowding out and forgone accumulation? Mobilization and unskilled labor scarcity? Embargoes, blockades and trade-suppressing world market conditions? In terms of labor's living standards, crowding out appears to have been the dominant force (0.56/0.73 = 77 per cent of the total over the six decades as a whole). Slow accumulation and thus slow rates of job creation (especially urban) account for most of the poor performance in living standards up to the 1820s, but war-induced price distortions played a major supporting role (0.30/0.73 = 41 per cent of the total). As we have seen, crowding out and forgone accumulation also account for most of slow aggregate growth, but they do *not* account for a large share of slow industrialization. Here, prices and world markets played a far greater role.

Inequality and the Kuznets curve

Earnings inequality and wage stretching were on the rise after the Napoleonic Wars. Most of this seems to have been due to the underlying forces of industrialization (Chapter 10), which created an aggregate unskilled-labor-saving and a skilled-labor-using bias, both of which served to create a relative scarcity of skills. Does it follow that any interruption in the pace of industrialization would have served to inhibit these earnings inequality trends? It is certainly true that the slower rates of accumulation during wartime prior to 1820 implied slower rates of capital-deepening and fewer new jobs for *all* workers, especially new jobs outside the farm sector. *All* workers would have shared in the poor real wage and standard-of-living performance up to 1820 as a result; but some would have suffered more than others. If wartime conditions favored unskilled-labor-intensive sectors like agriculture, and penalized skilled-labor-intensive sectors like industry, then *skilled* workers would have tended to lose some of their pay advantage over the unskilled.

So much for theory. What about fact? Tables 3.4 and 3.5 showed that the ratio of pay between skilled and unskilled actually declined a bit between 1781 and 1815, although stability is a better characterization of the larger 1781–1819 epoch. Can the wars explain this curious interlude of stability in pay ratios and, presumably, earnings inequality?

Table 12.4 offers an answer. Based on predictions about the skilled wage differential and unskilled labor's share in total wages, the table reports a counterfactual assessment (RAA only) of how differently earnings inequality would have behaved under peacetime conditions prior to 1820. The counterfactual supports my intuition that the wars had a far more deleterious impact on skilled labor than on unskilled labor – a result common to all twentieth-century wars (Williamson and Lindert, 1980). Thus, the skilled wage differential would have risen some 4.76 per cent per annum faster between 1790 and 1815 under peacetime conditions, and 2.56 per cent faster for the six decades as a whole. Since the skilled wage differential actually *fell* between 1781 and 1815 (Table 3.5), and since the counterfactual suggests

Table 12.4 *How differently would inequality have behaved under counterfactual peacetime conditions?*

Endogenous variable (per annum growth)	No war debt crowding-out effects dK^* (RAA only)	No mobilization effects $d\overset{*}{L}$	No war-distorted price effects $d\overset{*}{P}_j$	All effects combined (RAA only)
1790–1815:				
Real unskilled wage: $d(w - \overset{*}{P})$	0.89	−0.27	0.59	1.21
Real wage on skills: $d(q - \overset{*}{P})$	2.21	0.18	3.58	5.97
Skilled wage differentials: $d(q - \overset{*}{w})$	1.32	0.45	2.99	4.76
Unskilled labor's share in total wages	−0.23	−0.02	−0.53	−0.78
Return on equity: $d(r - \overset{*}{P})$	−1.81	0.19	−0.77	−2.39
Real land rents: $d(d - \overset{*}{P})$	0.50	0.28	−3.47	−2.69
Property income share:	−0.17	0.03	−0.73	−0.87
1760s–1810s:				
Real unskilled wage: $d(w - \overset{*}{P})$	0.56	−0.13	0.30	0.73
Real wage on skills: $d(q - \overset{*}{P})$	1.39	0.09	1.79	3.27
Skilled wage differentials: $d(q - \overset{*}{w})$	0.83	0.23	1.50	2.56
Unskilled labor's share in total wages	−0.15	−0.01	−0.26	−0.42
Return to equity: $d(r - \overset{*}{P})$	−1.14	0.09	−0.38	−1.43
Real land rents: $d(d - \overset{*}{P})$	0.31	0.14	−1.73	−1.28
Property income share:	−0.10	0.01	−0.36	−0.45

Notes: See notes to Table 12.2. All endogenous variables have been defined previously, but four may need a reminder: return to equity, $i = r/p$; unskilled labor's share in total wages, $wL/(wL + qS)$; property income share, $(dY + rK) \div Y$; and the cost-of-living index, $P = \phi_A P_A + \phi_M P_M + \phi_C P_C$. With the exception of unskilled labor's share in total wages and the property income share, all variables are in rates of change per annum. The shares are reported as absolute changes in percentage points per annum.

that the skilled wage differential would have risen at 4.76 per cent per annum under peacetime conditions, then it follows that this curious interlude *was* accounted for by the wars. Furthermore, during the 1790–1815 period, almost one-third of that counterfactual experience with wage differentials was due to accumulation effects (1.32/4.76 = 0.277) and almost two-thirds were due to price effects (2.99/4.76 = 0.628). Similar results apply to the six decades as a whole.

What was true for wage differentials was also true for unskilled labor's share in total wages, my proxy for earnings inequality. In the absence of war, earnings inequality is likely to have risen (common labor's share would have fallen) far sooner than was in fact the case. Although 1827 is the earliest year for which British earnings distribution can be reconstructed (Chapter 3, Table 3.2), suppose, for the sake of argument, that common (unskilled) labor's share in total wages averaged about 70 per cent between 1790 and 1815. In contrast with that wartime earnings distribution stability, Table 12.4 informs us that common labor's share would have declined from 70 per cent to about 50 per cent under the counterfactual peacetime conditions over the quarter century.

The accumulation, mobilization and trade effects associated with the wars appear to have had a profound impact on wage differentials and earnings inequality prior to 1820: the wars served to offset the earnings inequality trends set in motion by the underlying forces of the industrial revolution.

Income inequality is another matter entirely. Since the wars served to inflate grain prices, land rents tended to rise as well, especially after the early 1790s. While Table 12.4 illustrates that mobilization and slower accumulation during wartime tended to erode land rents in agriculture (suppressing the marginal *physical* product of farmland), the rise in grain prices tended to inflate land rents (raising the marginal *value* product of farmland), and the latter clearly dominated the former. Rents per acre rose as a result. With the stock of farm land relatively fixed, land's share in national income should have tended to rise as well. Since landlords were clearly at the top of the size distribution, it follows that war-distorted prices served to create inequality at the top of the distribution. What about the profit share? The story here is a bit more complex, but the bottom line is unambiguous. While the war served to *lower* the rate of accumulation by 2.27 per cent per annum between 1790 and 1815 (RAA estimate; see notes to Table 12.2), all three war effects combined served to *raise* the return to equity by about the same amount, 2.39 per cent per annum. The *net* impact of the war on the profit share must have been quite small. It follows that the vast majority of war-induced changes in the property income share must lie with changes in the land rental share. Now consider the counterfactual impact of peacetime conditions on the property income share. Table 12.4 reports that in the absence of wartime conditions the property income share would have fallen at 0.87 percentage points per annum between 1790 and 1815 over and above the influence of underlying forces associated with the industrial revolution. Since this counterfactual erosion in the property income share would have been due mostly to the behavior of land rents, it follows that most of the counterfactual erosion would have been due to the absence of war-distorting price effects that favored the rich landed interests.

Did wartime conditions serve to reinforce or offset the income inequality generated by the British industrial revolution? While the wars served to create a more equal distribution of income at the bottom, they also served to increase shares of the landed rich at the very top. The net effect on overall inequality is uncertain.

(6) War versus the industrial revolution: a final accounting

The wars *can* be factored out of the first industrial revolution, but it requires an explicit commitment to some economic model of the British economy. The revisionist gains are certainly great, but so are the costs. Some readers will take exception to the assumptions underlying the model or to the way the counterfactuals have been posed. Subsequent debate will, I hope, focus on assumptions and counterfactuals, rather than simply on further attempts to document precisely what happened. The counterfactual modeling appears to have yielded profound insights into the sources of British growth, industrialization and inequality experience before 1820.

Consider the main findings of this chapter.

Question: how much of Britain's slow growth during the first industrial revolution can be explained by war? *Answer:* most of it. Had peacetime conditions prevailed, British growth would have been augmented by about 0.8 per cent per annum from the 1760s to the 1810s, and by about 1.5 per cent per annum from 1790 to 1815. Most of the lower wartime growth rates seem to be the result of the lower rates of accumulation that wars and their financing produced.

Question: did the wars accelerate or retard the rate of industrialization? *Answer:* they retarded it. Indeed, British agriculture would have undergone no growth at all under peacetime conditions, and *all* of the measured doubling in industrial output growth between 1770–1815 and 1815–1840 (Chapter 11, based on Harley, 1982) is explained by the switch from war to peace. The impact of world market conditions, distorted by war's effects on trade, seems to account for most of this sectoral growth experience.

Question: 'What would have happened to living standards if there had been no wars?' (Hartwell and Engerman, 1975, p. 193). *Answer:* most of the dismal standard-of-living performance prior to the 1820s can be attributed to the wars and their financing. Indeed, had peacetime conditions prevailed over the six decades following the 1760s, workers' living standards would have grown 0.7–0.85 per cent per annum faster than was in fact the case. Furthermore, most of the dismal standard-of-living performance can be attributed to the war's effects on accumulation, not to the inflation of food prices.

Question: did the wars serve to produce a leveling in the distribution of earnings and a contraction in wage differentials? *Answer:* yes, like all major wars. Had peacetime conditions prevailed, the wage inequality trends that appeared with such drama after Waterloo would have appeared far earlier.

The wars served to postpone the influence of the industrial revolution on wage inequality.

While the wars served to generate a leveling in the earnings distribution, they also served to increase shares of the landed rich and thus created inequality at the top of the income distribution. *Question:* what was the net effect of these offsetting influences on income inequality? *Answer:* I simply cannot say. I do not know whether the British Kuznets curve would have appeared earlier in the absence of the wars.

Notes

1   Mokyr and Savin (1976, p. 221) feel that these estimates of the mobilization effects are too high. They estimate that those mobilized went from 2 to 5 per cent, rather than the 2 to 10 per cent reported in the text. What accounts for the difference? My estimate covers the period 1790–1812, while the Mokyr and Savin figure covers the period 1800–12. Furthermore, my estimate includes the navy and the marines, while it appears that the Mokyr and Savin estimate does not. I shall stick with my estimate in what follows, but if Mokyr and Savin are correct then the impact of war on the standard of living, on per capita income and on industrialization is *understated* in sections 4 and 5.

2   What about productivity change? There are some who might argue that excess demands on Britain's agricultural capacity encouraged an acceleration in productivity advance there. For example, the wave of enclosures seems to have been influenced by inflation in grain prices where rents were sticky (Allen, 1982), and, to the extent that enclosure led to more rational resource allocation on the farm, there may well have been some efficiency gains that would have served to augment productivity advance in British agriculture. One might also argue that expenditures on armaments fostered 'technological spillovers' into capital goods production, an argument made recently by Kozo Yamamura for Meiji and Taisho Japan (Yamamura, 1977). I do not support these arguments, and Ashton (1959, p. 83) doesn't either:

> It is possible to point to a few – a very few – technical inventions to which [the wars of the eighteenth century] gave rise.

3   Jeffrey Frankel (1982, p. 305) recently estimated that the American embargo raised British raw cotton prices by as much as 72 per cent in English markets, and that it served to lower the British terms of trade at home (cotton twist relative to Sea Island cotton) by some 42 per cent. It seems that Frankel's calculations are much too high to be applied to the Napoleonic Era as a whole. Furthermore, they cannot serve as a very effective proxy for the terms of trade between imported grains and raw materials relative to all manufactures.

4   Hueckel's paper 'War and the British Economy, 1793–1815' was the first such application to this problem in British history. While his effort was certainly innovative, the model is, in my opinion, too simplified to capture Britain's structural features during the first industrial revolution. There are only two sectors in Hueckel's model – agriculture and manufacturing – no raw material inputs to manufacturing, and no non-tradeables. Furthermore, Hueckel offers only qualitative assessments of the impact of capital formation.

5   O'Brien (1983, p. 31) culled the *Parliamentary Estimates*, and was able to get average expenditure distributions for 1804, 1809 and 1810. His categories were: pay, food and provisions, clothing, shipbuilding and repairs, hire for sea transport, building and construction, arms and ammunition, purchase and hire of horses, barrack stores, and prisoners of war. If military pay is allocated such that the combination of pay plus food and provisions plus clothing is distributed between food, clothing and 'other' according to rural workers' budgets in the South of England (Appendix Table A.1), then a military final demand allocation can be constructed from O'Brien's figures. These can then be compared with the 1821 peacetime final demand allocation given in Appendix Table D.5:

Supplying sector	Military final demand allocation %	1821 peacetime final demand allocation %
Agriculture	52.47	35.45
Manufacturing, construction and shipbuilding	34.14	29.44
Services and mining	13.39	35.11

Relative contraction of (urban) services is by far the most striking attribute suggested by this comparison. If it is even close to the truth, then it suggests that the long debate in the literature about the role of demand in the industrial revolution is misguided – first, because the wars played a far greater role in shifting the final demand mix than did long-run development forces, and, second, because the relative change in the fortunes of urban services was far more important than the agriculture versus manufacturing impact, which the literature debates almost exclusively.

6   The distributive impact of regressive indirect taxes would be more obvious had the economy-wide supply of unskilled labor been very elastic. Under 'labor surplus' assumptions, such taxes would have left the post-fisc wage unchanged, shifting the taxes back on to employers. This is *not* the labor supply assumption that this book advocates, but David Ricardo certainly did when he stated before the House of Commons in 1819 that

> He could not . . . agree, that [excise taxes] fell on the labourer, because imposed on the objects he consumed . . . the more the articles taxed approached the nature of necessaries, the more completely would they fall on those who employed labourers. (Ricardo, Vol. V, 1962, p. 26)

Indeed, in the Ricardian model such taxes would serve only to diminish the surplus available for accumulation, and thus diminish the number of jobs available in the future.

13

Data, Theory and Debate

(1) Key findings

British capitalism did breed inequality, and the inequality drift seems to have been a product of the forces associated with the industrial revolution. The rise in inequality can be dated around 1760, and it was manifested throughout the full income distribution: the income shares at the top rose, the shares at the bottom fell, the relative pay of the unskilled deteriorated, the premium on skills increased, and the earnings distribution widened. The French Wars interrupted the process, but the rise in inequality picked up following Waterloo. British inequality seems to have reached a peak somewhere around the 1860s or shortly thereafter. While not spectacular, the egalitarian leveling up to World War I was universal: the income shares at the top fell, the shares at the bottom rose, the relative pay of the unskilled improved, the premium on skills declined, and the earnings distribution narrowed.

These inequality facts support Simon Kuznets' (1955) conjecture that income inequality is likely to show an early rise and late decline as economic development proceeds. But the more interesting question is why? Why should the Kuznets curve appear in some countries and not in others? Why should some experience far more serious inequality problems than others? And what explains the turning points?

The advantage of working with 150 years of British economic history is that this offers the long perspective necessary to uncover the 'sources' of the Kuznets curve. Inequality changes only slowly over time, and it takes major economic and demographic events to influence the distribution of income significantly. What more major events can one imagine than the industrial revolution, the demographic transition, war on the far side of Waterloo and *Pax Britannica* on the near side – all packed into the century and a half from 1760 to World War I. So there is no shortage of events that theory tells us might have contributed to the British Kuznets curve and its timing.

How are the forces that drove inequality trends to be identified and isolated? How are the major forces to be separated from the minor ones? This book was guided in this quest by my reading of the evidence that most of the changes in inequality from 1827 to 1901 seem to have been driven by changes in factor rewards – the structure of pay from the lowest to the highest skill, rents on land relative to the wages of labor, and returns to conventional capital relative to all other inputs – *not* by changes in the distribution of factor ownership. Changes in earnings inequality are explained primarily by changes in the structure of pay rather than by employment shifts from occupations with low skill content to those with high. While skills may well have become more equally distributed in the late nineteenth century, it was the erosion in the premium on those skills, and the relative increase in the scarcity of unskilled labor, that did most of the work in driving earnings inequality. Similarly, the increase in the top 5 per cent's share in national income across the French Wars had little to do with increased concentration of landed wealth – although such an increase may well have taken place – but rather with the behavior of rents per acre. Changes in the distribution of wealth induced by accumulation served to reinforce the influence of changes in factor rewards on the distribution of income, but it was initial change in factor rewards that seemed to matter in setting the Kuznets curve in motion, and contributing to turning points.

To understand the joint determinants of unskilled wages, the skilled labor premium, rents and profit rates requires careful attention to macro forces driving conditions in factor markets for labor, skills, land and capital – just as Ricardo, Mill and Marx advised us. This book develops a general equilibrium model that is capable of predicting Britain's experience with growth, industrialization and inequality in response to the economic and demographic shocks that were the main interest of the classical economists too. The model seems to work well in accounting for British experience between 1821 and 1911. Thus encouraged, the model was used to sort out the main sources of the Kuznets curve.

Inequality and growth are complex events, and the reader is best advised to read Chapters 8–12 carefully for the complete narrative that this book offers. But the story is told in three parts: industrialization under unusual wartime conditions up to Waterloo; unfettered early industrialization under *Pax Britannica*; and late industrialization from mid-century to World War I. The key morals suggested by my interpretation can be summarized briefly:

- Labor 'surplus' conditions and the demographic transition never seem to have played an important role.
- World market conditions and British commercial policy seem to have muted the Kuznets curve. During the inequality upswing after 1820, world market conditions served partially to offset the underlying inequality forces associated with the industrial revolution. The opposite was true in the late nineteenth and early twentieth century.
- The key attribute of the industrial revolution that tended to produce inequality up to the mid-nineteenth century seems to have been unbalanced productivity advance, which favored those sectors that used skills and machines most intensively. As the rate and unbalanced character of technical progress slowed down later in the century, and especially during the Edwardian period, so too did the forces tending towards inequality quiet down.

- The resource commitments of war between 1760 and 1820 tended to inhibit growth, standard-of-living improvement, and industrialization. The impact of war on the rate of accumulation and on the relative price of agricultural products seems to have been central in explaining a whole host of 'paradoxes' associated with late eighteenth-century British development: little improvement in the standard of living among common laborers, sluggish rates of industrialization, slow per capita income improvement, very modest rates of capital-deepening, *and*, as it turns out, inequality trends that were very unlike those that followed Waterloo.
- Skill bottlenecks seem to have played a very important role in accounting for the Kuznets curve, especially in earnings and in the structure of pay. Much of the rise in earnings inequality up to mid-century can be explained by very inelastic skill supplies. Much of the leveling after mid-century can be explained by a much more elastic supply, which seems to have produced an acceleration in the rate of skills-deepening.

Through all of this, the book has found it very helpful to view the British Kuznets curve as reflecting the tension between disequilibrating factor demand forces associated with the industrial revolution and equilibrating factor supply forces, which served to have the opposite influence. The rise in inequality up to mid-century is seen as the result of the coincidence of very strong disequilibrating factor demand *and* inelastic factor supply. Industrialization had a bias – it tended to save on unskilled labor at the macro level. The more rapid the rate of industrialization after 1820, the greater the bias, and hence the upswing of the Kuznets curve. Retardation in the rate of industrialization implied a diminution in the bias. Thus, the downswing of the Kuznets curve up to World War I is seen as the result of the coincidence of elastic factor supply *and* weak disequilibrating factor demand.

These are the main findings, but they are hardly immutable. How might they be overturned by new evidence, by different interpretations of the same evidence, or by a different set of questions?

(2) New evidence?

A reading of Chapters 2–4 should make it clear that the data documenting real wage and inequality trends are weak and incomplete. Improved evidence might change one's interpretations of the timing and magnitude of the British Kuznets curve. Consider the points where the evidence is weakest.

Chapter 2 reports that common labor's real wage rose hardly at all up to about 1820, while it increased sharply thereafter. This finding is important in establishing the 1820s as a turning point separating the slow growth of wartime from the fast growth of *Pax Britannica*. The dating of that turning point is conditional on the imperfect cost-of-living index underlying the real wage calculation. Furthermore, the new cost-of-living index reported in this book relies heavily on new house rent and clothing indices, which seem certain to undergo sharp scrutiny by serious critics.

Nor does the cost of living appear as a critical issue only for the standard-of-living debate. Chapters 3 and 4 follow a time-honored convention and deal only with the *nominal* distribution of earnings and incomes, as well as with the *nominal* 'wage gap' between unskilled farm and urban labor. How much of the 1820 'wage gap' can be attributed to the higher cost of living in the cities? How much of the apparent rise in inequality between 1820 and 1860 is the result of the shift of labor to high cost-of-living cities, or of the greater rise in living costs in cities than in the countryside? I have no idea, and it is important to get spatial estimates of the cost of living to explore this issue fully.

Common labor's standard of living and measures of inequality depend on labor utilization rates as well as the real wage when fully employed. There are only incomplete public records, doubtful econometric backcasts and opinionated guesses about the behavior over time in unemployment, under-employment and pauperism. Until these variables can be better documented for the century following 1760, I shall always remain a bit uneasy about any standard-of-living generalization. In any case, Chapters 2 and 3 deal almost exclusively with adult males. The debate over inequality and living standards could certainly use more evidence on the secondary labor force – wives and children.

The income distribution data presented in Chapter 4 rely heavily on tax records. Reported incomes in those records have serious flaws, and they are of doubtful relevance by themselves anyway. Only the very richest had their income and assets taxed, and it is unlikely that changes in the distribution among them mattered much to overall inequality. Chapter 4 offered some heroic attempts to use inhabited house duty tax evidence to learn more about the middle of the income distribution, but the effort needs careful scrutiny by specialists. The 'social arithmetic' from Gregory King in 1688 to R. Dudley Baxter in 1868 fills out the complete size distribution from middle to bottom, but are such contemporary guesses to be believed? Chapter 4 offered lots of arguments in the negative, and tried to amend these guesses. I am not sure Chapter 4 was always successful; in particular I am not certain whether the new numbers allocated to occupation/social class by modern sampling techniques and econometrics are a real improvement over the old guesses by perceptive observers. New evidence is needed, especially for the pre-Census period.

Central to my measure of inequality is the effort reported in Chapter 3 to reconstruct pay ratios and the earnings distribution, the latter for the nineteenth century and the former back even earlier. The earnings distribution estimates are probably only as good as the occupational pay ratios underlying the reconstruction. One of my main goals has been to extend the earnings evidence well beyond farm laborers and the building trades to include the white-collar workers as well as urban service workers of lower skill. It turns out that wages in the urban service sector are crucial in understanding what happened to the pay structure more generally. So, how good are these new estimates? They are based very heavily on public sector pay quotations. Since there is little hard evidence on how public versus private white-collar pay differentials behaved over time, one should be equally uneasy about any real wage or inequality index that leans so heavily on the public sector. New evidence on private sector white-collar pay is urgently needed, from the late eighteenth century to the Playfair Commission in the 1870s.

Furthermore, post-fisc income concepts have been almost completely ignored in this book. How would one's perception of standard of living and inequality change if one took explicit account of taxes and transfers, especially in comparing the tax-heavy war years up to the 1820s with tax-light *Pax Britannica* thereafter?

Finally, what about the distribution of wealth? Here one can only await with excitement Peter Lindert's assessment of 'who owned England?' as his research reaches the publication stage.

Measures of inequality are not the only potential sources of error. Suppose the measures of inequality and real wage behavior presented in this book survive hard critical assessment and new evidence. What about the data that have been used to test the accuracy of the model (Chapter 9)? Could it be that revisions of measured rates of output growth, price and other variables endogenous to my general equilibrium model will be less kind to my assessment of the model's success in replicating history, especially the history between 1821 and 1861? Perhaps, but the more serious problem, it seems to me, is to improve the quality of the estimates of those variables that Chapter 10 argued were either trivial or central to the British Kuznets curve. Feinstein's (1978a) pioneering estimates of capital formation and the rate of accumulation will, no doubt, undergo tough scrutiny in the near future. Should his estimates be significantly revised, then my interpretation of capital accumulation's very modest role may also have to be revised. The same might be said for evidence documenting the drift in relative output prices that reflected changing world market conditions from the 1790s to World War I. My own hunch, however, is that relative price and accumulation estimates are unlikely to offer major revisionist gains to critics of this book.

The really *big* gains to our knowledge would be improvements in (i) sectoral rates of total factor productivity growth from the 1760s to World War I and (ii) British experience with skills-deepening across the nineteenth century. It is a bit unsettling to conclude in Chapter 10 that unbalanced productivity advance across sectors and the rate of skills-deepening economy-wide are the most critical factors driving British inequality across the nineteenth century, when these are variables about which the least is known! One can only hope that future economic historians will fill the gap, and that the effort will be kind to the tentative guesses used boldly in this book.

(3) Different theories?

I am often amused by some of my cliometric friends when they use the phrase 'theory tells us'. Different theories often, though not always, tell us different tales. Which theories are used here?

   This book relies heavily on general equilibrium theory. How should the reader decide whether or not s/he likes that theory, and thus whether or not s/he likes my interpretation of history? This answer should not hinge on the word 'general', since historians have long felt comfortable with 'general' views of history, i.e. as a seamless web. 'Partial' analysis of households, markets or industries may be quite satisfactory for some problems, but it simply won't do for almost all of the problems raised in this book – industrialization, distribution, growth and accumulation. The answer, then, must hinge on the word 'equilibrium'.

   The approach taken in this book is that markets *did* clear in the long run by changes in wages and prices, and that the economist's assumption of perfect competition came about as close to being satisfied as one will ever get. Many, perhaps most, readers of this book may disagree with that characterization. Does it matter? For some issues, it may not. For example, the finding that aggregate labor saving tends to breed inequality does not need flexible wages to get that result. Excess supplies of unskilled labor generated by unskilled labor saving would serve to create pauperism, unemployment and sagging earnings at the bottom of the distribution if wages were inflexible downwards. If, in contrast, wages tend to fall to clear that excess supply, then common labor's earnings would fall just as surely as if it were unemployment that served to 'clear' the unskilled labor market. The only difference would be *who* among the unskilled bore the brunt of the decline in unskilled labor's earnings – not a trivial social issue, I agree, but a difference that is unlikely to change one's view of the Kuznets curve.

   On the other hand, the finding that the slow growth in Britain up to 1820 was due to the wars *is* very much conditional on the model espoused. If one believes that private saving was interest-elastic, then the central government public debt issue in the 1790s, for example, would have had a far more modest impact on the rate of accumulation in the civilian sector than Chapters 11 and 12 estimated. If one believes that the British economy was far from full employment in the early 1790s, then the Keynesian view that war stimulated growth would dominate the opposite view in Chapters 11 and 12 where something closer to full employment is assumed. And what about my assumption in Chapters 8–12 that Britain was 'a small country' that had little or no long-run influence on relative prices in world markets? Certainly the supply of raw materials and foodstuffs facing Britain was never infinitely elastic, nor was the demand for British manufactures in world markets perfectly elastic. But were those elasticities high enough to justify the convenient 'small country assumption' used throughout the book? I think so, but others may disagree. As Chapters 5, 6 and 10 point out, these demand elasticities matter.

   Critics may, of course, strongly disagree with some of the assumptions maintained in Part III of this book. But for which problems does the disagreement really matter? To simply say 'I don't like his assumptions' is not enough.

(4) Could Britain have done better?

Modern economic historians seem to have drifted a long distance away from the original questions that started the whole controversy over capitalist growth in the 1830s and 1840s. We have been so busy trying to improve the documentation on what really happened to growth, industrialization, accumulation, distribution and the standard of living that often it seems as if we have forgotten the important questions for which the documentation was being sought. Why did British inequality and the standard of living behave as they did from the late eighteenth century to World War I? Which were the important driving forces? Why? Was it because the British economy was more sensitive to some technological, demographic or world market conditions than others? Did that sensitivity change over time as Britain matured? Or was it that changes in those conditions were 'big' in some epochs and 'small' in others? Why do we care? How else are we to assess the ability or failure of Britain to adjust to demographic, technological and world market shocks? How else are we to assess Britain's performance in the early nineteenth century against her performance during the Edwardian period? Indeed, how are we to assess Britain's performance against those of other industrial revolutions that were to follow?

We have been so busy debating what really happened that we've forgotten to look for the lessons of history that might guide industrial revolutions in the contemporary Third World. Indeed, most contemporary observers seem to think that British history is irrelevant to contemporary growth problems in Asia, Latin America and the Middle East. They are very wrong in this view, but the 'lessons' of history cannot be passed on to the contemporary Third World until economic historians are sure that they can control for at least the most important of the exogenous or environmental conditions that differ between them. Only after doing so can the economic historian expect to offer guidance regarding the impact of fuel scarcity, the gains from trade, coping with city growth, problems of accumulation, avoiding extreme inequality, and so on.

Could Britain have done better? How? These two questions were at the heart of the reformist debate in the 1830s. They have been at the heart of the 'did Britain fail?' debate since the late nineteenth century. They are at the heart of contemporary debates in mature economies as they confront productivity slowdown, in newly industrializing countries as they confront inequality and urban problems, and in the poorer Third World countries as they confront the problems of growth and accumulation.

This book contains no answer to the question 'could Britain have done better?' But if my explanations for British inequality experience hold up, then we shall be better equipped to assess Britain's performance. The jury is still out on capitalism's trial.

Appendix A: A New Cost-of-Living Index, 1781–1914

(1) Constructing cost-of-living estimates, 1781–1850

Price indices: improvements in the old chestnuts?
The four price indices most often cited in the standard-of-living debate are those offered by Gayer–Rostow–Schwartz (GRS, 1953), Silberling (1923), Rousseaux (1938) and Tucker (1936). These four series are listed in Table 2.7. Participants in the debate have used these series to measure trends in the cost of a market basket of goods that was typical for the working-class household. Any criticism of these pioneering efforts should focus on three issues: (1) the underlying price data used to construct the index; (2) the commodities included in the index; and (3) the budget weights attached to the individual commodities. This section will briefly list the shortcomings of these four old chestnuts in an effort to motivate the revision presented in Appendix Table A.5.

Silberling, Rousseaux and GRS all use wholesale prices in their index number construction. Indeed, the data used by GRS were actually collected by Silberling (who, in many cases, chose not to use them). Silberling's chief source was the *Price Current* lists 'which were issued by several private agencies in London for the use of business men' (Silberling, 1923, p. 224). Rousseaux also drew much of his data from Silberling, as well as from Jevons (1884) and Sauerbeck (1886). Tucker's chief sources were the contract prices paid by three London institutions: Greenwich, Chelsea and Bethlem hospitals. The use of both wholesale and institutional (*and* London-based) prices has been criticized extensively in the literature. For example, T. S. Ashton (in Taylor, 1975, p. 48) argues that early nineteenth-century wholesale and retail prices did not conform over time and thus indices like Silberling's are invalid. Deane and Cole have criticized the use of contract prices since they 'tend to lag behind open market prices in their response to changes in demand and supply [and they] tend, probably more than other kinds of price quotations, to mask quality changes behind a customary price' (Deane and Cole, 1962, p. 13). They do admit, however, that contract prices for food, coal and candles did move quite freely. Moreover, the use of wholesale prices when retail prices are unavailable has

been defended for analysis covering many decades since 'in the long run . . .
retail prices must move in sympathy with wholesale prices' (Flinn, 1974,
p. 402). I agree with Flinn.

For a cost-of-living index to have any relevance, it must be based on a
market basket that accurately reflects consumption habits. The four price
indices under discussion imply very different consumption baskets. There
are two separate issues here: first, which commodities to include in the
market basket and, second, what weights to assign to each commodity.

The most serious flaw in these four price series is that they exclude rent.
True, Tucker does attempt to account for rent by assuming that this item
moves with nominal wages. While the assumption is convenient, it is
unlikely to hold in an economy experiencing rising density and rapid
urbanization. Rents rose rapidly from the 1780s to the 1850s (see below),
and cost-of-living indices that exclude this item understate the rise in the
workingman's cost of living.

While rents are a sin of exclusion, there are also sins of inclusion in these
price series. The GRS, Silberling and Rousseaux indices all contain many
raw materials used to produce consumption goods as proxies for the
consumption goods themselves. The use of such proxies introduces an
upward bias in the cost-of-living indices since they ignore cost-reducing
innovations in the processing of raw materials that were so characteristic of
the period. The problem is especially apparent with clothing, where
technological advance is not reflected in the price of raw wool or cotton.
(Indeed, augmented consumer demands due to cost-reducing innovations
might well be expected to *raise* the price of intermediate inputs, further
compounding the bias.) Unfortunately, the Tucker series is little better
since it is based on institutional contract prices, which tended to be quite
sticky for clothing. This bias is likely to be especially serious for the GRS
index, where industrial raw materials such as iron, lead, tin, copper and
timber have a combined budget weight of 8 per cent. In a review of the GRS
index, Ashton wrote that the inclusion of raw materials rather than consumption goods meant that the index 'should not be used . . . to measure
changes in the purchasing power of consumers' (Ashton, 1955, p. 381). I
agree with Ashton.

The market basket should not only contain appropriate commodities, but
it should also include appropriate weights. Unfortunately, the exact weighting schemes used by Rousseaux and Tucker cannot be inferred from their
published work. Rousseaux's overall index is an unweighted average of two
other indices, an agricultural and an industrial commodity price index, a
procedure that clearly overstates the weight attached to industrial goods in
the workingman's budget. The weighting schemes used to create these two
sub-indices, and the commodities included in them, are not clear, although
Gayer, Rostow and Schwartz suggest that a simple geometric average was
applied. Tucker supplies aggregate commodity weights for food, clothing,
fuel and light, and sundry manufactures, but fails to supply the individual
commodity weights within these aggregates. His aggregate weights are
adjusted over time in the sense that he uses one for 1790–1814 and another
for 1815–50. The weights are 'based on studies by Wood, Chadwick, Nield

and Lowe, and on the official ration of the Chelsea veterans' hospital' (Tucker, in Taylor, 1975, p. 23). The weights for domestically produced commodities in the GRS index come from 'production figures', while weights for imported commodities come from estimates of home consumption (GRS, vol. 2, pp. 481–2). Both of these seem inappropriate representations of workingmen's budgets. Silberling's budget weights 'were drawn from studies by Nield, Wood, and Booth' (Silberling, 1923, p. 234). The close similarity between Tucker's and Silberling's aggregate budget weights can be explained, presumably, by the fact that they used similar sources. The major difference among the four series aggregate budget weights is the large weight given to 'other' goods in the GRS index. This figure is certainly too large for working-class or agricultural households. I intend to do better by going to working-class budgets directly.

There are also problems in the breakdown of food expenditures underlying the GRS and Silberling indices. In considering the two indices, Ashton commented on the 'overweighting of mutton as compared with beef' (Ashton, 1955, p. 381) in the GRS index, and on the large expenditures on meat and butter in the Silberling budget (Ashton, in Taylor, 1975, p. 49). Ashton was also disturbed by the absence of potatoes in the budgets, and I shall improve on this state of affairs.

Budget weights
In the context of modern demand theory, cost-of-living indices based on fixed budget weights may seem inappropriate. After all, the approach fails to let households respond to changes in relative prices, an especially serious behavioral restriction during, for example, the Napoleonic era when the relative price of grains shot up. Paul David and Peter Solar (1977) offer an excellent justification for this old-fashioned application of fixed budget weights. The Stone–Geary linear expenditure system (LES) and the extended linear expenditure system (ELES) have both had enormous popularity in current Third World applications (Lluch, Powell, and Williams, 1977; Kelley, Williamson and Cheetham, 1972). One of the main reasons for this popularity is that the LES and ELES stress the notion of subsistence, and this is exactly the reason that David and Solar found them useful in analyzing trends in American cost of living 1774–1974. I find it equally compelling for the British case, 1781–1914. That is, since I am estimating changes in the cost of living for low-income working-class households, the notion of subsistence – long embedded in the classical models of Ricardo, Malthus and Marx – is especially relevant and thus the 'old-fashioned' constant budget shares approach to the workers' cost of living seems to me quite defensible even in the face of modern demand theory.

Four sets of budget weights were constructed for the cost-of-living time series: northern urban, northern rural, southern urban and southern rural. My purpose is to see whether alternative budget weights matter to measured cost-of-living trends for working-class families.

Rural budget weights for both North and South were obtained from individual household data reported by county in David Davies (1795).

However, Davies supplied food expenditures only at high levels of aggregation. In order to break down Davies' aggregate expenditures on bread and
flour into their two expenditure components, I used 1904 working-class
budget weights (*Sixteenth Abstract of Labour Statistics*, 1914). Meat
expenditures were disaggregated into pork, beef and mutton expenditures
using W. A. MacKenzie (1921) augmented by the 1904 working-class
budgets. Expenditures on tea, butter and sugar were disaggregated using
weights obtained from Silberling (1923). The rural budget breakdown into
the larger aggregates of food, rent, fuel and light, and clothing was taken
from Davies without adjustment.

The rural breakdown on food expenditures obtained from the above
procedures was also used for the urban budgets. Weights for the larger
aggregates for food, rent, fuel and light, and clothing for urban areas,
however, were obtained by taking averages of those reported in Burnett
(1969), Tucker (1936) and Neale (1966). The Burnett figure was derived by
averaging the five urban household budgets he reports for the period 1795–
1845. Aggregate expenditure weights for urban areas (North and South
assumed to have the same aggregate expenditure shares, but not the same
disaggregated food composition) were then calculated as an unweighted
average of the Burnett figure, the household budget cited in Neale and the
two Tucker budgets (one for the pre-1815 period and one for 1815–50).

All four of these spatial-specific budgets are displayed in Appendix
Table A.1.

Appendix Table A.1   *Budget weights for cost-of-living estimation,*
1781–1850

Expenditure group	Northern rural %	Southern rural %	Northern urban %	Southern urban %
Food:	66.9	72.1	63.8	63.8
Bread	15.7	19.7	15.7	19.7
Flour (wheat)	39.1	48.9	39.1	48.9
Oats	7.7	0.0	7.7	0.0
Bacon (pork)	12.1	14.7	12.1	14.7
Beef	1.6	1.9	1.6	1.9
Mutton	0.8	1.0	0.8	1.0
Potatoes	7.9	0.0	7.9	0.0
Tea	3.0	2.8	3.0	2.8
Sugar	4.5	4.1	4.5	4.1
Butter	7.6	6.9	7.6	6.9
Rent	6.6	7.3	16.6	16.6
Fuel and light:	6.1	6.4	6.6	6.6
Candles	2.2	2.5	2.2	2.2
Fuel	3.9	3.9	4.4	4.4
Clothing:	20.4	14.2	13.0	13.0

Note: Food expenditure weights sum to 100%.

Appendix Table A.2 illustrates that these four budget weights matter very little to the long-term trends in the cost of living observed, with the possible exception of the northern rural weights, which exhibit somewhat lower price increases over the full six decades. Appendix Table A.6 illustrates even more clearly how little the remaining three weighting schemes matter to long run trends, and as a result I have chosen to use 'southern urban' in analysis in the text. This selection is arbitrary but at least consistent with so much of the standard-of-living debate, which stresses non-farm nominal wages in the South.

Commodity price and rent data
Price data for 1790–1850 were derived from Gayer, Rostow and Schwartz (GRS, 1953, microfilm of appendix tables) for the following goods: wheat (used as a proxy for flour), beets, oats, pork, tea, sugar, butter and tallow (used as a proxy for candles). Data for 1796–1850 for coal and mutton came from the same source. Coal prices for 1790–6 were taken from Beveridge (1939; prices paid by Greenwich Hospital). Eton College mutton prices for 1790–6 were also taken from Beveridge. Both coal and mutton prices for 1790–5 were linked to the GRS series using quotes from both series for 1796. Bread prices for 1790–1850 were taken from Mitchell and Deane (1971, p. 498). Potato prices were available only for the years 1790–1829, and were obtained from Beveridge (prices paid by the Lord Steward's Department). For the remainder of the period, I assumed that potato prices moved in the same way as did the aggregate of all other foods. Two sets of clothing prices were used. One set is from Tucker (1936), and is based on institutional prices, mainly those paid for clothing supplies by Greenwich Hospital. The other is based on cotton export piece good prices after 1820 (average declared value per year of plain cotton piece goods in the 'Report on Wholesale and Retail Prices in the U.K.', which in turn is based on Porter (1847), for 1820–39 and 'The Report on Prices of Exports and Imports', for 1840–50). The second clothing price series uses the first for the period 1790–1819.

What about rents? In Michael Flinn's words (1965, p. 6):

This sort of population pressure on housing must certainly have been reflected in trends of rents, and one of the more frustrating *lacunae* in the study of nineteenth-century economic and social history is the absence of any statistical study of house rents.

Thanks to Peter Lindert's efforts in collecting cottage rents from Trentham, Staffordshire (reported in Lindert and Williamson, 1980, Appendix C), I have now constructed a time series on dwelling rents (Appendix Table A.3). While the series is based on only one region, the data base is excellent, and furthermore the rent series conforms closely with the house rent estimates that become available in the mid-nineteenth century and beyond. Since the relative price of housing tended to rise faster than other consumer items throughout the industrial revolution, its inclusion in my revised series tends to support the pessimists. This can be seen clearly in Appendix Table D.6, where those cost-of-living indices with and without rents can be compared.

Appendix Table A.2   *Four cost-of-living series, 1790–1850, using various budget weights (rents included and using export cloth prices)*

Year	'Best guess' Southern urban	Alternative budget weights Southern rural	Northern urban	Northern rural
1790	125.9	136.8	124.7	147.5
1	121.2	131.5	121.2	143.8
2	118.3	127.4	118.1	139.8
3	127.3	137.0	127.5	149.1
4	130.7	140.8	133.8	155.6
1795	153.8	166.9	150.7	173.3
6	159.5	173.4	154.7	177.9
7	138.8	150.0	136.2	159.0
8	136.9	147.4	136.5	159.6
9	155.7	167.6	158.0	181.8
1800	207.1	225.7	202.9	229.3
1	218.2	238.7	207.8	235.3
2	160.9	173.7	157.4	183.0
3	156.8	168.7	155.9	181.7
4	160.2	172.4	158.1	184.4
1805	186.7	202.5	180.6	208.7
6	178.5	192.4	174.0	200.6
7	169.1	181.1	168.2	191.0
8	180.5	193.1	180.0	202.9
9	204.9	219.6	199.6	224.6
1810	215.4	230.8	208.0	232.9
1	204.5	217.9	200.1	223.6
2	235.7	252.4	232.8	257.8
3	230.0	246.1	226.0	250.3
4	203.3	215.4	203.0	228.8
1815	182.6	191.9	183.4	208.7
6	192.1	202.4	189.7	214.6
7	197.5	208.8	195.1	216.9
8	192.4	203.1	193.1	215.3
9	182.9	192.3	182.7	205.9
1820	170.1	177.7	170.7	192.8
1	155.5	161.2	157.2	177.8
2	139.8	143.7	143.2	160.6
3	146.0	150.7	147.7	163.6
4	154.6	160.6	155.4	171.5
1825	162.3	169.3	163.0	179.6
6	144.4	149.4	146.5	159.4
7	140.9	145.5	143.1	155.2
8	143.2	148.2	143.1	154.3
9	143.9	149.1	142.7	152.0

Appendix Table A.2   *Four cost-of-living series, 1790–1850, using various budget weights (rents included and using export cloth prices) continued*

Year	'Best guess' Southern urban	Alternative budget weights Southern rural	Northern urban	Northern rural
1830	141.3	146.0	141.1	150.5
1	141.3	146.2	141.4	150.1
2	133.9	138.0	133.0	139.9
3	124.7	127.6	124.1	130.5
4	117.6	119.4	118.7	124.9
1835	112.8	114.1	115.2	122.6
6	126.4	129.4	128.0	135.7
7	129.2	132.5	129.9	135.8
8	138.3	142.9	137.4	143.0
9	142.3	148.0	141.9	148.2
1840	138.4	143.6	138.7	143.8
1	133.3	137.9	132.8	137.2
2	123.4	126.8	122.5	125.2
3	109.6	111.4	109.6	111.4
4	114.5	116.4	114.7	116.6
1845	112.0	113.8	113.1	114.8
6	116.4	118.7	117.1	118.5
7	138.0	143.1	137.8	141.0
8	110.9	112.6	111.0	111.4
9	101.2	102.3	100.9	101.2
1850	100.0	100.0	100.0	100.0

Sources and Notes: The sources of the underlying price and rent data are described in the text to this appendix. The weights are taken from Appendix Table A.1.

Appendix Table A.3   *Average cottage rents, Trentham, Staffordshire, 1776–1897*

Year	Average rent (£ p.a.)	Year	Average rent (£ p.a.)	Year	Average rent (£ p.a.)
1776	0.788	1822	3.825	1860	4.812
1777	0.788	1823	3.824	1861	4.853
1778	0.794	1824	3.824	1862	4.928
1779	0.800	1825	3.824	1863	4.958
1780	0.800	1826	3.824	1864	5.029
1781	0.800	1827	3.824	1865	4.998
1782	0.800	1828	3.824	1866	5.104
1783	0.815	1829	3.868	1867	5.090
1784	0.860	1830	3.912	1868	5.090
1785	0.890	1831	3.912	1869	5.090
1786	0.890	1832	3.912	1870	5.090
1787	0.890	1833	3.988	1871	5.078
1788	0.890	1834	4.006	1872	5.066
1789	0.890	1835	3.867	1873	5.140
1790	0.890	1836	3.908	1874	5.140
1791	0.890	1837	3.908	1875	5.140
1792	1.113	1838	3.920	1876	5.255
1793	1.308	1839	3.744	1877	5.309
1794	1.336	1840	3.755	1878	5.346
1795	1.336	1841	3.768	1879	5.347
1796	1.337	1842	3.806	1880	5.349
1797	1.337	1843	3.799	1881	5.349
1798	1.417	1844	3.861	1882	5.349
1799	1.584	1845	3.861	1883	5.349
1800	1.584	1846	3.192	1884	5.349
1801	1.584	1847	3.861	1885	5.349
1802	1.584	1848	3.937	1886	5.502
1803	1.614	1849	3.727	1887	5.502
1804	1.675	1850	4.032	1888	5.502
1805	1.675	1851	3.988	1889	5.502
*		1852	3.888	1890	5.304
1812	3.471	1853	3.888	1891	5.503
1813	3.424	1854	3.826	1892	5.085
1814	3.424	1855	3.736	1893	5.255
*		1856	3.834	1894	5.255
1816	3.833	1857	3.946	1895	5.255
*		1858	4.278	1896	4.908
1820	3.811	1859	4.689	1897	5.645
1821	3.824				

*Denotes missing years.

Source: Lindert and Williamson, 1980, Appendix Table C.1. This is a linked series, 1838 = £3.92 as the base year.

For example, using southern urban weights and Tucker's clothing prices, the series with rents rises by 103.8 per cent between 1790 and 1812, whereas the series without rents rises by only 96.4 per cent. Between 1812 and 1850, the series with rents declines by only 51 per cent rather than 56 per cent.

Extending the cost-of-living series backwards to 1781
Relying heavily on Beveridge, and using the methods described above, these cost-of-living series were extended backwards an additional nine years, to 1781. These estimates are reported in Appendix Table A.4.

Appendix Table A.4   *Extending the cost-of-living indices back to 1781 (1850 = 100)*

| Year | Using Tucker clothing | | Using export clothing | |
	With rent	Without rent	With rent 'best guess'	Without rent
1781	94.4	109.2	118.8	138.5
1782	94.9	109.8	119.3	139.1
1783	97.5	112.9	121.9	142.2
1784	94.1	108.6	118.4	137.8
1785	88.0	101.1	112.3	130.3
1786	85.1	97.6	109.6	127.1
1787	87.7	100.7	112.5	130.5
1788	90.8	104.5	115.9	134.6
1789	96.9	111.8	122.3	142.2
1790	100.2	115.8	125.9	146.5

Notes: See notes to Appendix A.2. Southern urban budget weights applied.

A new cost-of-living index, 1781–1850
My 'best guess' cost-of-living index is reported in Appendix Table A.5. I shall summarize the main contributions that this revision of the 'old chestnuts' makes. First, rents have been added to the index. Since the relative price of housing rose faster than other consumer items during the industrial revolution, the inclusion of rents tends to support the pessimists who believe that the workers gained little. This can be seen clearly in Appendix Table A.6, where cost-of-living indices with and without rents can be compared. Second, my revisions include more relevant working class commodities (like potatoes), while excluding irrelevant industrial inter-mediate inputs (as in the GRS series) and minimizing the use of institutional contract prices (as in Tucker). It turns out that Tucker's series favors the pessimists' position while the GRS series favors the optimists' position. As Appendix Table A.6 illustrates, my index falls between these two extremes. Third, my revised index is based on budget weights that are grounded in the actual working-class household budgets of the time, namely the marvelous detail offered in Eden and Davies. This is in contrast with the weighting schemes used by Tucker, Silberling, Rousseaux and GRS. Of course, the critical reader may well be suspicious of my heavy reliance on Eden and

Appendix Table A.5   *A new cost-of-living index, 1781–1850 (1850 = 100)*

Year	'Best guess' cost-of-living index	Year	'Best guess' cost-of-living index
1781	118.8	1820	170.1
2	119.3	1	155.5
3	121.9	2	139.8
4	118.4	3	146.0
1785	112.3	4	154.6
6	109.6	1825	162.3
7	112.5	6	144.4
8	115.9	7	140.9
9	122.3	8	143.2
1790	125.9	9	143.9
1	121.2	1830	141.3
2	118.3	1	141.3
3	127.3	2	133.9
4	130.7	3	124.7
1795	153.8	4	117.6
6	159.5	1835	112.8
7	138.8	6	126.4
8	136.9	7	129.2
9	155.7	8	138.3
1800	207.1	9	142.3
1	218.2	1840	138.4
2	160.9	1	133.3
3	156.8	2	123.4
4	160.2	3	109.6
1805	186.7	4	114.5
6	178.5	1845	112.0
7	169.1	6	116.4
8	180.5	7	138.0
9	204.9	8	110.9
1810	215.4	9	101.2
1	204.5	1850	100.0
2	235.7		
3	230.0		
4	203.3		
1815	182.6		
6	192.1		
7	197.5		
8	192.4		
9	182.9		

Source: Appendix Tables A.2 and A.4.

Appendix Table A.6 *Long-period cost-of-living movements compared across sixteen indices, 1790–1850*

Index	1790–1812	Percentage price change over 1812–1850	1790–1850
Export/without rent/northern rural	72.7 Optimist extreme	−62.9 Optimist extreme	−36.0 Optimist extreme
Export/without rent/northern urban	80.4	−61.8	−31.1
Export/without rent/southern rural	82.0	−62.3	−31.4
Export/without rent/southern urban	81.0	−62.3	−31.7
Export/with rent/northern rural	74.8	−61.2	−32.2
Export/with rent/northern urban	86.7	−57.0	−19.8
Export/with rent/southern rural	84.5	−60.4	−26.9
Export/with rent/southern urban	87.2 'Best guess'	−57.6 'Best guess'	−20.6 'Best guess'
Tucker/without rent/northern rural	91.6	−53.9	−11.7
Tucker/without rent/northern urban	95.8	−55.4	−12.6
Tucker/without rent/southern rural	97.6	−56.2	−13.5
Tucker/without rent/southern urban	96.4	−56.0	−13.6
Tucker/with rent/northern rural	94.3	−52.0	−6.8
Tucker/with rent/northern urban	103.2 Pessimist extreme	−50.3 Pessimist extreme	+0.9 Pessimist extreme
Tucker/with rent/southern rural	100.5	−54.1	−8.1
Tucker/with rent/southern urban	103.8 Pessimist extreme	−51.0	−0.2

Sources and Notes: Lindert and Williamson (1980, Table 9, p. 46). 'Export' refers to clothing price series based on cotton export piece good prices. 'Tucker' refers to clothing price series based on institutional prices quoted in Tucker. The 'without' rent series is simply the cost-of-living index based on commodity prices only. 'Northern', 'southern', 'rural' and 'urban' refer to the budget weighting scheme in Appendix Table A.1.

Davies since their data were collected on poor agricultural households in the 1790s. The optimists might then argue that my weights favor the pessimists' view and that my cost-of-living index has an upward bias. The basis of the argument would presumably be that the Eden and Davies budgets are for families at the very bottom of the distribution for whom food expenditures were far higher shares of income than would have been the case for the average working-class family. Since the relative price of food appears to have risen over the period as a whole (Appendix E), the cost of living would have an upward bias – or so the optimists might allege. The allegation cannot be substantiated. Whether one uses budget weights based on urban workers' families (many of whom were skilled artisans and clerks) or on Eden and Davies' farm laborers matters very little to cost-of-living trends (Appendix Table A.6).

Appendix Table A.6 summarizes the behavior of sixteen alternative cost-of-living indices: with and without rents; using clothing prices from Tucker versus export values; and using four alternative budget weights. The range is wide, but for me the choice is clear. That is, I insist on including rents and I have little confidence in Tucker's institutional clothing prices, favoring the export value series instead. My 'best guess' (using southern urban weights) places me dead center between the optimist and pessimist extremes.

While I use the 'best guess' series for analysis of real wage growth throughout this book, I should emphasize just how important the cost-of-living index is to the debate. Appendix Table A.6 certainly exhibits a wide variance in changes in alternative indices over the six decades, 1790–1850.

Appendix Table A.7   *The importance of the cost-of-living index to the debate over real wage gains, 1797–1851: various real wage indices (1851 = 100)*

	(1)	(2)	(3)	(4)	(5)	(6)
		Building craftsmen			*Building laborers*	
			'Labor aristocracy'	*Phelps-Brown– Hopkins (PH)*		*'Middle Group'*
		Tucker	*'Best guess'*	*'Best guess'*		*'Best guess'*	*'Best guess'*
	Tucker	*'Best guess'*	*'Best guess'*	*PH*	*'Best guess'*	*'Best guess'*
Year	*COL*	*COL*	*COL*	*COL*	*COL*	*COL*
1797	74.54	58.36	46.73	61.34	48.05	52.54
1805	59.36	46.60	42.55	52.63	44.62	52.96
1810	64.42	49.03	42.73	54.09	45.03	51.54
1815	75.04	61.39	52.18	63.54	53.12	57.81
1819	69.81	56.48	50.26	62.47	53.03	54.35
1827	86.34	74.59	66.39	75.36	68.84	70.18
1835	96.46	87.68	78.62	90.68	85.99	85.97
1851	100.00	100.00	100.00	100.00	100.00	100.00

Sources and Notes: See text. Col. (1) – deflated by Tucker (1936, pp. 78–9);
Col. (2) – deflated by Appendix Table A.5.
Col. (3) – from Table 2.8.
Col. (4) – deflated by Phelps-Brown and Hopkins (1956, Appendix B, pp. 313–14).
Col. (5) – deflated by Appendix Table A.5.
Col. (6) – from Table 2.8.

But what about the implications for real earnings trends? Appendix Table A.7 gives some indication. Here I present two popular wage series that have been used by pessimists and optimists alike in the standard-of-living debate: Tucker's artisans in London and Phelps-Brown and Hopkins' building laborers in southern England. Now, we have already seen in Chapter 2 that my *nominal* earnings series for the 'labor aristocracy' corresponds closely with Tucker's nominal series, and that my 'middle group's' nominal earnings series also corresponds closely with the Phelps-Brown–Hopkins series, especially after 1797. This correspondence reappears in Appendix Table A.7 when all nominal series are deflated by the same cost-of-living index, the 'best guess' index. Striking differences appear only when the nominal wage series are deflated by different cost-of-living indices. In short, Appendix Table A.7 suggests that the standard-of-living debate is more about cost-of-living behavior than about nominal earnings experience.

(2) Constructing cost-of-living estimates, 1846–76

This period is documented far better than is the pre-1850 era. Appendix Table A.8 presents my working-class cost-of-living index for the three decades, 1846–76. What follows is a brief description of the sources.

Budget weights
With slight modification, this period relies on W. A. MacKenzie's (1921) 'lower quartile' working-class family budget in 1860. The modifications served to make her weights consistent with available price data. Thus, MacKenzie's total for meat is broken down into beef and mutton, and flour into bread and flour, the latter constructed by reference to 1904 working-class budgets in the *Sixteenth Abstract of Labour Statistics* (1914). Furthermore, her fuel and light aggregate is separated into fuel (coal, given a weight of 10) and light (tallow, given a weight of 3), the latter reported in the *Second Series of Memoranda, Statistical Tables and Charts* (1905). The following weights result from the exercise:

Food	66.9%
Flour	27.1
Potatoes	8.6
Bread	10.9
Beef	1.3
Mutton	0.6
Bacon	9.5
Butter	2.9
Tea	1.7
Sugar	4.3
Rent	16.1
Clothing	6.4
Fuel	3.7
Light	1.1
Other	5.8

Appendix Table A.8   *A new cost-of-living index, 1846–1914 (1900 = 100)*

Year	Cost-of-living index	Year	Cost-of-living index
1846	140.31	1880	117.45
7	158.71	1	115.45
8	127.89	2	114.38
9	117.45	3	114.06
1850	111.28	4	108.15
1	108.72	1885	102.17
2	112.97	6	99.36
3	140.12	7	96.89
4	158.76	8	97.10
1855	161.81	9	99.43
6	155.81	1890	99.09
7	145.29	1	99.64
8	121.97	2	99.18
9	123.32	3	97.12
1860	137.91	4	93.59
1	142.26	1895	91.57
2	135.89	6	91.62
3	127.97	7	93.95
4	127.08	8	96.66
1865	127.96	9	94.92
6	137.96	1900	100.00
7	155.02	1	100.16
8	149.02	2	100.12
9	128.86	3	101.26
1870	129.98	4	101.19
1	134.13	1905	101.43
2	145.30	6	101.16
3	150.64	7	103.70
4	138.13	8	104.91
1875	128.15	9	105.20
6	132.59	1910	105.98
7	123.82	1	106.12
8	116.09	2	110.42
9	111.73	3	110.57
		1914	111.08

Sources and Notes: See text.

Commodity price and rent data

Prices of flour, potatoes, beef, mutton, bacon, butter, tea and sugar all come from Sauerbeck (1886) and cover the whole period 1846–76. Beef and mutton prices use middling rather than prime; sugar prices use British West Indian (refined); and tea prices are a simple average of common Congou and the average import price from the Board of Trade. Bread prices are taken from Mitchell and Deane (1962, p. 498, for London).

Coal and tallow prices for 1846–1870 were taken from Sauerbeck: the coal prices are London quotations; and the tallow prices are apparently an average of Russian and Town tallow. For 1871–6, coal and tallow prices are taken from the *Second Series of Memoranda*, linked to Sauerbeck on 1871.

Clothing prices for the entire period are taken from the *Report on Wholesale and Retail Prices in the United Kingdom 1902* (1903), where the series refers to wholesale prices (export values) of plain cotton piece goods.

For 1846–69, I used Singer's (1941) rent series, interpolating for those years missing in his series. The years 1870–3 are taken from Cairncross (1953) and 1874–6 from Weber (1960), both linked to the Singer series.

Finally, 'other' consisted of domestic servants' wages for 1846–55 (from Layton, 1908), while for 1856–76 the index was constructed as a weighted average of domestic servants' wages (0.35 weight) and producer durables (0.65 weight, a proxy for consumer durables, from Feinstein, 1972, Table 63, 'plant and machinery'). These series were linked on 1855.

(3) Constructing cost-of-living estimates, 1877–1914

Appendix Table A.8 presents my working-class cost-of-living index for the late nineteenth century, 1877–1914. A brief description of the sources follows.

Budget weights
The aggregate commodity budget weights (food, rent, clothing, fuel and light, and other) are taken from Bowley (1937):

Food	60.0%
Rent	16.0
Clothing	12.0
Fuel and light	8.0
Other	4.0

The budget weights for individual foodstuffs are taken from 1904 working-class budgets reported in the *Sixteenth Abstract of Labour Statistics*. Owing to limited price data, the 1877–91 period is restricted to the same nine foodstuffs contained in the 1846–76 budget, while twenty-three items make up the aggregate for food 1892–1914:

1877–91

Flour	7.7%
Potatoes	6.9
Bread	19.2
Beef	18.4
Mutton	9.2
Bacon	7.3
Butter	15.7
Tea	8.4
Sugar	7.3

1892–1914

Bread	13.9%	Pork	4.2%
Flour	5.6	Bacon	5.3
Rice	0.8	Mutton (Brit.)	3.3
Tapioca	0.3	Mutton (Imp.)	3.3
Oatmeal	1.4	Milk	6.9
Potatoes	5.0	Butter	11.4
Beef (Brit.)	6.7	Eggs	5.3
Beef (Imp.)	3.3	Cheese	2.8
Tea	6.1%		
Coffee	0.6		
Cocoa	1.1		
Sugar	5.8		
Jams	2.2		
Currants	0.8		
Raisins	0.6		

Commodity price and rent data

Foodstuff prices are taken from the *Seventeenth Abstract of Labour Statistics* (1914–16) for 1892–1914, and from the *Memorandum on Cost of Living of the Working Classes* (1903) for 1877–91. Clothing prices for 1877–80 are taken from the same source as for 1846–76; those for 1881–99 come from the *Second Series of Memoranda*, which is based on 'the retail prices of 25 articles of clothing'; and those for 1900–14 are taken from Prest and Adams (1954). Fuel and light prices are taken from Prest and Adams for 1900–14, and from the *Second Series of Memoranda* for 1877–99. 'Other' expenditures' prices use Prest and Adams' price series 'other home expenses' for 1900–14, while the 1877–99 'other' price series is constructed exactly as that for 1856–76 and using the same sources. Finally, the rent data for 1877–99 come from Weber (1960) while those for 1900–14 come from Prest and Adams. Both rely on inhabited house duty returns.

(4) The 'sources' of cost-of-living drift

Which items in the working-class family's budget are mainly responsible for long-run trends in cost of living? Appendix Table A.9 decomposes the 'sources' of those trends into the five major expenditure items. The contribution of any item is the combined influence of the item's budget weight and its price change. An item whose price replicated general cost-of-living trends could still contribute the lion's share of the cost-of-living drift if its budget weight was very large. A key to *relative* price change is whether an item contributes *more* to the cost-of-living drift than its budget share. So it was with food.

It is clear that food prices drove the working-class cost of living between 1790 and 1914. Movements in the food price index never accounted for less than 78 per cent of total cost-of-living changes, and they often accounted for far more. Furthermore, despite the declining importance of food as a share in total working-class households' expenditures over the century, food prices did not relinquish their role as *the* central force driving the cost-of-living index. The only time that 'manufactures' played a significant role in

Appendix Table A.9   *The 'sources' of cost-of-living drift, 1790–1914*

Period	Total cost-of-living percentage change	(Percentage change in jth item) × (budget share weight)				
		Food	Rent	Fuel	Clothing	Other
1790–1812	+109.8	+85.5	+10.9	+4.7	+8.8	−0.1
1812–50	−135.7	−96.1	+2.1	−6.9	−34.7	−0.1
1847–58	−36.7	−36.0	+1.3	−0.1	−1.8	−0.1
1858–73	+28.6	+22.2	+2.7	+1.5	+1.5	+0.7
1873–1914	−37.6	−35.4	+3.3	−3.1	−3.5	+1.1

Sources and Notes: See text.

driving the cost-of-living index was during the 1812–50 deflation, when clothing prices accounted for a quarter of the decline, a share far exceeding the clothing budget weight. Finally, *note that rents consistently contributed to a rise in the cost of living even during periods of deflation*.

There are two morals that emerge from this exercise. Obviously, food remained the dominant wage-good throughout the century following 1790. Both housing and food are land-cum-labor intensive. Since economic growth generates land and labor scarcity, the first moral suggests that the working class suffered most from the cost-of-living drift over the century as a whole.

There is a second moral for the shorter run. Any period of price deflation implied a far greater decrease in the workers' cost of living generally, and the unskilled common laborers' particularly, than it did for the rich. Chapters 3 and 4 show that *nominal* earnings and income inequality leveled during the late nineteenth century. It now appears that price movements served, on the expenditure side, to reinforce those nominal egalitarian trends, making the leveling in *real* incomes even more pronounced, a finding also reported for America (Williamson, 1976b, 1977; Williamson and Lindert, 1980, Chapter 5). However, the same cannot be said of the post-Napoleonic deflation, a period of rising nominal inequality, or of the Napoleonic inflation, a period of leveling in the nominal earnings structure.

Appendix B: Constructing National Size Distributions of Income from Inhabited House Duty Tax Assessments and Window Tax Assessments

(1) Using the inhabited house duty (IHD) data

With minor manipulation, the IHD tax assessments supply mean annual rents (imputed to owner-occupants) and total number of families taxed, by rental class. One key to completing the national size distribution is an estimate for the average rent paid by those not taxed. This estimated average rent is then combined with the number of low-income households that escaped the tax, the latter derived as a residual when those households taxed are subtracted from total households enumerated by the Census. The second key ingredient to the analysis is a parameter linking rental expenditure to income. I would prefer to estimate

$$\ln R = \alpha' + \beta' \ln y_P + (1 + \gamma) \ln P_H + \delta \ln N \qquad (B.1)$$

where

y_P = individual household's real permanent income (deflated by some cost-of-living index),
P_H = annual rental per unit of housing, quality-adjusted, and deflated by some cost-of-living index,
N = size of household, and
$R = P_H \cdot H$ denotes annual rental expenditures on the quality-adjusted housing stock, H.

Unfortunately, the nineteenth-century micro data appear to allow the estimation of only the far simpler Engel function

$$R = \alpha Y^\beta. \qquad (B.2)$$

Appendix Table B.1   *Three British estimates of rental elasticities with respect to current income*

Date	Data base	Income range £	Rental range £	Elasticity
1852	Tax data, those charged	150–1,500	20–150	0.72
1910	Tax data, those charged	145–4,000	12–250	0.75
1938–9	Middle-class survey	n.a.	n.a.	0.83

Sources: Williamson (1979a, Table 1). The 1852 estimate is from the *Select Committee on Income Tax* for that year, while the 1910 estimate is from W. H. Mallock, both of which are cited in Stamp (1920, pp. 450–60). The 1938–9 estimate is from Prais and Houthakker (1955).

Hard evidence on nineteenth-century rental shares and rental elasticities is available only for the working class, since they 'suffer inquiries more gladly than the middle and upper classes . . .' (Stamp, 1920, p. 458). Thus, the famous studies by Bowley and Rowntree are for workers whose rental expenditures were below the minimum values at which the inhabited house duty was applied.

Appendix Table B.1 supplies two pre-World War I sources that are both well documented *and* apply to households that would have paid the inhabited house duty. Although these are rough estimates, they compare reasonably well with those from the 1930s reported in Prais and Houthakker's classic, *The Analysis of Family Budgets* (1955), thus making me more comfortable with the assumption of stability in that parameter from 1823, the first year for which there are inhabited house duty size distributions, and 1938–9, the date of the Prais and Houthakker middle-class survey. I use the Prais–Houthakker $\beta = 0.83$ estimate in what follows.[1]

The next problem is to establish an estimate for the intercept in the Engel function. All one requires here is an estimate of the rental share for any jth rental class, presumably the average non-taxed (NT) working-class household that is documented best. If one calls their rental share in total income ω_{NT}, it turns out that (B.2) implies

$$\alpha = \omega_{NT}^{\beta} \bar{R}_{NT}^{(1-\beta)}$$

Appendix Table B.2 supplies a set of late nineteenth-century estimates for ω_{NT}, an unweighted average of which is 0.0992. While I shall use this estimate in what follows, elsewhere I have shown that the measured inequality trends are fairly insensitive to the value of ω_{NT} assumed (Williamson, 1979a).

The final step is to estimate the mean rent for those households that did not pay the inhabited house duty (R_{NT}), since the official figures report rents only for assessed households. The procedure here is to select the value of $R_{NT}(t)$, say for 1890–1, that produces an estimate of total household income in England and Wales that replicates most closely Feinstein's independent estimates of national income. Similarly, given $\beta = 0.83$ and $\omega_{NT} = 0.0992$, the best estimate of $\bar{R}_{NT}(t)$ for all other years is sought. The

Appendix Table B.2   *Pre-World War I British estimates of the rental share in current income (below taxable limit)*

Date	Income £	Rent £	Rental share %	Source
Late 19th century	192	17.3	9.0	Rowntree
1885	100	13.4	13.4	Giffen
Late 19th century	104	7.6	7.3	Bowley
1889–90	100	9.98	9.98	US Commissioner of Labor (1890)
Unweighted average			9.92	

Source and Notes: Williamson (1979a, Table 2). All but one of these estimates have been conveniently collected and cited in Stamp (1920, pp. 450–60). The US Commissioner of Labor estimate is based on 363 renting working families in the following industries: pig iron, bar iron, steel, bituminous coal, coke, iron ore (US Commissioner of Labor, 1890, Table XXIV, p. 1374). I have taken a weighted average of Welsh and English and ignored those who own their own houses (only 10 out of 373).

Appendix Table B.3   *National income estimates, 1890–1 prices, England and Wales: indirect IHD estimates compared with direct Feinstein–Deane–Cole estimates, 1823–1915*

	(1)	(2)	(3)	(4)
		Estimated national income		
Year (t)	Best estimate of $R_{NT}(t)$ £	From IHD, 1890–1 prices $\omega_{NT} = 0.0992, \beta = 0.83$ £m.	From Feinstein–Deane–Cole, 1890–1 prices £m.	[(3) − (2)] ÷ (3)
1823	5.0	187.3	187.9	+0.0031
1830	5.0	237.3	225.8	−0.0509
1871	5.0	637.6	607.2	−0.1093
1891	7.96	1,050.0	1,047.0	−0.0028
1901	11.0	1,330.0	1,332.4	+0.0018
1911	13.0	1,454.0	1,460.0	+0.0041
1915	13.0	1,506.0	1,521.8	+0.0103

Sources and Notes: Williamson (1979a, Table 3) and see text. The current price UK or GB national income estimates are from Feinstein (1972, Appendix Tables) for 1855–1915 and from Deane and Cole (1962, Table 37, p. 166), where the 'off-census' years are estimated by geometric interpolation. These estimates are then converted to England and Wales aggregates by applying Baxter's (1868, pp. 53–6) shares. While Baxter's estimates are somewhat dated, the more recent regional income estimates by Kaser (1964) have been sharply criticized by Butlin (1967). In any case, the ratio of income in England and Wales to the UK was relatively stable between 1861 and 1911 (Kaser, 1964, p. 315), and Kaser's 1861 and 1871 figures average precisely to Baxter's.

results of this search for annual estimates of $\bar{R}_{NT}(t)$ are given in Appendix Table B.3 where my predicted values are compared with Feinstein's estimates (1890–1 prices).[2] With the sole exception of 1871, the 'best' estimates of national income coming from the IHD data never differ by more than 5 per cent from the direct national income estimates offered by Deane–Cole and Feinstein – a comforting result. This procedure generates my 'preferred' estimates of the size distribution of income since 1823. The inequality trends implied by these estimates appear to be quite robust in response to alternative assumptions regarding $\bar{R}_{NT}$ (Williamson, 1979a, Appendix Tables 26–28).

(2) Using the window tax data

As I pointed out in Chapter 4, the window tax has an even older history than the inhabited house duty, and it also reached lower in the income distribution than did the IHD. Yet, one is so accustomed to hearing tales of how the tax was avoided in the first seven decades of its existence that scholars have failed to make adequate use of the information for the years following the 1760s when the data are likely to be of higher quality. When first introduced in 1696, the 'new duties gave scope for scurrilous accusations that the government was taxing light and air' (Ward, 1952, p. 3). The tax got a bad reputation early in the eighteenth century. For example, in 1718 the Tax Office ascribed the declining yield 'mainly to the stopping up of windows to avoid the tax' (Ward, 1952, p. 5). The efforts of Henry Pelham in 1747 and Lord North in 1776, however, improved the tax-collecting efficiency enormously (Ward, 1952, pp. 8–22). In any case, by 1777 the improvements of real income, on the one hand, and the decline in the real cost of the duty (owing to inflation), on the other, made the tax hardly worth avoiding from the American Wars to the mid-nineteenth century when the tax was repealed. In short, the window tax offers data that are extremely valuable for inequality research on Britain: the data can be processed in the same fashion as the IHD data, supplying estimates of income distributions; they cover the eighteenth century; they overlap the IHD for the years 1823–49, thus making it possible to cross-check the veracity of both; and the tax was imposed on households lower in the distribution, thus supplying more complete information on the size distribution of income.

With minor manipulation, the window tax data supply the average number of windows, total number of houses, and total windows for each class of taxed families. To convert these data into income estimates by window size class requires three steps. First, since the Tax Office failed to report accurate estimates of those households that were exempt, one must do so indirectly by estimating the total number of houses in a given year and subtracting the official figures for those taxed. For the nineteenth century, the census supplies the total houses. For the eighteenth century, they must be constructed. Given total population reported in Mitchell and Deane (1962, p. 5, Part A, averaging Farr, Brownlee and Griffith), and applying Wall's (1974) estimates of dwellings per person, the total number of houses is easy enough to derive for the eighteenth century (Williamson, 1979a, Appendix Tables 15–25).

The second step requires more effort. How can one convert houses of a given number of windows into an estimated average annual rental value? Based on individual tax schedules still accessible in the Scottish Records Office, some 3,000 records have been collected from St Cuthbert's Parish in Edinburgh for the year 1801 (Williamson, 1979a). Each of these records reports the annual rental value of the house for IHD purposes and the number of windows for window tax purposes. From a random sample of 507 of these records, the data were then cross-tabulated to generate size classes conforming to that reported by the Tax Office. A number of non-linear regressions were estimated with these data and what follows yields the best explanation for rents (*t*-statistics reported in parentheses):[3]

$$\bar{R}_j = -34.0312 - 5.9028\ \bar{W}_j + 0.1402\ \bar{W}_j^2 + 41.3145\ ln\ \bar{W}_j$$
$$(2.0590)\quad (1.9121)\qquad (2.4614)\qquad (2\ .2699)$$

$$\bar{R}^2 = 0.9532$$
$$\text{DW stat} = 2.2925$$
$$\text{d.f.} = 22$$

This equation is used to estimate $\bar{R}_j(t)$, including the non-taxed class, for all years for which there are the nation-wide size distributions of dwellings by windows; i.e. 1777, 1781, 1812, 1823, 1830 and 1849. These rental value estimates, it must be remembered, are in constant 1801 prices. They are *not* nominal.

The third step follows that used for the IHD data in converting annual rental expenditures into annual income. Once again, average income in each window class is estimated (1801 prices) from the Engel function (B.2) where $\beta = 0.83$. The intercept, $\alpha(t) = \bar{\omega}_j^\beta\ \bar{R}_j^{1-\beta}$, is derived from Sir Frederick Eden's classic *The State of the Poor* (1928, listing on pp. 375–6 and excluding those families whose rents were supported by the parish) for the years 1794–6. On the basis of a sample of forty-one cottagers and converting to 1801 prices, one gets $\bar{R} = £3.29$ and $\bar{\omega}_{3.29} = 0.0771$. For all years (1801 prices), this implies $\alpha(t) = 0.1459$.

The data underlying the analysis reported in section 4 of Chapter 4 can be found in my earlier working paper (Williamson, 1979a, Appendix Tables 15–22). As Appendix Table B.4 indicates, however, the national income totals for England and Wales implied by the window tax size distributions are remarkably close to the direct estimates offered by Arthur Young, Phyllis Deane and W. A. Cole. From 1777 to 1830, the two estimates never differ by more than 4 per cent.

(3) Reconstructing the past from tax assessment data: two examples

The inequality statistics based on IHD tax assessment data in text Table 4.2 and the inequality statistics based on window tax assessment data in text

Appendix Table B.4   *National income estimates, 1801 prices, England and Wales: indirect window tax estimates compared with direct Young–Deane–Cole estimates, 1777–1849*

	(1)	(2)	(3)	(4)
		Estimated National Income		
	No. of window tax	*Predicted from*	*From Young–Deane–*	
	classes underlying	*window tax data*	*Cole estimates*	*[(2) − (3)]*
Year	*predicted income*	*£m.*	*£m.*	*÷ (3)*
1777	14	282.5	275.0	+0.03
1781	14	294.0	295.9	−0.01
1823	7	416.9	401.7	+0.04
1830	11	490.7	492.9	−0.00
1849	11	666.2	885.9	−0.25

Sources and Notes: Williamson (1979a, Table 5), and see text. The current price national income estimates for 1823–49 are from the same source as listed in Table 4.3. The eighteenth-century estimates use Arthur Young's figure (Deane and Cole, Table 35, p. 156), and the Deane and Cole (Table 19, p. 78) 'total real output index' (inflated) to interpolate 1781. The price index is the Schumpeter–Gilboy 'consumer goods other than cereals' index (Mitchell and Deane, 1962, pp. 468–9) for 1777–1801 and the Rousseaux 'Overall index' (Mitchell and Deane, 1962, p. 471) for 1801–49.

Appendix Table B.5   *The size distribution of 'permanent' income, based on inhabited house duty tax assessment data, England and Wales, 1830*

		Current price		Constant 1890–1 prices	
		Average	*Total*		
Rental class	*Total*	*rental*	*rental*	*Average*	*Total*
interval	*number of*	*value*	*value*	*income*	*income*
(£)	*households*	*£*	*£*	*£*	*£*
Untaxed	2,063,370	5.0	10,316,850	50.40	104,000,410
10–15	116,030	11.34	1,316,738	101.83	11,816,270
15–20	66,394	16.49	1,095,127	159.80	10,609,855
20–30	74,499	22.53	1,679,082	232.77	17,341,531
30–40	44,909	32.40	1,455,113	360.46	16,188,264
40–50	26,027	41.76	1,087,064	489.46	12,739,242
50–60	14,723	51.16	753,346	625.09	9,203,251
60–70	10,264	61.26	628,804	776.53	7,970,380
70–80	5,640	71.41	402,789	934.12	5,268,442
80–90	4,817	80.97	390,076	1,086.81	5,235,181
90–100	1,891	91.20	172,464	1,254.19	2,371,683
100–110	4,093	100.85	412,788	1,415.76	5,794,706
110–150	4,091	123.51	505,293	1,807.37	7,393,967
150–200	2,494	162.78	405,991	2,520.65	6,286,511
200–300	1,925	221.64	426,667	3,655.99	7,037,784
300–400	551	326.10	179,684	5,821.73	3,207,778
400+	438	554.98	243,083	11,047.72	4,838,902

Source: Williamson (1979a, Appendix Table 3, p. 63).

Appendix Table B.6   *The size distribution of 'permanent' income, 1801 prices, based on window tax assessments, England and Wales, 1777*

Window class interval	Total number of households	Windows	Average income £	Total income £
0–7	1,069,565	5,243,007	89.38	95,601,803
8	27,125	217,000	236.53	6,415,811
9	32,339	291,051	264.96	8,568,614
10	22,632	226,320	288.88	6,537,988
11	39,293	432,223	310.19	12,188,310
12	14,547	174,564	330.37	4,805,856
13	12,273	159,549	350.59	4,302,774
14–19	69,383	1,110,128	420.25	29,158,477
20	5,344	106,880	557.27	2,978,063
21	4,153	87,213	602.59	2,502,557
22	3,913	86,086	653.13	2,555,696
23	3,472	79,856	709.25	2,462,525
24	3,644	87,456	771.31	2,810,645
25+	33,590	1,377,190	3,025.86	101,800,000

Source: Williamson (1979a, Appendix Table 18, p. 83).

Table 4.3 all come from an earlier working paper where the 'reconstructed' size distributions are reported for every year (Williamson, 1979a, Appendix Tables 15–25 for window tax assessments and Appendix Tables 2–14 for IHD assessments). While some readers may wish to consult the working paper for details, most, no doubt, will be content with the sample in Appendix Tables B.5 and B.6.

Notes

1   It should be pointed out that international estimates from other countries between 1875 and 1928 are quite similar to the 0.83 estimate adopted here. Houthakker (1957, Table II, pp. 541–2) and Williamson (1967, Table 4, p. 116) offer the following estimates for Western countries:

Observation	Expenditure elasticities	Income elasticities
United States, 1901	0.839	0.755
Germany, 1907	0.913	0.822
Germany, 1928	0.881–0.887	0.793–0.798
Switzerland, 1919	0.824	0.742
Massachusetts, 1875	1.257	1.131
Washington, DC, 1916	0.930	0.837
Unweighted average	0.940	0.850

The income elasticities are estimated 'by diminishing the expenditure elasticities by about one-tenth' (Prais and Houthakker, 1955, p. 102).

2   Deflation is necessary, of course, since the Engel function is defined in terms of real income and relative housing rents. See expression (B.1). The appropriate deflator would be $P_H(t)$, but no such rental price index currently exists for the period 1823–1915. As a proxy, Appendix Table B.3 uses a consumer price index throughout.
3   The reader may well wonder why I have not simply used the Edinburgh sample to compute mean annual rents by window class, thus dispensing with the regression reported in the text. Unfortunately, the window class intervals reported by the Tax Office at various points in time vary a great deal. Regression is the only means, therefore, by which the size distribution of windows can be converted into an estimate of the size distribution of rents.

Appendix C: Estimating Skill per Worker Growth in Great Britain, 1821–1911

(1) The procedure

Following the discussion in Chapter 7, suppose one views skills as those advantages that command pay over that of common labor. The greater the pay advantage in a given occupation over that of common labor, the larger is the stock of skills per worker in that occupation. According to this view, the relevant wage for skills should be quoted as a premium, a gap or a markup. What follows is an estimate of the stock of skills in Britain between 1821 and 1911 using this approach.

The following definitions will prove useful. Let

S = the economy-wide stock of skills = $\sum s_j L_j$,
s_j = average stock of skills per person in the jth occupation,
L_j = persons employed in the jth occupation,
q_j = skill premium in the jth occupation = $w_j - w$,
w_j = average wage in the jth occupation,
q = the average wage rate for skills,
w = the average wage rate for common labor.

Since $q_j = s_j q$ by assumption (i.e. the economy-wide average wage for skills is equalized everywhere and thus a given occupation's skill premium reflects directly the amount of skills per person in that occupation), we have

$$S = \sum s_j L_j = \sum q_j L_j / q$$

or

$$S = \sum (w_j - w) L_j / q.$$

Arbitrarily, set the initial stock of skills equal to unity. By so doing, it follows that

$$q(0) = \sum [w_j(0) - w(0)] L_j(0).$$

Applying fixed (Laspeyres) weights, the stock of skills in t is simply

$$S(t) = \sum [w_j(0) - w(0)]L_j(t) \, / \, \sum [w_j(0) - w(0)]L_j(0). \qquad \text{(C.1)}$$

The *growth in skills* or labor quality, $\overset{*}{S}$, can be calculated directly from the stock estimates generated by expression (C.1). Furthermore, the *growth in skills per worker* can be easily derived as $\overset{*}{s} = \overset{*}{S} - \overset{*}{L}$. It should be emphasized, however, that both of these estimated growth rates may contain a serious downward bias. Nowhere have I admitted the possibility that all occupations underwent an increase in skills per worker, including common labor itself. To the extent that common labor underwent some skill accumulation across the nineteenth century, then $\overset{*}{S}$ will be underestimated. My own feeling is that this does not present a significant bias in the first half of the nineteenth century, but that it does become serious late in the century. This feeling is based on the knowledge that popular education began to 'trickle down' to lower-class families in an important way late in the century. It is also based on the knowledge that urban mortality and sickness–health conditions specific to the lower classes (see Williamson, 1981a, 1982a,c) underwent a marked downward drift following a period of relative stability prior to 1860. It is also based on the knowledge that children's labor participation rates in non-farm activities began to decline only a decade or two after the Factory Act of 1833, with the significant declines taking place later in the century (Nardinelli, 1980). Indeed, the traditional emphasis has been on the *increase* in child and female labor participation at least up to 1840 (Thompson, 1963, Ch. 3). The increase in the relative importance of 'secondary workers', with lower wages and therefore marginal productivity, would have tended to dilute average labor quality. Such influences suggest the wisdom of anticipating a downward bias in my $\overset{*}{S}$ estimates in the late nineteenth and early twentieth centuries. Thus, if one does find evidence of trend acceleration in skill per worker growth rates, it seems plausible to infer that the true extent of trend acceleration was somewhat higher.

(2) The estimates

The data required to implement estimates of $S(t)$ in equation (C.1) have already been used in Chapter 3. These are the annual earnings and employment estimates for seventeen non-agricultural, adult male occupations:

Low-wage non-agricultural employment:
- (1L)   General non-agricultural laborers
- (2L)   Messengers and porters
- (3L)   Government low-wage (e.g. messengers)
- (4L)   Police, guards and watchmen
- (5L)   Miners

High-wage non-agricultural employment:
- (1H)   Government high-wage (e.g. clerks)
- (2H)   Skilled in shipbuilding
- (3H)   Skilled in engineering
- (4H)   Skilled in the building trades
- (5H)   Skilled in textiles
- (6H)   Skilled in printing trades
- (7H)   Clergymen
- (8H)   Solicitors and barristers
- (9H)   Clerks (excluding government)
- (10H) Surgeons, medical officers and doctors
- (11H) Teachers
- (12H) Engineers and surveyors

This seventeen-occupation sample certainly does not exhaust the total non-agricultural labor force, since it is restricted to adult males and excludes retail trades, domestics and other service occupations where self-employment was important. As a share of Deane and Cole's (1962, Table 31, p. 143) total occupied population outside of agriculture, the sample exhibits the following trends:

1821	15.6%	1851	21.8%	1881	22.2%	1911	22.3%
1831	17.5	1861	21.1	1891	24.3		
1841	18.6	1871	20.7	1901	23.3		

The earnings data are available for the following years: 1819 (which I label '1821' in what follows), 1827 ('1831' in what follows), 1835 ('1841' in what follows) and at each census date 1851–1911. Employment figures for these seventeen occupations are supplied directly by published census compilations for 1851–1911. The earlier years, 1821–41, are estimates guided by the imperfect census data on occupations (see Williamson, 1982d). While all seventeen occupations are used to estimate equation (C.1) in what follows, the common laborer's wage is calculated as

$$w(t) = \sum_j w_j(t)/L_j(t), \text{ where } j = 1L, \ldots, 5L.$$

The results of this exercise are reported in Appendix Table C.1. A growth triangle is presented in that table partly to allow the reader to select those periods that are most relevant to his/her own interests. It also serves to point out that some of these benchmark years are flawed by an unknown combination of peculiarities in estimation, data source and stages of the business cycle. For example, by glancing down the diagonal, the reader will note that the decadal growth rates for the 1820s and 1840s are 'unusually' high, while those for the 1850s and 1900s are 'unusually' low. Obviously, the estimates are of much greater value the longer the period considered.

My interest, however, is not in the aggregate skill accumulation rates in these seventeen occupations, but rather in the growth of skills per worker. These are presented in Appendix Table C.3, which is derived by subtracting

Appendix Table C.1   *Skill stock growth rates, 1821–1911: estimates based on the unadjusted non-agricultural sample of seventeen occupations, S^*_{nas} (% per annum)*

End year	Base year								
	1821	1831	1841	1851	1861	1871	1881	1891	1901
1831	3.20 (3.20)								
1841	2.82 (2.81)	2.43 (2.43)							
1851	2.96 (2.97)	2.85 (2.85)	3.26 (3.27)						
1861	2.65 (2.51)	2.36 (2.28)	2.33 (2.20)	0.77 (1.13)					
1871	2.53 (2.28)	2.20 (2.05)	2.13 (1.93)	0.91 (1.26)	1.43 (1.41)				
1881	2.42 (2.22)	2.13 (2.03)	2.05 (1.93)	1.33 (1.49)	1.63 (1.62)	1.79 (1.69)			
1891	2.49 (2.24)	2.24 (2.09)	2.15 (2.00)	1.53 (1.71)	1.90 (1.89)	2.07 (2.09)	2.49 (2.42)		
1901	2.49 (2.30)	2.25 (2.18)	2.23 (2.14)	1.65 (1.91)	1.97 (2.07)	2.11 (2.24)	2.38 (2.42)	2.17 (2.25)	
1911	2.35 (2.05)	2.12 (1.91)	2.08 (1.84)	1.54 (1.60)	1.77 (1.71)	1.83 (1.80)	1.95 (1.81)	1.59 (1.54)	1.02 (0.93)

Notes: Figures in parentheses use end year (Paasche) weights, rather than beginning year (Laspeyres) weights. The wage and weight data, and the calculating procedure, are all discussed in the text.

the sample's employment growth (Table C.2) from its estimated skill stock growth (Table C.1). The table presents two estimates for each period, one using beginning year weights (Laspeyres) and one using end year weights (Paasche). For some periods, selection of wage weights matters a great deal. During the 1850s, for example, the wage structure changed enough to yield two quite different estimates (−0.38 versus −0.02 per cent per annum) depending on whether 1851 or 1861 wage weights are used. The same is true of longer periods over which the structure of pay by skill was changing dramatically, e.g. from the 1820s or 1830s to 1871.

The final step is to map the measured skill accumulation experience in my sample on to the total labor force. What should one assume about skill accumulation rates outside of my sample? Appendix Table C.4 offers two alternatives that serve to give a plausible range of estimates: in Case A, I assume that agriculture required only common labor and that all remaining non-agricultural sectors underwent the same skills per worker growth as did the sample. In Case B, I assume that *all* sectors underwent the same skills per worker accumulation experience as did the sample. The bottom two rows of Table C.4 report skills per worker growth economy-wide, where

Appendix Table C.2   *Employment growth rates in the unadjusted non-agricultural sample of seventeen occupations, 1821–1911, $\overset{*}{L}_{nas}$ (% per annum)*

End year	Base year								
	1821	1831	1841	1851	1861	1871	1881	1891	1901
1831	3.25								
1841	2.86	2.48							
1851	2.98	2.84	3.21						
1861	2.52	2.27	2.17	1.15					
1871	2.27	2.03	1.88	1.22	1.30				
1881	2.20	1.99	1.87	1.42	1.56	1.82			
1891	2.21	2.04	1.95	1.64	1.81	2.06	2.30		
1901	2.07	1.90	1.80	1.53	1.62	1.73	1.68	1.07	
1911	1.91	1.75	1.64	1.38	1.43	1.47	1.35	0.87	0.68

Notes: The sample and sources are described in the text.

Appendix Table C.3   *Growth in skills per worker in the unadjusted non-agricultural sample of seventeen occupations, 1821–1911: $\overset{*}{s}_{nas}$ (% per annum)*

End year	Base year								
	1821	1831	1841	1851	1861	1871	1881	1891	1901
1831	−0.05								
	(−0.05)								
1841	−0.04	−0.05							
	(−0.05)	(−0.05)							
1851	0.02	0.01	0.05						
	(−0.01)	(0.01)	(0.06)						
1861	0.13	0.09	0.16	−0.38					
	(−0.01)	(0.01)	(0.03)	(−0.02)					
1871	0.26	0.17	0.25	−0.31	0.13				
	(0.01)	(0.02)	(0.05)	(0.04)	(0.11)				
1881	0.22	0.14	0.18	−0.09	0.07	−0.03			
	(0.02)	(0.04)	(0.06)	(0.07)	(0.06)	(−0.13)			
1891	0.28	0.20	0.20	−0.11	0.09	0.01	0.19		
	(0.03)	(0.05)	(0.05)	(0.07)	(0.08)	(0.03)	(0.12)		
1901	0.42	0.35	0.43	0.12	0.35	0.38	0.70	1.10	
	(0.23)	(0.28)	(0.34)	(0.38)	(0.45)	(0.51)	(0.74)	(1.18)	
1911	0.44	0.37	0.44	0.16	0.34	0.36	0.60	0.72	0.34
	(0.14)	(0.16)	(0.20)	(0.22)	(0.28)	(0.33)	(0.46)	(0.67)	(0.27)

Notes: Calculated as the difference between skill stock growth rates in Appendix Table C.1 and employment growth rates in Appendix Table C.2, yielding an estimate of the growth in skills per worker for the non-agricultural sample of seventeen occupations.

Appendix Table C.4   *Growth in skills per worker: estimates for Great Britain, 1821–1911 (% per annum)*

Variable	1821–1861	1861–1911
Skills per worker growth in the nas sample: $\overset{*}{s}_{nas}$		
(1) Laspeyres weights $(t = 0)$	+0.13	+0.34
(2) Paasche weights $(t = 1)$	−0.01	+0.28
Employment growth in		
(3) The nas sample: $\overset{*}{L}_{nas}$	+2.52	+1.43
(4) All non-agricultural occupations: $\overset{*}{L}_{na}$	+1.75	+1.28
(5) All occupations: $\overset{*}{L}_{tot}$	+1.40	+0.90
Skill stock growth economy-wide: $\overset{*}{S}$		
Case A (assuming no skills in agriculture and all non-agricultural occupations follow nas experience):		
$\overset{*}{S}{}^0_A = \overset{*}{s}{}^0_{nas} + \overset{*}{L}_{na}$	+1.88	+1.62
$\overset{*}{S}{}^1_A = \overset{*}{s}{}^1_{nas} + \overset{*}{L}_{na}$	+1.74	+1.56
Case B (assuming all occupations, including agriculture, follow nas experience):		
$\overset{*}{S}{}^0_B = \overset{*}{s}{}^0_{nas} + \overset{*}{L}_{tot}$	+1.53	+1.24
$\overset{*}{S}{}^1_B = \overset{*}{s}{}^1_{nas} + \overset{*}{L}_{tot}$	+1.39	+1.18
Skills per worker growth economy-wide: $\overset{*}{s}$		
Case A: average	+0.41	+0.69
Case B: average	+0.06	+0.31

Notes and Sources: Lines (1) and (2) – from Appendix Table C.3.

Line (3) – from Appendix Table C.2.

For 1821–61, lines (4) and (5) are from Deane and Cole (1962, Table 31, p. 143), where L_{tot} is their 'total occupied labour force' and L_{na} excludes labor force in agriculture, forestry and fishing. For 1861–1911, lines (4) and (5) are from Feinstein (1972, Tables 57 and 60), where L_{tot} is working population less those in armed forces and L_{na} excludes those in agriculture and fishing.

Cases A and B are reported as an average of Laspeyres $(t = 0)$ and Paasche $(t = 1)$ weights.

For the period 1821–61, I prefer the Case B estimate of 0.06 per cent per annum. For the period 1861–1911, I have suggested that the estimates of $\overset{*}{s}$ are likely to have a downward bias. According to some competing estimates of labor 'quality' growth (Matthews *et al.*, 1982, Table 4.7, p. 113), it appears I was right. Including the influence on labor quality of age, sex, nationality and education, Matthews *et al.* estimate $\overset{*}{s}$ over 1856–1913 at 0.7 per cent per annum, more than double my Case B, but almost exactly my Case A. Guided by Matthews *et al.*, I shall use my 0.69 per cent per annum estimate in most of the calculation reported in the text unless otherwise noted.

Appendix D: Documenting Parameters and Initial Conditions

(1) Initial conditions: 1861, 1891 and 1911

The structure of production: input mix

There are four factors of production that are used in more than one sector in my model: capital (K), unskilled labor (L), skilled labor (S), and home-produced intermediate inputs (B). Since the remaining two factors of production – land $(\mathcal{J})$ and imported intermediate inputs (F) – are both sector specific, we need not concern ourselves with them further in this appendix. The sectoral distribution of the other four is, however, central to establishing the structure of the British economy at any point in time. Appendix Table D.1 reports the λ_{ij} used in Part III of the book, for three late nineteenth-century benchmarks. The remainder of this section will outline their source.

Capital stock distribution, λ_{Kj}. All of these estimates are taken from Feinstein (1978b), sectoral net capital stocks in constant prices.

Appendix Table D.1 *Input mix, 1861, 1891 and 1911*

λ_{ij}	1861	1891	1911
λ_{LA}	0.2754	0.1606	0.1201
λ_{LM}	0.3795	0.3883	0.3792
λ_{LC}	0.3068	0.3998	0.4362
λ_{LB}	0.0383	0.0513	0.0645
λ_{KA}	0.2150	0.1221	0.0748
λ_{KM}	0.1631	0.1879	0.2413
λ_{KC}	0.5959	0.6627	0.6577
λ_{KB}	0.0259	0.0273	0.0263
λ_{SM}	0.4530	0.4073	0.4363
λ_{SC}	0.5470	0.5927	0.5637
λ_{BM}	0.8367	0.6966	0.7055
λ_{BC}	0.1633	0.3034	0.2945

Unskilled labor force distribution, λ_{Lj}. All of these estimates are taken from Feinstein (1972, Table 60), total working population less defense, by sector, UK males and females.

Skilled labor force distribution, λ_{Sj}. The procedure here is first to estimate each sector's share of the total wage bill that represents payments to 'skills', where the latter is simply the difference between the sector's average wage and the non-agricultural unskilled wage. Both of these wages are constructed from Williamson (1982d, Appendix Table 4), the difference representing skills per worker in manufacturing and services. This wage differential is then multiplied by the sectoral employment figures in Mitchell and Deane (1962, p. 60). Given these estimates of S_M and S_C, the λ_{Sj} can be computed directly.

Home-produced intermediate inputs distribution, λ_{Bj}. Deane and Cole (1962, Table 55, p. 219) report the distribution of coal use for 1869, 1887 and 1913. Their estimates imply the B_M and B_C figures necessary to compute the λ_{Bj}.

The structure of production: demand and output mix

The basic national accounts data for 1861, 1891 and 1911 (actually 1907) are taken primarily from Deane and Cole (1962). However, their definitions had to be bent to conform to the model structure in Chapter 8. The result of that effort is summarized in Appendix Table D.2. The remainder of this section will outline the sources and methods used to construct the underlying national accounts that yield the demand and output mix documented in Appendix Table D.2.

Manufacturing output. Deane and Cole (1962, pp. 166 and 175) report the value of manufacturing, mining and construction combined, and in current prices. I have subtracted an estimate of mining output to make the aggregate conform to 'manufacturing' in the model. The mining output estimate is derived by applying the time series on the 'value of coal at pithead' (Deane and Cole, 1962, Table 54, p. 216) to the 1907 estimate for mining and quarrying output (Deane and Cole, 1962, Table 40, p. 175).

Service output. This series is constructed using the same sources as for manufacturing. It excludes construction and rents on dwellings; it includes trade, transport, domestics, personal services, government, professional, public utilities, etc.

Agricultural output. Deane and Cole (1962, pp. 166 and 175).

Home-produced intermediate production. First, I constructed the mining and quarrying output series described above under 'manufacturing'. Since the model treats B as a non-tradeable that is used only as an input into M and C, I needed a means by which exports and household final demand use of the home-produced intermediate could be subtracted out. The Deane and

Appendix Table D.2 *Demand and output mix, 1861, 1891 and 1911*

Share	1861	1891	1911
National income shares:			
$\hat{\phi}_A$	0.2012	0.1048	0.0715
$\hat{\phi}_M$	0.3754	0.3904	0.3495
$\hat{\phi}_C$	0.3986	0.4574	0.5453
$\hat{\phi}_B$	0.0249	0.0473	0.0337
Final demand shares:			
$\tilde{\phi}_A$	0.2936	0.2235	0.1721
$\tilde{\phi}_M$	0.3319	0.3374	0.2931
$\tilde{\phi}_C$	0.3745	0.4391	0.5348
Agriculture's demand shares:			
α_{A_M}	0.3627	0.5636	0.5999
α_A	0.6373	0.4364	0.4001
Manufacturing's demand shares:			
α_M	1.4794	1.4682	1.5542
α_{M_x}	0.4794	0.4682	0.5542
Import shares:			
z_A	0.4652	0.5542	0.5186
z_F	0.5348	0.4458	0.4814
z_M	0.6951	0.6950	0.8157

Cole (1962, p. 219) estimates on coal use were assumed to apply for that purpose, producing my 'home-produced intermediate' B and its allocation between M and C.

Trade. The model confronts commodity trade only. Furthermore, it deals only with *net* trade. Mitchell and Deane (1962) supply annual data on the value of 'principal imports' (pp. 298–301), 'principal domestic exports' (pp. 303–6), and 'principal re-exports' (pp. 307–8). These have been used to derive estimates of the net import of agricultural goods ($P_A A_M$), the net export of manufactures ($P_M M_X$), and the import of foreign-produced intermediate products ($P_F F$). A_M includes grain, flour, coffee, sugar, wine, tea, meat, animals, butter, margarine and tobacco. F includes timber, cotton, wool, silk, oils, flax, hemp, jute, hides, dyestuffs, rubber, paper materials and petroleum. M includes all remaining items. This information is sufficient to derive all the $\hat{\phi}$'s, $\tilde{\phi}$'s, α's, and z's in Appendix Table D.2.

Sectoral technologies: factor shares

Factor shares in home-produced intermediates production, θ_{iB}. Bowley (1919, p. 43) reports factor payments for coal mining in 1911. Lacking data for any earlier years, I assume that the 1911 coal mining θ's apply to sector B throughout the nineteenth century.

Appendix Table D.3   *Sectoral factor shares, 1861, 1891 and 1911*

Shares	1861	1891	1911
Agriculture:			
θ_{JA}	0.2364	0.2279	0.1934
θ_{KA}	0.2502	0.2088	0.2115
θ_{LA}	0.5127	0.5634	0.5951
Manufacturing:			
θ_{LM}	0.3217	0.3444	0.3401
θ_{KM}	0.2632	0.2714	0.2735
θ_{SM}	0.1264	0.1176	0.1257
θ_{BM}	0.0395	0.0620	0.0503
θ_{FM}	0.2493	0.2045	0.2104
Services:			
θ_{LC}	0.2945	0.3034	0.2984
θ_{SC}	0.1937	0.1634	0.1619
θ_{KC}	0.5017	0.5028	0.5218
θ_{BC}	0.0101	0.0304	0.0179
Home-produced intermediates:			
θ_{LB}	0.6848	0.6848	0.6848
θ_{KB}	0.3152	0.3152	0.3152

Factor shares in manufacturing, θ_{iM}. One needs payments shares in *gross* output rather than value added, so the first step is to augment the 'manufacturing output' estimate by home-produced resources and net resource imports consumed by manufacturing. (All of these estimates can be found above under 'The structure of production: demand and output mix'.) Labor (both skilled and unskilled) and capital's share in value added are taken from Bowley's (1919, p. 45) summary of the 1907 census. Finally, labor's share is then split into skilled and unskilled factor payments, the split determined by the differential between the average manufacturing wage and the unskilled non-agricultural wage (based on Williamson, 1982d, Appendix Table 4, and see 'Skilled labor force distribution' section above).

Factor shares in agriculture, θ_{iA}. The problem here, of course, is imputing wage income to farmers. Bellerby (1956, Table 1, p. 56) reports total factor incomes in British agriculture from 1867–9 onwards, but his figures require two adjustments to conform to my model. First, Bellerby's 'wages' are only payments to hired labor. I have converted the 'wage bill' in agriculture to include imputations to farmers by simply multiplying average annual earnings of male farm labor (Williamson, 1982d, Appendix Table 4) by total occupied in agricultural employment (Mitchell and Deane, 1962, p. 60). Given Bellerby's total factor income, net rent and my imputation for the wage bill, one finds a residual, which I treat as returns to capital.

Factor shares in services, θ_{iC}. As with agriculture, the problem here lies with wage imputation and I solve it the same way. The average wage in the service sector is derived from Williamson (1982d, Appendix Table 4), which in turn is multiplied by employment reported in Mitchell and Deane (1962, p. 60). This wage bill is then decomposed into skilled and unskilled wage payments. The unskilled wage payment is estimated by multiplying the Mitchell and Deane total employment figure by the average unskilled non-agricultural wage (Williamson, 1982d, Appendix Table 4). Skilled wage payments appear as a residual when the unskilled payments are subtracted from total wage payments. Finally, subtracting the total wage bill (and the intermediate input payments) from my estimate of 'service output' (see 'The structure of production: demand and output mix' above) yields returns to capital.

Parameters

Technology. Chapter 8 stated my assumptions regarding substitution elasticities in production. I repeat them here:

Agriculture: $\sigma_{KL}^A = \sigma_{K\mathcal{J}}^A = \sigma_{\mathcal{J}K}^A = \sigma_{L\mathcal{J}}^A = 1$ (Cobb-Douglas)

Manufacturing: $\sigma_{KL}^M = 1$, $\sigma_{KS}^M = \sigma_{LS}^M = 0.5$ (CES)

Services: $\sigma_{KL}^C = 1$, $\sigma_{KS}^C = \sigma_{LS}^C = 0.5$ (CES)

B-goods: $\sigma_{KL}^B = 1$ (Cobb-Douglas)

Demand. Based on 'stylized facts of demand', the price elasticity of demand for manufactures is assumed elastic, for agriculture inelastic, and for services unit elasticity. Thus,

$$\epsilon_A = -0.6, \quad \epsilon_M = -1.3, \quad \text{and} \quad \epsilon_C = -1.0.$$

In addition, Engel effects are captured by assumptions on income elasticities – high for manufactures and low for agriculture:

$$\eta_A = 0.4 \quad \text{and} \quad \eta_M = 1.35.$$

The elasticity of demand for services is derived as a residual (satisfying the aggregate budget constraint)

$$\eta_C(t) = [1 - \bar{\phi}_M(t)\eta_M - \bar{\phi}_A(t)\eta_A]/\bar{\phi}_C(t)$$

which, as it turns out, is close to unity.

The cross-price elasticities are implied by the following adding-up conditions that must be preserved:

$$\epsilon_A + \epsilon_{AM} + \epsilon_{AC} + \eta_A = 0$$

$$\epsilon_M + \epsilon_{AM} + \epsilon_{MC} + \eta_M = 0$$

$$\epsilon_C + \epsilon_{AC} + \epsilon_{MC} + \eta_C = 0$$

Solving this sytem of equations implies

$$\epsilon_{AM} = 0.075, \quad \epsilon_{AC} = 0.125, \quad \text{and } \epsilon_{MC} = -0.125.$$

These demand parameters are maintained in all experiments 1861–1911 (although the implied η_C may vary over the late nineteenth century as the $\dot\phi_j(t)$ vary).

(2) Initial conditions: 1821

The structure of production: input mix
For the 1790–1861 experiments, Chapters 10 and 11 use initial conditions from around 1821. Appendix Table D.4 reports the λ_{ij} used in Part III of this book.

Appendix Table D.4   *1821 input mix*

λ_{ij}	*1821*
λ_{LA}	0.284
λ_{LM}	0.357
λ_{LC}	0.333
λ_{LB}	0.026
λ_{KA}	0.4730
λ_{KM}	0.2134
λ_{KC}	0.3041
λ_{KB}	0.0095
λ_{SM}	0.3058
λ_{SC}	0.6942
λ_{BM}	0.9504
λ_{BC}	0.0496

Capital stock distribution, λ_{Kj}. The distribution is based on Feinstein's (1978a, Table 8, p. 42) estimates, gross stocks at 1851–60 replacement cost, including land improvements. The 1821 estimates are linear interpolations between Feinstein's 1800 and 1830 figures. K_A includes farm buildings, equipment and land improvements. K_B is mining and quarrying stocks. K_C includes public works and buildings, transport, gas and water, and commercial buildings (the latter derived by applying the share of $P_C C/(P_C C + P_M M)$ – Deane and Cole, 1962, Table 37, pp. 166–7 – to Feinstein's 'industrial and commercial buildings' estimate). K_M includes industrial machinery and equipment, and industrial buildings.

Unskilled labor force distribution, λ_{Lj}. Deane and Cole (1962, Table 30, p. 142) supply the 1821 sectoral employment distributions, but with B and M

aggregated. It appears that 1841 is the first year for which mining and quarrying are separated out (Deane and Cole, 1962, Table 31, p. 143), and thus I assume that the 1841 share of B and M holds for 1821 as well.

Skilled labor force distribution, λ_{Sj}. These are derived in exactly the same way as those for 1861–1911, and using the same sources. The calculation uses 1819 wages and 1821 employment weights.

Home-produced intermediate inputs distribution, λ_{Bj}. Based on Deane and Cole (1962, Table 55, p. 219) for 1840, the earliest observation on coal use. The calculation nets out mining, domestic and exports usage (see the discussion above for 1861–1911).

The structure of production: demand and output mix
The estimates for 1821 follow closely the methods described above for 1861–1911. The 1821 estimates are documented in Appendix Table D.5, and the reader is guided to the sections above for discussion of their source.

Sectoral technologies: factor shares
Here I simply use the 1861 θ_{ij} reported in Appendix Table D.3.

Appendix Table D.5   *1821 demand and output mix*

Share	1821
National income shares:	
$\hat{\phi}_A$	0.2853
$\hat{\phi}_M$	0.3042
$\hat{\phi}_C$	0.3803
$\hat{\phi}_B$	0.0301
Final demand shares:	
$\bar{\phi}_A$	0.3545
$\bar{\phi}_M$	0.2944
$\bar{\phi}_C$	0.3511
Agriculture's demand shares:	
α_{A_M}	0.2600
α_A	0.7400
Manufacturing's demand shares:	
α_M	1.2957
α_{M_x}	0.2957
Import shares:	
z_A	0.5497
z_F	0.4503
z_M	0.5193

Parameters

Technology. The assumptions for substitution elasticities in production used for 1861–1911 are applied here to 1821 as well.

Demand. What follows is a listing of those 1821 demand parameters that differ from those assumed for 1861–1911.

To reflect the fact that the income elasticity of demand for foodstuffs tends to be higher closer to subsistence, I set $\eta_A = 0.60$ for 1821. This changes the cross-price elasticities required to satisfy adding-up conditions:

$$\epsilon_{AM} = 0.0302, \quad \epsilon_{AC} = -0.0302, \quad \text{and } \epsilon_{MC} = -0.0802.$$

Appendix E: Estimating Shift Parameters, 1821–1911

Appendix Tables E.1 and E.2 list all the exogenous variables used in the analysis in Chapters 9 and 10. The exogenous variables in rates of change, or 'shift parameters', are given separately for 1821–61 in Table E.1 and for 1861–1911 in Table E.2, primarily because they are of different quality. In some cases, the pre-1861 data are outright guesses. Each of the tables lists the variable name, its estimated value and the evidence supporting that estimate. Where I have simply exploited other scholars' estimates, the tables make a brief comment to that effect. Where other scholars' estimates have been extensively revised, or where the estimate is my own, the tables will direct the reader to a more detailed defense in the text following.

Industrial price index, 1821–61, $\overset{*}{P}_M$. The industrial price index is a composite, consisting of the following four price series:

Price series	$\overset{*}{P}_j$	Period	Source
Cotton textiles	−2.64%	1819/23– 1859/61	Imlah (1958, Table II, pp. 208–10), 'exports of cotton manufactures with "much fabrication"'.
Woolen textiles	−1.24	1819/23– 1859/61	Imlah (1958, Table III, pp. 211–13), 'exports of woolen manufactures with "much fabrication"'.
Iron products	−1.17	1819/23– 1859/61	Mitchell and Deane (1962, pp. 492–3), Porter's (1851) English merchant bar iron at Liverpool and Meade/Sauerbeck Scottish pig iron, linked.
All others	−1.07	1819/23– 1859/61	Imlah (1958, Table IV, pp. 214–15), 'exports omitting cottons and woolens'.

To get the composite price index, these four price series were weighted by a recombination of Hoffman's (1955, pp. 18–19) industrial weights:

Cotton	0.204
Wool	0.135
Iron	0.156
Other	0.504
(excl. coal)	

Appendix Table E.1　*Shift parameter estimates, 1821–61*

Shift parameter	Estimated per annum rate %	Source of estimate
$\overset{*}{L}$	1.40	Deane and Cole (1962, Table 31, p. 143), 'total occupied' British labor force, 1821–61.
$\overset{*}{K}$	2.50	Feinstein (1978a, Tables 8 and 15, pp. 42, 70–2), revised by Field (1981, Table 3, p. 16). British capital stock (producer durable equipment plus non-residential structures) in 1851–60 prices, 1830–60.
$\overset{*}{S}$	1.46	Taken from Appendix Table C.4, 1821–61, average of the two Case 'B' estimates.
$\overset{*}{\mathcal{J}}$	0.03	Feinstein (1978a, Table 15, p. 68 and discussion pp. 72–3). Farmland values in 1851–60 prices, Great Britain, 1830–60.
$\overset{*}{Pop}.$	1.23	Mitchell and Deane (1962, pp. 8–9), Great Britain, 1821–61.
$\overset{*}{P}_A$	−0.36	Rousseaux price index for 'total agricultural products', from Mitchell and Deane (1962, p. 471), 1819/23–1859/63. Beginning and end year observation centered on 1821 and 1861, five-year average for smoothing.
$\overset{*}{P}_M$	−1.43	See text of this appendix.
$\overset{*}{P}_F$	−0.54	A linked series of Gayer–Rostow–Schwartz 'imported commodities' and Rousseaux 'principal industrial products', both in Mitchell and Deane (1962, pp. 470–1), linked on 1839–43 average. Beginning and end year observation centered on 1821 and 1861, five-year average for smoothing, 1819/23–1859/63.
$\overset{*}{T}_A$	0.30	There is no evidence of significant productivity advance in British agriculture until very late in this period. A modest rate of total factor productivity growth of 0.3 per cent per annum is assumed, half of that for the 1861–1911 period (see Appendix Table E.2).
$\overset{*}{T}_C$	0.37	There is no evidence of more rapid productivity advance in services prior to 1861 than after. The rate of total factor productivity growth estimated for 1861–1911 (see Appendix Table E.2) is therefore assumed for this period too.
$\overset{*}{T}_B$	0.50	The rate of total factor productivity growth estimated for 1861–1911 is 0.37 per cent per annum (see Appendix Table E.2). Since Deane and Cole (1962, p. 217) tell us that coal mining grew fastest between 1830 and 1865, one would have thought that productivity advance would have been high as well. While Sidney Pollard (1980, p. 212) asserts that labor 'productivity per man increased very little' between 1750 and 1850, the total factor productivity growth estimate used here, 0.50 per cent per annum, still seems reasonable.
$\overset{*}{T}_M$	1.0475	Derived as a residual. See text of this appendix.

Appendix Table E.2   *Shift parameter estimates, 1861–1911*

Shift parameter	Estimated per annum rate %	Source of estimate
$\overset{*}{L}$	0.90	Feinstein (1972, Table 57), total UK working population less those in armed forces, 1861–1911.
$\overset{*}{K}$	1.97	Feinstein (1978b, Table 'Domestic capital formation – all fixed assets'), net stock of domestic reproducible fixed assets in 1900 prices, 1861–1911
$\overset{*}{S}$	1.74	The Appendix Table C.4 figure has been raised to reflect the likely presence of downward bias discussed in Appendix C, section 1.
$\overset{*}{j}$	0.18	Mitchell and Deane (1962, pp. 78–9 and 80–1), UK 'acreage in crops', 1867–1911.
$\overset{*}{Pop}$	0.90	Mitchell and Deane (1962, pp. 8–10), UK population, 1861–1911.
$\overset{*}{P_A}$	−0.37	Mitchell and Deane (1962, pp. 472–3), Rousseaux 'total agricultural products' index. Beginning and end year observation centered on 1861 and 1911, five-year average for smoothing, 1859/63–1909/13.
$\overset{*}{P_M}$	−0.24	Current price index of industrial production (see Appendix D) divided by Feinstein's (1972, Table 8) index of industrial production at constant factor cost, 1861–1911.
$\overset{*}{P_F}$	−0.71	Weighted average of Sauerbeck–Statist indices of textile fibers and sundry, Mitchell and Deane (1962, pp. 474–5), where the weights are based on import shares, textile fibers at 77 and 80 per cent in the early and late periods, respectively. Beginning and end year observation centered on 1861 and 1911, five year average for smoothing, 1859/63–1909/13
$\overset{*}{T_A}$	0.60	See text of this appendix.
$\overset{*}{T_M}$	0.26	See text of this appendix.
$\overset{*}{T_C}$	0.37	See text of this appendix.
$\overset{*}{T_B}$	0.37	See text of this appendix.

Total factor productivity growth in manufacturing, 1821–61, $\overset{*}{T_M}$. Manufacturing total factor productivity growth is derived as a residual, given the aggregate rate, $\overset{*}{T}$, the rates in each of the other three sectors, and one remaining parameter, z :

$$\overset{*}{T} = (1 - z)^{-1} (v_A \overset{*}{T_A} + v_M \overset{*}{T_M} + v_C \overset{*}{T_C} + v_B \overset{*}{T_B})$$

or

$$\overset{*}{T}_M = {}_M{}^{-1}\left[(1-z)\overset{*}{T} - v_A\overset{*}{T}_A - v_C\overset{*}{T}_C - v_B\overset{*}{T}_B\right]$$

where the v_j are 1821 sectoral value added weights (Appendix D)

$$v_A = 0.2853 \quad v_M = 0.3042 \quad v_C = 0.3803 \quad v_B = 0.0301$$

and $\overset{*}{T} = 1.0$, based on Feinstein (1978a, Table 26, p. 86), 1801–60. Economy-wide total factor productivity growth is composed of two parts: *inter-industry* total factor productivity growth resulting from improved resource allocation between sectors whose factor marginal products differ, an effect of which much has been made in the development literature ($\overset{*}{T}_{RA}$); and *intra-industry* total factor productivity growth resulting from productivity improvements within the sectors themselves ($\overset{*}{T}_j$). The following expression must hold:

$$\overset{*}{T} = \sum_j v_j\overset{*}{T}_j + \overset{*}{T}_{RA}$$

or

$$\overset{*}{T} = \sum_j v_j\overset{*}{T}_j + z\overset{*}{T}$$

or

$$\overset{*}{T} = (1-z)^{-1}\left(v_A\overset{*}{T}_A + v_M\overset{*}{T}_M + v_C\overset{*}{T}_C + v_B\overset{*}{T}_B\right)$$

where z is the parameter that expresses inter-industry total factor productivity growth as a share of $\overset{*}{T}$. While there is no evidence on z for 1821–61, there is an enormous amount of information on its value in twentieth-century growing economies. For post-World War II Northwest Europe, z was only 0.22 (Denison, 1967, p. 300), and the same value obtained for America from 1929 to 1967 (Denison, 1974, p. 344). It seems likely that developing economies would exhibit much higher values of z since they are industrializing more rapidly while also exhibiting far greater disequilibria in sectoral factor markets. As a result, I have arbitrarily doubled the 1821–61 estimate of z to 0.44, but I expect it to have fallen across the nineteenth century.

Sectoral total factor productivity growth, 1861–1911, $\overset{*}{T}_j$. These have all been estimated directly from input data, using the standard 'sources of growth' fixed-weight calculation, but where gross output rather than value added concepts are used. The sectoral output growth rates used in the calculation are reported in Table 9.1; the estimates of $\overset{*}{K}_j$ are taken from Feinstein (1978b, net capital stock by sector, constant prices); the estimates of $\overset{*}{L}_j$ are taken from Feinstein (1972, Table 60); $\overset{*}{\jmath}$ is from Appendix Table E.2; $\overset{*}{S}_j$ and $\overset{*}{B}_j$ are derived from the stock series underlying the aggregate growth rate estimates for $\overset{*}{S}$ and $\overset{*}{B}$ in Appendix Table E.2 and Table 9.1, distributing the aggregate stocks between sectors by use of the λ's described in Appendix D; and $\overset{*}{F}$ is taken from Appendix D. The data underlying the calculation of the $\overset{*}{T}_j$ (1861–1911) are summarized below:

Sector j	$\overset{*}{K}_j$	$\overset{*}{L}_j$	$\overset{*}{S}_j$	$\overset{*}{\jmath}$	$\overset{*}{B}_j$	$\overset{*}{F}$	Output growth (constant price) %
A	−0.14	−0.76	—	0.18	—	—	0.01
M	2.79	0.90	1.74	—	1.29	1.99	2.01
C	2.19	1.61	1.88	—	2.84	—	2.05
B	2.01	1.95	—	—	—	—	2.34

Given these input and output growth rates, and given input cost shares (the θ's), one can compute

$$\overset{*}{T}_A = \overset{*}{A} - (\theta_{jA}\overset{*}{\jmath} + \theta_{KA}\overset{*}{K}_A + \theta_{LA}\overset{*}{L}_A) = 0.60$$
$$\overset{*}{T}_M = \overset{*}{M} - (\theta_{KM}\overset{*}{K}_M + \theta_{LM}\overset{*}{L}_M + \theta_{SM}\overset{*}{S}_M + \theta_{BM}\overset{*}{B}_M + \theta_{FM}\overset{*}{F}_M) = 0.26$$
$$\overset{*}{T}_C = \overset{*}{C} - (\theta_{KC}\overset{*}{K}_C + \theta_{LC}\overset{*}{L}_C + \theta_{SC}\overset{*}{S}_C + \theta_{BC}\overset{*}{B}_C) = 0.37$$
$$\overset{*}{T}_B = \overset{*}{B} - (\theta_{KB}\overset{*}{K}_B + \theta_{LB}\overset{*}{L}_B) = 0.37$$

Using 1891 value added weights and $z = 0.1$ (based on UK 1950–62, in Denison, 1967, p. 300), these $\overset{*}{T}_j$ imply an aggregate rate of total factor productivity growth equal to 0.32 per cent per annum. This estimate is not far below McCloskey's (1970, p. 450) estimate of 0.5, and it is certainly consistent with the nineteenth-century retardation in British technological advance, which has been so long debated.

References

Abramovitz, M. and David, P. (1973), 'Reinterpreting economic growth: parables and realities', *American Economic Review*, 63, 2 (May), pp. 428–439.

Adelman, I. and Morris, C. T. (1978), 'Growth and impoverishment in the middle of the nineteenth century', *World Development*, 6, 3 (March), pp. 245–273.

Ahluwalia, M. (1976), 'Inequality, poverty and development', *Journal of Development Economics*, 3 (December), pp. 307–342.

Allen, R. C. (1982), 'The efficiency and distributional consequences of eighteenth century enclosures', *Economic Journal*, 92, 368 (December), pp. 937–953.

Asher, E. (1972), 'Industrial efficiency and biased technical change in American and British manufacturing: the case of textiles in the nineteenth century', *Journal of Economic History*, 32, 2 (June), pp. 431–442.

Ashton, T. S. (1949), 'The standard of life of the workers in England, 1790–1830', *Journal of Economic History*, Supplement, 9, pp. 19–38.

Ashton, T. S. (1955), *An Economic History of England: The 18th Century*. London: Methuen.

Ashton, T. S. (1959), *Economic Fluctuations in England, 1700–1800*. Oxford: The Clarendon Press.

Ashton, T. S. and Sykes, J. (1964), *The Coal Industry of the Eighteenth Century*. Manchester: University of Manchester Press.

Atkinson, A. B. (1970), 'On the measurement of inequality', *Journal of Economic Theory*, 2 (September), pp. 244–263.

Ball, R. J. and Drake, P. S. (1964), 'The relationship between aggregate consumption and wealth', *International Economic Review*, 5, 1 (January), pp. 63–81.

Barro, R. J. (1974), 'Are government bonds net wealth?', *Journal of Political Economy*, 82, 6 (November/December), pp. 1095–1117.

Baumol, W. (1967), 'Macroeconomics of unbalanced growth: the anatomy of urban crisis', *American Economic Review*, 57, 3 (June), pp. 415–426.

Baxter, R. D. (1868), *National Income: The United Kingdom*. London: Macmillan.

Becker, G. S. (1962), 'Investment in human capital: a theoretical analysis', *Journal of Political Economy*, 70 (October, Supplement), pp. 9–49.

Becker, G. S. (1964). *Human Capital*. New York: National Bureau of Economic Research.

Bellerby, J. R. (1956), *Agriculture and Industry Relative Income*. London: Macmillan.

Beveridge, W. (1939), *Prices and Wages in England*. London: Longmans.

Binswanger, H. P. (1974), 'The measurement of technical change biases with many factors of production', *American Economic Review*, 64, 6 (December), pp. 964–976.

Blaug, M. (1963), 'The myth of the Old Poor Law and the making of the New', *Journal of Economic History*, 23, 2 (June), pp. 151–184.

Bowley, A. L. (1898), 'The statistics of wages in the United Kingdom. Part I. Agricultural wages', *Journal of the Royal Statistical Society*, 61 (December).

Bowley, A. L. (1900a), *Wages in the U.K. in the Nineteenth Century*. Cambridge: Cambridge University Press.

Bowley, A. L. (1900b), 'The statistics of wages in the United Kingdom during the last hundred years. Part VII. Wages in the building trades', *Journal of the Royal Statistical Society*, 63 (June).

Bowley, A. L. (1901), 'The statistics of wages in the United Kingdom during the last hundred years. Part VIII. Building trades', *Journal of the Royal Statistical Society*, 64 (March).

Bowley, A. L. (1914), 'The British super-tax and the distribution of income', *Quarterly Journal of Economics*, 28 (February), pp. 255–268.

Bowley, A. L. (1919), *The Division of the Product of Industry*. Oxford: The Clarendon Press.

Bowley, A. L. (1920), *The Change in the Distribution of the National Income, 1880–1913*. Oxford: The Clarendon Press.

Bowley, A. L. (1937), *Wages and Income in the United Kingdom since 1860*. Cambridge: Cambridge University Press.

Bowley, A. L. (1938), 'The change in the distribution of national income, 1800–1913', in Arthur L. Bowley and Sir Josiah Stamp, *Three Studies in the National Income*. London: London School of Economics and Political Science.

Bowley, A. L. and Wood, G. H. (1899), 'The statistics of wages in the United Kingdom during the last hundred years. Part V. Printers', *Journal of the Royal Statistical Society*, 62 (December).

Bowley, A. L. and Wood, G. H. (1905), 'The statistics of wages in the United Kingdom during the last hundred years. Parts X–XIII. Engineering and ship-building', *Journal of the Royal Statistical Society*, 68 (March, June, September, December).

Bowley, A. L. and Wood, G. H. (1906), 'The statistics of wages in the United Kingdom during the nineteenth century. Part XIV. Engineering and shipbuild-ing', *Journal of the Royal Statistical Society*, 69 (March).

Boyer, G. (1982), 'The English Poor Law as an endogenous response to peak requirements for seasonal labor, 1795–1834', Paper presented to the *Eighth International Conference on Economic History*, Budapest, Hungary (16–21 August).

Briggs, A. (1967), 'The language of "class" in early nineteenth-century England', in A. Briggs and J. Saville (eds), *Essays in Labor History*. London: Macmillan.

Buchanan, J. H. (1976), 'Barro on the Ricardian equivalence theorem', *Journal of Political Economy*, 84, 2 (April), pp. 337–342.

Buer, M. C. (1926), *Health, Wealth and Population in the Early Days of the Industrial Revolution*. London: Routledge.

Burnett, J. (1969), *A History of the Cost of Living*. Middlesex, England: Penguin.

Butlin, N. G. (1967), 'Kaser on England and Wales gross national product', *Bulletin of the Oxford University Institute of Economics and Statistics*, 29, 1 (February), pp. 67–88.

Cain, G. G. (1976), 'The challenge of segmented labor market theories to orthodox theory: a survey', *Journal of Economic Literature*, 14, 4 (December), pp. 1215–1257.

Caird, J. (1852), *English Agriculture in 1850–51*, 2nd edn. New York: Augustus M. Kelley, 1967.

Cairncross, A. K. (1953), *Home and Foreign Investment, 1870–1913*. Cambridge: Cambridge University Press.

Cairnes, J. E. (1874), *Some Leading Principles of Political Economy Newly Expounded*. London: Macmillan.

Cameron, R. (1967), 'Scotland, 1750–1845', in R. Cameron (ed.), *Banking in the Early Stages of Industrialization*. New York: Oxford University Press.

Chalmers, G. (1794), *An Estimate of the Comparative Strength of Great Britain*. London: J. Stockdale.

Chamberlayne, E. (1695), *Magnae Britanniae Notitia, or the Present State of Great Britain*. London: Hodgkin.

Chamberlayne, J. (1755), *Magnae Britanniae Notitia, or the Present State of Great Britain*. London: Ward, 17th edn.

Chambers, J. D. (1940), 'Enclosure and the small landowner', *Economic History Review*, 10, pp. 118–127.

Chambers, J. D. and Mingay, G. E. (1966), *The Agricultural Revolution: 1750–1880*. London: Botsford.

Chenery, H. B. *et al.* (1974), *Redistribution with Growth*. Oxford: The Clarendon Press.

Chenery, H. and Syrquin, M. (1975), *Patterns of Development, 1950–1970*. Oxford: The Clarendon Press.

Christensen, L. R., Cummings, D., and Jorgenson, D. W. (1980), 'Economic growth, 1947–73: an international comparison', in J. W. Kendrick and B. N. Vaccara (eds), *New Developments in Productivity Measurement and Analysis*. Chicago, Ill.: University of Chicago Press.

Clapham, J. H. (1926), *An Economic History of Modern Britain*. Cambridge: Cambridge University Press.

Clark, C. (1940), *The Conditions of Economic Progress*. London: Macmillan.

The Clerical Guide and Ecclesiastical Directory, various years.

The Clergy List, various years.

Cline, W. R. (1975), 'Distribution and development: a survey article', *Journal of Development Economics*, 2, 1 (February), pp. 359–400.

Colquhoun, P. (1806), *A Treatise on Indigence*. London: J. Hatchford.

Colquhoun, P. (1815), *A Treatise on the Wealth, Power, and Resources of the British Empire*. London: Bryer.

Crafts, N. F. R. (1976), 'English economic growth in the eighteenth century: a re-examination of Deane and Cole's estimates', *Economic History Review*, 2nd series, 29, 2 (May), pp. 226–235.

Crafts, N. F. R. (1980), 'National income estimates and the British standard of living debate: a reappraisal of 1801–1831', *Explorations in Economic History*, 17, 2 (April), pp. 176–188.

Crafts, N. F. R. (1983), 'British economic growth, 1700–1831: a review of the evidence', *Economic History Review*, 2nd series, 36, 2 (May), pp. 177–199.

Crouzet, F. (1972), *Capital Formation in the Industrial Revolution*. London: Methuen.

David, P. A. (1975), *Technical Choice, Innovation and Economic Growth: Essays on American and British Experience in the Nineteenth Century*. Cambridge: Cambridge University Press.

David, P. A. and Scadding, J. L. (1974), 'Private savings: ultrarationality, aggregation, and "Denison's Law"', *Journal of Political Economy*, 82, 2, Pt. 1 (March/April), pp. 225–249.

David, P. A. and Solar, P. (1977), 'A bicentenary contribution to the history of the cost of living in America', in P. Uselding (ed.), *Research in Economic History*, Vol. 2. Greenwich, Conn.: Johnson Associates.

Davies, D. (1795), *The Case of Labourers in Husbandry*. Bath, England.

Deane, P. (1961), 'Capital formation in Britain before the railway age', *Economic Development and Cultural Change*, 9, 3 (April), pp. 352–368.

Deane, P. (1968), 'New estimates of gross national product for the United Kingdom, 1830–1914', *Review of Income and Wealth*, Series 14, no. 2 (June), pp. 95–112.

Deane, P. and Cole, W. A. (1962), *British Economic Growth, 1688–1959*. Cambridge: Cambridge University Press (2nd edn, 1967).

DeCanio, J. and Mokyr, J. (1977), 'Inflation and wage lag during the American Civil War', *Explorations in Economic History*, 14, 4 (October), pp. 311–336.

Denison, E. F. (1962), *The Sources of Economic Growth in the United States*. New York: Committee for Economic Development.

Denison, E. F. (1967), *Why Growth Rates Differ*. Washington, DC: The Brookings Institution.

Denison, E. F. (1974), *Accounting for United States Economic Growth, 1929–1969*. Washington, DC: The Brookings Institution.

Denison, E. F. and Chung, W. K. (1976), *How Japan's Economy Grew So Fast*. Washington, DC: The Brookings Institution.

Dewald, W. G. (1983), 'Federal deficits and real interest rates: theory and evidence', Federal Reserve Bank of Atlanta, *Economic Review*, 68, 1 (January), pp. 20–29.

Douty, H. M. (1953), 'Union impact on wage structure', *Proceedings of the Sixth Annual Meeting of the Industrial Relations Research Association* (28–30 December), pp. 61–76.

Douty, H. M. (1961), 'Sources of occupational wage and salary dispersion within labor markets', *Industrial and Labor Relations Review*, 15 (October), pp. 67–74.

Dowell, S. (1893), *The Acts Relating to the Tax on Inhabited Dwelling-Houses*. London: Butterworths.

Drake, M. ed. (1969), *Population in Industrialization*. London: Methuen.

Easterlin, R. (1981), 'Why isn't the whole world developed?', *Journal of Economic History*, 41, 1 (March), pp. 1–20.

Edelstein, M. (1975), 'Realized rates of return on UK home and overseas portfolio investment in the age of high imperialism', mimeo, Department of Economics, Queens College–City University of New York.

Edelstein, M. (1982), *Overseas Investment in the Age of High Imperialism: The United Kingdom, 1850–1914*. New York: Columbia University Press.

Eden, F. (1797), *The State of the Poor*, original edition. London: J. Davis, vols 2 and 3.

Eden, F. M. (1928), *The State of the Poor*. London: Routledge.

Emsley, C. (1979), *British Society and the French Wars, 1793–1915*. Totawa, NJ: Rowman and Littlefield.

Engels, F. (1974), *The Condition of the Working Class in England*. Translated from the 1845 German edition, with an introduction by J. Hobsbawm. St Albans, Herts: Panther.

Engerman, S. L. and O'Brien, J. P. (1981), 'Income distribution in the industrial revolution', in R. Floud and D. N. McCloskey (eds), *The Economic History of Britain since 1700*. Cambridge: Cambridge University Press.

Fallon, P. R. and Layard, P. R. G. (1975), 'Capital–skill complementarity, income distribution, and output accounting', *Journal of Political Economy*, 83, 2 (May), pp. 279–301.

Farr, W. (1837), *Vital Statistics*. Reprinted with an introduction by Richard Wall. London: Gregg International, 1974.

Farr, W. (1885), *Vital Statistics*. London: Sanitary Institute.

Fei, J. C. H. and Ranis, G. (1964), *Development of the Labor Surplus Economy: Theory and Policy*. Homewood, Ill.: Irwin.

Feinstein, C. H. (1972). *National Income, Expenditure and Output of the UK, 1855–1965*. Cambridge: Cambridge University Press.

Feinstein, C. H. (1976), 'Capital accumulation and economic growth in Great Britain', mimeo. Subsequently published in the *Cambridge Economic History of Europe*.

Feinstein, C. H. (1978a), 'Capital formation in Great Britain', Chapter 2 in *The Cambridge Economic History of Europe: Volume VII: The Industrial Economies: Capital, Labour, and Enterprise*. Part I. Ed. by P. Mathias and M. M. Poston. Cambridge: Cambridge University Press.

Feinstein, C. H. (1978b), mimeographed tables. Department of Economics, Cambridge University.

Field, A. J. (1981), 'Land abundance, factor returns, and nineteenth century American and British technology: a Ricardian general equilibrium perspective', mimeo, Department of Economics, Stanford University (February).

Fishlow, A. H. (1966), 'Levels of nineteenth-century American investment in education', *Journal of Economic History*, 26, 4 (December), pp. 418–436.

Flinn, M. W. (1965), 'Introduction', to Edwin Chadwick, *Report on the Sanitary Condition of the Labouring Population of Great Britain*, 1842, ed. M. W. Flinn. Edinburgh: Edinburgh University Press.

Flinn, M. W. (1974), 'Trends in real wages, 1750–1850', *Economic History Review*, 2nd Series, 27, 3 (August), pp. 395–413.

Floud, R. and D. McCloskey (1981), *The Economic History of Britain Since 1700, Volume 1: 1700–1860*. Cambridge: Cambridge University Press.

Fogel, R. W. (1967), 'The specification problem in economic history', *Journal of Economic History*, 27, 3 (September), pp. 283–308.

Frankel, J. A. (1982), 'The 1807–1809 embargo against Great Britain', *Journal of Economic History*, 42, 2 (June), pp. 291–308.

Friedman, B. M. (1978), 'Crowding out or crowding in? Economic consequence of financing government deficits', *Brookings Papers on Economic Activity*, 3, pp. 593–641.

Galpin, W. F. (1925), *The Grain Supply of England During the Napoleonic Period*. New York: Macmillan.

Gayer, A., Rostow, W. W., and Schwartz, A. J. (1953), *The Growth and Fluctuations of the British Economy*. Oxford: The Clarendon Press.

Giffen, R. (1883), 'The progress of the working classes in the last half-century', Statistical Society, 20 November. Reprinted in *Essays in Finance*, 2nd series. New York: G. P. Putnam, 1886.

Giffen, R. (1889), *The Growth of Capital*. New York: Augustus M. Kelley Reprints, 1970.

Gilboy, E. W. (1934), *Wages in Eighteenth Century England*. Cambridge, Mass.: Harvard University Press.

Gollop, F. M. and Jorgenson, D. W. (1980), 'US productivity growth by industry, 1947–73', in J. W. Kendrick and B. N. Vaccara (eds), *New Developments in Productivity Measurement and Analysis*. Chicago, Ill.: Chicago University Press.

Greg, W. R. (1853), *Essays of Political and Social Science*. London: Longmans.

Grigg, D. B. (1963), 'The land tax returns', *Agricultural History Review*, 11, pp. 82–94.

Griliches, Z. (1969), 'Capital–skill complementarity', *Review of Economics and Statistics*, 51, 4 (November), pp. 465–468.

Habakkuk, H. J. (1962), *American and British Technology in the Nineteenth Century*. Cambridge: Cambridge University Press.
Habakkuk, H. J. (1972), *Population Growth and Economic Development Since 1750*. Leicester: Leicester University Press.
Hamermesh, D. and Grant, J. (1979), 'Econometric studies of Labor–Labor substitution and their implications for policy', *Journal of Human Resources*, 14, 4 (Fall), pp. 518–542.
Hammond, B. (1928), 'Urban death-rates in the early nineteenth century', *Economic History*, 1, 3 (January), pp. 419–428.
Hammond, J. L. (1930), 'The industrial revolution and discontent', *Economic History Review*, 1st Series, 2 (January), pp. 215–228.
Harley, C. K. (1974), 'Skilled labour and the choice of technique in Edwardian industry', *Explorations in Economic History*, 11, 4 (Summer), pp. 391–414.
Harley, C. K. (1982), 'British industrialization before 1841: evidence of slower growth during the industrial revolution', *Journal of Economic History*, 42, 2 (June), pp. 267–290.
Hartwell, R. M. (1959), 'Interpretations of the industrial revolution in England: a methodological inquiry', *Journal of Economic History*, 19, 2 (June), pp. 229–249.
Hartwell, R. M. (1961), 'The rising standard of living in England, 1800–1850', *Economic History Review*, 13, 3 (April), pp. 397–416.
Hartwell, R. M. and Engerman, S. (1975), 'Models of immiseration: the theoretical basis of pessimism', in A. J. Taylor (ed.), *The Standard of Living in Britain in the Industrial Revolution*. London: Methuen.
Hicks, J. R. (1932), *The Theory of Wages*. London: Macmillan.
Hobsbawm, E. J. (1957), 'The British standard of living, 1790–1850', *Economic History Review*, 2nd Series, 10 (August), pp. 46–68.
Hobsbawm, E. J. (1964), *Labouring Men: Studies in the History of Labour*. New York: Basic Books.
Hobsbawm, E. J. (1969), *Industry and Empire*. London: Pelican Books.
Hobsbawm, E. J. (1974), *Labour's Turning Point: 1880–1900*. Rutherford, NJ: Fairleigh Dickenson University.
Hobsbawm, E. J. and Rudé, G. (1969), *Captain Swing*. New York: Pantheon Books.
Hoffman, W. G. (1955), *British Industry, 1800–1950*, English edn. Oxford: Oxford University Press.
Hollingsworth, T. H. (1977), 'Mortality in the British peerage families since 1600', *Population*, numéro special, pp. 323–335.
House of Commons, Accounts and Papers (1797–), 'Annual Estimates'.
Houthakker, H. S. (1957), 'An international comparison of household expenditure patterns, commemorating the centenary of Engel's law', *Econometrica*, 25 (October), pp. 532–551.
Hueckel, G. (1973), 'War and the British economy, 1793–1815: a general equilibrium analysis', *Explorations in Economic History*, 10, 4 (Summer), pp. 365–396.
Hughes, J. R. T. (n.d.), 'The cadre Adonis – A bourgeois reactionary view', mimeo, Department of Economics, Northwestern University, Evanston, Illinois.
Hunt, E. H. (1973), *Regional Wage Variations in Britain, 1850–1914*. Oxford: The Clarendon Press.
Hunt, H. G. (1958), 'Landownership and enclosure, 1750–1830', *Economic History Review*, 2nd series, 11 (April), pp. 497–505.

Huzel, J. P. (1969), 'Malthus, the Poor Law, and population in early 19th century England', *Economic History Review*, 2nd Series, 22, 3 (December), pp. 430–452.
Huzel, J. P. (1980), 'The demographic impact of the Old Poor Law', *Economic History Review*, 2nd Series, 33, 3 (August), pp. 367–381.

IBRD (1980), International Bank for Reconstruction and Development, *World Tables*, 2nd edn. Baltimore, Md: Johns Hopkins Press.
Imlah, A. H. (1958), *Economic Elements in the Pax Britannica*. Cambridge, Mass.: Harvard University Press.

Jevons, W. S. (1884), *Investigations in Currency and Finance*. London: Macmillan.
John, A. H. (1967), 'Farming in wartime: 1793–1815', in E. L. Jones and G. E. Mingay (eds), *Land, Labour and Population in the Industrial Revolution*. London: Edward Arnold.
Jones, E. L. (1964), *Seasons and Prices: The Role of Weather in English Agricultural History*. London: Allen & Unwin.
Jones, E. L. (1974), *Agriculture and the Industrial Revolution*. New York: John Wiley.
Jones, R. W. (1965), 'The structure of simple general equilibrium models', *Journal of Political Economy*, 73, 6 (December), pp. 557–572.

Kaser, M. C. (1964), 'The share of England and Wales in the national income of the United Kingdom, 1861–1958', *Bulletin of the Oxford University Institute of Economics and Statistics*, 26, 1 (February), pp. 311–321.
Kelley, A. C. and Williamson, J. G. (1974), *Lessons from Japanese Development: An Analytical Economic History*. Chicago, Ill.: University of Chicago Press.
Kelley, A. C. and Williamson, J. G. (1984), *What Drives Third World City Growth? A Dynamic General Equilibrium Approach*. Princeton, NJ: Princeton University Press.
Kelley, A. C. Williamson, J. G. and Cheetham, R. J. (1972), *Dualistic Economic Development: Theory and History*. Chicago, Ill.: University of Chicago Press.
Kesselman, J. R., Williamson, S. H., and Berndt, E. R. (1977), 'Tax credits for employment rather than investment', *American Economic Review*, 67, 3 (June), pp. 339–349.
Keynes, J. M. (1939), 'Relative movements in real wages and output', *Economic Journal*, 49 (March), pp. 34–51.
Kindleberger, C. P. (1967), *Europe's Postwar Growth: The Role of Labor Supply*. Cambridge, Mass.: Harvard University Press.
King, G. (1936), *Natural and Political Observations and Conclusions upon the State and Condition of England*, in G. E. Barnett (ed.), *Two Tracts by Gregory King*. Baltimore, Md: Johns Hopkins Press. First published 1696.
King, W. (1915), *The Wealth and Income of the People of the United States*. New York: Macmillan.
Knowles, K. G. J. C. and Robertson, D. J. (1951), 'Differences between the wages of skilled and unskilled workers, 1880–1890', *Bulletin of the Oxford University Institute of Statistics*, 13 (April), pp. 109–127.
Kuznets, S. (1950), *Shares of Upper Income Groups in Income and Savings*, Occasional Paper No. 35. New York: National Bureau of Economic Research.
Kuznets, S. (1955), 'Economic growth and income inequality', *American Economic Review*, 45, 1 (March), pp. 1–28.
Kuznets, S. (1966), *Modern Economic Growth*. New Haven, Conn.: Yale University Press.

Kuznets, S. (1973), *Population, Capital and Growth*. New York, Norton.
Kuznets, S. (1979), *Growth, Population, and Income Distribution*. New York: Norton.

Landes, W. and Solomon, L. (1972), 'Compulsory schooling legislation: an economic analysis of law and social change in the nineteenth century', *Journal of Economic History*, 32, 1 (March), pp. 54–91.
Layton, W. T. (1908), 'Changes in the wages of domestic servants during fifty years', *Journal of the Royal Statistical Society*, 71 (September), pp. 515–524.
Levi, L. (1885), *Wages and Earnings of the Working Class*. London: John Murray.
Lewis, W. A. (1954), 'Economic development with unlimited supplies of labour', *Manchester School of Economic and Social Studies*, 22 (May), pp. 139–191.
Lindert, P. H. (1974), 'Land scarcity and American growth', *Journal of Economic History*, 34, 4 (December), pp. 851–884.
Lindert, P. H. (1978), *Fertility and Scarcity in America*. Princeton, NJ: Princeton University Press.
Lindert, P. H. (1980a), 'English occupations, 1670–1811', *Journal of Economic History*, 40, 4 (December), pp. 683–712.
Lindert, P. H. (1980b), 'English occupations, 1670–1811', Working Paper no. 144, Department of Economics, University of California, Davis, California (March).
Lindert, P. H. (1982), 'Who owned Victorian England?' mimeo, Department of Economics, University of California, Davis, California (September).
Lindert, P. H. (1984 forthcoming), 'The distribution of personal estates among male household heads, England and Wales, 1670–1875'.
Lindert, P. H. and Williamson, J. G. (1980), 'English workers' living standards during the industrial revolution: a new look', Economic History Discussion Paper Series, University of Wisconsin, Madison (September).
Lindert, P. H. and Williamson, J. G. (1982), 'Revising England's social tables, 1688–1867', *Explorations in Economic History*, 19, 4 (October), pp. 385–408.
Lindert, P. H. and Williamson, J. G. (1983a), 'English workers' living standards during the industrial revolution: a new look', *Economic History Review*, 2nd Series, 36, 1 (February), pp. 1–25.
Lindert, P. H. and Williamson, J. G. (1983b), 'Reinterpreting Britain's social tables, 1688–1913', *Explorations in Economic History*, 20, 1 (January), pp. 94–109.
Lindert, P. H. and Williamson, J. G. (1984 forthcoming), 'Growth, equality, and history', *Journal of Economic Literature*.
Lluch, C., Powell, A., and Williams, R. (1977), *Patterns in Household Demand and Saving*. Oxford: Oxford University Press.
Lockwood, W. W. (1954), *The Economic Development of Japan*. Princeton, NJ: Princeton University Press.
Lydall, H. (1968), *The Structure of Earnings*. Oxford: The Clarendon Press.
Lydall, H. and Lansing, J. B. (1959), 'A comparison of the distribution of personal income and wealth in the U.S. and Great Britain', *American Economic Review*, 49, 1 (March), pp. 43–67.

McCloskey, D. N. (1970), 'Did Victorian England fail?', *Economic History Review*, 2nd Series, 23 (December), pp. 446–459.
McCloskey, D. N. (1973), 'New perspectives on the Old Poor Law', *Explorations in Economic History*, 10, 4 (Summer), pp. 419–436.
McCloskey, D. N. (1980), 'Magnanimous Albion: free trade and British national income, 1841/1881', *Explorations in Economic History*, 17, 3 (July), pp. 303–320.

McCulloch, J. R. (1854), *Descriptive and Statistical Account of the British Empire*, vol. 2. London: Longmans.

MacKenzie, W. A. (1921), 'Changes in the standard of living in the United Kingdom, 1860–1914', *Economica*, 1, 3, pp. 211–230.

McKinnon, R. (1972), *Money and Capital in Economic Development*. Washington, DC: The Brookings Institution.

Macpherson, D. (1805), *Annals of Commerce*.

Maddison, A. (1970), *Economic Progress and Policy in Developing Countries*. London: Allen & Unwin.

Marshall, A. (1910), *Principles of Economics*, 6th ed. London: Macmillan.

Marshall, J. D. (1968), *The Old Poor Law, 1795–1834*. London: Macmillan.

Martin, J. M. (1966), 'Landownership and the land tax returns', *Agricultural History Review*, 14, pp. 96–103.

Marx, K. (1947), *Capital*, Volume I. New York: International Publishers.

Marx, K. and Engels, F. (1930), *The Communist Manifesto*. New York: International Publishers. First published 1848.

Mathias, P. (1957), 'The social structure in the eighteenth century: a calculation by Joseph Massie', *Economic History Review*, 2nd Series, 10, 1 (October), pp. 30–46.

Mathias, P. and O'Brien, P. (1976), 'Taxation in Britain and France, 1715–1810: a comparison of the social and economic incidence of taxes collected for the central governments', *Journal of European Economic History*, 5, 3 (Winter), pp. 601–650.

Matthews, R. C. O., Feinstein, C. H., and Odling-Smee, J. C. (1982), *British Economic Growth, 1856–1973*. Stanford, Calif.: Stanford University Press.

Mayhew, H. (1861/2), *London Labour and the London Poor*, vol. III. New York: Augustus M. Kelley, 1967.

Memorandum on Cost of Living of the Working Classes (Cd 1761), Parliamentary Papers 1903.

Mill, J. S. (1824), 'Observations on the effects produced by the expenditure of government during the restriction of cash payments', *The Westminster Review*, 2 (July), Art. II, pp. 27–48.

Mill, J. S. (1848 and 1852), *Principles of Political Economy*, 1st and 3rd edns, 2 vols. London.

Mill, J. S. (1909), *Principles of Political Economy*, 5th edn, 2 vols. New York: Appleton.

Minami, R. (1973), *The Turning Point in Economic Development: Japan's Experience*. Tokyo: Kinokuniya Bookstore.

Mincer, J. (1974), *Schooling, Experience and Earnings*. New York: National Bureau of Economic Research.

Mingay, G. E. (1964), 'The land tax assessments and the small landowner', *Economic History Review*, 2nd Series, 17, 2 (December), pp. 381–388.

Mingay, G. E. (1968), *Enclosure and the Small Farmer in the Age of the Industrial Revolution*. London: Macmillan.

Mingay, G. E. (1976), *The Gentry: The Rise and Fall of a Ruling Class*. London: Longmans.

Mitchell, B. R. and Deane, P. (1962 and 1971), *Abstract of British Historical Statistics*. Cambridge: Cambridge University Press.

Mitchell, W. C. (1903), *A History of the Greenbacks*. Chicago, Ill.: The University of Chicago Press.

Mitchell, W. C. (1908), *Gold, Prices, and Wages Under the Greenback Standard*. Berkeley, Calif.: The University of California Press.

Modigliani, F. (1961), 'Long-run implications of alternative fiscal policies and the burden of the National Debt', *Economic Journal*, 71 (December), pp. 730–755.

Modigliani, F. (1966), 'The life cycle hypothesis of savings, the demand for wealth and the supply of capital', *Social Research*, 33, 2 (Summer), pp. 160–217.

Mokyr, J. and Savin, N. E. (1976), 'Stagflation in historical perspective: the Napoleonic Wars revisited', in P. Uselding (ed.), *Research in Economic History*, Vol. 1. Greenwich, Conn.: Johnson Associates.

Morawetz, D. (1974), 'Employment implications of industrialization in developing countries: a survey', *Economic Journal*, 84 (September), pp. 491–542.

Morris, C. T. and Adelman, I. (1980), 'Patterns of industrialization in the nineteenth and early twentieth centuries', in P. Uselding (ed.), *Research in Economic History*, Vol. 5. Greenwich, Conn.: Johnson Associates.

Nardinelli, C. (1980), 'Child labor and the Factory Acts', *Journal of Economic History*, 15, 4 (December), pp. 739–755.

Neal, L. (1977), 'Interpreting power and profit in economic history: a case study of the Seven Years War', *Journal of Economic History*, 37, 1 (March), pp. 20–35.

Neale, R. S. (1966), 'The standard of living, 1780–1844: a regional and class study', *Economic History Review*, 2nd Series, 19, 3 (December), pp. 590–606.

Neale, R. S. (1968), 'Class and class-consciousness in early nineteenth century England: three classes or five?' *Victorian Studies*, 12, pp. 4–32.

Nordhaus, W. and Tobin, J. (1972), 'Is growth obsolete?', in National Bureau of Economic Research, *Economic Growth: Fiftieth Anniversary Colloquium V*. New York: Columbia University Press.

O'Brien, P. K. (1983), 'The impact of the Revolutionary and Napoleonic Wars, 1793–1815, on the long run growth of the British economy', mimeo, Davis Center Seminar, Princeton University (1 April).

O'Brien, P. K. and Engerman, S. L. (1981), 'Changes in income and its distribution during the industrial revolution', in R. Floud and D. McCloskey (eds), *The Economic History of Britain Since 1700: Volume 1: 1700–1860*. Cambridge: Cambridge University Press.

O'Driscoll, G. P. O. (1977), 'The Ricardian nonequivalence theorem', *Journal of Political Economy*, 85, 1 (February 1977), pp. 207–210.

Offer, A. (1980), 'Ricardo's paradox and the movement of rents in England, c. 1870–1910', *Economic History Review*, 2nd series, 33 (May), pp. 236–252.

Ohkawa, K. and Rosovsky, H. (1973), *Japanese Economic Growth: Trend Acceleration in the Twentieth Century*. Stanford, Calif.: Stanford University Press.

Olson, M. (1963), *The Economics of Wartime Shortage*. Durham, NC: Duke University Press.

Perkin, H. (1969), *The Origins of Modern English Society*. London: Routledge & Kegan Paul.

Phelps-Brown, E. H. (1977), *The Inequality of Pay*. Berkeley, Calif.: University of California Press.

Phelps-Brown, E. H. and Browne, M. H. (1968), *A Century of Pay*. London: Macmillan.

Phelps-Brown, E. H. and Hopkins, S. V. (1955), 'Seven centuries of building wages', *Economica*, New Series, 22, 87 (August), pp. 195–206.

Phelps-Brown, E. H. and Hopkins, S. V. (1956), 'Seven centuries of the prices of consumables, compared with builders' wage-rates', *Economica*, New Series, 23, 92 (November), pp. 296–314.

Phelps-Brown, E. H. and Hopkins, S. V. (1959), 'Builders' wage-rates, prices and population: some further evidence', *Economica*, 26, 101 (February), pp. 18–38.

Phelps-Brown, E. H. and Hopkins, S. V. (1981). *A Perspective of Wages and Prices*. London: Methuen.

Phillips, A. W. (1958), 'The relationship between unemployment and the rate of change in money wage rates in the United Kingdom, 1862–1957', *Economica*, New Series, 25, 100 (November), pp. 283–299.

Phillips, W. H. (1982), 'Induced innovation and economic performance in late Victorian British industry', *Journal of Economic History*, 42, 1 (March), pp. 97–103.

Pollard, S. (1980), 'A new estimate of British coal production, 1750–1850', *Economic History Review*, 2nd series, 33, 2 (May), pp. 212–235.

Pollard, S. and Crossley, D. W. (1968), *The Wealth of Britain, 1085–1966*. London: Batsford.

Porter, G. R. (1851), *The Progress of the Nation*. London: John Murray.

Prais, S. J. and Houthakker, H. S. (1955), *The Analysis of Family Budgets*. Cambridge: Cambridge University Press.

Prest, A. R. and Adams, A. (1954), *Consumers' Expenditure in the United Kingdom, 1900–1919*, Studies in the National Income and Expenditure of the United Kingdom, No. 3. Cambridge: Cambridge University Press.

Preston, S. H., Haines, M. R., and Pamuk, E. (1981), 'Effects of industrialization and urbanization on mortality in developed countries', Paper presented to the IUSSP General Conference, Manila (9–16 December).

Reich, M. (1980), 'Empirical and ideological elements in the decline of Ricardian economics', *Review of Radical Political Economics*, 12, 3 (Fall), pp. 1–14.

Report on Wholesale and Retail Prices in the U.K. 1902, Parliamentary Papers 1903, Vol. 68.

Rhee, H. A. (1949), *The Rent of Agricultural Land in England and Wales*. London: Central Landowners Association.

Ricardo, D. (1962), *The Works and Correspondence of David Ricardo*, ed. by P. Sraffa. Cambridge: Cambridge University Press.

Ricardo, D. (1971), *Principles of Political Economy*, ed. by R. M. Hartwell. Harmondsworth, Middx: Penguin Books.

Richardson, T. L. (1976), 'The agricultural labourer's standard of living in Kent, 1790–1840', in D. Eddy and D. Miller (eds), *The Making of the Modern British Diet*. London: Croom Helm.

Richardson, T. L. (1977), 'The standard of living controversy, 1790–1840', PhD dissertation, University of Hull.

Robinson, Sherman (1976), 'A note on the U Hypothesis relating income inequality and economic development', *American Economic Review*, 66, 3 (June), pp. 437–440.

Rose, M. E. (1972), *The Relief of Poverty, 1834–1914*. London: Macmillan.

Rostow, W. W. (1948), *British Economy of the Nineteenth Century*. Oxford: The Clarendon Press.

Rostow, W. W. (1961), *The Stages of Economic Growth: A Non-Communist Manifesto*. Cambridge: Cambridge University Press.

Rousseaux, P. (1938), *Les Mouvements de fond de l'economie anglaise 1800–1913*. Louvain.

Routh, G. (1954), 'Civil service pay, 1875 to 1950', *Economica*, New Series, 21, 83 (August), pp. 201–223.

Routh, G. (1965), *Occupation and Pay in Great Britain, 1906–60*. Cambridge: Cambridge University Press.

Rowe, J. W. (1928), *Wages in Practice and Theory*. London.

Sauerbeck, A. (1886), 'Prices of commodities and precious metals', *Journal of the Royal Statistical Society*, 49 (September), pp. 581–648.

Sayer, B. (1833), *An Attempt to Shew the Justice and Expediency of . . . an Income or Property Tax*. London: Hatchard and Son.

Schultz, T. W. (1960), 'Capital formation by education', *Journal of Political Economy*, 68, 6 (December), pp. 571–583.

Schultz, T. W. (1961), 'Investment in human capital', *American Economic Review*, 51, 1 (March), pp. 1–17.

Scitovsky, T. (1966), 'An international comparison of the trend of professional earnings', *American Economic Review*, 66, 1 (March), pp. 25–42.

Second Series of Memoranda, Statistical Tables and Charts, Part II: Changes in the Cost of Living of the Working Classes in Large Towns (Cd 2337), Parliamentary Papers 1905, vol. 84.

Seventeenth Abstract of Labour Statistics (Cd 7723), Parliamentary Papers 1914–16, vol. 61.

Siegal, J. J. (1979), 'Inflation-induced distortions in government and private saving statistics', *Review of Economics and Statistics*, 61, 1 (February), pp. 83–90.

Silberling, N. (1923), 'British prices and business cycles, 1779–1850', *Review of Economics and Statistics*, 5 (October), pp. 223–261.

Simon, H. (1947), 'Effects of increased productivity upon the ratio of urban to rural population', *Econometrica*, 15, 1 (January), pp. 31–42.

Singer, H. W. (1941), 'An index of urban land rents and house rents in England and Wales, 1845–1913', *Econometrica*, 9, 2 (April), pp. 221–230.

Sixteenth Abstract of Labour Statistics, Parliamentary Papers 1914, vol. 80.

Slicher van Bath, B. H. (1963), *The Agrarian History of Western Europe*. London: Arnold.

Smelser, N. J. (1959), *Social Change in the Industrial Revolution*. Chicago, Ill.: University of Chicago Press.

Soltow, L. (1968), 'Long-run changes in British income inequality', *Economic History Review*, 21, 1 (April), pp. 17–29.

Soltow, L. (1971), 'An index of the poor and rich of Scotland, 1861–1961', *Scottish Journal of Political Economy*, 18, 1 (February), pp. 49–67.

Stamp, J. (1920), *British Incomes and Property*. London: P. S. King.

Stern, W. M. (1964), 'The bread crisis in Britain, 1795–1796', *Economica*, New Series, 31, 122 (May), pp. 168–187.

Stone, R. (1954), *The Measurement of Consumer's Expenditure Behavior in the UK, 1920–1938*, vol. 1. Cambridge: Cambridge University Press.

Taylor, A. J. ed. (1975), *The Standard of Living in Britain in the Industrial Revolution*. London: Methuen.

Thatcher, A. R. (1968), 'The distribution of earnings of employees in Great Britain', *Journal of the Royal Statistical Society*, 130, Pt 2, pp. 133–170.

Thompson, E. P. (1963), *The Making of the English Working Class*. New York: Random House.

Thompson, R. J. (1907), 'An inquiry into the rent of agricultural land in England and Wales during the nineteenth century', *Journal of the Royal Statistical Society*, 70 (December), pp. 587–616.

Titmuss, R. M. (1943), *Birth, Poverty and Wealth: A Study of Infant Mortality*. London: Hamish Hamilton Medical Books.

Tobin, J. (1971), *Essays in Economics. Vol. 1: Macroeconomics*. Amsterdam, North Holland.

Tooke, T. (1838), *A History of Prices*, vol. 1. London.

Tucker, R. S. (1936), 'Real wages of artisans in London, 1729–1935', *Journal of the American Statistical Association*, 31 (March), pp. 73–84.

Turner, H. A. (1952), 'Trade unions, differentials and the levelling of wages', *Manchester School of Economics and Social Studies*, 20 (September), pp. 227–282.

US Commissioner of Labor (1890), 'Report of the Commissioner of Labor: Part III: Cost of living', *House Executive Documents No. 265* (2867, Pt 2), 51st Cong., 2nd Sess., 1890–91.

US Commissioner of Labor (1891), *Sixth Annual Report*. Washington, DC: Government Printing Office, Part III.

US Commissioner of Labor (1892), *Seventh Annual Report*, Washington, DC: Government Printing Office, Part III.

Usher, D. (1973), 'An imputation to the measure of economic growth for changes in life expectancy', in M. Moss (ed.), *The Measurement of Economic and Social Performance*, NBER Studies in Income and Wealth, vol. 38. New York: Columbia University Press.

Vedder, R. K. and Gallaway, L. E. (1980), 'Population transfers and post-bellum adjustments to economic dislocation, 1870–1920', *Journal of Economic History*, 40, 1 (March), pp. 143–150.

von Tunzelmann, G. N. (1979), 'Trends in real wages, 1750–1850, revisited', *Economic History Review*, 2nd Series, 32, 1 (February), pp. 33–49.

von Tunzelmann, G. N. (1982), 'The standard of living, investment, and economic growth in England and Wales, 1760–1850', Paper presented to the *Eighth International Conference on Economic History*, Budapest, Hungary (16–21 August).

Wall, R. (1974), 'Mean household size in England from printed sources', in P. Laslett and R. Wall (eds), *Household and Family in Past Time*. Cambridge: Cambridge University Press.

Ward, W. R. (1952), 'The administration of the window and assessed taxes, 1696–1798', *The English Historical Review*, 67, 265 (October), pp. 1–29.

Ward, W. R. (1953), *The English Land Tax in the Eighteenth Century*. London: Oxford University Press.

Webb, S. J. and Webb, B. (1909), *The Break-Up of the Poor Law*. London: Longmans, Green.

Weber, B. (1960), 'A new index of residential construction in 1838–1950', *Scottish Journal of Political Economy*, 7, 3 (November), pp. 232–237.

West, E. G. (1965), *Education and the State*. London: The Institute of Economic Affairs.

West, E. G. (1970), 'Resource allocation and growth in early nineteenth-century British education', *Economic History Review*, 2nd Series, 23, 1 (April), pp. 68–95.

West, E. G. (1975a), 'Educational slowdown and public intervention in 19th-century England', *Explorations in Economic History*, 12, 1 (January), pp. 61–87.

West, E. G. (1975b), *Education and the Industrial Revolution*. London: Batsford.

Whitaker, T. P. (1914), *The Ownership, Tenure and Taxation of Land*. London: Macmillan.

Wiles, P. (1974), *Distribution of Income: East and West*. Amsterdam: North Holland.

Williamson, J. G. (1967), 'Consumer behavior in the nineteenth century: Carroll D. Wright's Massachusetts workers in 1875', *Explorations in Entrepreneurial History*, 4, 2 (Winter), pp. 98–135.

Williamson, J. G. (1974a), *Late Nineteenth Century American Development: A General Equilibrium History*. Cambridge: Cambridge University Press.

Williamson, J. G. (1974b), 'Watersheds and turning points: conjectures on the long term impact of Civil War financing', *Journal of Economic History*, 34, 3 (September), pp. 636–661.

Williamson, J. G. (1976a), 'The sources of American inequality, 1896–1948', *Review of Economics and Statistics*, 58, 4 (November), pp. 387–397.

Williamson, J. G. (1976b), 'American prices and urban inequality since 1820', *Journal of Economic History*, 36, 2 (June), pp. 387–397.

Williamson, J. G. (1977), 'Strategic wage goods, prices and inequality', *American Economic Review*, 67, 1 (March), pp. 29–41.

Williamson, J. G. (1978), 'British income inequality, 1688–1913: political arithmetic and conventional wisdom', mimeo, Department of Economics, University of Wisconsin, Madison, Wisconsin.

Williamson, J. G. (1979a), 'Two centuries of British income inequality: reconstructing the past from tax assessment data, 1708–1919', Economic History Discussion Paper Series, University of Wisconsin, Madison, Wisconsin (April).

Williamson, J. G. (1979b), 'The distribution of earnings in nineteenth century Britain', Economic History Discussion Paper Series, University of Wisconsin, Madison, Wisconsin (December).

Williamson, J. G. (1979c), 'Inequality, accumulation and technological imbalance: a growth equity conflict in American history?', *Economic Development and Cultural Change*, 27, 2 (January), pp. 231–253.

Williamson, J. G. (1980a), 'Earnings inequality in nineteenth century Britain', *Journal of Economic History*, 40, 3 (September), pp. 457–476.

Williamson, J. G. (1980b), 'Urban disamenities, dark satanic mills and the British standard of living debate', Economic History Discussion Paper Series, University of Wisconsin, Madison, Wisconsin (July).

Williamson, J. G. (1981), 'Urban disamenities, dark satanic mills, and the British standard of living debate', *Journal of Economic History*, 41, 1 (March), pp. 75–83.

Williamson, J. G. (1982a), 'Was the industrial revolution worth it? Disamenities and death in 19th century British towns', *Explorations in Economic History*, 19, 3 (July), pp. 221–245.

Williamson, J. G. (1982b), 'Trickle-down during the first industrial revolution', Paper presented to the *Eighth International Conference on Economic History*, Budapest, Hungary (16–21 August).

Williamson, J. G. (1982c), 'British mortality and the value of life: 1781–1931', Paper presented to the *Conference on British Demographic History*, Asilomar, Calif. (7–9 March).

Williamson, J. G. (1982d), 'The structure of pay in Britain, 1710–1911', in P. Uselding (ed.), *Research in Economic History*, Vol. 7. Greenwich, Conn.: Johnson Associates.

Williamson, J. G. (1983), 'Why was British growth so slow during the industrial revolution?', Paper presented to the *Cliometrics Conference*, Iowa City, Iowa (29 April–1 May).

Williamson, J. G. (1984 forthcoming), 'The great egalitarian leveling under twentieth century capitalism', in Peter Berger (ed.), *Capitalism and Inequality: Europe*.

Williamson, J. G. and DeBever, L. (1977), 'Savings, accumulation and modern economic growth: the contemporary relevance of Japanese history', *The Journal of Japanese Studies*, 4 (Fall), pp. 125–167.

Williamson, J. G. and Lindert, P. H. (1980), *American Inequality: A Macroeconomic History*. New York: Academic Press.

Wood, G. H. (1909), 'Real wages and the standard of comfort since 1850', *Journal of the Royal Statistical Society*, 72 (March), pp. 91–103.

Wrigley, E. A. and Schofield, R. S. (1981), *The Population History of England, 1541–1871: A Reconstruction*. Cambridge: Cambridge University Press.

Yamamura, Kozo (1977), 'Success ill-gotten? The role of Meiji militarism in Japan's technological progress', *Journal of Economic History*, 37, 1 (March), pp. 113–135.

Yelling, J. A. (1977), *Common Field and Enclosure in England, 1450–1850*. London: Macmillan.

Index